Lecture Notes in Business Information Processi 52

Raj Sharman H. Raghav Rao
T. S. Raghu (Eds.)

Exploring the Grand Challenges for Next Generation E-Business

8th Workshop on E-Business, WEB 2009
Phoenix, AZ, USA, December 15, 2009
Revised Selected Papers

Springer

Volume Editors

Raj Sharman
State University of New York at Buffalo
School of Management, Dept. of Management Science and Systems
Buffalo, New York, 14260, NY, USA
E-mail: rsharman@buffalo.edu

H. Raghav Rao
State University of New York at Buffalo
School of Management, Dept. of Management Science and Systems
Buffalo, New York, 14260, NY, USA
and
Sogang University, Dept. of SSME
Seoul 121-742, Korea
E-mail: mgmtrao@buffalo.edu

T. S. Raghu
Arizona State University
Dept. of Information Systems
301G, Box 874606, Tempe, 85287, AZ, USA
E-mail: Raghu.Santanam@asu.edu

Library of Congress Control Number: 2010939795

ACM Computing Classification (1998): J.1, K.4.4, I.2, H.3.5, H.4

ISSN 1865-1348
ISBN-10 3-642-17448-5 Springer Berlin Heidelberg New York
ISBN-13 978-3-642-17448-3 Springer Berlin Heidelberg New York

springer.com

Printed in Germany

Typesetting: Camera-ready by author, data conversion by Scientific Publishing Services, Chennai, India
Printed on acid-free paper 06/3180 5 4 3 2 1 0

Preface

While information systems continue to transform organizations, organizational IT infrastructures and business models are themselves beginning to change. There is an increased focus on service orientation and performance levels of IT infrastructures and systems. Outsourcing and off-shoring strategies are evolving to include utility-based approaches to computing. These developments are showing promises of a renewed period of innovative thinking in e-business technologies. The progress in e-commerce and the global information infrastructure has increased access and improved the promise for a better tomorrow. New initiatives such as cloud computing and collective intelligence are rapidly becoming active research areas. Directions for future research and development in e-commerce include the area of Web-based multi-sided platforms (MSP) supporting micro-transactions. The workshop on e-business provided an opportunity for the interaction and exchange of ideas among IT researchers and practitioners wishing to explore and respond to the grand challenges of next generation e-business systems.

The primary objective of this Lecture Notes on Business Information Processing volume on *Exploring the Grand Challenges for Next Generation E-Business* is to mobilize a collective awareness in the research community of the leading and emerging developments in e-business. The contributions in the lecture notes highlight the enormous potential in e-business as we usher in a new era of cloud computing, collective intelligence, and multi-sided platforms. The volume is a compendium of some of the cutting-edge work going on in various areas of fundamental and applied areas of e-business research.

The papers in this volume have been shepherded from the papers presented at the Eighth Workshop on E-Business, held in Phoenix Arizona. Out of nearly 70 research papers that were featured at the workshop, we invited a select set of papers for the lecture notes. As a result, the volume contains a total of 30 chapters. These chapters have been organized into two broad themes: core organizational e-business information system issues and contemporary issues in e-business. The papers grouped within the first theme cover the areas of ontology, semantic issues and cognitive absorption, supply chain and RFID issues, process modeling and standardization, and security, privacy and extreme events. The papers grouped within the second theme focus on the areas of social networking, gender and mobility, e-services and market mechanisms, IT portfolio management, and special topics in e-business.

As program chairs and editors of this volume, we would like to express our gratitude to the conference co-chairs, Prof. Michael Shaw (University of Illinois at Urbana Champaign) and Prof. Ting-Peng Liang (National Sun Yat-sen University) for their unrelenting support throughout the process. There were a number of members of the AIS Special Interest Group on E-Business who helped in the organization of the workshop and served in various capacities such as organizing committee members, international liaisons, focused session chairs, and program committee members. The Workshop on E-Business is organized as an activity of the AIS Special Interest group on E-Business and garners much support for the Assoication of Information Systems. As a workshop we received logistical support for AIS staff and our gratitude and thanks go to them. We interacted closely with Ms. Lise M. Fitzpatrick, who was patient with us and we are indeed grateful for the help we received and we would like to acknowledge her for that. Finally the conference and this volume would not have been possible without the support of the authors who submitted their papers to the workshop and to this volume. Our gratitude also goes to Andrew B. Whinston (The University of Texas, Austin) for serving as the honorary chair for the workshop. The workshop was sponsored by (a) the University of Florida, (b) the W. P. Carey School of Business, Arizona State University, (c) the College of Business Administration, Sacramento State University, (d) the College of Business, University of Illinois at Urbana-Champaign, (e) the School of Management, University at Buffalo, The State University of New York and (f) the Springer Information Systems Frontiers Journal. In this regard, our sincere thanks go to Prof. Selwyn Piramuthu serving as the sponsorship chair and helping the workshop secure these sponsorships. Several students volunteered during the workshop to ensure the smooth functioning of the event and we acknowledge their contributions. A number of graduate students (Karthic R. Raghupathi, Haricharan Rangamani, Mahesh Thiagarajan Venkatramani, Divya Narayana, Insu Park) at The State University of New York at Buffalo helped with the publication of this proceedings. Graduate students from Arizona State University (Aaron Baird and Karthik Janardhan) provided invaluable local support during the workshop. Prof. Ron Freeze (Emporia State University, Kansas) and Prof. Beom-Jin Choi (California State University, Sacramento) handled all the local arrangements at the workshop. Prof. Divakaran Liginlal has contributed to the organization of the Workshop on E-Business for the past several years and this year was no exception. We would like to take this opportunity to thank him for his service for his help. A lot of conference-related work gets accomplished by people behind the scene. Prof. Sanjukata Das-Smith served as the review chair and helped with the management of all pre-workshop activities as a review coordinator, and this preface would not be complete without our acknowledgement of her efforts. Our thanks go to her as well. Finally we would like to express our thanks to Prof. Mike Shaw (University of Illinois at Urbana-Champaign) and Ralf Gerstner and Christine Reiss of Springer for agreeing to support the publication of this Lecture Notes in Business Information Processing volume.

September 2010

Raj Sharman
T.S. Raghu
Raghav Rao

Organization

Focused Sessions Chairs

Customer Centric and Service Oriented Enterprises	Chen, Minder, California State University, USA Shang, Shari, National Chengchi University, Taiwan
E-Business Standards	Xia, Mu, University of Illinois at Urbana-Champaign, USA
E-Business and Poverty Alleviation	Iyer, Lakshmi S., The University of North Carolina at Greensboro, USA
Economic Models for Mashups and Cloud Systems	Neumann, Dirk, University of Freiburg, Germany Rana, Omer F., Cardiff University, UK Sen, Ravi, Texas A&M University, USA
Economics of E-Commerce	Subramanian, Chandra, The University of North Carolina at Charlotte, USA
Mobile Technologies	Tunnanen, Tuure, The University of Auckland, New Zealand
Multiagent-based System, Semantic Web and Context Aware Computing	Russell, Stephen, George Washington University, USA Yoon, Victoria Y., University of Maryland, Baltimore County, USA
Multi-Agent-Based Business Process and Supply Chain Management	Ketter, Wolf, RSM Erasmus Rotterdam, The Netherlands Müller, Jörg P., Clausthal University of Technology, Germany
Organizational Implications of Electronic Markets	Zhang, John, University of Connecticut, USA Boeck, Harold, Université de Sherbrooke Canada
RFID Technology, Models, Issues and Supply Chain Management	Piramuthu, Selwyn, University of Florida, USA Wamba, Samuel Fosso, University of Wollongong, Australia
Security Informatics	Goel, Sanjay, State University of New York at Albany, USA Zeng, Daniel, University of Arizona, USA
Social Computing Applications and Collective Intelligence	Benbunan-Fich, Raquel, City University of New York, USA

Social Networks	Kumar, Nanda, City University of New York, USA
	Ganesh, Jai, Infosys Technologies Ltd, India
Web 2.0 and Beyond	Nath, Anupam, The University of North Carolina at Greensboro, USA
	Singh, Rahul, The University of North Carolina at Greensboro, USA
Web Intelligence	Lin, Lin, Lehigh University, USA
Web Services and Architecture	Zhang, Dongsong, University of Maryland, Baltimore County, USA

International Liaisons

Shankar Aggarwal	Dept. of IT, Govt. of India
Subash A. Babu	Indian Institute of Technology, Bombay, India
Mahil Carr	Institute for Development and Research in Banking Technology, India
Gregory Kersten	Concordia University, Canada
Wolf Ketter	Erasmus University, Netherlands
Stefan Klein	Universität Münster, Germany
Stefan Luckner	Universität Karlsruhe, Germany
Ambuj Mahanti	Indian Institute of Management, Calcutta, India
Arunabha Mukhopadhyay	Indian Institute of Management, Calcutta, India
Jörg P. Müller	Clausthal University of Technology, Germany
Dirk Neumann	University of Freiburg, Germany
Omer F. Rana	Cardiff University, UK
Debashis Saha	Indian Institute of Management, Calcutta, India
Tuure Tunnanen	The University of Auckland, New Zealand
Shalini Urs	International School of Information Management, India
Sridhar Varadharajan	Sasken Communication Technologies, India
Samuel Fosso Wamba	University of Wollongong, Australia
Christof Weinhardt	Universität Karlsruhe, Germany

Program Committee

Manish Agrawal	University of South Florida, USA
Gove Allen	Brigham Young University, USA
Subash A. Babu	Indian Institute of Technology, Bombay, India
Richard Baskerville	Georgia State University, USA
Ernst Bekkering	Northeastern Oklahoma State University, USA
Rui Chen	Ball State University, USA
Wm. Arthur Conklin	University of Houston, USA
Gurpreet Dhillon	Virginia Commonwealth University, USA
Xiao Fang	Toledo University, USA

Fang Fang	CSU San Marcos, USA
Zhiling Guo	University of Maryland, Baltimore County, USA
Manish Gupta	M&T Bank, USA
Alan R. Hevner	University of South Florida, USA
Paul Hu	University of Utah, USA
Derrick Huang	Florida Atlantic University, USA
Kai Lung Hui	Hong Kong University of Science and Technology, Hong Kong
Mark Keith	Arizona State University, USA
Jin Ki Kim	Korea Aerospace University, South Korea
Karl Reiner Lang	The City University of New York, USA
Jin Q. Lee	Oklahoma State University, USA
Nirup Menon	George Mason University, USA
Gautam Pant	University of Utah, USA
Manoj Parmeswaran	Santa Clara University, USA
Selwyn Piramuthu	University of Florida, USA
Paul Pavlou	Temple University, USA
Sandeep Purao	Penn State University, USA
Daniel O. Rice	Technology Solutions Experts Inc, USA
Sagnika Sen	California State University, Fullerton, USA
Thomas Setzer	Technische Universität München, Germany
Sushil Sharma	Ball State University, USA
Olivia Sheng	University of Utah, USA
J.P. Shim	Mississippi State University, USA
Simha, Maghal	Grand Valley State University, USA
Singh, Rahul	University of North Carolina at Greensboro, USA
Shobha Chengalur Smith	State University of New York at Albany, USA
Jochen Stoesser	Universität Karlsruhe (TH), Germany
Matt Thatcher	University of Louisville, USA
Avinash Waiker	Southeastern Louisiana University, USA
Jingguo Wang	University of Texas at Arlington, USA
Han Zhang	Georgia Tech, USA
John Zhang	University of Connecticut, USA
Lina Zhou	University of Maryland, Baltimore County, USA

Table of Contents

Core Organizational E-Business Information System Issues

Ontology; Semantic Issues and Cognitive Absorption

Supply Chain and RFID Issues

Process Modeling and Standardization

Security; Privacy and Extreme Events

Contemporary Issues in E-Business

Social Networking, Gender and Mobility

E-Services and Market Mechanisms

IT Portfolio Management

Special Topics in E-Business

An Architecture to Support Web-Based Information Extraction Using Domain Ontologies

Vijayan Sugumaran[1,2] and Farid Meziane[3]

[1] Department of Decision and Information Sciences
School of Business Administration
Oakland University, Rochester, MI 48309, USA
[2] Department of Service Systems Management and Engineering
Sogang University
1 Shinsoo-Dong, Mapo-Gu, Seoul 121-742, South Korea
[3] School of Computing Science and Engineering, Newton Building
The University of Salford, Salford M5 4WT, UK
sugumara@oakland.edu, f.meziane@salford.ac.uk

Abstract. The web is the world's most valuable information resource. However, a wide gap has emerged between the information available for software applications vis-à-vis human consumption. In response to this problem, new research initiatives have focused on extracting information available on the web with machine-processable semantics. Ontologies play a large role in information extraction, particularly in the context of semantic web, and applications should be able to find appropriate ontologies on the fly. However, existing tools do not adequately support information extraction and ontology selection. This research-in-progress paper presents the architecture for an information extraction system which relies on domain ontologies and lexical resources. We also provide an approach for easy identification of appropriate ontologies for a particular task.

Keywords: Information Extraction, Semantic Web, Ontology, Ontology Selection.

1 Introduction and Motivation

1.1 Introduction

The development of the web has seen an exponential expansion of information available to users. It contains huge collections of documents that span different domains, languages and levels. Hence, turning the web into the primary source of information for many users and its associated information services will undeniably be the richest source of information. The web serves a huge, widely distributed, and diverse community of users.

The diversity and density of the web has created a significant data extraction problem as its present structure makes it difficult to make use of that information in a systematic way [4]. The content of the web is created and managed by many individuals and organizations and adhere to various standards and formats, which provide

R. Sharman, T.S. Raghu, and H.R. Rao (Eds.): WEB 2009, LNBIP 52, pp. 1–9, 2010.

undeniably convenient and intuitive ways of representing and using information to humans. However, this imposes a real challenge to machines and the automatic extraction of relevant knowledge and information. Hence, this limits the benefits the web could bring to some communities and is frustrating when searching for incomplete, imprecise and ambiguous information. Hence, knowledge discovery from web resources is becoming a priority for many researchers and industries. The most common way currently in use for searching and retrieving information from the web is based on keywords search or similarity based search using one or more search engines, and then in order to extract relevant information, the user has to browse the large number of returned URLs. Moreover, these approaches can encounter many major difficulties including synonymy and polysemy problems.

On the other hand, the development of the semantic web aims at reducing these difficulties by stressing more on the semantics associated with the web content than its keyword based search. There are various definitions and developments of the semantic web which is becoming the main research interest of many communities that include artificial intelligence, and information retrieval and extraction communities. Ontologies are seen as the backbone of the semantic web research. In this paper, we present an architecture to support efficient information extraction from web resources. This architecture is based on domain specific ontologies and is aimed to be generic enough to be applied to various domains. In addition, we present an approach for the selection of the best ontology for specific domain searches.

1.2 Research Context and Limitations

There are two approaches to information extraction, the knowledge engineering approach and the automated training approach [7]. In the knowledge engineering approach, a knowledge engineer will develop some hand crafted rules to use on a specific corpus. Being an interactive process, the rules will be improved until they yield a satisfactory result. Although intuitive, relatively easy to develop and not requiring high computational resources, it is hard to generate rules that are general enough to be used on unseen documents and applied to different domains [15]. On the other hand, extensive corpora annotation is used in the automated training approaches. The Information Extraction (IE) system has to learn extraction patterns from the annotated corpora. This approach requires human intervention for the annotation of large corpora and is known to require extensive computational resources. In our research, we adopt a knowledge engineering approach for two main reasons.

1. The model we are developing is not a single architecture that will fit all domains, but a generic one whose instances can be applied for specific domains. Hence the rules will be specific to a single domain and different domains will require different sets of rules.
2. We attempt to minimize human intervention and particularly the manual annotation of large corpora. It is just not feasible to annotate large corpora for systems that attempt to extract knowledge from the web.

The proposed architecture does not support the development of ontologies but attempts to use existing ones. Indeed, experts suggest that in the semantic web, it is unlikely that we will have a large number of comprehensive, high-quality ontologies but rather many smaller, domain-specific ontologies [6,13]. Based on these assumptions, our system attempts to make use of this plethora of ontologies and incorporate in the architecture a component that selects the most suitable ontology for the application to be considered.

The rest of the paper is organized as follows. Section 2 summarizes the benefits and vision of the semantic web and in section 3 we introduce the concept of ontologies and their use in information retrieval. We describe our proposed system in section 4 and the ontology selection process in section 5. Section 6 concludes the paper.

2 Semantic Web

The web contains a huge collection of documents, which are read, understood, and processed mainly by humans and its current structure is not machine friendly. The amount of electronic information keeps on growing and the internet users are facing the information overload paradox and existing tools and techniques do not provide adequate relief from this problem. Moreover, they are not able to exploit the semantic content of these information sources, so it can be hard at times to find out meaningful relationships between different pieces of information.

These and many other similar problems are the bottlenecks for the future growth and utilization of the web, and in order to overcome them, web contents should be processed by computers if we want to achieve the vision of the semantic web which aims at providing an information enriched with machine processable semantics. This will allow various intelligent services to understand the information and to perform knowledge level information transformation, search, retrieval and extraction [2].

Ontologies are no doubt the most important form of knowledge representation currently in use for the semantic web. In order to overcome the problems caused by present search and retrieval techniques to access information, ontologies are providing ways to retrieve and extract information based on the actual content of a page and help navigate the information space based on semantic concepts. Tools like ontologies facilitate access to and description of the content of documents and are an important step towards offering efficient resource discovery on the web. They can be generic, for example WordNet (http://wordnet.princeton.edu/), or can be domain dependant covering the concepts related to a particular domain. The proposed architecture will be using domain ontologies, which will provide concepts related to a domain of interest, in order to disambiguate word sense, automatic query expansion and for efficient information retrieval and extraction.

3 Role of Ontologies in Information Extraction

The use of ontologies to overcome the limitations of keyword-based search has been put forward as one of the motivations of the semantic web since its emergence in the late 90's [14]. Ontology driven information extraction methods extract relatively shallow information from a very large corpus of documents, instead of performing more exhaustive (and expensive) processing of a small set of documents [9]. Ontologies can be used for both knowledge engineering and automated training approaches [15]. In the knowledge engineering approach, ontologies can be used in the development of rules as well as automated training for the annotation of corpora.

The advantages of using ontology driven information extraction include:

- Driving the entire information extraction process directly from the ontology presents a very natural path for exploiting all kinds of ontological data [9].
- Search-based system using ontologies, allow users to consider a much larger set of documents than could be handled via individual, document-driven processing for example [9].
- Ontology-driven information extraction can be easily focused on the desired results rather than processing all the content from some documents [9].
- Domain knowledge in form of an ontology makes it possible to develop portable Information Extraction system [15].

4 The Proposed Architecture

We propose a generic ontology based information extraction system that constitutes a suitable basis for building an effective solution to extracting unstructured information from the web by providing an extensible architecture and will provide fast and accurate selective access to this information; performing selective dissemination of relevant documents depending on filtering criteria.

The architecture aims at providing a set of integrated software components for accessing heterogeneous data sources and extracts the required information based on domain dependent ontologies. However, ontology selection will be based on the search criteria and the information users are requesting. The architecture of our system is shown in Fig.1. It is composed of 5 modules, which are briefly described below.

Query Processing Module: The query component handles the user's query which is expected to be in a free format probably in natural language or some known keywords. A suitable interface will be developed and this is the main input to the system and if necessary, the query will be pre-processed to remove stop words, stemming etc.

Ontology Selection Module: This component has two tasks. The first is to identify the domain of the ontology if this is not known to the system or provided by the user. This task will rely mainly on the components of the user query and will attempt to link the query to a known domain. The second task is the selection of the best ontology among a set of ontologies. This task is described in details in section 5 of this paper.

Searching Module: This component performs the usual web search based on users' requirements and the ontology. Query expansion and refinement can be performed at this stage. The output of this component would be a set of documents or websites containing the requested information.

Information Extraction Module: Once the documents are retrieved, this module attempts to extract the required information. It uses a variety of natural language processing techniques, text summarization, etc. As mentioned earlier, in its early implementation, our system will adopt a rule based approach for information retrieval.

User Interaction and Presentation Module: This module's task is to gather user input and present the results in a layout suitable to the user needs such as tables, templates etc. The module can be extended to personalize the output taking into account user profiles.

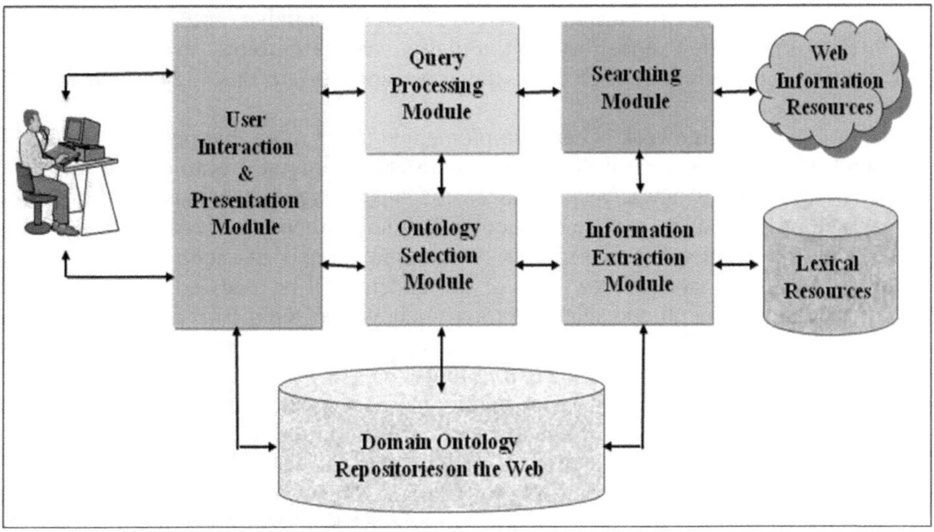

Fig. 1. Proposed Information Extraction System Architecture

5 Ontology Searching and Selection Methodology

Some ontology search engines have been discussed in the literature. For example, SWOOGLE [5] uses traditional Information Retrieval (IR) techniques to retrieve ontologies using keywords. It indexes ontologies primarily designed using OWL language which supplies a set of metadata that could be used for identification of semantic web documents. Since the terms are usually compounded into Uniform Resource Index (URI) reference terms, this approach is not very effective in identifying relevant ontologies. Similarly, link analysis is used to rank ontologies with respect to queries in the OntoSearch system [16] and in the OntoKhoj system [10]. These approaches are limited in focus and do not scale up. Also, they place the burden on the user to determine the appropriateness of the ontologies for the task at hand [1].

Another issue in ontology selection is the difficulty in assessing the quality of ontologies. As the number of available ontologies increases, the evaluation of these ontologies becomes more difficult. A few ontology evaluation approaches have been discussed in the literature. For example, Porzel and Malaka [11] propose an evaluation approach that primarily focuses on the syntactic aspects of ontologies. However, it does not take into account the semantic aspects and user context. The OntoMetric approach [8] establishes a set of processes to evaluate ontologies. It uses predefined characteristics such as ontology language, the methodology used to develop the ontology, and the software environment used. While this is an interesting approach, it greatly depends on the user's familiarity with the domain and is applicable for only small ontologies. The proposed approach attempts to minimize the cognitive burden on the end user who may not be well versed in ontology engineering.

One of the goals of this research is to develop a framework using a novel approach for assessing and selecting the most appropriate ontology for a particular task on the semantic web and implement it in a proof-of-concept prototype system. This system will make use of external knowledge sources available on the web, as well as an internal knowledge repository that contains various ontology evaluation metrics for ranking ontologies and selecting the most appropriate ontology based on task characteristics.

The proposed framework is being implemented using a suitable open source CASE tool and other open source utilities such as inference engines, ontology editors, dictionaries and natural language processors for supporting the various functionalities. The resulting system is expected to enhance the efficiency of systems analysts in developing different types of semantic web applications that require the use of ontologies. The utility and effectiveness of the system will be assessed by comparing it to other ontology search and selection tools such as SWOOGLE. It is anticipated that the users and applications can find their web resources, namely ontologies, on the web more effectively compared to the existing tools.

Our approach for the selection of ontologies on the semantic web consists of the following three steps (Fig. 2): 1) identification of the initial ontology set, 2) ontology evaluation and 3) ontology selection. Users can start the search for ontologies using a natural language query and specifying the domain. The system will initiate the search for the available ontologies in the knowledge-base (KB) repository and identify ontologies within that domain. Then, the ontologies are evaluated and ranked using appropriate metrics. With user feedback and taking into account the task characteristics, the system will recommend the best ontologies to use. The individual steps are briefly discussed below.

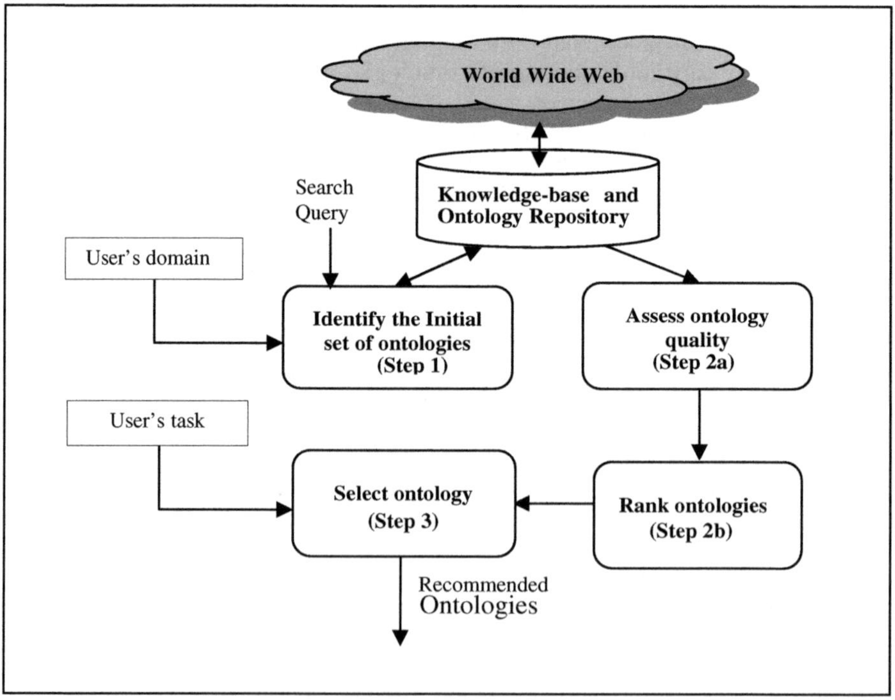

Fig. 2. Ontology Selection Approach

Step 1: Initial set of ontologies

There are a large number of ontologies on the web and many ontologies are being created every day. However, finding and accessing these ontologies has been difficult. Hence, we will design a knowledge-base of ontology repositories to identify potential candidate ontologies. Our system will provide an interface for the user to access a particular ontology on the web directly or use our knowledge-based ontology repository as a starting point. For example, ResearchCyc (http://research.cyc.com) is a well-known ontology library with more than 300,000 concepts, 3,000,000 assertions (facts and rules), and 26,000 relations, that interrelate, constrain, and define the concepts. However, it doesn't provide a flexible user interface for searching. Similarly, DARPA Agent Markup Language (DAML) ontology library (http://www.daml.org/ontologies) is the well-known ontology library, which contains 282 publicly available ontologies. Our system will provide an interface to such libraries and the user can search these libraries by providing keywords and domain information. For example, assume that the user submits a query related to air travel. Using the ontology repository, the system identifies travel domain ontologies as a starting point. At the end of this step, the system provides a set of ontologies to consider.

Step 2: Ontology evaluation

The most important step in ontology selection is ontology evaluation. The ontology evaluation step consists of two sub-steps, namely, ontology quality assessment (step 2a) and ontology ranking (step 2b). The quality assessment activity requires a suite of metrics that can be used to assess the quality of ontologies. Burton-Jones et al. [3] have proposed a metric suite for ontology auditing. This metric suite comprises of ten metrics derived from the theory of semiotics that assess the syntactic, semantic, pragmatic and social quality of an ontology. We examine the suitability of the individual metrics in the context of semantic web and adopt only those metrics suitable for SW and operationalize them. We develop an ontology auditing tool to assess the quality of the initial set of ontologies. For each ontology, a numerical score for each metric is computed. The ontology ranking step involves computing the overall quality score for the ontology depending upon the relative importance of the quality dimensions (weights) specified by the user and ranking them based on the overall score. Thus, at the end of this step, the ontologies to consider are further reduced based on the threshold score set by the user.

Step 3: Ontology selection

After evaluating and ranking the ontologies, one can select the highest ranked ontology. However, it may not always be the right ontology to use. For example, assume that the user needs an ontology for a task related to airline reservation. In the previous step, the user may start with travel domain ontologies in general and evaluate and rank them. However, not all of them may be directly applicable for the task at hand. For example, the highest ranked ontology may specialize in other forms of transportation such as train or cruise reservation. Thus, the highest ranked ontology may not always be the best ontology to use. In this step, the ontology selection takes into account the task-artifact fit [12]. In addition to task characteristics, other factors such as reputation of the source, usage of the ontology, and user feedback are used in selecting the ontology. At the end of this step, the most appropriate ontology to use is suggested.

6 Conclusion and Future Work

We have discussed the need for effective information extraction systems for the web and presented an architecture for such a system. These systems rely heavily on domain ontologies and selecting an appropriate ontology for the task at hand is not trivial. We have presented an approach for ontology selection in a systematic way. The work outlined in this paper is research in progress and the proposed system is currently under implementation. There are many areas which can enhance and influence the current architecture. The processing and expansion of natural language based queries will have an impact on the proposed architecture particularly since ontologies are central to the architecture. Another enhancement could be the development of a module for automatic generation of rules as suggested by [15]. An issue that is becoming inherent to the information extracted from the web is its quality. Indeed, the web is replete with less reliable and untrustworthy information, contradictory statements, and fake data. Any future information extraction system that relies on the web should include some quality assessment. This would require the development of modules that will rely on intelligent techniques to filter and assess the extracted information. This would undoubtedly lead to the more challenging task of data personalization as quality is subjective and users have different needs. Users have different perception of information quality which depends on their experience, their use of the information and the risks they are ready to take in using unknown information.

Acknowledgements

The work of the first author has been partly supported by Sogang Business School's World Class University Program (R31-20002) funded by Korea Research Foundation.

References

1. Alani, H., Brewster, C.: Ontology ranking based on the analysis of concept structures. In: Proceedings of the 3rd International Conference on Knowledge Capture, pp. 51–58 (2005)
2. Aldea, et al.: An Ontology-Based Knowledge Management Platform. In: Proceedings of IJCAI 2003 Workshop on Information Integration on the Web (IIWeb 2003), Mexico, pp. 177–182 (2003)
3. Burton-Jones, A., Storey, V.C., Sugumaran, V., Ahluwalia, P.: A Semiotic Metrics Suite for Assessing the Quality of Ontologies. Data and Knowledge Engineering 55(1), 84–102 (2005)
4. Chaudhry, W., Meziane, F.: Information Extraction from Heterogeneous Sources Using Domain Ontologies. In: IEEE International Conference on Emerging Technologies, Islamabad, Pakistan, September 17-18, pp. 511–516 (2005)
5. Ding, L., Finin, T., Joshi, A., Pan, R., Cost, R.S., Peng, Y., Reddivari, P., Doshi, V., Sachs, J.: Swoogle: a search and metadata engine for the semantic web. In: Proceedings of the 13th ACM Conference on Information and Knowledge Management, pp. 652–659 (2004)
6. Hendler, J.: Agents and the Semantic Web. IEEE intelligent Systems 16(2), 30–37 (2001)
7. Kushmerick, N., Thomas, B.: Adaptive Information Extraction: Core Technologies for Information Agents. In: Klusch, M., Bergamaschi, S., Edwards, P., Petta, P. (eds.) Intelligent Information Agents. LNCS (LNAI), vol. 2586, pp. 79–103. Springer, Heidelberg (2003)

8. Lozano-Tello, A., Gómez-Pérez, A.: OntoMetric: A method to choose the appropriate ontology. Journal of Database Management 15(2) (April-June 2004)
9. McDowell, L.K., Cafarella, M.: Ontology-Driven Information Extraction with OntoSyphon. In: Cruz, I., Decker, S., Allemang, D., Preist, C., Schwabe, D., Mika, P., Uschold, M., Aroyo, L.M. (eds.) ISWC 2006. LNCS, vol. 4273, pp. 428–444. Springer, Heidelberg (2006)
10. Patel, C., Supekar, K., Lee, Y., Park, E.K.: OntoKhoj: a semantic web portal for ontology searching, ranking and classification. In: Proceedings of the 5th ACM International Workshop on Web Information and Data Management, pp. 58–61 (2003)
11. Porzel, R., Malaka, R.: A Task-based Approach for Ontology Evaluation. In: ECAI Workshop on Ontology Learning and Population, Valencia, Spain (2004)
12. Simon, H.: Sciences of the artificial. MIT Press, Cambridge (1981)
13. Stephens, L.M., Huhns, M.N.: Consensus ontologies: reconciling the semantics of web pages and agents. IEEE Internet Computing 5(5), 92–95 (2001)
14. Vallet, D., Fernández, M., Castells, P.: An Ontology-Based Information Retrieval Model. In: Gómez-Pérez, A., Euzenat, J. (eds.) ESWC 2005. LNCS, vol. 3532, pp. 455–470. Springer, Heidelberg (2005)
15. Yildiz, B., Miksch, S.: Motivating Ontology-Driven Information Extraction. In: International Conference on Semantic Web and Digital Libraries (ICSD 2007), Bangalore, pp. 45–53 (2007)
16. Zhang, Y., Vasconcelos, W., Sleeman, D.: Ontosearch: An ontology search engine. In: Proceedings of the 24th SGAI International Conference on Innovative Techniques and Applications of Artificial Intelligence, Cambridge, UK, December 13 – 15, pp. 58–69 (2004)

A Framework for Ontology Evaluation

Jinie Pak and Lina Zhou

Department of Information Systems
University of Maryland, Baltimore County
Baltimore, MD 21250
{jpak3,zhoul}@umbc.edu

Abstract. The rapid growth in the number of ontologies has not met with the wide adoption of ontology in practice. Ontology evaluation can promote ontology use by facilitating the selection of a good ontology. Despite that a host of ontology evaluation methodologies are available, many of them are fragmentary and strongly tied to ontology development methodologies. Based on a review of extant ontology evaluation methods, we propose a framework for ontology evaluation. The framework provides a holistic view of ontology evaluation, suggesting both fundamental ontology dimensions and concrete criteria.

Keywords: Ontology, Ontology evaluation, Ontology quality.

1 Introduction

Ontology has witnessed significant growth and widespread application in many fields such as knowledge management, information retrieval, and semantic web. For example, ontology technologies are popular in inference engines, annotation tools, ontology-based crawlers, and mining tools [25]. Ontology is a formal, explicit specification of a shared conceptualization [12], which can capture semantic information at both concept and instance levels. Ontology can represent a set of objects and their associated relationships in a declarative language. The effectiveness of the ontological knowledge relies on the quality of the ontology.

Ontology evaluation is a technical judgment of the content of the ontology with respect to a frame of reference during every phase and between phases of its lifecycle [9]. Ontology evaluation is critical to the adoption and improvement of ontologies both in academics and industry. Nonetheless, it remains a challenging task to evaluate ontologies due in part to the fact that ontology is semantic oriented. By nature semantics involves ambiguity. Unlike software evaluation, the evaluation of ontology does not have access to concrete specifications for inputs and outputs. Therefore, ontology evaluation deserves separate attention.

Although there is extensive discussion of ontology evaluation in the literature [1], [7], [14], [25], systematic guidelines for performing ontology evaluation are still rare. Therefore, this research aims to improve our theoretical understanding of ontology evaluation and to provide guidance for ontology evaluation by proposing a framework. As a secondary objective, this research identifies future research issues in ontology evaluation, which call for new effort to advance the field.

R. Sharman, T.S. Raghu, and H.R. Rao (Eds.): WEB 2009, LNBIP 52, pp. 10–18, 2010.

2 Existing Methods for Ontology Evaluation

In the literature, various ontology evaluation approaches have been proposed with respect to domains, scopes, and purposes of ontologies Although Hartmann et al. [14] and Yu et al. [30] attempted to provide systematic guidelines for ontology evaluation, most ontology evaluation approaches are rather fragmentary. Some approaches may address certain evaluation dimensions to some extent and often involve more than one quality evaluation criterion. Other approaches evaluate ontologies from the application perspective by comparing ontologies against pre-defined gold standards [23]. There is a need to take a holistic look at ontology evaluation to gain a better understanding of the problem. This section presents a summarization of current ontology evaluation approaches and methods in two major categories: quality attributes based and task-oriented methods.

2.1 Quality Attribute-Based Approaches

Quality attributes-based approaches rely on a set of pre-define quality criteria in evaluation. Metrics are usually defined to measure individual quality attribute of an ontology (e.g. a score and a weight). This type of approach is particularly useful for checking for errors in ontologies such as redundant terms, inconsistencies between definitions and missing definitions. However, some quality attributes such as clarity and expandability can be difficult to evaluate as they may not be easily quantifiable. Thus, manual inspection by human experts is required.

OntoClean [28] is based on philosophical notions of formal evaluation of taxonomical structures. There are four core ontological notions: rigidity, unity, identity, and dependence. OntoClean was the first attempt to formalize notions of ontological analysis for information systems. The idea is to detect both formal and semantic inconsistencies in the properties defined in an ontology.

Content and technology evaluation [11] focuses on the definition of a set of criteria useful in the evaluation process and empirically applies some of these criteria in the evaluation of bibliographic-data ontology. This approach proposes a global technical evaluation that ensures well-defined properties in: 1) the definition of the ontology, 2) the software environment used to build, reuse and share definition, and 3) documentation. Each evaluation step involves three notions: consistency, completeness, and conciseness. In addition, this approach draws a distinction between two main evaluation dimensions: content evaluation and technology evaluation. Content evaluation is related to the Knowledge Representation (KR) paradigm that underlies the language in which ontology is implemented. Ontology technology evaluation is to ensure smooth and correct integration with industrial software environment. This evaluation is directed at the expressiveness of the KR model underlying the ontology editor, the tool's interoperability, quality of import and export functions, scalability, navigability, usability, and content evaluation functions.

Yao et al. [29] proposes a number of cohesion metrics that are specific to ontologies. Grounded on a number of mathematical theories such as Graph theory and Metric theory, cohesion metrics are used to describe and measure structures. There are three main cohesion metrics or functions for evaluating ontologies: 1) number of root classes, 2) average depth of inheritance, and 3) tree of leaf nodes. However, this metric is not suitable for direct application to ontology evaluation. As a result, cohesion metrics is used to measure specific items such as modularity (e.g. relatedness of elements in ontologies). The metrics can also be used to measure the degree of the relatedness of OWL classes and relations by properties.

Gold standard based approach [23] aims to improving the evaluation procedures by proposing criteria for good evaluation measures. The criteria allow for a multi-dimensional evaluation and ensure that errors are weighted differently based on their position in a concept hierarchy. This approach can evaluate the lexical term layer of an ontology as well as the concept hierarchy and non-taxonomic relations contained in an ontology. On the lexical term layer, precision and recall measures are used to compare the terms from the reference and the learned ontology based on string match. For the comparison of concept hierarchies, measures are divided into two categories: local and global. The local measure compares the similarity of the positions of two concepts in the learned and the reference hierarchies. The global measure is computed by averaging the results of the local measure for concept compares from the reference and the learned ontology.

2.2 Task-Oriented Approaches

Task-oriented approaches focus on the practical use of ontology in applications. Such evaluation focuses on user types, usefulness, usability, and use cases. Although this type of approaches can directly benefit practical applications by putting ontology to use, it does not provide generic viewpoints about the quality of an ontology outside the application context.

The task-based approach [19] is to evaluate ontologies at three basic levels: vocabulary, taxonomy and (non-taxonomic) semantic relations. It presents an evaluation scheme that allows ontology engineers to employ a number of different ontologies and to measure their performance on specific tasks. This approach provides performance measures as follows; quantify the respective gains and losses of insertion, deletion, and substitutions errors; populate and improve the ontology as derived from the results of individual specific error types; and re-evaluate the respective performance increases resulting from the improvements.

Structure and function based evaluation [19] views ontology evaluation from customers' perspectives. It emphasizes practical ways (functions) for ontology consumers to discover and evaluate ontologies. This approach suggests ontology summarization, e-pinions for ontologies, views and customization.

OntoMetric [17] is a method that helps choose the appropriate ontologies for a new project or a new system among existing candidate ontologies. OntoMetric provides a set of processes that the user should follow to obtain the measures of suitability of existing ontologies, regarding the requirements of a particular system. The main drawback of OntoMetric is related to its usability: specifying the characteristics of ontologies is a complicated and time-consuming process; assessing its characteristics is quite subjective. Moreover, the number of use cases is limited, which is an important obstacle to specifying parameters based on a large number of comparable cases.

Hartmann et al. [14] provides a classification of various ontology evaluation methods and tools for industrial practice. The method and tools are classified by the following tasks: 1) selecting existing ontologies, 2) measuring the similarities between textual source and its corresponding ontologies, 3) evaluating the impacts of ontology on IS applications, 4) checking the quality and consistency of ontologies, and 5) monitoring ontology in use.

3 A Framework for Ontology Evaluation

Based on the review of ontology evaluation approaches, we propose a framework for ontology evaluation. The framework provides a set of dimensions for classifying ontology evaluation methods, and for each dimension, it proposes measurement criteria for ontology evaluation. Additionally, we also propose guidelines for choosing ontology evaluation methods based on the objectives of an ontology.

Table 1. Taxonomy of Ontology Evaluation Approaches

Ontology Evaluation Dimensions	Articles
Scope	(Gómez-Pérez 2003), (Hartmann et al. 2004), (Lozano-Tello et al. 2004), (Porzel et al. 2004), (Daelemans et al. 2004),(Noy et al. 2004), (Staab et al. 2006)
Layer	(Welty et al. 2001), (Porzel et al. 2004), (Daelemans et al. 2004), (Yao et al. 2005), (Spyns et al. 2005), (Staab et al. 2006)
Life Cycle	(Welty et al. 2001), (Gómez-Pérez 2003), (Hartmann et al. 2004), (Lozano-Tello et al.2004), (Brewster et al. 2004), (Spyns et al. 2005)
Quality Principles	(Welty et al. 2001), (Gómez-Pérez 2003), (Yao et al. 2005)
Methods	(Hartmann et al. 2004), (Brewster et al. 2004), (Yao et al. 2005), (Spyns et al. 2005)

3.1 Ontology Scopes

Determining the domain and scopes of an ontology is important to both evaluation and building of the ontology. In ontological engineering, ontology scope is equivalent to specification and design aspects for the representation of knowledge underlying things, concepts, and phenomena [4]. Also ontology scope can be useful to confirming whether the specification and design aspects in ontologies are appropriately implemented. The scope of ontologies can be classified in three aspects.

- **Domain Scope** is to evaluate whether the scopes of ontologies are relevant to the tasks that ontologies are meant to accomplish in the intended domain.
- **Conceptual Scope** is to evaluate whether ontologies well-represent hierarchical and taxonomical concepts.
- **Technical Scope** is to evaluate whether the specifications and requirements for ontologies are integrated smoothly and correctly in terms of ontology integration and application in practice.

3.2 Ontology Layers

Ontology has a complex structure and it is not practical to directly evaluate ontology as a whole. Accordingly, it would be more efficient to focus on the evaluation of different layers of ontology separately. In addition, the layer-based approach allows for the use of distinctively different automatic techniques for different layers [15].

- **Lexicon/vocabulary layer.** This includes criteria relevant to knowledge representation and conceptualization of ontologies such as naming criteria in concepts, instances, and facts. Naming criteria assesses how well terms and definitions are formulated. Evaluation on this layer tends to involve comparisons with various sources of data concerning the problem domain (e.g. domain-specific corpora), as well as techniques such as string similarity measures (e.g. edit distance).
- **Structure/ architecture layer.** The structural attributes of ontologies are of primary interest in this layer. This layer is more relevant to hierarchical and taxonomic elements of ontology such as hierarchical relations among concepts, reasoning, and modularization. Usually this layer can be evaluated with both pre-defined principles or criteria and the suitability for further development [8].
- **Representation/ semantic layer.** This layer contains criteria relevant to the semantic elements of ontologies. Accordingly, the evaluation focuses on how adequately the semantic elements conceptually describe the structural elements that have been defined [2].
- **Context/application layer.** An ontology may be part of a large collection of ontologies, and may reference or be referenced by various definitions in these other ontologies [1]. It is very important to take this context into account when evaluating ontology. Another relevant issue is the application context where the ontology is to be used in. Typically evaluation looks at how the outcomes of the application are affected by the use of ontology.

3.3 Ontology Life Cycle

A technical evaluation must be performed throughout the life cycle of an ontology. The purpose is to detect the absence of some well-defined properties in the definitions in specification, knowledge acquisition, conceptualization and integration [9]. Ontology life cycle is the set of stages through which the ontology moves during its time. Each stage involves different levels of activities with regard to management, development, and support of ontologies. Accordingly, specific techniques used in each activity and the outputs from each activity need to be evaluated [10].

- **Specification.** The purpose of this phase is to develop informal, semi-formal or formal ontology requirement specification, using a set of intermediate representations or using competence questions. Accordingly, the intended scope, domain, and purpose of the ontology should be identified. Well-characterized specification is important to the design, evaluation, and reuse of an ontology. The specification needs to be checked for problems such as incompleteness, inconsistency, and conciseness and for feasibility. Thus, the evaluation is performed in the following areas: the degree of required formality, the set of terms to be represented, their characteristics and the required granularity of contents.
- **Knowledge acquisition.** As an independent activity in ontology development process, most acquisition is done simultaneously with the requirements specification phase. Knowledge can be elucidated, inspecting potential relevant glossary and refining the list of terms and their meanings. Sources span the complete range of domain experts who hold knowledge. Motivating scenarios and informal competency questions are collected. The competency questions, informal and formal text analysis are used to check whether the ontology is fit for purpose. Thus, this phase

verifies the domain facts and the abstract inference rules by using collected competency questions.

- **Conceptualization.** This phase is to identify the key concepts that exist in the domain, their properties and the relationships that hold between them, and is to structure the domain knowledge in a conceptual model that describes the problem and its solution in terms of the domain vocabulary identified in specification activity. As an outcome of the conceptualization, a complete Glossary of Terms is built, including concepts, instances, verbs and properties. Thus, this phase needs to checks consistency and completeness of identified domain terms such as concepts, instances, verbs relations or properties and their applicable informal representations.
- **Integration.** Sometimes an ontology uses or specializes existing ontologies to speed up the construction of the ontology. This phase is closely related to the reusability. When reusing the existing definitions, a task may be frequently hindered by the inadequate documentation of existing ontologies and their implicit assumptions. This phase assesses some uniformity in definitions across ontologies.

3.4 Ontology Quality Principles

Ontology is semantic oriented and may take a variety of forms. This leads to ambiguity in ontology evaluation. Therefore, ontology evaluation deserves more precise and clear principles. The following principles are most commonly identified in the ontology evaluation literature [8], [13].

- **Consistency.** This principle refers to the capability of getting no contradictory conclusions simultaneously from valid input data [9]. For example, ontology engineers check whether an ontology has semantic consistency in the definitions, the meanings of formal and informal definitions, and sentences that may be inferred by using other definitions and axiom that may or may not belong to the same ontology.
- **Completeness.** Sometimes some of important information about concepts in ontologies can be overlooked. Such incompleteness often leads to ambiguity and a lack of reasoning mechanisms. Precision and recall, set-based measures can be used for examining the incompleteness errors of ontologies. Precision is a measure of the ability of an ontology present only relevant item and recall is a measure of the ability of an ontology to present all relevant items. The completeness of a definition depends on the level of granularity agreed to in the whole ontology. To detect incompleteness of an ontology and its definition, the class hierarchy, the domains and scopes of the functions and relations, and classes need to be verified. The incompleteness errors in ontologies can be classified by incomplete concept classification, partition errors, and disjoint knowledge omission [11].
- **Conciseness.** This principle is related to whether all the information collected in an ontology is useful and precise. Conciseness doesn't imply absence of redundancies. Sometimes, some degree of controlled redundancy can be useful in identifying definitions. Explicit redundancies do not exist among definitions and redundancies cannot be derived using axioms attached to other definitions. Finally, the set of properties in the definitions of a class can be precisely and exactly defined.
- **Reusability.** Ontologies can import and export modules among ontologies. However, the effectiveness to interoperate modules among ontologies is often reduced

due to the use of different ontological scheme, that is, structural and semantic heterogeneity between ontologies. String matching metric can be used for measuring similarity between two strings.

3.5 Ontology Evaluation Methods

The choice of ontology evaluation methods can be contingent upon ontology development methodologies. Such a consideration is also related to other factors such as degree of formality and domain coverage or future extensions of ontology. Nonetheless, along this dimension, there are three main methods that cover all possible aspects of ontology evaluation.

- **Independent method.** They are used for various types of ontologies developed with different tools and different knowledge representation and formalization. These methods can be applied to ontology evaluation, no matter which methodology or approach is used for ontology development [16]. Precision, recall and string matching matrix are the examples of the independent methods.
- **Verification.** The verification of ontologies is to detect anomalies can occur due to the combination of ontology definitions and rules. Taxonomy evaluation and OntoClean are examples of this type of approach.
- **Validation.** This refers to a diagnostic task over ontology elements, process, and attributes. Structural measures, functional measures and usability -profiling measures are the examples of validation [7].

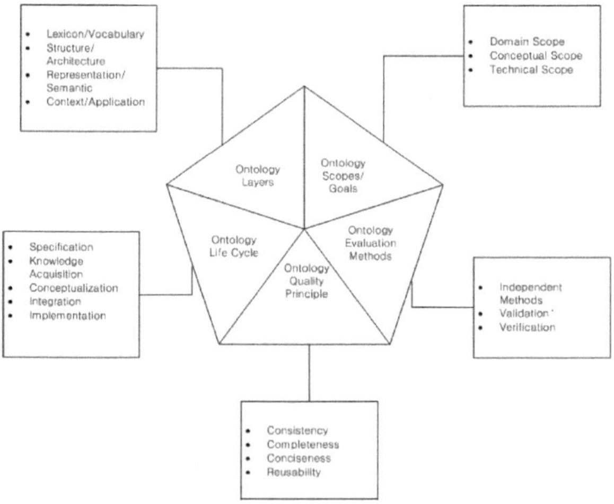

Fig. 1. Proposed Framework for Ontology Evaluation

4 Conclusion and Further Research

Ontology evaluation is a complex and time-consuming process. It is impossible for a single approach to ontology evaluation to work best for all application contexts.

Instead, the selection of an evaluation approach should consider a number of factors, including the phases where the ontology is evaluated, the application and domain in which the ontology is to be used, and the aspects of the ontology to be evaluated.

The proposed framework lays the groundwork for developing a comprehensive approach to ontology evaluation, addressing both basic ontology dimensions and concrete criteria. It allows conducting a multi-dimensional evaluation. It also supports the view that ontology evaluation should be considered throughout the entire life cycle of an ontology [8], [10]. This research can be continued in the following directions:

- Development of guidelines for choosing and prioritizing different dimensions of ontology evaluation in research and practice. High quality ontology measures and a set of agreed-on evaluation measures will support the general development and evolution of ontology engineering environment. Nonetheless, the importance of specific ontology evaluation criteria is likely to vary with ontology context.
- Identification of evaluation tools and methods that can be used to support each dimension of the framework. Tools can be used to automatically check if certain quality criteria are satisfied during the engineering phases, and if not, issue appropriate warnings.
- Implementation of the framework to demonstrate the validity and effectiveness of the framework.

The ontology evaluation framework proposed in this research is expected to help improve the use of ontologies by providing a set of dimensions for selecting good ontologies.

References

1. Brank, J., Grobelnik, M., Mladenic, D.: A survey of ontology evaluation techniques. In: The Conference on Data Mining and Data Warehouses, SiKDD (2005)
2. Brewster, C., Alani, H., Dasmahapatra, S., Wilks, Y.: Data Driven Ontology Evaluation. In: The Language Resources and Evaluation Conference (LREC), Lisbon, Portugal (2004)
3. Daelemans, W., Reinverger, M.L.: Shallow Text Understanding for Ontology Content Evaluation. IEEE Intelligent Systems 19(4), 74–81 (2004)
4. Devedzic, V.: Understanding Ontological Engineering. Communications of the ACM 45, 135–144 (2005)
5. Fernández, M., Gòmez-Pérez, A., Juristo, N.: METHONTOLOGY: From Ontological Art Towards Ontological Engineering. In: The AAAI Spring Symposium on Ontological Engineering, pp. 33–40. Stanford University, AAAI Press, Stanford, CA (1997)
6. Fernández-López, M.: Overview of Methodologies for Building Ontologies. In: The IJCAI 1999 Workshop on Ontologies and Problem-Solving Methods, Stockholm, Sweden (1999)
7. Gangemi, A., Catenacci, C., Ciaramita, M., Lehmann, J.: A theoretical framework for ontology evaluation and validation. In: The 2nd Italian Semantic Web Workshop (SWAP) (2005)
8. Gómez-Pérez, A.: Some ideas and examples to evaluate ontologies. In: The 11th Conference on Artificial Intelligence for Applications (CAIA 1995), Washington DC, p. 299 (1995)
9. Gómez-Pérez, A.: Towards a framework to verify knowledge sharing technology. Expert Systems with Applications 4, 519–529 (1996)
10. Gómez-Pérez, A.: Knowledge sharing and reuse. In: Liebowitz, J. (ed.) The Handbook of Applied Expert Systems, p. 10.1–10.35. CRC, Boca Raton (1998)

11. Gómez-Pérez, A.: Ontology Evaluation. In: Staab, S., Studer, R. (eds.) Handbook on Ontologies, pp. 251–274. Springer, Heidelberg (2003)
12. Gruber, T.R.: A translation approach to portable ontology specifications. Knowledge Acquisition 5, 199–220 (1998)
13. Guarino, N., Welty, C.: Evaluating ontological decisions with OntoClean. Comm. of the ACM 45(2), 61–65 (2002)
14. Hartmann, J., Sure, Y., Giboin, A., Maynard, D., Suárez-Figueroa, M., Cuel, R.: Methods for Ontology Evaluation. KWeb Deliverable D1.2.3, University of Karlsruhe (2004)
15. Kehagias, D.D., Papadimitriou, I., Hois, J., Tzovaras, D., Bateman, J.: A methodological approach for ontology evaluation and refinement. In: 2nd International ASK-IT Final Conference, Nuremberg, Germany (2008)
16. Lovrencic, S., Cubrilo, M.: Ontology Evaluation-comprising verification and validation. In: The 19th Central European Conference on Information and Intelligent Systems, pp. 657–663 (2008)
17. Lozano-Tello, A., Gómez-Pérez, A.: ONTOMETRIC: A Method to Choose the Appropriate Ontology. Journal of Database Management. Special Issue on Ontological analysis, Evaluation, and Engineering of Business Systems Analysis Methods 15(2), 1–18 (2004)
18. Maedche, A., Staab, S.: Measuring Similarity between Ontologies. In: Gómez-Pérez, A., Benjamins, V.R. (eds.) EKAW 2002. LNCS (LNAI), vol. 2473, pp. 251–263. Springer, Heidelberg (2002)
19. Noy, N.F.: Semantic Integration: A Survey Of Ontology-Based Approaches. SIGMOD Record, Special Issue on Semantic Integration 33(4), 65–70 (2004)
20. Porzel, R., Malaka, R.: A Task-based Approach for Ontology Evaluation. In: ECAI 2004 Workshop on Ontology Learning and Population, Valencia, Spain (2004)
21. Spyns, P., Meersman, R., Jarrar, M.: Data modelling versus Ontology engineering. In: Sheth, A., Meersman, R. (eds.) SIGMOD Record Special Issue 31 (4), 12–17 (2002)
22. Spyns, P., Reinberger, M.-L.: Lexically evaluating ontology triples automatically generated from text. In: Gómez-Pérez, A., Euzenat, J. (eds.) ESWC 2005. LNCS, vol. 3532, pp. 563–577. Springer, Heidelberg (2005)
23. Dellschaft, K., Staab, S.: On How to Perform a Gold Standard Based Evaluation of Ontology Learning. In: Cruz, I., Decker, S., Allemang, D., Preist, C., Schwabe, D., Mika, P., Uschold, M., Aroyo, L.M. (eds.) ISWC 2006. LNCS, vol. 4273, pp. 228–241. Springer, Heidelberg (2006)
24. Stojanovic, N., Maedche, A., Staab, S., Studer, R., Sure, Y.: SEAL-A Framework for Developing Semantic PortALs. In: The 1st International Conference on Knowledge captures (ACM K-CAP), Vancouver, pp. 155–162 (2001)
25. Sure, Y., Gómez-Pérez, A., Daelemans, W., Reinberger, M., Guarino, N., Noy, N.F.: Why Evaluate Ontology Technologies? Because It Works! IEEE Intelligent Systems 19(4), 74–81 (2004)
26. Uschold, M., Gruninger, M.: Ontologies: Principles, methods, and applications. Knowledge Engineering Review 11(2), 93–155 (1996)
27. Ushold, M.: Creating, integrating and maintaining local and global ontologies. In: The First Workshop on Ontology Learning (OL-2000) in Conjunction with the 14th European Conference on Artificial Intelligence (ECAI). IOS Press, Berlin (2000)
28. Welty, C.A., Guarino, N.: Supporting ontological analysis of taxonomic relationships. Data & Knowledge Engineering 39, 51–74 (2004)
29. Yao, H., Orme, A.M., Etzkorn, L.: Cohesion metrics for ontology design and application. Journal of Computer Science 1(1), 107–113 (2005)
30. Yu, J., Thom, J., Tam, A.: Requirements-oriented methodology for evaluating ontologies. Information Systems, Sixteenth ACM 34(8), 686–711 (2009)

An Idealet-Centric Scheme for Large Scale Open Innovation Systems

Matti Hämäläinen[1], Qing Li[2], Zhangxi Lin[3], Alin Tomoiaga[3], and Jia Wang[2]

[1] Aalto University
[2] Southwestern University of Finance and Economics
[3] Texas Tech University
matti.hamalainen@tkk.fi, liq_t@swufe.edu.cn,
{zhangxi.lin,alin.tomoiaga}@ttu.edu, xiaojiajia198796@sina.com

Abstract. This paper intends to demonstrate how open innovation systems could be developed by tackling the challenging knowledge management problems that are encountered when aiming at involving very large audiences. This is the case when generalizing open innovation approach beyond companies to a wider societal context like in the case of national innovation systems. The Open Innovation Banking System (OIBS) project, funded by the European Social Fund (ESF) and the participating higher education institutions in Finland, is used as a basis for our discussion. It specifically aims at bringing the largely underutilized creativity of students and senior citizens to play. Among several technologies to develop OIBS, mashups as hybrid web applications can play an important role in such constantly evolving system and contents. However, relying only on unstructured text inputs, the services of textual content sharing for OIBS would require intelligent text processing that far exceeds the capability of such applications. In this paper, we propose an "idealet"-centric solution for representing the data submitted by users, enabling concise description, refinement and linking of ideas as input for innovation processes. An idealet is defined as the core knowledge about an innovative idea. The relationships among idealets and essays can be represented in a semantic network in terms of their relationships. This scheme allows the mashup applications for OIBS to more effectively retrieve, process, extract, and deliver the most important knowledge from an ocean of information contributed by participating information composer, reviewers, and users. The paper also discusses how the idealet-centric approach can be employed for a functional open innovation system.

Keywords: Open Innovation, Mashup, Semantic Network, Knowledge Modeling, "Wicked" Problems.

1 Introduction

The idea of open innovation has gained exceptional momentum with web 2.0 enabled social media and collaborative services and has quickly gained popularity since it was promoted by Henry Chesbrough in 2003 [2]. The central idea behind open innovation is that in a world of widely distributed knowledge, companies cannot afford to

R. Sharman, T.S. Raghu, and H.R. Rao (Eds.): WEB 2009, LNBIP 52, pp. 19–29, 2010.

rely entirely on their own research, but should instead buy or license processes or inventions (e.g. patents) from other companies. In addition, internal inventions not being used in a firm's business should be taken outside the company, for example, through licensing, joint ventures, or spin-offs. While Chesbrough originally focused on firm's perspective the open innovation approach has potential to foster solution of many of today's challenging problems - or so called "wicked problems" - when generalized from organizations to wider societal context and supported by appropriate discourse mechanisms. Here a "wicked problem" is referred to as "to describe a problem that is difficult or impossible to solve because of incomplete, contradictory, and changing requirements that are often difficult to recognize. Moreover, because of complex interdependencies, the effort to solve one aspect of a wicked problem may reveal or create other problems." [12].

This paper is intended to demonstrate how such systems could be developed by tackling the knowledge management problems in Open Innovation Banking System (OIBS) project, an EU sponsored open innovation system project in Finland aiming at bringing the largely underutilized creativity of the students and senior citizens to play [13]. Specifically, OIBS is a kind of textual contents sharing system, which is similar to Wikipedia in its open content service [14] but with the focus on innovative ideas contributed by the users.

When applying the open content approach to the development of the idea bank system – not just to the process of producing its content - it becomes important to support approaches that enable very easy and lightweight linking of various value adding services as well as composition of new services. The mashup approach [10] can be applied in the ongoing development and extension of such a system by providing support for analyzing information and evaluating contributions, for identifying related items and supporting composition, and for ranking, visualizing, and various other forms of processing. There are a number of most well-known mashup implementations, such as Microsoft Popfly (discontinued on August 24, 2009), Google Mashup Editor (Deprecated, since January 14, 2009), Mozilla Ubiquity, Yahoo! Pipes, and Open Mashup Alliance. However, relying only on unstructured text inputs, these services for typical idea banking and brainstorming support systems would require intelligent text processing that far exceeds the capability of such applications. In the last couple of decades great efforts have been exerted to develop various techniques, methods, and algorithms for automatically processing and summarizing unstructured text documents, but there is no practically feasible resolution that is applicable to our specific application context. The challenging problems include:

- How to effectively and efficiently manage a large amount of textual contents, and
- How to support composition, refinement and more structured processing and discourse on the submitted contents.

To address these problems, we suggest a solution, *idealet-centric* knowledge modeling, for structuring the information elements (i.e. inputs and possible outputs of the mashups) in a more meaningful way, so that the information can be better understood and processed. The structuring also supports discourse, idea refinement, and composition processes for providing input for the innovation process. The analogous problem of supporting of scientific collaboration has been earlier addressed by proposing a structured discourse model [5] based on the IBIS-model [12]. With the current pervasive

Internet connectivity and social network systems even very large scale of introduction of such approach has become viable. An *idealet* is defined as the core knowledge about a piece of innovative idea. Based on the idealet-centric model, we show how the essays contributed by the users of an open innovation system can be processed incorporating with the information retrieval techniques, such as the latent Dirichlet allocation (LDA) model [1]. Then a semantic mashup approach using the latest text snippet extraction technique can be employed to extract innovative ideas. This scheme allows the mashup applications for OIBS to more effectively process the most important knowledge from an ocean of information contributed by participating information composer, reviewers, and users. In this way, the suggested idealet concept and structure as a lightweight knowledge representation scheme that can be applied in Web environment both from technology and from user perspectives thus promoting scalability and adoption of open innovation systems. The idealet model and tools making use of it is suggested to provide value both to idea contributors and to participants looking to further processing of ideas in the innovation process. Thus, we can expect it to help boosting the initial adoption and scaling of use of OIBS and other such systems, which is typically a major challenge in their successful introduction.

2 Challenges in OIBS - Mashing Up the Innovative Ideas

The OIBS concept is based on the idea that Online Social Networks can be utilized as a critical part of National Innovation System i.e. National Open Innovation Systems (NOIS) as illustrated in Fig. 1 that presents the general Innovation Triangle framework which consolidates NOIS [13].

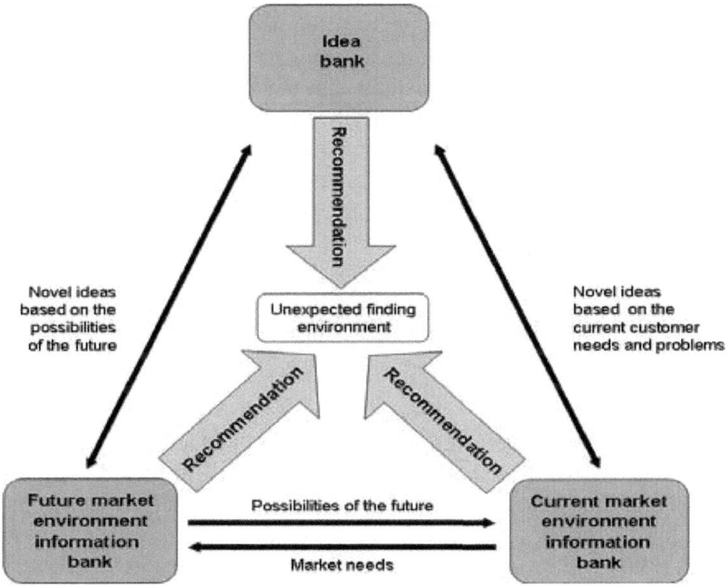

Fig. 1. General Innovation Triangle framework [13]

With the aim of generating new ideas (i.e. the top box) NOIS framework includes two complementary innovation sources: first, future market environment information, presenting visions of the future (i.e. the left box) and second, current market environment information, presenting today's challenges (i.e. the right box). By combining these, the approaches of collaborative content production and intelligent content recommendation will significantly boost the possibilities of unexpected findings, which have been identified as a major innovation source. It has also been recognized by [13] and others that a successful innovation system must include options for rewards for all key actors.

The OIBS project launched in 2008 aims at creating an environment that supports the OIBS approach and takes it into large scale operational use starting from a network of higher education institutions. The challenges in the development of such a system are described in [6]. The intended widespread use of OIBS requires that the system should be easy to learn and use. Still it should have very powerful features for the management, processing and presentation of huge amounts of fairly unstructured data. Once the user community gets large, the OIBS system will contain huge amounts of valuable pieces of information just waiting to be combined intelligently to form innovative solutions to the needs of companies and the society. The technology development subproject adopts the open approach that is basis for the content creation. It is based on enabling development of the web based applications collaboratively and has made the technology entirely open source. Specifically, the potential of mash-up type of approach has been recognized for supporting community innovation. As a relatively new concept, the project has a challenge to attract developers and content contributors.

Among several technologies to develop OIBS, mashups as hybrid web applications play an important role in the system as they can combine contents from multiple web sites into a single application. They have become popular because of the emphasis on interactive user participation in which they aggregate and stitch together the data from multiple sources. However, before mashups can make the transition from cool toys to sophisticated applications, much work will have to go into distilling robust standards, protocols, models, and toolkits. Due to complexity of the input information, most of current mashup applications have limited functions and majority of them are based on Google map applications [11]. Therefore, they are incapable of aggregating a large amount of textual information.

3 The Idealet-Centric Knowledge Modeling Scheme

3.1 The General Idea

We suggest a knowledge structuring approach - the "idealet" that can help boost the open development approach of both the environment itself as well as the content of OIBS. Idealets can represent the knowledge embedded in the previously unstructured text inputs at least semi-structured with the focus on the innovative components. In this way, they allow new functionalities and services, like intelligent text analysis, incentive mechanisms and reward systems to be developed and plugged on the core OIBS services. In addition, by incorporating the text mining techniques into mashup applications based on the semantic representation of the input information, the idealet-centric modeling scheme will enrich the knowledge being processed. The basic mechanism for semantics are provided using the "idealet" attributes and can be enriched with user defined tags.

Our model is expected to increase the dynamics of the individual's creativity by creating an online environment where a conventional habit is easily exceeded. The collaborative content production and intelligent content recommendation approach together will significantly boost the possibilities of unexpected findings which are a major innovation source. We conceive a new people-to-people interaction based approach to support the innovation system. This way, people with fresh ideas and people with practical knowledge can effectively combine their forces in an open innovation based social networking community.

To better illustrate the knowledge modeling scheme we narrow down our discussion to open textual content systems, where the pieces of textual contents produced by users are named as "essays". These essays are short articles that may contain limited multimedia information that are associated to some part of text information. As the basic inputs, essays are contributed by content composers – a subcategory of users. The idea behind this phenomenon is that the content users may take the role of content composers if they want to contribute. This kind of user-driven services has been studied and advocated recently [4].

The essays in the open innovation system are short articles consisting of one or multiple idealets. Fig. 2 shows the structure of such a system for managing shared textual contents. The essays in the database are converted into knowledge via a semantic network, which appear as the innovative ideas at the user end. There are three user interfaces. The Innovation Services interface is the main one to content users, which allows content users to create, edit, retrieve, summarize, aggregate, and market essays. The System Admin interface is used to manage the system and services by the

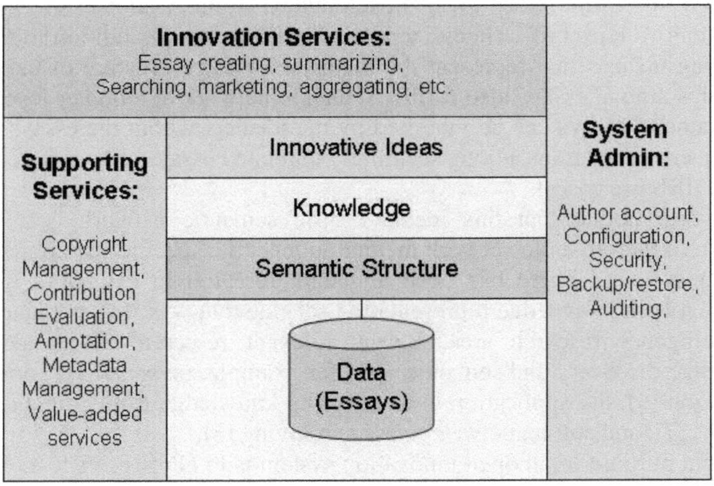

Fig. 2. The logic structure of an open innovation system with textual content services

system administrators. The Supporting Services interface provides advanced services, such as copyright management, essay evaluation, annotation, user-configurable services, etc., mainly for those advanced or power users. The idealet-centric approach can help composers to structure their essays in the way that will ease the access of them. Most importantly, the essays organized in idealets with relationships among them are more informative for mashups to aggregate innovative contents in better quality to users.

3.2 Knowledge Modeling with Idealets

A semantic network based knowledge modeling approach for idealets can be applied to the open innovation system with a specific focus on the identified innovative contents. Idealets are then associated to each other with regard to their categories and attribute values in conjunction with the relationship among essays. The attributes also enable implementation of relevant models of structured discourse for argumentation-based approaches [5].

When users input their essays they will be advised to input key information of the essay as its attributes, such as the theme of the essay, keywords, references, category, type of the essay, etc. Some of the attributes are generic and some are specific to the context and user group (e.g. in the context of OIBS this ranges from course assignment with students to open ideation for thematic area, or locally or situationally relevant issue, with elderly people). Importantly, inputting the attributes happens as natural part or side effect of the process minimizing the user efforts. These attributes obviously enrich the input information and will serve as a good source for the applications to mash multiple inputs up into a piece of new essay. Since an essay may contain more than one idea, idealets then become the fundamental components in a semantic network formed by essays. An example of semantic network for the relationships among idealets is shown in Fig. 3. There are two major types of relationships among idealets – 1:1 Relation and 1:M Relation. Examples of 1:1 Relations are "extended from", "referred to", and "differentiated from"; examples of 1:M Relations include "multi-referred to", "integrated from", and so on. In addition to the relationships among idealets that represent the major knowledge structure of the essays, the relationships among essays also form a semantic network at a higher level. The relationships among essays can be inherited by the idealets within the essays. Also, they help discovery of relations among seemingly unrelated essays (e.g. as described above on in the OIBS use cases).

It is worth noting that this idealet-centric semantic network is a customized application of the semantic network method to meet the specific requirements of open innovation systems. There has been abundant research in extending the classical semantic network knowledge representation scheme that was very popular in the artificial intelligence research area. Recent relevant research efforts include those in knowledge discovery and semantic web, for example, personalized knowledge recommendation [9], the application in discovering knowledge from computer-mediated discussions [7], and automatic web content archiving [3].

The main purpose of an open innovation system is to allow users to exchange their ideas and generate input for innovation process. This involves knowledge creation, dissemination, integration, and refinement. Naturally, idealets become the elemental

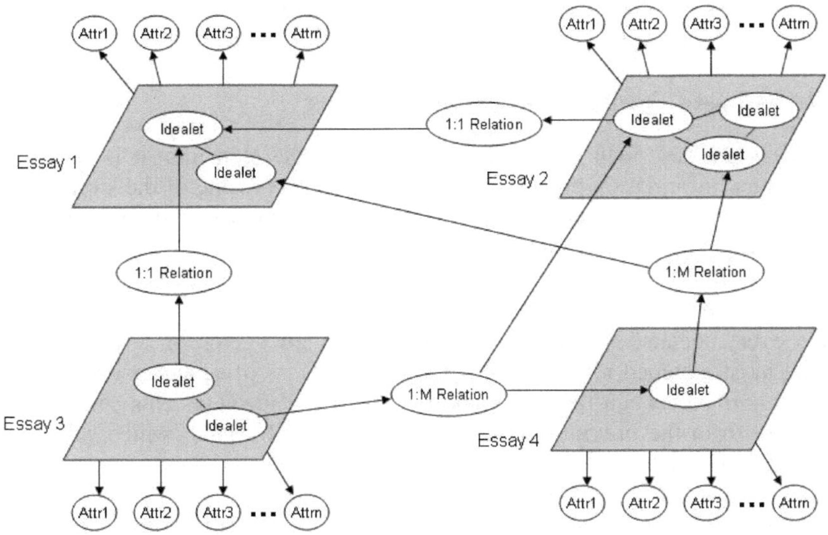

Fig. 3. The semantic network at the idealet level

unit of the knowledge in the semantic network. The essay is the carrier of idealets and predetermines its idealets' attributes. In this way, the two-level semantic network becomes the basic form of the idealet-centric knowledge model.

Idealets in an essay are normally tied to each other closely as they are tightly integrated together by a stream of textual contents. Theoretically, they can be identified in terms of latent Dirichlet allocation (LDA) [1], which stems from the Dirichlet distribution, a family of continuous multivariate probability distributions characterized by a vector of positive real values. LDA allows sets of observations explained by unobserved groups which explain why some parts of the data are similar. Once the vector of terms with their frequencies is generated from an essay, the terms can be partitioned into subgroups according to the number predefined. In this way, the outcome of an essay processed by the LDA model will be a set of idealets, each being associated with a term vector that comes with the probabilities for each term. To ensure that the automatically created idealets are meaningful, the results of this process may be verified by the one who submitted the essay – or by other members of the community. Thus, this combined process would provide substantial boost in idea processing, refinement and linking.

Our application of semantic network approach differs from others in that we focus on the level of idealet and the formation of the semantic network based on combining it with the web 2.0 approach. The better quality the description of the idealet is, the more comprehensive the semantic network is, and the more likely the innovative idea will be adopted. Therefore, essay composers have incentive to conceive their essay in a way making use of the idealet-centric knowledge representation scheme. In the best case, an essay composer can readily outline each idea with detailed information. By default, there is only one idealet in the essay but the composer may specify number of idealets. In summary, the idealets are identified by two approaches, either defined by essay composers or generated by the LDA model. Each idealet is characterized by a vector of terms, each of the terms having a probabilistic value.

3.3 Idealet-Based Textual Information Processing

As the ideas are described by text (and optional media elements) it is important to support textual information processing in addition to processing of the structured data elements. Below we describe the basic textual information processing functions for an open innovation system idea bank:

- Idealet search
  Since every idealet is characterized in a weighted vector of terms, the search for the most matched idealets is a calculation process of semantic distance or cosine-similarity between the query and the candidate idealets. This can be seen an extension from the previous semantic network based search, which relies on the semantic links among idealets.
- Idealet comparison
  The "innovativeness" is an important criterion to justify the contribution of an essay. The weighted vector of terms for idealets allows the calculation of the distance between two idealets to determine the extent of innovativeness - in case we choose to use such a criterion as a measure of "innovativeness". Again, this automatic processing is meant as input for final judgment to be done by human users, and it remains to be studied what would be the appropriate criteria in various cases.
- Idealet aggregation
  Based on the enriched inputs of textual information in the idealet semantic network, we will apply text snippet extraction technique to reconstruct an essay based on many idealets [8]. Text snippet extraction is a special text processing technique based on language statistical model to identify certain personalized patterns in a textual document for the applications such as web search engine construction, customized text summarization and automated question answering. Li and Chen proposed that text snippet extraction can be generalized if a user's intention is utilized. This is achieved by constructing and using statistical language models which effectively capture the commonalities between a document and the user intention. In particular, this approach first employs a document filter to retrieve a set of documents from the corpus that are relevant to a profile representing a user's intention. Since this step is orthogonal to the subsequent text snippet extraction, any good filters can be applied to retrieve documents. Typically, a document filter conducts a certain similarity comparison between the profile and a subset of documents in the corpus which contain at least part of the profile. Next, a pair of statistical language models is constructed. One pertinent to the user's intention and the other is independent of this intention. Using these two models, two probabilities of each word in the relevant document being generated by either model are calculated. In this approach, a relevant document is treated as a sequence of words, each associated with these two probabilities. Thus, from every relevant document, one or more snippets that are deemed to best satisfy the user's intention can be extracted. In this way, the system can overcome the rigidness of existing approaches by dynamically returning more flexible start-end positions of text snippets, and is semantically coherent.

When a user enters a string of keywords to summarize relevant ideas proposed by others, the system will do the following steps based on the idealet-based knowledge representation:

- Step 1: retrieve a number of relevant essays and rank them in accordance with the semantic distance from the query
- Step 2: use a configurable cut-off level to keep those most relevant essays for further processing
- Step 3: these top-N relevant essays are treated as one document and fed into the text snippet extraction engine [8] to construct a new condensed essay.

This is in fact the main idea of text mining based mashup applications.

4 Implementing an Open Innovation System

Based on the idealet-centric approach, an open innovation system for text information sharing is depicted in Fig. 4. The idealet-centric data model is built upon a network infrastructure, normally the Internet or an intranet. These idealets organized by the model are constructive blocks for open innovation services delivered by semantic mashups, and technically implemented in the advanced methods, such as text summarization. A series of services may be configured to form certain business processes upon needs.

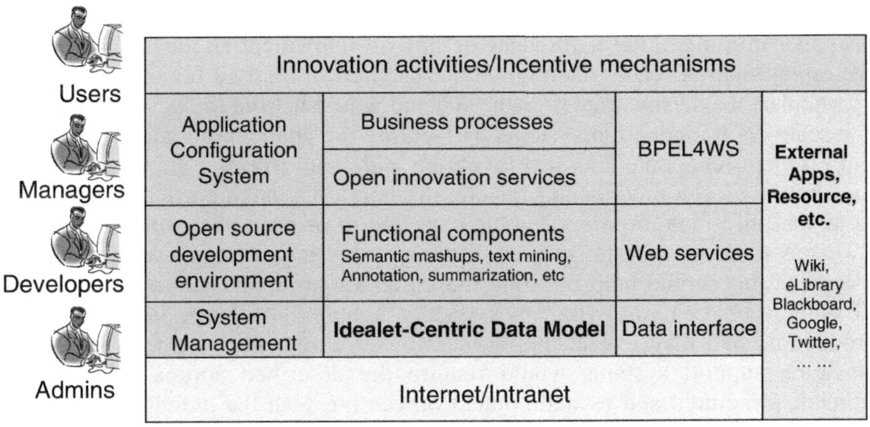

Fig. 4. The anatomy of idealet-centric open innovation system

There are four types of users: system administrators (Admins), who support the operation of the system, service developers (Developers), who provide the evolving functions of the system to users, project managers (Managers), who are leaders of specific projects which are configurable upon needs, and normal users (Users), who contribute the knowledge to the open innovation system. Users of the system could play different roles, including idealet contributor, idealet reviewer, and idealet follower.

To facilitate different needs of the open innovation system, a number of utilities must be available. In the left column of the system diagram in Fig. 4, the Application

Configuration System is for project managers to define their projects, the Open Source Development Environment is for service developers to enhance the functions of the system, and the System Management module is dedicated for system administration purposes.

There must be several incentive-compatible mechanisms to guarantee the effective operation of the system. For example, the following are the most important incentive-compatible mechanisms for an open innovation system:

- The incentive for users to contribute idealets. The idealet contributors should not be bothered by the copyright problem. Their contributions to the system must be clearly identified and properly evaluated.
- The incentive for idealet contributors to input the contents in the way that can better organize the text information for further processing.
- The incentive for users to follow the innovative ideas available in the system. Obviously, the number of followers can well indicate the value of an idealet or a set of idealets.
- The mechanism to promote high quality idealets that will attract better followers and keep the thread moving forward. For this purpose, some users of the system will be playing the role of reviewers of the idealets. Their contributions must be accounted and encouraged.

5 Concluding Remarks

This paper introduces the main ideas on how to implement an idealet-centric knowledge representation scheme and how this scheme can be used for semantic mashups. In particular, we demonstrate how the scheme would help in the development of very large scale open innovation systems by tackling the challenging knowledge management problems encountered when involving wide and diverse audiences. The combination of the idealet model and semantic mashup tools making use of both structured and textual information processing are expected to provide value to idea contributors as well as to those looking to their further processing as inputs for the innovation processes. This should help boosting the initial adoption and scaling of use of OIBS and other such systems, which is typically a major challenge in their successful introduction. We may expect that successful development of very large scale open innovation support systems would require the described approach of combining automatic structured and textual content processing with the individual and community judgment and efforts. To take this approach further, the research tasks, among others, include the development of content aggregation algorithm, and experiments using text corpus.

References

1. Blei, D.M., Ng, A.Y., Jordan, M.I.: Latent Dirichlet Allocation. Journal of Machine Learning Research (3), 993–1022 (2003)
2. Chesbrough, H.W.: Open Innovation: The new imperative for creating and profiting from technology. Harvard Business School Press, Boston (2003)

3. Du, T.C.: Building an automatic e-tendering system on the Semantic Web. Decision Suppor Systems 47(1), 13–21 (2009)
4. Hamalainen, M.: Crowdsourcing and a Living Lab on Campus: enabling research in user driven service innovation. Presented in IBM Academic Days, Zurich, Switzerland (May 13-14, 2008)
5. Hamalainen, M., Hashim, S., Holsapple, C., Whinston, Y.: Structured Discourse for Scientific Collaboration: a Framework for Scientific Collaboration Based on Structured Discourse Analysis. Journal of Organizational Computing and Electronic Commerce 2, 1–26 (1992)
6. Heino, P., Pippola, T., Peltonen, J., Piispanen, P.: Innovative development of an environment for innovations. In: Proceedings of the Beyond the Dawn of Innovation 2009 Conference, Laurea University of Applied Sciences, Finland, June 15 – 17, pp. 256–260 (2009)
7. Khalifa, M., Liu, V.: Semantic network representation of computer-mediated discussions: Conceptual facilitation form and knowledge acquisition. Omega 36(2), 252–266 (2008)
8. Li, Q., Chen, Y.P.: Personalized Text Snippet Extraction Using Statistical Language Models. Pattern Recognition (2009) (in press)
9. Liang, T.P., Yang, Y.F., Chen, D.N., Ku, Y.C.: A semantic-expansion approach to personalized knowledge recommendation. Decision Support Systems 45(3), 401–412 (2008)
10. Palfrey, J., Gasser, U.: Case Study - Mashups Interoperability and eInnovation. Berkman Publication Series (November 2007), `http://cyber.law.harvard.edu/interop/pdfs/interop-mashups.pdf` (retrieved on September 10, 2009)
11. Reamy, T.: Mashup Mindset Moving Mashups to Next Level. Knowledge Architecture Professional Services, `http://www.kapsgroup.com/presentations/Mashup%20Mindset.ppt` (retrieved on June 1, 2009)
12. Rittel, H.W., Webber, M.M.: Dilemmas in a General Theory of Planning. Policy Sciences (4), 155–169 (1973); Reprinted in Cross, N. (ed.): Developments in Design Methodology, pp. 135–144. J. Wiley & Sons, Chichester (1984)
13. Santonen, T., Kaivo-Oja, J., Antikainen, M.: National Open, Innovation System (NOIS): Defining a Solid Reward Model for NOIS. In: Huizingh, K.R.E., Torkkeli, M., Conn, S., Bitran, I. (eds.) Proc. of the 1st ISPIM Innovation Symposium - Managing Innovation in a Connected World, Singapore, December 14-17 (2008)
14. Viégas, F.B., Wattenberg, M., McKeon, M.M.: The Hidden Order of Wikipedia. IBM Watson Research Center, Technical Report #07-12 (2007)

The Effects of Sense of Presence, Sense of Belonging, and Cognitive Absorption on Satisfaction and User Loyalty toward an Immersive 3D Virtual World

Dan J. Kim[1] and Dongsong Zhang[2]

[1] Computer Information Systems, University of Houston-Clear Lake, 2700 Bay Area Blvd. Houston, TX 77058, USA
kimdan@uhcl.edu

[2] Department of Information Systems, University of Maryland, Baltimore County, 1000 Hilltop Circle, Baltimore, MD 21250
zhangd@umbc.edu

Abstract. Avatar-based 3D virtual worlds such as Second Life have drawn increasing attention from users and researchers in the past few years as an emerging online environment for social, entertainment, and virtual business. However, there are very limited empirical studies that have examined the influence of social-technonlogical constructs (i.e., sense of presence, sense of belonging, and cognitive absorption) on users' satisfaction and their loyalty to a virtual world. An aggregate second-order construct that consists of multiple-dimensions seems a reasonable approach. Moreover, due to the multi-dimensional characteristics of socio-technological constructs, examining those constructs needs to use more stable and reliable higher-order measurements than before. Therefore, in this study, we empirically investigate the effect of three social-technological constructs as a multi-dimensional second-order construct on the first-time users' satisfaction with and loyalty to avatar-based virtual world. The results and their theoretical and practical implications are also discussed.

Keywords: Virtual world, sense of presence, sense of belonging, cognitive absorption, satisfaction, loyalty.

1 Introduction

A virtual world (VW) is an electronic artificial environment where users assume an identity as a made-up character and interact with other users in real time in a somewhat realistic manner. People who join a virtual world often establish social relationship with other community members and develop social norms and expectations of the community [1]. Some 3D virtual worlds such as Second Life (SL, www.secondlife.com) are designed to simulate the real world with sufficient fidelity. They possess unique features such as personalized avatars (i.e., visual representations of users created by themselves), real-time multi-modal communication, diverse social networking activities, teleport, and virtual business. Users can interact with each other

R. Sharman, T.S. Raghu, and H.R. Rao (Eds.): WEB 2009, LNBIP 52, pp. 30–43, 2010.

through avatars. On the practical side, many companies such as Mercedes-Benz, Coca-Cola, and IBM have their presence in SL. Although currently they use their virtual stores in SL more for product demonstration and marketing than for direct sales, the latter could well be a desirable long-term goal. Thus, understanding influential factors that can affect users' decision to use an immersive virtual world like SL offers potential value to businesses.

Both immersive 3D virtual worlds and Web 2.0 technologies can be described as social computing or social technology[1] [1-3]. Despite their importance, popularity, and potential, the research on the effects of social-technological constructs such as users' perceptions on the presence, belonging, and cognitive absorption in virtual worlds is scarce[2]. Moreover, socio-technological constructs have multiple dimensions. Sense of presence, for example, has at least two dimensions, namely virtual presence ("being there") and social presence ("being together"). Sense of belonging consists of four dimensions: feelings of membership, feelings of influence, feelings of supporting each others, and feelings of relationships [4]. An aggregate second-order construct comprised of multiple dimensions seems a reasonable approach. As a result, examining those constructs needs to use more stable and reliable higher-order measurements than what were used before.

This research is aimed to empirically investigate the effect of three socio-technological variables (i.e., sense of presence, sense of belonging, and cognitive absorption) as second-order constructs on the user satisfaction with and loyalty to avatar-based 3D virtual worlds such as SL. This study not only provides theoretical and methodological contributions to the research on socio-technological constructs in avatar-based 3D virtual worlds, but also potentially assists developers of such virtual environments with system interface design.

2 Literature Review and Theoretical Background

2.1 Sense of Presence

In Webster's New Collegiate Dictionary, the term 'presence' is defined as "the fact or condition of being present" or "something… felt or believed to be present". Lombard & Ditton [5] interpret presence as a perceptual illusion of non-mediation; presence is what happens when a participant 'forgets' that his perceptions are mediated by technologies. Sense of presence (SoP) is the subjective sensation of "being there" [6],

---

[1] This sociological view of technology was first proposed by Jacques Ellul in his 1964 seminal book entitled 'The Technological Society'. Ellul defined seven characteristics of modern technology: rationality, artificiality, automatism of technical choice, self-augmentation, monism, universalism, and autonomy. According to Ellul [2], technology is progressively effacing the two previous environments, nature and society. He argued that "The machine represents only a small part of technique…we could say not only that the machine is the result of a certain technique, but also that its social value and economic applications are made possible by other technical advances (p. 4)."

[2] Although the sociological view of technology is discussed before, the unique features and social norms of virtual worlds such as SL are significantly different from traditional virtual teams and online communities examined in the literature. As a result, previous findings on those constructs may likely not be applicable.

which is obtained by successful arousal of the emotional reasoning of the human brain. SoP has been described as a perceptual flow requiring directed attention and is based on the interaction of sensory stimulation, environmental factors, and internal tendencies [7].

There have been many terms associated with sense of presence, such as copresence [8], social presence [9], telepresence [10], virtual presence [11], and para-social presence [12]. Jsselsteijn et al. [13] argue that that the conceptualization of Lombard and Ditton [5] can be grouped into two broad categories: physical and social presence. The first is the sense of being physically in a remote space and the second is the sense of being together with someone in a virtual space. In this research, we use two reflective constructs of sense of presence, namely virtual presence and social presence. Virtual presence can be considered as a special case of telepresence where a remote environment is artificially created [14]. *Social presence* is the sense of "being with" someone instead of feeling of "*being there*" in a virtual world. Social presence can be defined as "the degree to which a medium facilitates awareness of the other person and interpersonal relationships during the interaction" [15, p. 118]. Social presence is a subjective quality of a communication medium and relates to the social psychology concepts of intimacy, determined by physical distance, eye contact, smiling, and personal topics of conversation, as well as immediacy, determined by the medium's capacity in transmitting information [9].

2.2 Sense of Belonging

Sense of belonging or sense of community refers to the feeling of connection and attachment to a social group [16]. Jones [17] makes a distinction between virtual settlement and virtual community. Without sense of belonging, virtual community is just virtual settlement. In other words, when this sense of connection is present, a virtual settlement can be called a "virtual community".

Some researchers have examined a variety of constructs related to sense of belonging. Many of those constructs are originated from psychological or sociological theories or the literature exploring issues of person-environment (P-E) fit. The concept of P-E fit, a measure of a person's general sense of belonging within a particular environment, indicates that alignment between characteristics of people and their environments results in positive outcomes for individuals and organizations [18]. McMillan and Chavis [4] proposed four dimensions of sense of belonging: feelings of membership (i.e., feelings of belonging to a community), feelings of influence (i.e., feelings of having influence on or being influenced by a community), integration and fulfillment of needs (i.e., feelings of supporting each other in a community), and shared emotional connection (i.e., feelings of relationships within a community). They serve as a foundation for users to form loyalty to a group.

2.3 Cognitive Absorption

Cognitive absorption (CA), a state of deep involvement or a holistic experience that an individual has with a virtual world, can be best manifested by the level of individual involvement with Internet and video games [19]. Agarwal and Karahanna [19] posit that CA, an intrinsic motivation related variable, is important to the study of technology usage behavior because it serves as a key antecedent to salient beliefs about an information technology. They define cognitive absorption as "a state of deep involvement with software" that is exhibited through five dimensions: 1) temporal dissociation, or the inability to register the passage of time while engaging in interaction; 2) focused immersion, or the experience of total engagement where other attentional demands are ignored; 3) heightened enjoyment, capturing the pleasurable aspects of the interaction; 4) control, representing the user's perception of being in charge of the interaction, and 5) curiosity, tapping into the extent the experience arouses an individual's sensory and cognitive curiosity. A sense of being in charge and exercising control over software interaction should reduce the perceived difficulty of tasks.

Yang and Teo [20] report in a study that CA positively influences a trial player's willingness to purchase computer games. In addition to leading to positive outcomes such as behavioral intention to use a technology, higher levels of CA are also found to result in increased user satisfaction and decision performance [21]. On the other hand, individuals who exhibit problematic usage behavior often report total immersion, time distortion, and a sense of control [22]. Therefore, it is important to examine the effect of CA on user intention to use a virtual world.

3 Research Model and Hypotheses

In this study, to investigate the effects of the second-order constructs on users' satisfaction with an immersive 3D virtual world (i.e., SL) and their intention to use it continuously (i.e., Vw-Loyalty), we propose a research model with three second-order constructs as presented in Figure 1.

3.1 Satisfaction and Virtual World Loyalty

The ultimate endogenous construct of this study, a user's *loyalty to the virtual world (Vw-Loyalty),* has its root in the consumer behavior literature. Rowley and Dawes

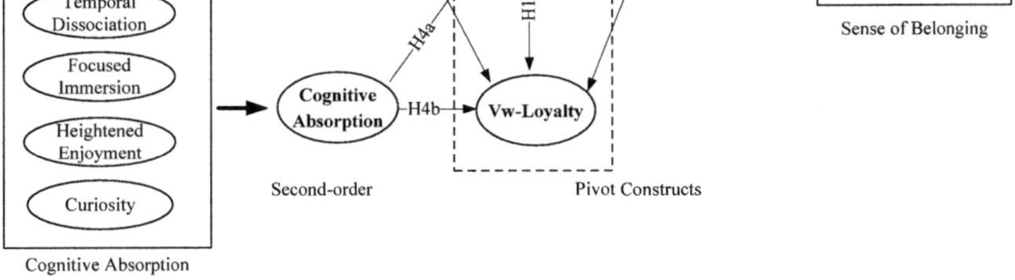

Fig. 1. Virtual World Loyalty Model

[23] conceptualized consumer loyalty as a positive attitude reflecting three concepts: repeated patronage to a retailer, intention to repurchase from a retailer, and willingness to recommend a retailer to others. In this study, by adapting the concept of loyalty suggested by Rowley and Dawes [23], we define Vw-Loyalty as a positive attitude toward a virtual world that includes retaining, participating, and engaging in the services and activities provided by the virtual world, as well as recommending the virtual world to others.

Satisfaction refers to a user's specialized form of judgment resulting from the previous experiences of the virtual world. The causal relationship between satisfaction and loyalty has been discussed and empirically tested in different contexts in many studies [e.g., 24-31].

Users who are satisfied with a service tend to have a higher usage level than those who are not [32]. They may stay loyal to the service because they feel that they receive a greater value than they would from other competitors [33]. We argue that a user's satisfaction with a virtual world is a significant determinant of his or her Vw-Loyalty. It is reasonable to argue that after initial use, users who are satisfied with a virtual world are more likely to continue using it (i.e., loyalty to the virtual world). Therefore, we propose that:

Hypothesis H1: Satisfaction with a 3D virtual world has a positive effect on Vw-Loyalty.

Aforementioned, *sense of presence* can be in diverse forms such as virtual presence and social presence in a computer-mediated communication environment. Social presence implies psychological connections among users in a virtual world, who perceive a virtual world as a personal, sociable, and warm environment, thus creating a feeling of human contact [34].

Several prior empirical studies suggested the relationship between different types of presence and attitude in virtual environmental settings, including virtual communities and online stores. The greater virtual presence that customers experience, the more favorable attitude or performance they show [35, 36]. An environment with a high level of social presence promotes positive attitude and behaviors such as information sharing [37], trust in online stores [38, 39], and participation in a virtual community [40]. Considering virtual presence and social presence at the same time, Jung [41] empirically tested the direct relationship between those two types of presence and behavioral intention (i.e., intention to participate in a virtual community). Drawing from the evidence of previous studies, we propose that sense of presence as a second-order construct positively affects users' satisfaction and their attitude (i.e., loyalty) toward an immersive 3D virtual world. Thus, we propose that:

Hypothesis H2a: Sense of presence has a positive effect on satisfaction with the virtual world.
Hypothesis H2b: Sense of presence has a positive effect on Vw-Loyalty.

By adopting four dimensions of sense of community proposed by McMillan and Chavis [4], namely feelings of membership, feelings of influence, integration and fulfillment of needs, and shared emotional connection, this study proposes *sense of belonging* as a four-dimensional second-order construct. In computer-mediated communication, users' satisfaction and performance are found to be dependent on the degree of social presence of the communication medium [42]. Several studies have investigated the relationship between sense of community and other important outcomes in face-to-face environments. Surprisingly, there have been very few empirical studies on the relationship between sense of belonging and loyalty in virtual community context.

To feel a sense of belonging to a virtual world, one needs to feel he or she is a member of the community; members can influence and support each other; and they share experience in some senses. The increased sense of belonging to a virtual community promotes positive and active involvement [4, 43], and in turn leads to important outcomes such as satisfaction, commitment, and copying behaviors (e.g., loyalty) in virtual settings [44]. Thus, we propose that:

Hypothesis H3a: Sense of belonging has a positive effect on satisfaction with a 3D virtual world.
Hypothesis H3b: Sense of belonging has a positive effect on Vw-Loyalty.

CA consists of several dimensions (Agarwal and Karahanna [19]: temporal dissociation, focused immersion, heightened enjoyment, control, and curiosity. If users experience temporal dissociation, they will lose track of time and feel completing a task with less time than they actually did. This feeling of being immersed into virtual environments, sometimes manifested as addiction to a virtual community via daily computer-mediated communication, is what people experience as virtual community members [45]. With focused immersion and heightened enjoyment, all of the attentional resources of a user are focused on a particular task, thus the level of cognitive burden is reduced. Curiosity invokes the act of intensive interaction with the technology. Thus, in this study, CA is conceptualized as a multi-dimensional second-order construct.

CA is reported to be a proximal antecedent of two dominating technology acceptance factors: perceived ease of use and perceived usefulness (Agarwal and Karahanna, [19]. Consistent with the result of previous studies, Lin [46] identifies that users with higher CA experience in the virtual community are likely to have a higher level of positive usefulness and ease of use beliefs. The previous research (e.g., [47]) reveals CA as an important antecedent to user's beliefs in relation to IT usage. However, there have been limited empirical studies examining the relationship between CA and the pivot constructs (i.e., satisfaction, and loyalty) in a virtual world. Thus, this study mainly focuses on the direct effect of cognitive absorption on pivot constructs.

Drawing upon previous studies, we expect cognitive absorption, a second-order aggregated construct of four dimensions[3], has positive influence on user's satisfaction with and loyalty to a 3D virtual world. In other words, when people are absorbed into a 3D virtual world, they generally believe interaction with the virtual world is more useful and effortless and are more likely to be satisfied with it. Hence, they will intend to use it more frequently and likely recommend it to others [46]. Thus, we propose that:

---

[3] Control dimension is not used in this study because there is a conceptual overlap with virtual presence.

Hypothesis H4a: Cognitive absorption has a positive effect on satisfaction with a 3D virtual world.
Hypothesis H4b: Cognitive absorption has a positive effect on Vw-Loyalty.

4 Research Methodology and Data Collection

To assess the research model and test the hypotheses, a survey research methodology was adopted. We followed the three stages of instrument development suggested by Moore and Benbasat [48]: item creation, scale development, and instrument testing. For the survey item creation, all measurement items were initially adopted from previous literature sources. To improve the measurement scale, a panel of experts carefully reviewed the instruments, identified ambiguous items, and modified them to fit the research context. Most of the scales were anchored as 7-point Likert-type with such end points as "strongly disagree/strongly agree" and "very dissatisfy/very satisfy". The instrument items[4] were tested for reliability, construct validity, and convergent and discriminant validity.

4.1 Data Collection

A careful data collection method is required because of several reasons: i) the decision to adopt and use a technology innovation is a multi-stage process [49, 50]; ii) all three second-order variables are meaningful mainly for those who have already been exposed to the 3D virtual world of interest (i.e., Second Life); and iii) the concept of loyalty adopted from Rowley and Dawes [23] is related to transaction experiences from a longitudinal perspective. Therefore, we followed a multi-stage data collection plan for the first-time SL users. Three rounds of survey were administrated to a group of students at two public universities in the United States.

Students participated in the surveys voluntarily as an optional bonus assignment for an introductory IS class. In the first step, Second Life was introduced and demonstrated in the class. Since SL is a relatively new 3D virtual world, this introduction section was a necessary step to provide basic understanding of SL. The 30-minute introduction section covered the definition and examples of virtual worlds, general information about SL, various social, entertainment, educational activities that can be performed, and virtual economy in SL. Right after the introduction section and tutorial, students were asked to fill out the first-round survey, which contained questions about their try-out intentions and basic demographics. We also gathered data on whether participants had any prior experience with Second Life.

After the first-round survey, respondents who did not have any prior experience with SL were asked to create a free Second Life user account within a two-week timeline and gaining some actual experience with SL. The detailed instructions on how to create a free SL account were provided to participants. The bonus assignment required participants to accomplish several tasks designed for Second Life, including, but not limited to, navigating SL, communicating with other SL residents, earning SL money in LD$, and went shopping in virtual stores in SL. After they gained initial SL

[4] Due to the space limitation, the measurement items are not included, but are available from the authors upon request.

experience, participants were asked to fill out the second-round survey, which comprised questions related to their initial-usage experience and initial satisfaction. A total of 78 students participated in the second round survey.

The third-round survey about post-usage was conducted four weeks after the second-round survey was done. In that survey, all respondents were asked to provide information about the sense of presence, sense of belonging to SL, cognitive absorption, their satisfaction about SL experience, and their intention to continue using SL. A total of 75 responses were received. After eliminating invalid responses, a total of 71 usable responses were available for measurement model testing and structure model testing. The average age of 71 participants was 25.6 years old; 58.6 percent were male; participants rated a relatively high level of experience with computers (mean = 5.77) and Internet technology (mean = 6.05) on a scale of 1 to 7 (1-novice/ 7-expert).

5 Data Analysis and Results

To test the proposed research model, we employed SmartPLS 2.0 M3 for data analysis. Since the number of maximum arrowheads in the model pointing to the

Table 1. Descriptive Statistics and Reliability Coefficients for Constructs

Constructs	Mean+	S.D.+	Cronbach Alpha	Composite Reliability	AVE	Concept & Scales adapted from
Sense of Presence	3.843	1.347	0.961	0.966	0.705	Second-order++
Virtual Presence	3.211	1.746	0.959	0.969	0.861	[52]
Social Presence	4.474	.948	0.930	0.944	0.708	[52]
Sense of Belonging	3.127	1.438	0.969	0.973	0.719	Second-order
Feelings of Membership	3.231	1.489	0.943	0.959	0.855	[53]
Feelings of Influence	2.918	1.463	0.796	0.881	0.715	[53]
Feelings of Support	3.314	1.582	0.932	0.957	0.881	[53]
Emotional Connection	3.042	1.219	0.919	0.943	0.806	[53]
Cognitive Absorption	3.747	1.530	0.957	0.968	0.695	Second-order
Temporal Dissociation	3.839	1.527	0.800	0.867	0.628	[54]
Focused Immersion	3.558	1.125	0.647	0.826	0.659	[55, 56]
Heightened Enjoyment	3.780	1.733	0.952	0.966	0.875	[56]
Curiosity	3.811	1.734	0.946	0.965	0.903	[56]
Satisfaction	4.170	1.638	0.940	0.957	0.847	[57, 58]
Vw-Loyalty	3.222	1.977	0.978	0.984	0.937	[59-61]

Note: +: Mean and standard deviation (S.D.) are calculated using the average of construct items.. ++: Second-order constructs are calculated based on the aggregation of its' first-order constructs.

Vw-Loyalty is four, this study has enough samples to test the proposed model. Following the suggestion of Chin [51], we conducted a two-step assessment process (i.e., the assessment of the outer and inner model, respectively).

5.1 Outer Model (Measurement Model) Assessment

We tested reliability, construct validity, and convergent and discriminant validity of the first-order and second-order constructs. Reliability was tested by Cronbach Alpha and Composite Reliability, and convergent and discriminate validity was evaluated using Average Variance Extracted (AVE) reported by SmartPLS. Table 1 summarizes the descriptive statistics of constructs and literature sources from which the measurement items of the constructs were adopted. Table 2 shows the square root of the AVE and the cross correlations of latent variables.

The results show that all Cronbach Alpha coefficients and Composite Reliability scores are greater than 0.7, indicating adequate internal consistency. For convergent and discriminate validity, AVE values of all constructs are much higher than 0.5, the minimum requirement [62], and the square root of the AVE of all constructs are larger than the cross-correlations among latent variables (see Table 2), indicating that more variance is shared between the latent variable component and its group of indicators than with another group representing a different group of indicators [63].

Table 2. Correlations of Latent Variables

	1	2	3	4	5	6	7	8	9	10	11	12
1. Virtual Presence	**0.95**											
2. Social Presence	0.83	**0.96**										
3. Feelings of Membership	0.72	0.81	**0.97**									
4. Feelings of Influence	0.80	0.73	0.83	**0.88**								
5. Feelings of Support	0.83	0.75	0.87	0.78	**0.92**							
6. Emotional Connection	0.68	0.81	0.92	0.77	0.82	**0.95**						
7. Temporal Dissociation	0.87	0.79	0.81	0.67	0.78	0.85	**0.95**					
8. Focused Immersion	0.82	0.82	0.77	0.81	0.85	0.86	0.76	**0.96**				
9. Heightened Enjoyment	0.88	0.80	0.78	0.81	0.84	0.84	0.78	0.77	**0.97**			
10. Curiosity	0.86	0.75	0.81	0.70	0.78	0.85	0.89	0.76	0.87	**0.95**		
11. Satisfaction	0.78	0.79	0.79	0.70	0.75	0.80	0.76	0.81	0.80	0.79	**0.85**	
12. Vw-Loyalty	0.67	0.86	0.74	0.67	0.82	0.88	0.60	0.75	0.67	0.58	0.84	**0.95**

Note: Diagonal elements are the Square root of the AVE. These values should exceed the inter-construct correlations for adequate discriminant validity.

Following the guidelines for hierarchical latent variable models using PLS path modeling, we constructed a second-order hierarchical construct model in PLS path modeling. Figure 2 represents the results of second-order structural model testing, which includes estimated path coefficients, factor-loadings of the second-order constructs, and R-square.

The results of the structural model testing show a strong positive effect of satisfaction on Vw-loyalty (beta = 2.81, $p < .01$), supporting H1; significant impacts of sense of presence on both satisfaction (beta =1.85, $p < 0.05$) and Vw-loyalty (beta=3.50, $p < .001$), supporting H2a and H2b; positive effects of sense of belonging on satisfaction (beta=1.64, $p < .05$), supporting H3a; and strong positive effects of cognitive absorption on both satisfaction (beta =2.38, $p < 0.01$) and Vw-loyalty (beta=4.33, $p < .001$), supporting H4a and H4b. The effect of sense of belonging on Vw-loyalty (beta=1.85, $p > .05$) is not statistically significant, so H3b is not supported.

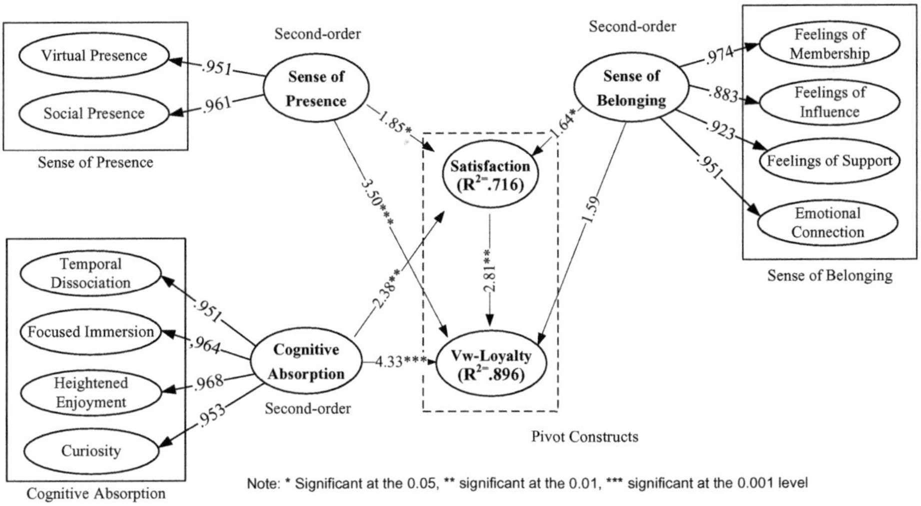

Fig. 2. Structural Model – Results

6 Discussion and Conclusion

The major findings of this study reveal the important roles of three social-technological constructs (i.e., sense of presence, sense of belonging, and cognitive absorption) in determining users' satisfaction with and their loyalty to SL. Since the main applications of SL are social networking, virtual business, and virtual entertainment, the result is somewhat understandable.

There are multi-fold theoretical contributions of the results. First, this is the one of pioneer studies focusing on three major socio-technological constructs as second-order constructs at the same time, particularly in the context of 3D virtual world. Second, we empirically tested the effects of second-order constructs on the pivot constructs (i.e., satisfaction and loyalty) in an immersive 3D virtual world. Many previous studies proposed those constructs individually in e-Commerce and computer-assisted virtual team contexts, which are different from immersive avatar-based 3D virtual worlds. This study also provides practical implications. It explores and validates the important roles of social-technological variables in users' satisfaction and loyalty. The findings reveal several operators of influential factors (i.e., sense of presence, sense of belonging, and cognitive absorption) that can affect user satisfaction and persistence with a 3D virtual world. They suggest that the designers and managers of such virtual worlds should enhance the levels of those factors in their environment in order to attract and keep users.

There are several limitations of this study and research issues that merit further research. First, we focused on SL only in this study. The results may differ from other virtual worlds in various ways. Therefore, it is necessary to validate the findings of this study in other virtual world contexts in the future research. Second, in this study, we only used data collected from those participants who actually used SL. It could provide us additional insights if we also collected and analyzed data from those who don't intend to use SL. Further research will be helpful on finding the difference between those two groups. Third, in order to control the complexity of research model and survey questionnaire, we mainly focused on three major second-order constructs in this study. There are other dimensional factors that could influence user satisfaction with and loyalty to a 3D virtual world, such as pre-usage expectation, service quality, social influences, as well as technological aspects (e.g., system speed). Examining those additional factors in the future studies can make the proposed theoretical model more comprehensive. Fourth, the questions in our survey sought mainly for participants' perception and attitude towards the use of SL as whole rather than specific types of activities in SL such as social interaction or virtual business. Focusing on specific activities or contexts in a virtual world may provide extra insights for the improvement of system design in support of those activities.

References

1. Sproull, L., Faraj, S.: Atheism, Sex, and Databases: The Net As A Social Technology. In: Kiesler, S. (ed.) Culture of The Internet, pp. 35–51. Lawrence Erlbaum Associates, Mahwan (1997)
2. Ellul, J.: The technological society. Vintage, New York (1964)
3. Parameswaran, M., Whinston, A.B.: Social Computing: An Overview. Communications of the Association for Information Systems 19, 762–780 (2007)
4. McMillan, D.W., Chavis, D.M.: Sense of community: A definition and theory. Journal of Community Psychology 14, 6–23 (1986)
5. Lombard, M., Ditton, T.B.: At the Heart of It All: The Concept of Presence. Journal of Computer Mediated Communication 3(2) (1997)
6. Barfield, W., et al.: Presence and performance within virtual environments. In: Barfield, W., Furness, T.A. (eds.) Virtual environments and advanced interface design, pp. 473–541. Oxford University Press, New York (1995)
7. Singer, M.J., Witmer, B.G.: Presence; Where are we now? In: Smith, M., Salvendy, G., Koubek, R. (eds.) Design of Computing Systems: Social and Ergonomic Considerations, pp. 885–888. Elsevier Science Publishers, Amsterdam (1997)
8. Goffman, E.: Behavior in Public Places. The Free Press, New York (1963)
9. Short, J., Williams, E., Christie, B.: The Social Psychology of Telecommunication. John Wiley and Sons, London (1976)
10. Minsky, M.: Telepresence. Omni 2(9), 45–51 (1980)
11. Sheridan, T.B.: Musings on Telepresence and Virtual Presence. Presence 1(1), 120–126 (1992)
12. Kumar, N., Benbasat, I.: Para-Social Presence and Communication Capabilities of a Web Site: A Theoretical Perspective e-Service Journal 1.3, 5–24 (2002)
13. IJsselsteijn, W.A., et al.: Presence: concept, determinants and measurement. In: SPIE, Human Vision and Electronic Imaging, San Jose, CA (2000)

14. Schloerb, D.W.: A quantitative measure of telepresence. Presence 4(1), 64–80 (1995)
15. Fulk, J., Schmitz, J., Steinfield, C.: A social influence model of technology use. In: Fulk, J., Steinfield, C. (eds.) Organizations and Communication Technology, pp. 117–142. Sage, Newbury Park (1990)
16. Blanchard, A.L., Markus, M.L.: The experienced "sense" of a virtual community: Characteristics and Processes. The Data Base for Advances in Information Systems 35(10), 64–79 (2004)
17. Jones, Q.: Virtual communities, virtual settlements and cyber-archaeology: A theoretical outline? Journal of Computer Mediated Communication 3(3) (1997)
18. Ostroff, C., Shin, Y., Feinberg, B.: Skill acquisition and person-environment fit. In: Feldman, D.C. (ed.) Work careers: a developmental approach, pp. 63–90. Jossey-Bass, San Francisco (2002)
19. Agarwal, R., Karahanna, E.: Time Flies When You're Having Fun: Cognitive Absorption and Beliefs about Information Technology Usage. MIS Quarterly 24(4), 665–694 (2000)
20. Yang, X., Teo, H.: The Conflict Between Absorption and Self-Control in Playing Computer Games: How Do Free Trial Restrictions Influence Playing Experience and Purchase Decision Making. In: ICIS 2008 (2008)
21. Hess, T.J., Fuller, M.A., Mathew, J.: Involvement and Decision-Making Performance with a Decision Aid: The Influence of Social Multimedia, Gender, and Playfulness. Journal of Management Information Systems 22(3), 15–54 (2006)
22. Jia, R., Hartke, H., Pearson, J.: Can Computer Playfulness and Cognitive Absorption Lead to Problematic Technology Usage? In: ICIS 2007, Montreal, Canada (2007)
23. Rowley, J., Dawes, J.: Customer Loyalty - a Relevant Concept for Libraries? Library Management 20(6), 345–351 (1999)
24. Oliver, R.L.: Expectation Processes in Satisfaction Formation. Journal of Service Research 1(3), 196–214 (1999)
25. Ranaweera, C., Prabhu, J.: The influence of satisfaction trust and switching barriers on customer retention in a continuous purchasing setting. International Journal of Service Industry Management 14(4), 374–395 (2003)
26. Lam, S.Y., et al.: Customer Value, Satisfaction, Loyalty, and Switching Costs: An Illustration From a Business-to-Business Service Context. Journal of the Academy of Marketing Science 32(3), 293–311 (2004)
27. Shankar, V., Smith, A.K., Rangaswamy, A.: Customer Satisfaction and Loyalty in Online and Offline Environments. International Journal of Research in Marketing 20, 153–175 (2003)
28. Yi, Y., La, S.: What Influences the Relationship Between Customer Satisfaction and Repurchase Intention? Investigating the Effects of Adjusted Expectations and Customer Loyalty. Psychology & Marketing 21(5), 351–373 (2004)
29. Taylor, S.A., Hunter, G.: An exploratory investigation into the antecedents of satisfaction, brand attitude, and loyalty within the (B2B) eCRM industry. Journal of Consumer Satisfaction, Dissatisfaction and Complaining Behavior 16, 19–35 (2003)
30. Lee, E.-J., Overby, J.W.: Creating Value for Online Shoppers: Implications for Satisfaction and Loyalty. Journal of Consumer Satisfaction, Dissatisfaction and Complaining Behavior 17, 54–67 (2004)
31. Singh, J., Sirdeshmukh, D.: Agency and Trust Mechanisms in Consumer Satisfaction and Loyalty Judgments. Journal of Academy of Marketing Science 28(1), 150–167 (2000)
32. Bolton, R.N., Lemon, K.N.: A dynamic model of customers usage of services: usage as an antecedent and consequence of satisfaction. Journal of Marketing Research 36(2), 171–186 (1999)

33. Sirdeshmukh, D., Singh, J., Sabol, B.: Consumer Trust, Value, and Loyalty in Relational Exchanges. Journal of Marketing 66(1), 15–37 (2002)
34. Yoo, Y., Alavi, M.: Media and group cohesion: relative influences on social presence, task participation, and group consensus. MIS Quarterly 25(3), 371–390 (2001)
35. Hoffman, D.L., Novak, T.P.: Marketing in Hypermedia Computer-Mediated Environments: Conceptual Foundations. Journal of Marketing 60(3), 50–68 (1996)
36. Li, H., Daugherty, T., Biocca, F.: Impact on 3-D advertising on product knowledge, brand attitude, and purchase intention: the mediating role of presence. Journal of Advertising 31(3), 43–57 (2002)
37. Miranda, S.M., Saunders, C.S.: The Social Construction of Meaning: An Alternative Perspective on Information Sharing. Information Systems Research 14(1), 87–107 (2003)
38. Gefen, D., Straub, D.: Managing user trust in B2C e-Services. e-Service Journal 2(2), 7–24 (2003)
39. Pavlou, P.A., Liang, H., Xue, Y.: Understanding and Mitigating Uncertaintyin Online Environments: A Longitudinal Analysis of Trust and Social in Academy of Management Conference, Honolulu (2005)
40. Khalifa, M., Shen, N.: System Design Effects on Social Presence and Telepresence in Virtual Communities. In: ICIS, Washington (2004)
41. Jung, Y.: Influence of Sense of Presence on Intention to Participate in a Virtual Community. In: HICSS 2008 (2008)
42. Biocca, F., Harms, C., Burgoon, J.K.: Toward a More Robust Theory and Measure of Social Presence: Review and Suggested Criteria. Presence 12(5), 456–480 (2003)
43. Brodsky, A.E., O'Campo, P.J., Aronson, R.E.: PSOC in Community Context: Multi-Level Correlates of a Measure of Psychological Sense of Community in Low-Income, Urban Neighborhoods. Journal of Community Psychology 27(6), 659–679 (1999)
44. Kim, W.G., Lee, C., Hiemstra, S.J.: Effects of an online virtual community on customer loyalty and travel product purchases. Tourism Management 25(3), 343–355 (2003)
45. Koh, J., Kim, Y.G.: Sense of Virtual Community: A Conceptual Framework and Empirical Validation. International Journal of Electronic Commerce 8(2), 75–93 (2003-2004)
46. Lin, H.-F.: Examination of cognitive absorption influencing the intention to use a virtual community. Behaviour & Information Technology, iFirst article, 1–11 (2008)
47. Saade, R., Bahli, B.: The impact of cognitive absorption on perceived usefulness and perceived ease of use in on-line learning: an extention of the technology acceptance model. Information & Management 42(2), 317–327 (2005)
48. Moore, G.C., Benbasat, I.: Development of an Instrument to Measure the Perceptions of Adopting an Information Technology Innovation. Information Systems Research 2(3), 192–222 (1991)
49. Rogers, E.M.: Communication: The new media in society. The Free Press, New York (1986)
50. Rogers, E.M.: Diffusion of innovations, 4th edn. The Free Press, New York (1995)
51. Chin, W.W.: The Partial Least Squares Approach to Structural Equation Modeling. In: Marcoulides, G.A. (ed.) Modern Methods for Business Research, pp. 295–336. Lawrence Erlbaum Associates, Mahwah (1998)
52. Qiu, L., Benbasat, I.: An Investigation into the Effects of Text-to-Speech Voice and 3D Avatars on the Perception of Presence and Flow of Live Help in Electronic Commerce. ACM Transactions on Computer-Human Interaction 12(4), 329–355 (2005)
53. Ma, M., Agarwal, R.: Through a Glass Darkly: Information Technology Design, Identity Verification, and Knowledge Contribution in Online Communities. Information Systems Research 18(1), 42–67 (2007)

54. Koh, J., Kim, Y.G.: Sense of Virtual Community: A Conceptual Framework and Empirical Validation. International Journal of Electronic Commerce 8(2), 75–93 (2004)
55. Konana, P., Balasubramanian, S.: The Social–Economic–Psychological model of technology adoption and usage: an application to online investing. Decision Support Systems 39(3), 505–524 (2005)
56. Hsu, C.-L., Lu, H.-P.: Why do people play on-line games? An extended TAM with social influences and flow experience. Information and Management 41(7), 853–868 (2004)
57. Bhattacherjee, A.: Understanding Information Systems Continuance: an Expectation-Confirmation Model. MIS Quarterly 25(3), 351–370 (2001)
58. McKinney, V., Yoon, K., Zahedi, F.: The Measurement of Web-Customer Satisfaction: An Expectation and Disconfirmation Approach. Information Systems Research 13(3), 296–315 (2002)
59. Jarvenpaa, S.L., Tractinsky, N., Vitale, M.: Consumer Trust in an Internet Store. Information Technology and Management 1(1-2), 45–71 (2000)
60. Mathieson, K.: Predicting User Intentions: Comparing the Technology Acceptance Model with the Theory of Planned Behavior. Information Systems Research 2(3), 173–191 (1991)
61. Gefen, D.: E-commerce: The Role of Familiarity and Trust. Omega: The International Journal of Management Science 28(6), 725–737 (2000)
62. Fornell, C., Larcker, D.: Evaluating Structural Equation Models with Unobservable Variables and Measurement Error. Journal of Marketing Research 18(1), 39–50 (1981)
63. Chin, W.W.: Issues and Opinion on Structural Equation Modeling. MIS Quarterly 22(1), 7–16 (1998)

Analyzing Market Interactions in a Multi-agent Supply Chain Environment

William Groves[1], John Collins[1], Wolfgang Ketter[2], and Maria Gini[1]

[1] Department of Computer Science and Engineering
University of Minnesota, USA
{groves,jcollins,gini}@cs.umn.edu
[2] Rotterdam School of Management
Erasmus University, Netherlands
wketter@rsm.nl

Abstract. Enterprises continuously seek decision support tools that can help automate and codify business decisions. This is particularly true in the business of consumer electronics manufacturing where components are often interchangeable and several manufacturers can supply the same component over the life of a product. In this kind of dynamic environment, businesses are faced with the choice of signing long-term (possibly quite risky) contracts or of waiting to procure necessary components on the spot market (where availability may be uncertain). Having analytical tools to analyze previous and forecast future market conditions is invaluable. We analyze a supply chain scenario from an economic perspective that involves both component procurement and sales uncertainties. The data we analyze comes from a multi-agent supply chain management simulation environment (TAC SCM) which simulates a one-year product life-cycle. The availability of simulation logs allows us access to a rich set of data which includes the requests and actions taken by all participants in the market. This rich informational access enables us to calculate supply and demand curves, examine market efficiency, and see how specific strategic behaviors of the competing agents are reflected in market dynamics.

Keywords: decision support, supply chain management, economic simulation, market forecasting, agent-mediated electronic commerce.

1 Introduction

The expectations of agile business and the push toward more closely coupled processes, both within and across organizations, have generated a need for greater sophistication in managing an enterprise's supply chain. Providing operational guidance and formulating business strategies in an automated way is a natural extension of the push toward greater sophistication in business operations. While many business transactions in supply chains are regulated by combinations of overlapping and binding long-term contracts, it is useful to have procurement and sales strategies that can anticipate and accommodate changes in the underlying market conditions. Unfortunately, development and testing of such strategies can be risky in

R. Sharman, T.S. Raghu, and H.R. Rao (Eds.): WEB 2009, LNBIP 52, pp. 44–58, 2010.

real-world markets, making it impossible to do the rigorous experiments needed to develop detailed understanding of the interactions between new strategies and market dynamics.

We use a competitive economic environment designed for autonomous trading agents to study market dynamics and their responses to actions of the participants. The Trading Agent Competition for Supply Chain Management [4] simulates a one-year product life-cycle in a three-tier supply chain, including parts suppliers, end customers, and a set of competing manufacturing agents. They must purchase parts in a competitive procurement market, manufacture finished goods, and sell them in a competitive sales market. A schematic overview of TAC SCM is shown in Figure 1. This kind of market scenario is common to many fast moving electronic goods markets, such as Dell[1].

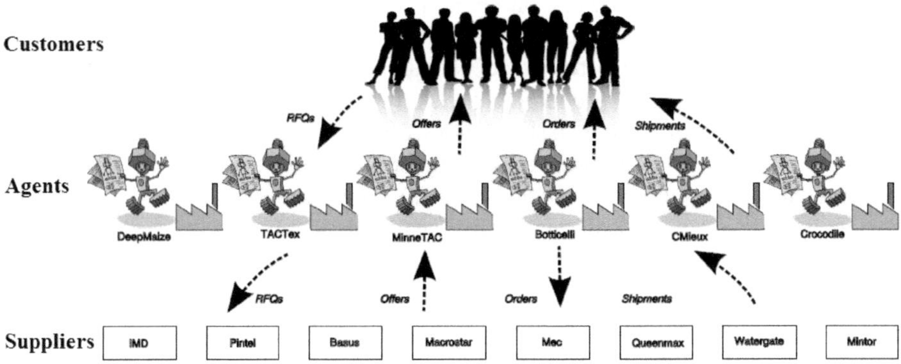

Fig. 1. This graphic provides an overview of the TAC SCM simulation. The TAC SCM game has six competing manufacturing agents who buy parts in the "Supply" market (bottom) and sell finished goods in the "Customer" market (top). A customer sends an individual request (RFQ) to all manufacturers for specific computer configuration, quantity, maximum price, and due date. Each manufacturer can respond to the request with an offer stating its selling price for that configuration. The lowest price offer will receive an order for that computer from the customer. The product is then shipped on the specified due date. The supplier market functions similarly, and is driven by requests (RFQs) for parts sent by agents. An agent can send a parts request (RFQ) to a supplier for a specific part type, quantity, maximum price, and delivery date. A supplier will send an offer in response to agent RFQ indicating the actual price and quantity available for the request. The agent can decide to accept the offer with an order message.

One objective in this study is to gain a detailed understanding of the dynamics of both the procurement and sales markets in the final round of the seventh-annual TAC SCM competition, held in July 2009. The phenomena we observe emerge from the interactions among the competing agents—these are not inherent in the design of the game. Understanding such phenomena can help us design better decision processes for both autonomous agents and for human-centered decision support systems.

---

[1] Dell Computer Corporation, with its direct sales model, was an inspiration for the design of TAC SCM.

The paper is organized as follows. After a survey of related literature, section 3 introduces the agents that participated in the 2009 finals and provides a brief statistical overview of the outcome. Section 4 explores agent strategies for procurement and inventory management, and their effects on the component market. Section 5 examines supply and demand patterns in the customer market, and shows how the oligopoly nature of the market allows agents to manipulate prices. Finally, we conclude with a few thoughts on where these visualizations and strategies could be directly applied to improve real-world business decision making.

2 Related Work

We consider techniques from both the business literature as well as from the TAC SCM community. Previous work on economic analysis to enable business decision making and efforts to visualize economic processes are quite relevant to this work.

Authors from HP Labs offer practical insights into how a large enterprise like Hewlett-Packard mitigates procurement risk in [10]. The authors outline a three layered approach to procuring flash memory for use in printers involving low-price, large quantity contracts, medium price variable quantity contracts, and spot market procurement. Literature on trading agents in continuous double auctions markets provides inspiration on visualizing supply and demand in an auction clearing house scenario [3]. In [7], the authors present an approach to identify current and predicted future market conditions, such as scarcity or oversupply, called economic regimes. They show a dynamic graphical presentation of the economic regimes, which can be used by managers to improve decision-making in the overall supply chain.

Not all assistive business technologies are graphical in nature. For instance, the authors of [12] describe an automated data mining program for price prediction of commodity laptops on the consumer auction site, eBay. The authors envision the price output as a means of determining which products are undervalued and could therefore be resold at a profit. Their algorithm vastly increases the speed of what was previously a manual filtering and prediction process. Another example of an assistive prediction mechanism is described in [6] where a price prediction algorithm is used to assist users in determining the best time to buy airline tickets based on historical price trends.

Various works in the literature provide methods of computing price predictions for real-world markets including electricity ([5], [11]), currencies [1], and commodities [8] using machine learning algorithms. The price predictions that come out of these algorithms can then be used for many business purposes including speculation or hedging.

Even when we have almost complete observability of market behaviors, it is non-trivial to determine what performance measures are useful to employ when attempting to improve agent performance. Various performance measures ([2], [9], [13]) related to bidding performance have been introduced in the TAC SCM literature.

The critical difference between our work and previous work in TAC SCM, is that we approach many of the phenomena discussed from a business purpose basis, not simply from the approach of the TAC SCM competition. Insights presented here could be used to support the development of human-augmented TAC SCM agents or be applied to real business domains.

3 High-Level Analysis of the 2009 TAC SCM Finals

While a complete description of the TAC SCM scenario is beyond the scope of this paper, there are several key economic and technical aspects of the simulation that are important for this analysis. First, each of the (up to 6) competing manufacturer agents experience the same market environment in both the component procurement as well as computer sales markets. The agents cannot communicate with each other. Also, agents can only communicate with customers and suppliers using explicit market requests. The competition has been repeated for several years and the rules have been changed to negate the effectiveness of strategies that exploit technical weaknesses. For example, a buyer reputation mechanism was introduced in the procurement market to prevent overt price manipulation.

Data collected from the trading agent competition provides a unique opportunity to study markets. There are three aspects of the game which make analysis particularly fruitful in this domain. First, the simulation server collects and logs its own internal state along with all its interactions with the competing agents, giving researchers the ability to observe detailed actions of all market participants once a simulation is complete. Second, the scenario has a well-defined stochastic set of inputs which generate the supply and demand profile of the game. Finally, because the final round of the competition includes a number of individual games, we have an opportunity to observe the same oligopoly of agents operating under significantly different market conditions (levels of supply and demand, balance between procurement market and sales market, etc.).

Due to the complexity of behaviors enabled by the simulation, only a small selection can be addressed in this paper. In the next sections, we present examples of several strategic market behaviors and show how these behaviors can be visualized. But first, we give an overview of the 2009 competition, because it serves to introduce the two top agents, and because it shows that top performance in the competition can be approached by at least two very distinct strategies.

The final 18-game round of the 2009 TAC SCM tournament was run on 14 July 2009. Finalists, their institutions and final scores are given in Table 1. For most of the detailed analyses in this paper, we will be primarily interested in the behavior and performance of the two top agents, DeepMaize and TacTex. The Mean Score column is the bank balance at the end of the simulation averaged over the 18 games in the final round. Mean score is the scoring measure used to determine the winner of the competition.

Table 1. Participants in the final round of the 2009 TAC SCM tournament

Agent	Institution	Mean Score (in $'000,000s)
DeepMaize	University of Michigan	4.605
TacTex	University of Texas	4.269
MinneTAC	University of Minnesota	-0.192
Botticelli	Brown University	-0.819
CMieux	Carnegie-Mellon University	-2.025
CrocodileAgent	University of Zagreb	-7.788

The two top agents are virtually tied, but the similarity in overall score hides large differences in detailed behavior. DeepMaize did well by selling relatively small numbers of finished products, while TacTex did well by selling larger numbers of finished products. Table 2 shows the results for DeepMaize and TacTex over a range of summary statistics, along with the *p*-value for the paired-means t-test for each of them.

Table 2. Aggregate performance measures for the two top agents in the 2009 final round

Comparison Measure	DeepMaize	TacTex	ratio	p-value
Score (millions)	4.606	4.270	---	0.547
Total Revenue (millions)	83.22	110.9	0.750	0.000
Selling Price (normalized)	0.778	0.788	0.988	0.010
Total material cost (millions)	75.78	103.2	0.735	0.000
Unit cost (normalized)	0.710	0.720	0.986	0.000
Interest cost (millions)	0.2627	0.5380	0.472	0.000
Storage Cost (millions)	1.158	2.411	0.486	0.000
Factory utilization (percentage)	66.2%	88.0%	0.751	0.000

We can see from Table 2 that while the difference in overall scores is statistically insignificant, the differences in all the other interesting measures are quite significant.[2] In this table, selling price and material cost is "normalized" to the nominal cost of the components. Prices in the procurement market are discounted from the nominal cost according to the ratio of suppliers' uncommitted capacity to total capacity over the interval between the order date and the committed delivery date. A few of these measures stand out:

- First, TacTex had higher selling prices than DeepMaize, not lower prices as one might expect by the difference in sales volume.
- Second, the largest difference between these agents was in interest and storage costs. This reflects the fact that TacTex on average carried much larger inventories than DeepMaize, which it used effectively to raise its market share during periods of high demand and high prices.
- Third, neither agent was constrained on average by factory capacity.

[2] As is evident from the *p*-values. A *p*-value greater than 0.05 indicates that the difference between the values measured is not statistically significant (with 95% confidence).

We now turn to two aggregate observations of agent behavior that will illustrate some of these differences more clearly.

3.1 Daily Profit and Loss

The large number of actions that a competitive manufacturer undertakes to achieve good performance makes the contribution of individual events difficult to analyze. To address this we can use aggregate measures, such as daily profit and loss, to see if there may be areas of particular interest for further analysis. For example, the plot in Figure 2 enables us to discover when agents spend the most money and make the most profit.

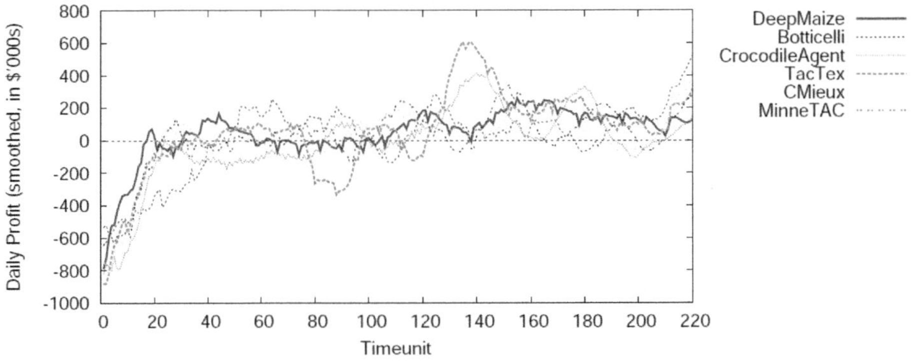

Fig. 2. Smoothed daily agent profit and loss for game tac02—#2069. All agents have strongly negative daily profit early in the game due to the simultaneous, acute need to begin production. In this instance, TacTex, who invested the most early in the game, had the highest total profit.

Several conclusions can be drawn from this plot: the strongest agents (the agents that win most frequently) tend to invest more money at the beginning than the weaker agents, and the strongest agents tend to achieve consistently profitable days earlier than their opponents. In this game, we discover that TacTex took significant losses around day 80, and unusually high daily profits around day 150. This is evidence of strategic behavior which is discussed in section 3.2. We can also see that DeepMaize was profitable early and was more consistently profitable late in the game.

Because each run of the game approximates a one-year product lifecycle beginning with no initial inventory, the TAC SCM environment can be useful for studying strategies at all phases of the product lifecycle from introduction to decline. Also, the game is repeatable, so market conditions of different runs can be quantified and the effect of market environment on strategy can be analyzed.

3.2 Significant Inventory Build-Up

If an agent can predict significant profit opportunities ahead, it may decide to build inventory in preparation for an aggressive selling period. Figure 3 shows an example: a steady increase in demand over time (plotted in the figure is one sixth of the global demand) and a concurrent inventory buildup for agent TacTex, starting around day

80. The agent is able to increase its profit by reducing sales until the sales price peaks around day 130 when the agent begins selling aggressively. The agent's sales activity can be observed through the *sales velocity* series which shows the number of units sold each day. The agent's procurement activity can be observed in the figure through the *agent procurement* impulses. Days with non-zero quantity procurement deliveries are shown and the height represents the total quantity delivered. The agent's running inventory is also plotted (the actual value divided by five is shown to facilitate a more compact visual display). "Playing the market" in this way by intentionally reducing sales velocity as prices are rising serves to increase this agent's overall profit margin.

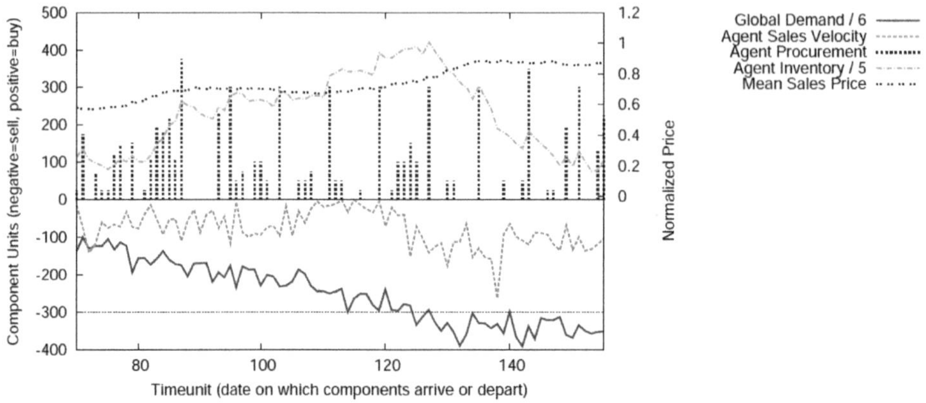

Fig. 3. Component Inventory, Supply Velocity, and Sales Velocity for agent TacTex for component 111 for selected dates of game tac02-#2069. As product demand increases up (becomes more negative), the agent reduces sales velocity while simultaneously increasing procurement velocity. When the demand exceeds some threshold, the agent increases sales velocity just as the per-unit price peaks.

4 Component Market Strategic Behaviors

The TAC SCM component market includes eight suppliers, each of which carries two product lines. Each supplier produces its components on a make-to-order basis, and the capacity of each supplier production line varies from day to day using a mean-reverting random walk. To build a finished product, an agent needs one each of four different component types: a CPU, a motherboard, a disk drive, and a memory card. Agents may request price quotes from suppliers by specifying quantity, delivery date, and reserve price. Quoted prices are based on the ratio of total demand to the supplier's total capacity between the current date and the requested delivery date.

The procurement market generally yields lower prices for longer lead-times, but at times of oversupply, prices can be lower for very short-term requests. Order lead-times can extend to the end of the game, which is 220 days at the beginning of a game. The longest lead-time in the customer market is 12 days, and supplier prices tend to peak in the range of 8-15 days lead-time. Because the procurement market allows long-term commitments (usually at a lower price) to be made far in advance of the longest customer order, agents must commit to procurement long before a corresponding product order is finalized. The method by which the lead time gap between procurement commitments and sales orders can be handled is a principle strategic consideration. If components arrive before they can be used in production, the agent must pay to store them. Supplier orders require a 10% down-payment, and so the cost of funds can be a significant factor for long lead-time orders.

4.1 Long-Term and Short-Term Procurement Mixture

To reliably make a profit in the wide range of possible market demand levels and market supply capacities, it is important to balance long-term and spot market procurement. Normally, long term prices are lower than short term prices, even when down payment and storage costs are factored in, as we show in Section 4.2. But long term contracts are risky for two reasons: 1) long term prices are highly dependent on the actions of the other market players, and 2) long term contracts allow agents to significantly over-commit relative to the actual future demand. Figure 4 shows how the procurement mixture has varied in the top performing agents over time.[3]

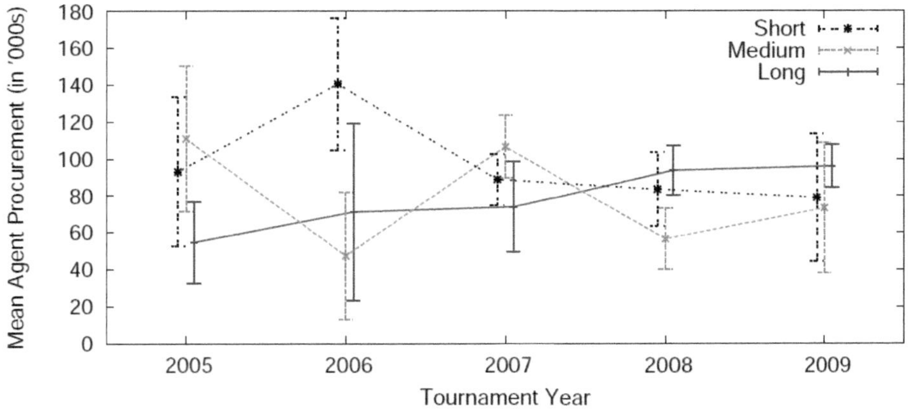

Fig. 4. Variation in the mean mixtures of long term, medium term, and short term procurement for the top 3 agents in the TAC SCM tournament. Error bars show first standard deviation.

Clearly, the proportion of long-term procurement has increased steadily as competition has stiffened and agents have become more sophisticated. We suggest that the increase in long term procurement is a consequence rather than a cause of good agent performance in this market. Indeed, there are instances of weak agents badly over-committing in with long-term contracts, resulting in poor overall performance. This statistic has been determined by the actions of development teams working to improve their performance in the competition. It is also possible to arrive at an optimal mixture for other markets. The authors of [10] balance long-term,

[3] For classification, a short term event is defined as a procurement order with a lead time of less than 10 days. Long term is defined as a procurement event initiated within the first 10 days having lead time greater than or equal to 10. Medium term is for the remaining unclassified requests.

medium-term, and spot market procurement needs of the production of consumer printers at Hewlett Packard. It is likely that the same approach could be applied to other fast moving electronic goods markets. The next subsections will address how additional profit can be obtained by operating in the spot market.

4.2 Capitalize on Low Short-Term Prices

The general price trend in the procurement market is for high short-term prices with price decreasing as lead time increases. This general trend shown as "normal" in Figure 5 is almost universal at the beginning of the game. However, there are periods where the price trend is "inverted," where the short-term price is below the long-term price. These inversions occur when a supplier has made significant long-term sales to manufacturers with large lead times and has also had an unexpected increase in its manufacturing capacity. The supplier has a relatively low committed capacity to available capacity ratio, so it uses reduced offer prices to entice manufacturers to commit to additional short-term requests.

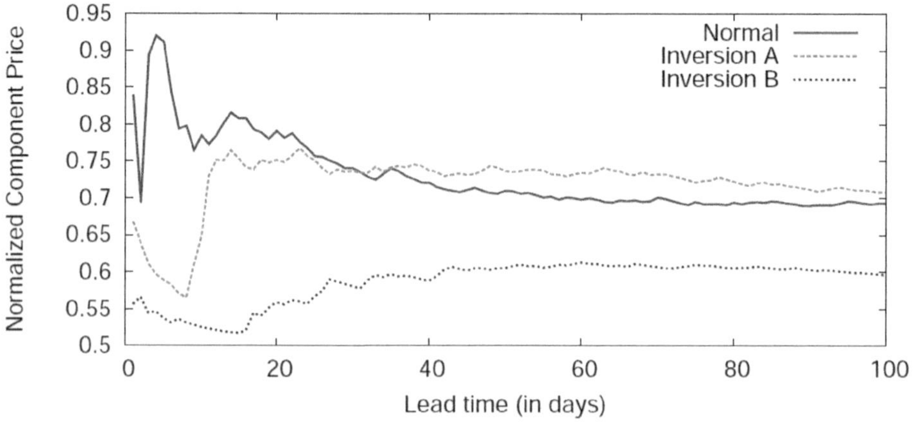

Fig. 5. Set of common price vs. lead time relationships for individual components. These series observed in game tac02-#2069 for component 100 on days 20 (Normal), 67 (Inversion A), and 118 (Inversion B). The specific values are not important for the discussion; instead, these series are included to illustrate common scenarios agents can face when making procurement requests.

Agents must make requests in order to observe prices and maintain their pricing models in the component market. They typically use "price probes"[4] and time procurement actions to ensure maximal observability of price curves. In the next section we will see how price probing can be repurposed to capture unusually low prices.

[4] Price probes are requests to suppliers for zero quantity (i.e. a price query).

4.3 Opportunistic Procurement

Opportunistic procurement occurs when an agent is able to buy a particular part significantly below the predicted price. These opportunities occur infrequently, due to short-term variations in supplier capacity, and often vanish in the next bidding cycle. MinneTAC takes advantage of this situation by consistently making low quantity requests at a low reserve price (perhaps 20% or more below the predicted price).

In Figure 6, we see prices for a single component type normalized to MinneTAC's mean price estimate. When the agent is not very interested in acquiring additional stock, it makes requests at a very low reserve price, and usually is unsuccessful as we see by the price quotes labeled "unsuccessful opportunistic proc. events." However, it sometimes receives offers for very low cost requests, which it can then use to sell profitably at a higher price in the customer market.

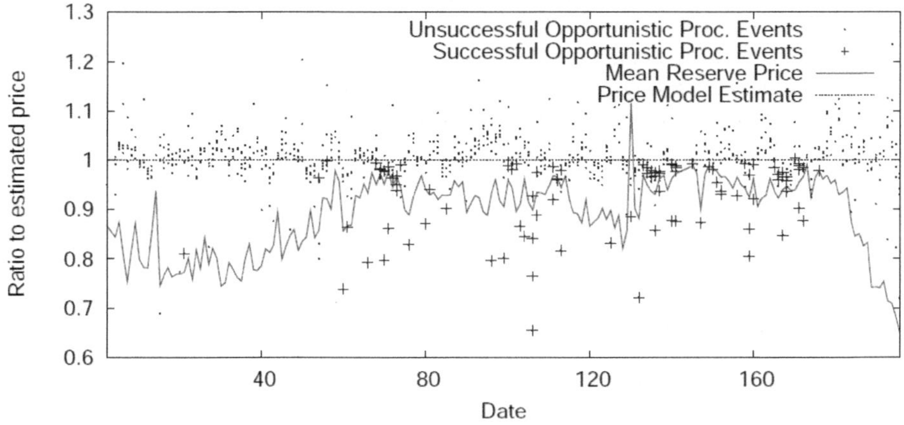

Fig. 6. Opportunistic procurement events plotted in proportion to agent's price estimate for today as predicted on previous day. The 1.0 value on the y-axis represents the value of the price prediction model for the current day. The mean reserve price of opportunistic procurement requests for the agent increases to near (or above) 1.0 as the agent becomes more aggressive due to expected procurement needs. The range of days between 130 and 180 represents a period when the agent was more aggressively procuring this component.

Sales and procurement decisions are tightly intertwined. For example, sales must account for the cost of parts, and procurement must set reserve prices based on expected sales prices. Due to the normal fluctuations in the market, there are situations where the estimates of price (and thus profitability) are incorrect. If a component is 20% cheaper than predicted, it is very likely to be profitable. Buying at such a low price will offset the need for short term procurement later, serve to update the price prediction model, and may increase the sales velocity because the agent will now have a lower cost basis. These infrequent but highly favorable procurement events can lead to higher overall profit for the agent.

5 Customer Market Strategic Behaviors

The TAC SCM customer market is a reverse sealed-bid auction market. Each simulated day, customers issue requests for quotes (RFQs) for the products they wish to buy, specifying model, quantity, delivery date, and maximum (reserve) price. The market trades in 16 product types, segmented into high-end, medium, and low-end products. Customer demand varies from day to day independently in each of the market segments, controlled by a trend value that changes daily using a bounded random walk.

Supply is generated by an oligopoly of six manufacturing agents. Each agent must decide whether to bid on each customer request and at what price. Customers collect all valid bids from agents, and choose the bids with the lowest prices. The shape of the demand curve is controlled by the current overall demand, and by the distribution of reserve prices in customer RFQs. The demanded quantity does not increase as prices fall below of 0.75 because customer RFQs have reserve prices uniformly distributed between 0.75 and 1.25 of nominal. The shape of the supply curve is constrained at the high-quantity end by the inventory status and aggregate production capacities of the competing agents, and at the low-price end by the minimum cost of components. The supply price can go below 0.5 when agents decide to sell parts below cost; this can occur when agents are trying to dump unsold inventory near the end of the simulation. The detailed shape of the supply curve is a function of the combined bidding strategies of the competing agents. It is not directly observable within a game, but can be deduced through post-game examination of data as we shall see below.

5.1 Visualizing Supply and Demand

We have a qualitative notion of what supply and demand curves should look like in the customer market, but the reality is somewhat surprising. It appears that many agents quote a single price for each product (regardless of RFQ parameters such as quantity, lead time). The only limiting factor appears to be reserve price. This tends to lead to an all-or-nothing result of the auction where a single agent usually wins all of the demand for a single product on a given day. The result is that the supply curve is often completely flat, as we see in the second graph in Figure 7 (bottom).

Early in the competition, raw materials are scarce and expensive, so the limiting factor is reserve price. Figure 7 (top) shows just such a situation early in the game when agents are only bidding on the portion of demand that exceeds some threshold. Because each agent's cost basis, procurement schedule, and risk aggressiveness are different, each agent is likely to bid a different price for each request. Figure 7 (bottom) highlights a common situation when manufacturers bid fixed prices on all demand. In this situation, one agent receives all contracts for a given product on a given day, and the second lowest price agent loses the bidding round by just a few dollars. This is normally an undesirable situation, because an agent rarely has the capacity to serve 100% of the market for any product. Some agents, among them MinneTAC, randomize offer prices slightly in an attempt to achieve more consistent sales volume.

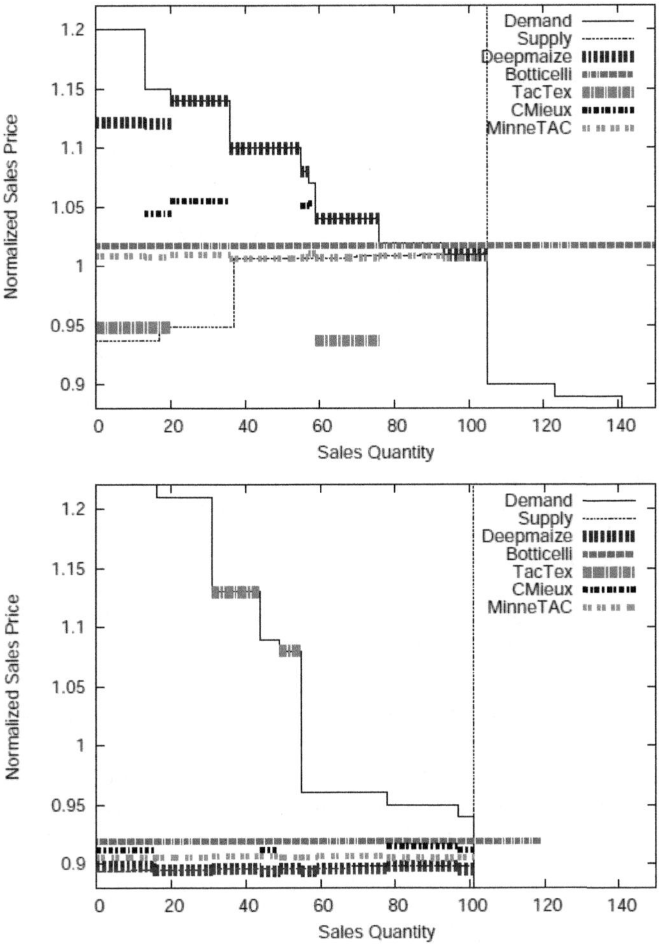

Fig. 7. Customer market supply and demand for product #8 on day 9 (top) and day 18 (bottom) of game tac02-2069. The demand line corresponds to the total market demand for that day, sorted by decreasing reserve price. The dotted lines correspond to the offers made by each manufacturer and the height of the line indicates the offer price. The agent with the lowest offer price for a given demand request will receive the order from the customer.

5.2 Price Manipulation

The TAC SCM customer market is an oligopoly, and agents that act as price-takers often miss significant profit opportunities that might result from manipulating prices. In Figure 8, we can see cases where agents are clearly attempting to drive prices either down (DeepMaize between days 80 and 100) or up (TacTex around day 130). The effect can be seen in the daily profitability shown in Figure 2. In general, the product price change over one day will be small (at less than 1% change in price).

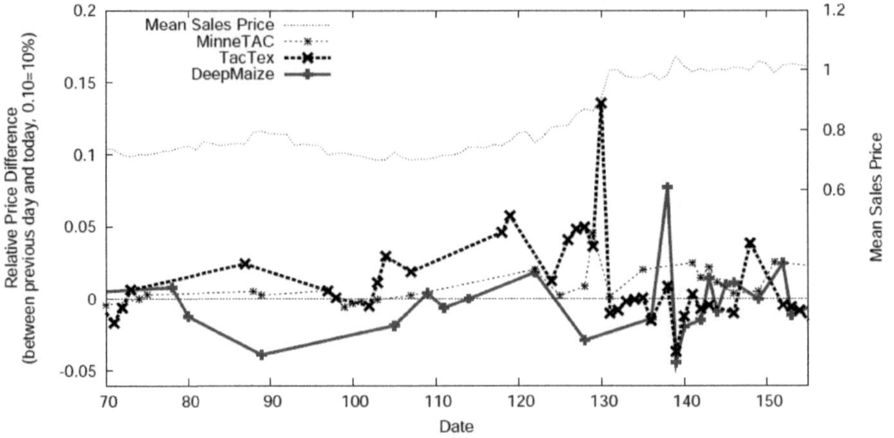

Fig. 8. Bidding price trends of the top 3 agents for product 8 in game tac02-#2069. Each point along an agent's series denotes an instance when the agent placed a winning bid (all winning bids for the selected agents are shown, bids of other agents are omitted for clarity). The y-axis value denotes the difference between the agent's bid price and yesterday's mean winning bid price. Yesterday's mean winning bid price is the mean price across all sales of the product for the previous day. Because daily price changes are small, we expect the previous day's mean price to be a good estimate of the current day's price.

Agents that are adept at price prediction and who only seek to bid at (or near) the previous price are defined as price followers. Price following is a safe strategy designed to maximize profit for individual winning bids. In a price following strategy, an agent would be likely to bid within a small range of the previous day's price; in Figure 8, this would correspond to bids near zero on the y-axis. Agents can attempt to move prices by taking risks and bidding far from the previous day's price. This is shown by winning bids that are far from the zero value on the y-axis. The figure shows that many bids are very close to the previous day mean price, but the bids far from the previous day's value can presage persistent shifts in the mean sales price.

6 Conclusions and Future Work

When automating business processes, designers should be concerned with how the automated process will respond to particular situations where the standard conceptions of the market are violated. We have identified several common situations where the normal economic paradigm of supply and demand cannot be relied upon to deliver highest profit.

These analyses help to elucidate general economic behaviors that are not always intuitive given knowledge of the basic market mechanisms. In hindsight, many of these behaviors seem obvious, but only through careful analysis can these behaviors be seen and their effectiveness determined.

The evolution of the TAC SCM scenario resembles the evolution of real markets in several ways. First, the market behaviors and performance have changed with time.

Year after year, the overall market's reliance on long term procurement has increased. Concurrently, the profit margin (both per unit and in absolute terms) has decreased. There are even games for which all agents cease to make a profit. Manufacturers often need to make long-term investment decisions that include exposure to risk due to uncertainties in eventual product demand. These characteristics are seen in many real world markets from service industries such as airlines and restaurants, to manufactured goods such as consumer electronics and automobiles. Only through careful analysis can these risks be understood and mitigated.

We believe that TAC SCM is a particularly useful environment for studying supply chains for several reasons. First, the actions available to agents are similar to the contractual agreements that can be made in real supply chains. While more complex communication and coordination mechanisms are seen in real supply chains, the action set here represents the minimum set available in most markets. Second, pricing advantages found by making procurement commitments far in advance are too compelling to ignore despite the fact that product demand at the time of delivery is uncertain. How agents address the risk of engaging in long lead time requests is a critical issue that must be addressed in an optimized supply chain. This is not to say that businesses should not engage in such risk, but the risk of committing to supply far in advance of demand must be carefully considered.

We leave many areas to be explored in future work, but this work could be readily extended in several ways. First, many of the visualizations were generated with the benefit of the enhanced observations only available after a game. It would be useful to generate many of these from the limited perspective of an on-line agent. Additionally, there has long been interest in human-augmented agents that could trade in the TAC SCM competition. The complexity and speed of the decisions required to act rationally in this space are considerable. Analytical tools such as those presented here would be invaluable in aiding a human to act quickly enough in this environment.

References

1. Barbosa, R.P., Belo, O.: Autonomous Forex Trading Agents. In: Proceedings of the 8th Industrial Conference on Advances in Data Mining: Medical Applications, E-Commerce, Marketing, and Theoretical Aspects, pp. 389–403
2. Benisch, M., Sardinha, A., Andrews, J., Sadeh, N.: CMieux: Adaptive Strategies for Competitive Supply Chain Trading. In: Proceedings of the 8th ACM International Conference on Electronic Commerce, pp. 47–58 (2006)
3. Cliff, D.: Explorations in evolutionary design of online auction market mechanisms. Electronic Commerce Research & Applications Journal 2(2), 162–175 (2003)
4. Collins, J., Arunachalam, R., Sadeh, N., Ericsson, J., Finne, N., Janson, S.: The Supply Chain Management Game for the 2006 Trading Agent Competition (Technical Report) CMU-ISRI-05-132, Carnegie Mellon University, Pittsburgh, PA (November 2005)
5. Contreras, J., Espinola, R., Nogales, F., Conejo, A.: ARIMA models to predict next-day electricity prices. IEEE Transactions on Power Systems 18(3), 1014–1020 (2003)
6. Etzioni, O., Tuchinda, R., Knoblock, C.A., Yates, A.: To buy or not to buy: mining airfare data to minimize ticket purchase price. In: Proceedings of the ACM Conference on Knowledge Discovery and Data Mining, pp. 119–128 (2003)

7. Ketter, W., Collins, J., Gini, M., Gupta, A., Schrater, P.: Detecting and Forecasting Economic Regimes in Multi-Agent Automated Exchanges. Decision Support Systems 47(4), 307–318 (2009)
8. Kohzadi, N., Boyd, M., Kermanshahi, B., Kaastra, I.: A comparison of artificial neural network and time series models for forecasting commodity prices. In: Neurocomputing (1996)
9. Kovalchuk, Y., Fasli, M.: Adaptive Strategies for Predicting Bidding Prices in Supply Chain Management. In: Proceedings of the International Conference on Electronic Commerce, pp. 6–12 (2008)
10. Nagali, V., Hwang, J., Sanghera, D., Gaskins, M., Pridgen, M., Thurston, T., Mackenroth, P., Branvold, D., Scholler, P., Shoemaker, G.: Procurement Risk Management at Hewlett-Packard. Interfaces 38(1), 51–60 (2008)
11. Nogales, F., Contreras, J., Conejo, A., Espinola, R.: Forecasting next-day electricity prices by time series models. IEEE Transactions on Power Systems 17(2), 342–348 (2002)
12. Raykhel, I., Ventura, D.: Real-time automatic price prediction for ebay online trading. In: Proceedings of the Innovative Applications of Artificial Intelligence Conference, pp. 135–140 (July 2009)
13. Wellman, M.P., Reeves, D.M., Lochner, K.M., Vorobeychik, Y.: Price prediction in a trading agent competition. Journal of Artificial Intelligence Research (21), 19–36 (2004)
14. Smith, T.F., Waterman, M.S.: Identification of Common Molecular Subsequences. J. Mol. Biol. 147, 195–197 (1981)

Distinct Impact of Information Access Patterns on Supplier's Non-contractible Investments and Adaptation for Supply Chain Agility

Jeffrey C.F. Tai[1], Eric T.G. Wang[2], Her-Sen Doong[1], and Kai Wang[3]

[1] Department of Management Information Systems, School of Management, National Chiayi University, Chiayi City, Taiwan 600, R.O.C.
{jeffreycftai,hsdoong}@mail.ncyu.edu.tw
[2] Department of Information Management, School of Management, National Central University, Chung-Li, Taiwan 320, R.O.C.
ewang@mgt.ncu.edu.tw
[3] Department of Information Management, School of Management, National University of Kaohsiung, Taiwan 811, R.O.C.
kwang@nuk.edu.tw

Abstract. This study explores how distinct information access patterns affect a supplier's supply chain agility. A supplier's specific investments for IT-enabled supply chain coordination and relational adaptation in supply chain operations are identified as the technical and behavioral antecedents to its supply chain agility. Because both are non-contractible elements in formal contracts and complementary to buyer's supply chain coordination information and buyer's specific investments in monitoring and control, either buyer or supplier may hold up their counterpart based on their own information assets. Therefore, this study draws on the theory of incomplete contracts and suggests that both buyer and supplier need to make their idiosyncratic information assets alienable and accessible to their counterpart so that the rent-seeking problem can be alleviated and the supplier's investment and adaptation incentives improved. This study contributes to the literature by demonstrating that distinct information access patterns can improve a supplier's supply chain agility through the mediation of the non-contractible investments and adaptation made by the supplier.

Keywords: Information access patterns, non-contractible investments, relational adaptation, supply chain agility, theory of incomplete contracts.

1 Introduction

Prior research on inter-firm information sharing for supply chain management (SCM) predominantly emphasizes its value about reducing demand distortion, facilitating synchronous operations and enabling strategic collaboration [18, 19]. While this line of literature answers what values of information sharing are achievable, it rarely tests how these values are realized empirically. All too often, information sharing is treated as a bilateral, holistic phenomenon [26]. The approach does not consider the fact that upward- and downward- information sharing in an supply chain can distinctively

R. Sharman, T.S. Raghu, and H.R. Rao (Eds.): WEB 2009, LNBIP 52, pp. 59–66, 2010.

change supply chain members' incentives to improve their coordination and performance monitoring [20]. Drawing on this idea, this study attempts to shed light on the study of business value of information sharing by exploring the effects of distinct information access patterns on a supplier's non-contractible investments and adaptation for achieving its supply chain agility.

2 Conceptual Background and Research Model

2.1 Supply Chain Agility and Its Antecedents

Supply chain agility has been increasingly recognized as a pivotal capability for firms to adapt to changing market demands [7]. In the literature, there has been general ambivalence of defining supply chain agility as chain- or firm-level construct [28]. This study bases on [3] and regards supply chain agility as a firm-level construct, focusing on a firm's capability to deal with its adjacent customers or suppliers (i.e., internal supply chain). Thus, a supplier's supply chain agility is defined as its capability, internally and in conjunction with its customer, to respond in a speedy manner to market changes or to seize market opportunities with speed and quickness. Since there is scant theoretical research about supply chain agility, this study follows [17] and identifies relevant antecedents from the technical and behavioral perspectives of a supply chain linkage.

Transaction-specific Investments for IT-enabled Process Coordination as Technical Antecedent to Achieving Supply Chain Agility. From a technical perspective, agility is theoretically linked to flexibility in terms of capability- competence relationship [33]. In this vein, agility can be seemed as an extrinsic capability, deriving from a firm's intrinsic competences - such as range and adaptability flexibility of the firm's resources [28]. Range flexibility refers to the number of different states that a firm's resources can achieve; adaptability flexibility represents the timeliness and cost effectiveness of the resources to change from one state to another. Because procurement/sourcing, manufacturing and distribution processes are the focal resources an supplier bases upon for achieving agility [8], this study focuses on analyzing supply chain process flexibility for identifying the technical antecedents to supply chain agility.

It is suggested that inter-organizational information infrastructures can be designed to facilitate distinct modes of coordination for supply chain process flexibility: coordination by plan vs. coordination by feedback [10]. Thus, firms can either structure inter-organizational information flows and interconnected processes (i.e. advanced structuring approach) to reduce the efforts involved in adjusting to changing business environments or effectively and quickly reconfigure a set of inter-organizational processes appropriate for changed business environments through IT-supported learning and adaptation (i.e. dynamic adjustment approach). The research reveals that the coordination efforts in business processes and information infrastructures might require IT-related, transaction-specific investments from supply chain members, because these efforts are not common or standardized practices in typical inter-firm exchange relationships [10]. Other studies also echo the necessity of integrating supply chain processes and customer knowledge with the support of information technologies for enabling agile supply chain [22].

Specifically, [27] suggests business process and domain knowledge as the primary specific investments a supplier utilizes to leverage its IT use for improving supply chain performance. The former focuses on unique operating, administrative and quality-control processes, and the latter concentrates on idiosyncratic knowledge about competitive analysis, strategy formulation and new-product development. Both types of transaction-specific investments (hereafter, termed transaction-specific investments for IT-enabled supply chain coordination) have the potential to mediate the value creation of IT use on supply chain relationships due to their complementary role in facilitating IT-enabled supply chain coordination. Once these investments are realized by an supplier, further, the reach and richness of its processes and knowledge with respect to a specific customer can be greatly enhanced [22]. Process and knowledge reach can increase the supplier's ex ante information processing capacities, because the closer integrated business processes and the more comprehensive, codified domain knowledge invested enable the supplier to spend less efforts to adjusting to changed environments. Process and knowledge richness can increase the supplier's ex post information processing capacities, since high-quality information available through integrated business processes and improved absorptive capacity to customer-specific knowledge provide the supplier with greater sensing capability to environmental changes and facilitate timely, accurate and customized adjustments in supply chain operations. Since the improved ex ante and ex post information processing capacities increase the range and adaptability flexibility of a supplier's supply chain processes, the created digital options can facilitate the supplier to achieve greater supply chain agility [24]. Therefore, this study posits that:

> H_1: A supplier's transaction-specific investments for IT-enabled supply chain coordination are positively related to its supply chain agility.

Relational Adaptation in Supply Chain Operations as Behavioral Antecedent to Achieving Supply Chain Agility. While transaction-specific investments for IT-enabled supply chain coordination improve supply chain agility through enhancing information processing capacities (and, hence, flexibility) of supply chain processes, short-term yet recurrent responses of a supplier to sudden, often unanticipated customer needs contribute to supply chain agility through realizing the requested adaptive adjustments in its supply chain operations (hereafter, termed as relational adaptation in supply chain operations)[32]. The most widely cited cases of relational adaptation in the supplier part are product customization, production capacity adjustment and stockholding or delivery schedule modifications [6, 21]. These efforts probably but not necessarily involve transaction-specific investments, and they are performed frequently over time rather than on a one-time basis [9]. Thus, interfirm relationship, beside economic transaction, has been treated as the unit of analysis for studying interfirm adaptation [6]. In a similar vein, this study identifies relational adaptation as a behavioral characteristic of supply chain relationships [17] and posits it to be complementary to supply chain process flexibility in contributing to supply chain agility [15].

Theoretically, relational adaptation refers to that a firm performs "adaptive, sequential decision-making" in the face of uncertainty [2]. It needs not to be necessarily involved with specific investments and hence the hold-up problem [9]. According to the theory of incomplete contracts, the major merit of relational adaption is that it plays an important role in filling the gap of adaptation requirements incompletely safeguarded by formal contracts in volatile environments [30]. Relational adaptation is particularly necessary for adaptive asset utilization decisions because they are usually noncontractible both ex ante and ex post [9]. It is noncontractible ex ante because unforeseen contingencies make it costly to specify contingent-claims contracts. It is noncontractible ex post due to that adaptation behavior is usually observable but non-verifiable by a third party (e.g., court) ex post [11, 12]. Even though ex post renegotiation is permitted, the incentives of both supplier and buyer might not be the same and so renegotiating a jointly acceptable decision or asset ownership is time-consuming or suboptimal [2]. Since relational adaptation is self-enforcing, it can avoid costly and time-consuming bargaining in the face of uncertainty [5, 16, 29]. As a result, this study argues that a supplier's relational adaptation in supply chain operations can increase its supply chain agility.

> H_2: A supplier's relational adaptation in supply chain operations is positively related to its supply chain agility.

2.2 Relating Information Access Patterns to the Antecedents of Supply Chain Agility

Supplier's Access to Buyer's Supply Chain Coordination Information. According to the theory of incomplete contracts, transaction-specific investments for IT-enabled supply chain coordination are also non-contractible because they may be observable but non-verifiable ex post by a third party (e.g., court)[11, 12]. Thus, supply chain partners cannot enter into a contract based on the outcomes of these non-contractibles and they must negotiate and divide the value created by these investments ex post, based their relative bargaining power. The theory suggests that ownership structure matters to the ability to appropriate this value ex post, because the party who owns a property can hold up the other party who makes non-contractible investments based on such property by withdrawing from the relationship, hence, possessing greater bargaining power against the other. This in turn reduce the latter's incentive to make non-contractible investments, detrimental to the overall value created. To resolve this problem, it is suggested that the allocation of property ownership must be aligned with the incentive of the invested party in order to maximize the exchange value [11, 12].

To achieve supply chain agility, a buyer's information assets (e.g., demand, planning or scheduling information) are suggested to be "indispensable" or "complementary" to its supplier's business process and domain knowledge investments for IT-enabled coordination [4, 27]. Because of the buyer's rent-seeking potential, according to the theory of incomplete contracts, the supplier should own the buyer's information assets (or vice versa) in order to increase its investment incentives [4, 12]. When the supplier cannot readily integrate with the buyer to own the latter's information assets, an alternative solution is the buyer makes its information assets "alienable" so that the supplier can "access" them for making transaction-specific investments for IT-enabled supply chain coordination [4]. As long as the buyer's information assets are alienable, they become contractible assets and the buyer has no "residual rights of control" to these assets [23]. Thus, the supplier has greater investment incentives because it is no longer afraid of being held up by the buyer. Moreover, the supplier also can create greater bargaining power against the buyer since it has full control over its own investments [23, 31]. Again, this strengthens the supplier's incentives to specialize the investments for IT-enabled supply chain coordination for the buyer. Consequently, this study posits that:

> H_3: A supplier's access to its buyer's supply chain coordination information is positively related to its extent of transaction-specific investments for IT-enabled supply chain coordination.

Buyer's Access to Supplier's Supply Chain Operations Information. The difficulty of inducing a supplier's relational adaptation is that the adaptation decisions are non-contractible both ex ante and ex post and, hence, cannot be safeguarded by formal contracts. The reason for the former case is that it is costly to write contingent-claims contracts as environments are unforeseen. For the latter case, there is a moral-hazard problem ex post and so makes renegotiation, after uncertainty is resolved, difficult to achieve first-best adaptation. When environments are too volatile to renegotiate the allocation of decision right ex post back and forth [9], the second-best solution for effective adaptation is to delegate the control of decision right ex ante to the party (e.g., a boss) whose adaptation requirements are most important to joint value creation [25, 30]. Thus, the party delegated with authority can then make self-interested adaptation decisions after uncertainty is resolved while the counterpart (e.g., a subordinate) can receive an incentive payment based on its performance of adaptation [9].

In the supply chain context, a supplier often has control of decision rights over its own assets and operations. However, its decisions might not be aligned with a buyer's interests for achieving supply chain agility. Therefore, according to the theory of incomplete contracts (as discussed above), this study posits that buyer should be delegated with control of decision rights so that it can control its supplier's adaptation decisions once uncertainty is resolved. Nevertheless, the supplier may cheat or shirk due to the presence of asymmetric information and hidden actions [1, 14]. Therefore, the buyer also needs to invest in monitoring the supplier's output or behavior in order to decrease the latter's opportunism [13]. As a result, the buyer is suggested to make specific investments for both monitoring and control in order to increase a supplier's relational adaptation in supply chain operations. Similar to the arguments for hypothesis 3 discussed above, a buyer's specific investments in monitoring and control are complementary to its supplier's information assets associated with supply chain operations. Since the buyer cannot own its supplier's information assets through integration, it does not have enough incentive to make such specific investments. An alternative solution is that the supplier makes its information assets alienable and grants the buyer with access to the alienable information as much as possible [4, 12]. This can let the buyer avoid being hold up by its supplier while strength its bargaining power and investment incentives, thereby, leading to improved relational adaptation in the supplier side [23, 31]. Accordingly, this study posits that:

> H_4: A buyer's access to its supplier's information for monitoring and control is positively related to its supplier's relational adaptation in supply chain operations.

Based on the above discussion, the research model is presented as Figure 1.

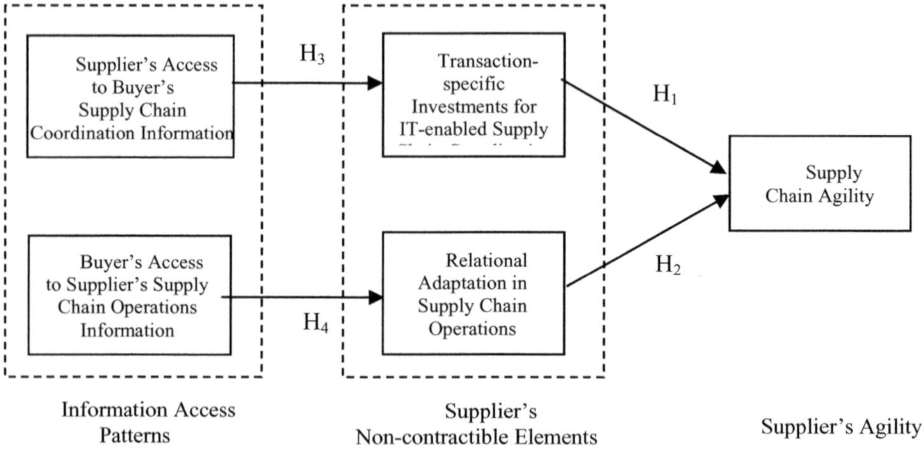

Fig. 1. Research Model

3 Conclusion

This study contributes to the literature by demonstrating that distinct information access patterns can improve a supplier's supply chain agility through the mediation of non-contractible investments and adaptation by the supplier. Our hypotheses explicitly examine how the access of partner's information assets can be utilized to mitigate rent-seeking and mal-adaptation problems, as has long been studied in the transaction costs economics. The distinct effects of upstream- and downstream-information access patterns show that the "ownership" of information assets matters to partner's (in our case, supplier) incentives to make relation-specific investments and adaptation. Thus, future research is suggested to open the black box of the notion of "information sharing" and "information flow integration" in order to advance our knowledge about the impact of the allocation of the property rights of information assets on their business value. From a practitioner's perspective, how and why supply chain members are willing to grant access of their information assets to others is the next issue, which deserves further exploration by future research.

References

1. Alchian, A.A., Demsetz, H.: Production, Information Costs, and Economic Organization. American Economic Review 62, 777–795 (1972)
2. Baker, G., Gibbons, R., Murphy, K.J.: Relational Contracts and the Theory of the Firm. The Quarterly Journal of Economics, 39–84 (2002)
3. Braunscheidel, M.J., Suresh, N.C.: The Organizational Antecedents of a Firm's Supply Chain Agility for Risk Mitigation and Response. Journal of Operations Management 27, 119–140 (2009)
4. Brynjolfsson, E.: Information Assets, Technology, and Organization. Management Science 40(12), 1645–1662 (1994)
5. Bull, C.: The Existence of Self-Enforcing Implicit Contracts. Quarterly Journal of Economics CII, 147–159 (1987)
6. Cannon, J.P., Perreault Jr., W.D.: Buyer-Seller Relationships in Business Markets. Journal of Marketing Research 36(4), 439–460 (1999)
7. Christopher, M.: The Agile Supply Chain: Competing in Volatile Markets. Industrial Marketing Management 29(1), 37–44 (2000)
8. Dong, S., Xu, S.-X., Zhu, K.X.: Information Technology in Supply Chains: The Value of IT-enabled Resources under Competition. Information Systems Research 20(1), 18–32 (2009)
9. Gibbons, R.: Four Formal(izable) Theories of the firm? Journal of Economic Behavior & Organization 58, 200–245 (2005)
10. Gosain, S., Malhotra, A., El Sawy, O.A.: Coordinating for Flexibility in e-Business Supply Chains. Journal of Management Information Systems 21(3), 7–45 (2004-2005)
11. Grossman, S., Hart, O.: The Costs and Benefits of Ownership: A Theory of Vertical and Lateral Integration. Journal of Political Economy 94, 691–719 (1986)
12. Hart, O., Moore, J.: Property Rights and the Nature of the Firm. Journal of Political Economy 98, 1119–1158 (1990)
13. Heide, J.B., Wathne, K.H., Rokkan, A.I.: Interfirm Monitoring, Social Contracts and Relationship Outcomes. Journal of Marketing Research XLIV, 425–433 (2007)
14. Jensen, M., Meckling, W.H.: Theory of the Firm: Managerial Behavior, Agency Costs and Ownership Structure. Journal of Financial Economics 3, 305–360 (1976)
15. Jones, C., Hesterly, W.S., Borgatti, S.P.: A General Theory of Network Governance: Exchange Conditions and Social Mechanisms. Academy of Management Review 22(4), 911–945 (1997)
16. Klein, B., Leffler, K.: The Role of Market Forces in Assuring Contractual Performance. Journal of Political Economy LXXXIX, 615–641 (1981)
17. Knoppen, D., Christiaanse, E.: Interorganizational Adaptation in Supply Chains: A Behavioral Perspective. International Journal of Logistics Management 18(2), 217–237 (2007)
18. Lee, H.L., Padmanabhan, V., Whang, S.: Information Distortion in a Supply Chain: the Bullwhip Effect. Management Science 43, 546–558 (1997)
19. Lee, H.L., So, K., Tang, C.: Supply Chain Re-engineering through Information Sharing and Replenishment Co-ordination. Working Paper, Department of Industrial Engineering, Stanford University (1996)
20. Lee, H.L., Whang, S.: Decentralized Multi-Echelon Supply Chains: Incentives and Information. Management Science 45(5), 633–640 (1999)
21. Mukherji, A., Francis, J.D.: Mutual Adaptation in Buyer-Supplier Relationships. Journal of Business Research 61, 154–161 (2008)

22. Overby, E., Bharadwaj, A., Sambamurthy, V.: Enterprise Agility and the Enabling Role of Information Technology. European Journal of Information Systems 15, 120–131 (2006)
23. Rajan, R.G., Zingales, L.: Power in a Theory of the Firm. The Quarterly Journal of Economics 113(2), 387–432 (1998)
24. Sambamurthy, V., Bharadwaj, A., Grover, V.: Shaping Agility through Digital Options: Reconceptualizing the Role of Information Technology in Contemporary Firms. MIS Quarterly 2(27), 237–263 (2003)
25. Simon, H.: A Formal Theory of the Employment Relationship. Econometrica 19, 293–305 (1951)
26. Straub, D., Rai, A., Klein, R.: Measuring Firm Performance at the Network Level: A Nomology of the Business Impact of Digital Supply Networks. Journal of Management Information Systems 21(1), 83–114 (2004)
27. Subramani, M.: How Do Suppliers Benefit from Information Technology Use in Supply Chain Relationships? MIS Quarterly 28(1), 45–73 (2004)
28. Swafford, P.M., Ghosh, S., Murthy, N.: The Antecedents of Supply Chain Agility of a Firm: Scale Development and Model Testing. Journal of Operations Management 24, 170–188 (2006)
29. Telser, L.: A Theory of Self-Enforcing Agreements. Journal of Business LIII, 27–44 (1981)
30. Williamson, O.: Markets and Hierarchies: Analysis and Antitrust Implications. Free Press, New York (1975)
31. Windsperger, J.: Allocation of Decision Rights in Joint Ventures. Managerial and Decision Economics 30(8), 491–501 (2009)
32. Wong, C.W.Y., Lai, K., Nagi, E.W.T.: The Role of Supplier Operational Adaptation on the Performance of IT-enabled Transport Logistics under Environmental Uncertainty. International Journal of Production Economics 122(1), 47–55 (2009)
33. Zhang, Q.U., Vonderembse, M.A., Lim, J.-S.: Value Chain Flexibility: A Dichotomy of Competence and Capability. International Journal of Production Research 40(3), 561–583 (2002)

Drivers for RFID Implementations

Frank G. Goethals[1], G. Yazgi Tütüncü[1,2], and Chieh-Yu Lin[3]

[1] IESEG School of Management, 3 Rue de la Digue, 59000 Lille, France
[2] Izmir University of Economics, Department of Mathematics, Izmir, Turkey
[3] Department of International Business, Chang Jung Christian University, Taiwan
f.goethals@ieseg.fr, y.tutuncu@ieseg.fr, jylin@mail.cjcu.edu.tw

Abstract. This workshop paper studies drivers for RFID (Radio Frequency IDentification) adoption. The research in progress reported here puts forward several types of mindless and mindful decision making drivers. Hypotheses are tested using a questionnaire that was answered by 122 Chinese companies. The promise to reach higher efficiency seems to be the most important driver for mindful RFID adoption decisions. The early implementers were more driven to adoption by the promise of higher efficiency, better supply chain monitoring and better collaboration than late implementers. Tests show that mindless decision making shows up in RFID adoption.

Keywords: RFID adoption, survey, mindlessness, mindfulness.

1 Introduction

Radio Frequency Identification (RFID) technology is a tracking technology that can be used to create a network of things. Every object can be identified by reading the tag that is attached to it. This tag can contain any data valuable for the user. Data is transferred from the tag to the reader via radio-waves. Reading data thus not requires being in line-of-sight as bar-code technology does [1]. In general it can be stated that RFID has more potential to provide freedom and supply-chain visibility to any process [2] but it becomes much easier to implement when it is standardised.

Several organizations, such as the Massachusetts Institute of Technology‘s Auto-ID Centre and the International Standard Organisation (ISO), have been developing standards. It is obvious that standardisation of RFID is not an easy thing. The frequency is part of the complexity. For instance the North American standard for Ultra-high-frequency is not accepted in France as it interferes with French military bands [3]. One of the solutions to this issue was to design agile readers which could read several frequencies, therefore avoiding doubling costs of readers for companies dealing with international suppliers or buyers [2]. Furthermore, different types of waves have been categorized, each of them having their positive and negative sides [4]. Since it is a wireless technology, the environment, the air, the humidity, the components of scanned objects or containers can influence the signal. This prevents the possibility of a fit-to-all solution. Therefore, every usage needs a customised solution. Moreover, the lack of software dedicated to the integration of back-end applications

R. Sharman, T.S. Raghu, and H.R. Rao (Eds.): WEB 2009, LNBIP 52, pp. 67–79, 2010.

has made the implementation difficult. Additional costs for programming can be necessary to match the languages of the software, and if this issue is not carefully considered, may threaten the implementation of the RFID system [2].

It is important to weigh costs against profits that can be achieved by the company. This Workshop paper reports on exploratory research-in-progress that investigates drivers of RFID adoption. In what follows, we first present the current state of RFID usage, to get an image of the advantages that can be achieved through RFID technology. After that, we present one specific theory that could help explain what drives companies to adopt RFID technology: the mindlessness/mindfulness theory. Next we put forward a number of hypotheses and the research methodology. Subsequently the research results are presented and discussed.

2 RFID in Practice

RFID technology was implemented by huge entities such as Wal-Mart [6] [7], the Department of Defence of the United States of America [8], Best-Buy [9] [10] in the USA, Metro [11], Tesco [7] and Marks & Spencer [7] in Europe. The Chinese government also applied the technology for its Identification Cards [12].

The global market of RFID including tags, systems and services was estimated to be of $4.93 billion in 2007, and to increase to $27 billion by 2018. In volume, the quantities of tags sold have more than doubled, from 2006 with 1.02 billion tags, 2008 is expected to have seen 2.16 billion tags sold [13]. Researchers have increasingly turned their attention toward this topic [14] and studied technical aspects, application areas, and security and policy issues. Ngai identified that 80% of literature has been oriented towards the tags and antennae and that the first step was to solve all technical issues, to focus later on the implementations and their outcomes [14].

Later in this paper we will present a survey we conducted on RFID in China. Therefore, it is interesting to shortly investigate the situation in China first. The Chinese market's value for RFID has become the largest in the world. In 2008, $1.96 billion were spent in the country. The delivery of identification cards, which is a gigantic project of $6 billion, accounted for $1.65 billion in 2008. Once these cards are delivered and requests for ID cards are saturated, the Chinese RFID market is expected to decrease below the US and Japan, but to keep on its fast growth. Table 1 shows how the volume of tags is expected to increase in every sector of the Chinese economy [15]. As the technology evolves, actors tend to get the best benefits out of RFID and look for new usage. Wireless information can provide benefits in a large amount of industries.

In the airlines and airports sector, RFID promises a better traceability during transportation and supply of numerous parts. RFID was applied by the McCarran International Airport and Hong Kong International Airport to tag baggage. Since airports represent a vast structure, RFID has been considered for managing food trolleys, enabling a fluid access to car parks, organising taxi arrivals, etc.

Also, RFID has been considered as a technology that could have great results once adapted to the management of livestock. It can enable automation of farming activities such as weighing and feeding. Lack of traceability, fears of illegally imported meat and current health issues can be mitigated with a tag tracing the animal from its origin [17]. In China, the number of pigs tagged is expected to reach a number of 1.3 billion every year by 2018 [15].

The difficulty with library management has been the large quantity of references. Often applied as a sticker in the inside cover of a book, RFID can speed-up the book identification, enable self checkout, fight book-theft, and sort and control the inventory faster [18] [19].

Table 1. RFID Projects in China planned for 2008-2018 [16]

End User	Category	Application	Tag Volume
China Railway nationwide rollouts	Passenger Transport, Automotive	RFID ticketing	3 billion
Nationwide rollouts	Animal and Farming	Live pig tagging	1.3 billion
Food and Drug Administration	Financial Security Safety	Anti-counterfeiting drugs	over 1 billion
Nationwide rollouts	Books, Libraries, Archiving	Book tagging	500 million
Major appliance manufacturers	Manufacturing	Product line management	hundreds of
Nationwide rollouts	Animal and Farming	Pet dog tagging	150 million
National Tobacco Project	Retail Consumer Goods	Anti-counterfeiting	37.5 billion packs
China Post nationwide rollouts	Land and Sea Logistics, Postal	Mailbag tracking	100 million
Chinese government mandate	Financial Security Safety	Firework Tagging	45 million
Level 3 hospitals rollouts	Healthcare	Hospital inpatient tagging	20 million
Major Sea Ports Rollouts	Land and Sea Logistics, Postal	Container Tracking	Tens of millions
Chinese Army	Military	Logistics	Tens of millions
Alcohol	Retail Consumer Goods	Anti-counterfeiting alcohol	Tens of millions

There have been studies about automatic identification of customers. Banks hope they can improve their services by identifying their customers as soon as they enter the bank via the tag mounted on their credit card [21]. Nowadays, over 17 million cards are in circulation with 95% of Hong Kong people aged between 16 and 65 using this system [16].

Healthcare industry has seen the use of RFID as a means to prevent errors which can have dramatic consequences in this industry. Hospitals have implemented RFID to monitor patient movements and to maximise room utilisation. The market of RFID tags and systems dedicated to healthcare is expected to increase from $120.9 million in 2008 to $2.03 billion in 2018 [22].

The increasing sizes of sea carriers and ports have encouraged the use of RFID to track containers [2].

Manufacturing has also been a relevant domain of RFID applications. This was especially the case in the car manufacturing industry as it requires a large number of parts and a strong flexibility to provide high diversity of models and options. RFID has been used to identify containers, pallets, organize the inventory better and track the forklifts [2].

The mandate issued by the Department of Defence of the United States is the most resounding example that military industry could show us. In extreme conditions, RFID enables a quick identification of the ammunition left, but also the food, water and other supplies that can be needed during military operations. It is also used to track shipments of containers [23].

Clearly, RFID technology could be useful in many companies. However, organizations often suffer from mindlessness behaviour when it comes to new technologies: they implement some technology because others have implemented it, without investigating whether such a technology investment really fits their specific company. Such projects often fail. It is the goal of this paper to investigate whether the mindlessness theory also applies to the RFID technology. In what follows we first shortly present the mindfulness/mindlessness theory and develop hypotheses with respect to RFID adoption. Next, we present the research methodology and survey results and we discuss the results.

3 Mindlessness-Mindfulness Theory

One of the elements that will be considered in this paper to investigate adoption is the mindlessness/mindfulness theory. Here we shortly introduce that theory.

IT (Information Technology) innovations are supposed to be grounded in organizational facts and specifics, but often they are not. The mindlessness and mindfulness perspective enlightens the way in which a company may consider investing in a new technology and has been discussed by Swanson and Ramiller in MISQuarterly [5].

The mindless firm pays no attention to the firm's own circumstances. It engages in some innovation because it is impressed by success stories that appear to validate the innovation as a good or even an irresistible idea. It invests in some technology because 'everyone is doing it' or it is 'time to catch up'. The mindless firm typically turns to the dominant vendor within the industry, as there is no need to consider anything else. After all, the adoption decision was not guided by attention to organizational specifics. Assimilation is regarded as unproblematic: end-users will get some application and have to fend for themselves. If the end-user does not like the application, not the application is considered wrong but the user is considered to be at fault. The mindless firm believes that the technology under consideration is not critical to its distinctive competence ant it is content to be a follower rather than a leader. It will therefore wait for innovations to come to the firm, rather than seeking intelligence about innovations. It is confident that others will call the important innovations to its attention [5].

Companies often choose to be mindless. After all, mindfulness represents a costly and demanding sensemaking regime. Mindful decisions are "discriminating choices that best fit a firm's unique circumstances, rather than familiar and known behaviours based on what others are doing". A mindful decision is based on elements grounded in the firm's own specifics and helps decide whether, when, and how the investment should be done.

Mindless decision taking might also show up in RFID implementation decisions. For instance, a company might blindly copy the pallet-level-tagging that is used in another company, while case-level-tagging would be better in their case. This could lead to project failure.

3.1 Mindful Decision Making

Mindful decision making is the way of deciding that is usually assumed to exist in reality: companies analyse their own situation and choose a technology that is suited to resolve their specific problem. A study that investigates the drivers for RFID adoption should thus in the first place consider mindful decision making. For early implementers the choice to adopt a new technology is more likely to be grounded in organisational specifics because there is still little knowledge about successes that have been achieved with the new technology and it is thus still unclear whether the technology is likely to be appropriate for all companies. This is no longer true for late implementers. This leads to the following hypothesis:

H1: Companies that are still planning to implement RFID technology show less mindful decision making than companies that have already implemented the technology.

Companies can pursue different goals with RFID implementations. They could try to become more efficient, try to reach a higher quality, to monitor closely what others in a Supply Chain are doing, collaborate with other companies in the Supply Chain etcetera. Given the higher expected mindfulness of early implementers (and thus a better knowledge of the goals to achieve), we put forward the following hypotheses (related to hypothesis 1):

H2a: Early implementers were motivated more to adopt the technology by the promise of improved efficiency than late implementers.

H2b: Early implementers were motivated more to adopt the technology by the promise of improved quality than late implementers.

H2c: Early implementers were motivated more to adopt the technology by the promise of improved Supply Chain monitoring than late implementers.

H2d: Early implementers were motivated more to adopt the technology by the promise of improved inter-organizational collaboration than late implementers.

Inter-organizational practices seem more advanced and far-reaching than intra-organizational practices. Therefore, we put forward the following hypothesis:

H3: Achieving higher efficiency and higher quality are more important drivers for adoption than the ability to monitor others in the supply chain and to collaborate with them.

Given the fact that RFID technology is only now gaining momentum (The technology is currently at the start of the slope of enlightenment of the Gartner Hype cycle.), we expect this hypothesis to hold for both, early implementers and (relatively) 'late implementers'.

A mindful company would consider acceptance by users an important issue. According to the TAM (Technology Acceptance Model [24]), a technology is more likely to be accepted by users if it has a higher perceived usefulness and ease of use. The elements mentioned in the TAM should thus be considered when making an implementation decision.

H4a: Companies that consider RFID technology to be easy to use and useful are more likely to implement it.

Companies often make implementation decisions that may look useful and easy from a business standpoint while they neglect the technological complexity of the implementation. For example, many mergers and acquisitions went wrong (e.g. in the banking industry) because the difficulty of integrating the computer systems of the different companies was much more complex than assumed. As an extension to what is suggested by the TAM, not only the ease of use, but also the ease of implementation would thus be considered by a mindful company:

> **H4b:** Companies that consider RFID technology to be easy to implement in their company are more likely to implement it.

3.2 Mindless Decision Making

This paper intends to report on research in progress concerning different kinds of drivers for RFID adoption, exploring the mindfulness/mindlessness theory. Therefore, we also put forward hypotheses related to mindlessness. Prior research often only considered either mindfulness or mindlessness. This paper intends to deal with both at once. Mindless behaviour can show in many ways and several variables should thus be considered when determining whether a company behaves mindlessly or not. Companies may be influenced to invest in a technology because it is fashionable. RFID, which is seen as a technological breakthrough, can be considered as *fashionable* and this aspect has to be considered as a variable possibly leading to mindless behaviour. The fact that the number of implementations can positively influence the perception and adoption of a technology is also described by the Mindlessness Theory. *Observations* of implementations done by competitors, buyers, suppliers and companies in other industries should thus also be taken into account when determining the role of mindlessness. Similarly, *demands* (e.g. from buyers) to implement the technology should be considered. We then define mindless decision making as decision making where such fashionableness, observations or demands play a role.

As stated above, mindless firms are content to be followers rather than leaders. Therefore, we would expect companies that have not yet implemented RFID technology (but plan to implement it) to show more mindless behaviour than companies that have already implemented it. To explore the field of mindlessness theory, we thus put forward the next hypothesis:

> **H5:** Companies that are still planning to implement RFID technology show more mindless decision making than companies that have already implemented the technology.

The mindless company is said to regard assimilation as unproblematic: it is "a simple matter of rolling out the innovation to its end-users, who will in effect be left to fend for themselves. Initial confusion, frustration, or resistance may be dismissed as anomalous or attributed to shortcomings in the users themselves" [5, p 564]. While hypothesis 5 suggests that late adopters are more mindless than early adopters, we here investigate whether both, early and late adopters, can be considered mindless decision makers. We therefore hypothesize:

H6a: Early implementers would not be demotivated to use the technology if employees would feel threatened by it.

H6b: Late implementers would not be demotivated to use the technology if employees would feel threatened by it.

4 Research Methodology

A survey was conducted to test our hypotheses. A questionnaire was created with the aim of discovering drivers and inhibitors of RFID adoption by companies. It has been translated from English to Chinese and distributed to a list of 500 companies based in mainland China. The questionnaire was in Word format and sent by e-mail to the contact list. 136 questionnaires have been received back and 122 of them were usable. Questions were designed to provide all the information needed to test the hypotheses reported here and to test more advanced hypotheses in further studies.

Respondents evaluate different statements on a 7-point Likert scale ("1" meaning they strongly disagree with the statement and 7 meaning they strongly agree). We questioned different drivers that either motivated or would motivate the investment in RFID. We included a question asking if the person considered him or herself as the most knowledgeable to fill out the questionnaire. This enabled us to check whether the distribution of the questionnaire was well-targeted.

Respondents were mainly IT Directors (39%) and Responsible of Logistics (36%) with a less significant part of Managing Directors (14%), General Managers (8%) and CEO's (3%). The knowledge of each respondent regarding RFID was measured from 1 to 7 and resulted with a mean "knowledge" of 5.61 and a standard deviation of 0.74. A large majority of the companies stay open to new technologies but do not belong to the innovators (61%). 16% try to use the latest technologies, while, in the contrary, 22% avoid them. In our sample, 12% of the companies are using RFID technology. 13% plan to use it in the short term (within a year), 25% may use it within 5 years, and 4% dropped the project after trying. The biggest share is for the companies who are currently not planning to implement RFID technology (45%).

To test our hypotheses, we divided the sample in three different groups:

- *Group 1: the early implementers.* This group includes all companies which already use RFID extensively or plan to use it more extensively in the future and those that attempted to implement the technology in the past but dropped it (20 observations).
- *Group 2: the late implementers.* This group includes those running tests and which will start using it shortly and those planning to start using it the next few years (47 observations).
- *Group 3: the non-implementers.* This group includes companies that are currently not thinking about implementing this technology (55 observations).

To test the drivers and inhibitors we used the Student's t-test. This is the most "appropriate whenever you want to compare the means of two groups" and enables to conclude whether these are statistically different from each other. To test the hypotheses, we mainly compared the means of groups 1 and 2, and the means of groups (1+2) and 3.

5 Research Results

Hypothesis 1 states that early implementers show more mindful decision making than late implementers. The test results in Table 2 confirm this hypothesis ($p<0.005$). The results are based on the average response of each implementer with respect to the four following questions: Were you motivated to start using RFID in your company because it allows you to ….

- be more efficient (e.t., material receipts,…).
- monitor closely what others in your Supply Chain are doing.
- collaborate with other companies in your Supply Chain.
- reach a higher quality.

Table 2. Test results for Hypothesis 1 (*no equal variances assumed*)

mean group1	*mean group2*	*t-value*	*df*	*Sig. (1-tailed)*
5.8625	5.4149	4.657	33	0.000

Early implementers thus show more mindful decision making than late implementers.

To test Hypotheses 2a through 2d, a t-test was performed to compare the mean replies on the four questions mentioned for Hypothesis 1 for early and late implementers. The results are shown in Table 3. The hypothesis is confirmed in 3 of the four cases. No statistical significant difference is detected between early and late implementers in the motivation created by the possibility to achieve a higher quality.

Hypothesis 3 suggests that companies would rather be motivated by quality improvements and efficiency improvements than by the possibility to collaborate with other companies and to improve Supply Chain monitoring. The results of the t-test that was performed to test this hypothesis are shown in Table 4 for the early implementers and in Table 5 for the late implementers.

Table 3. Test results for Hypothesis 2a, 2b, 2c and 2d (*no equal variances assumed*)

	mean group1	*mean group2*	*t-value*	*df*	*Sig. (1-tailed)*
Efficiency	6.75	6.13	4.922	43.041	0.000
Quality	5.55	5.34	1.278	37.594	0.104
Monitoring	5.50	5.04	2.707	40.587	0.005
Collaboration	5.65	5.15	3.027	41.968	0.002

As suggested in hypothesis 3, efficiency seems a more important driver than the possibility to monitor and to collaborate with other companies. However, the possibility to deliver a higher quality is not a significantly more important driver than the improved monitoring (except for the late implementers) and collaboration.

Table 4. Test results for hypothesis 3, early implementers

mean 1	*mean 2*	*t-value*	*df*	*Sig. (1-tailed)*
Efficiency: 6.75	Monitoring: 5.5	7.804	19	0.000
Efficiency: 6.75	Collaborate: 5.65	7.678	19	0.000
Efficiency: 6.75	Quality: 5.55	13.077	19	0.000
Monitoring: 5.5	Collaborate: 5.65	-1.000	19	0.165
Monitoring: 5.5	Quality: 5.55	-0.252	19	0.402
Collaborate: 5.65	Quality: 5.55	0.567	19	0.288

Table 5. Test results for hypothesis 3, late implementers

mean 1	*mean 2*	*t-value*	*df*	*Sig. (1-tailed)*
Efficiency: 6.13	Monitoring: 5.04	8.012	46	0.000
Efficiency: 6.13	Collaborate: 5.15	7.289	46	0.000
Efficiency: 6.13	Quality: 5.34	5.948	46	0.000
Monitoring: 5.04	Collaborate: 5.15	-1.219	46	0.115
Monitoring: 5.04	Quality: 5.34	-2.141	46	0.019
Collaborate: 5.15	Quality: 5.34	-1.386	46	0.085

Hypothesis 4a (concerning the role of perceived usefulness and perceived ease of use) was tested using the following questions: Do you agree on the following statement:

- RFID is a technology that is easy to use.
- RFID can be useful for your company.

The average of the replies to these questions was compared for two groups: the early and late implementers on one side and the non-implementers on the other side. The test results in Table 6 show there is a statistically significant difference between both groups ($p < 0.005$). Consequently, the higher the perceived usefulness and ease of use, the higher the chance a company is implementing RFID technology.

Hypothesis 4b (concerning the role of perceived ease of implementation) was tested using the following question:

Table 6. Test results for Hypothesis 4a (equal variances assumed after successful Levene's Test for equality of variances)

mean group1+2	*mean group3*	*t-value*	*df*	*Sig. (1-tailed)*
5.9203	3.6226	18.537	120	0.000

- Do you agree on the following statement: RFID is a technology that is easy to implement?

The test results, shown in Table 7, indicate there is a statistically significant difference between implementers and non-implementers ($p < 0.005$). Companies that find the technology harder to implement are thus less likely to have implemented the technology.

Table 7. Test results for Hypothesis 4b (*no equal variances assumed*)

mean group1+2	*mean group3*	*t-value*	*df*	*Sig. (1-tailed)*
3.94	2.68	8.214	116	0.000

The confirmation of hypotheses 4a and 4b reveals that companies generally show signs of mindful decision making: the higher the considered usefulness, ease of use and ease of implementation, the higher the chance the technology gets implemented.

To test H5 (whether late implementers show more mindless decision making than early implementers) the means of the answers to the following questions of groups 1 and 2 were compared: Were you motivated to start using RFID in your company because …

- companies in other industries are implementing it,
- some of your important suppliers have implemented it,
- some of your important buyers have implemented it,
- some of you competitors have implemented it,
- it gives credibility to the organization and appears as technologically updated.
- your important suppliers asked you to use it,
- your important buyers asked you to use it.

The results of the test are shown in Table 8. Hypothesis 5 is confirmed by the data ($p < 0.05$).

Hypotheses 6a and 6b are confirmed by the data too. Both, early implementers and late implementers in our sample seem to show signs of not taking customer perceptions into account. When asked if they would be demotivated to start using RFID technology if they thought their employees would feel threatened by the implementation of the new technology, both groups gave a response that was statistically significantly lower than 4 (the neutral value). This is shown in Table 9.

Table 8. Test results for Hypothesis 5 (equal variances assumed after successful Levene's Test for equality of variances)

mean group1	*mean group2*	*t-value*	*df*	*Sig. (1-tailed)*
4.1714	4.3556	-2.011	65	0.048

Table 9. Test results for hypotheses 6a and 6b

	mean	*compared to*	*t-value*	*df*	*Sig. (1-tailed)*
group1	2.6500	4	-9.000	19	0.000
group2	2.7021	4	-12.916	46	0.000

6 Discussion and Limitations

A higher efficiency seems to be the most important driver for implementing RFID technology, both for early and late implementers. Contrary to what was expected, companies are not more motivated by the promise of achieving higher quality than by the possibility to better monitor the supply chain and to collaborate with other companies. The early implementers were more driven by the promise of higher efficiency, better supply chain monitoring and better collaboration than late implementers.

The fact that hypotheses 5 and 6a are confirmed seems worrying. It leads to the conclusion that mindless followers follow leaders that show mindless behavior. Late implementers might assume that early implementers did not take decisions mindlessly, but such assumption seems invalid. Mindless companies have been said not to believe they can get competitive advantages by implementing some technology [5]. Therefore, the test results seem to suggest that companies don't consider RFID technology as a technology that can give them competitive advantages. The fanaticism of early and late implementers 'to move forward' suppresses demotivations that could arise because of potential problems with employees. The fear from what other companies might achieve and the fear of missing an opportunity seems bigger than the fear from internal problems. Internal factors are supposed to be under control or are at least not supposed to cause big problems. This fits Swanson and Ramiller's view on mindless companies, which regard assimilation for example as unproblematic. On the basis of these preliminary results, more advanced research towards mindlessness is recommended.

While the fact that *mindless followers follow leaders that show mindless behavior* might be worrying, the confirmation of hypothesis 1 also points out that early implementers show more mindful decision making than late implementers. The followers thus at least follow leaders that seem *more* mindful than them. Neither early nor late implementers can be qualified as purely 'mindless' or 'mindful' decision makers. They combine both, characteristics of mindful and mindless decision taking. As mindfulness is an expensive approach, a 'healthy' mix of mindfulness and mindlessness may be appropriate. The mix is different for early implementers than for late implementers. Further research is needed to investigate the function describing the change in mix. Also, further research is currently conducted to understand the consequences of the change in mix over time. For researchers this case illustrates there is no straight line between the perceived ease of use and perceived usefulness and the decision to implement the technology. Factors related to mindless decision taking are also part of the picture.

There are several limitations to the research reported here. First, the research was conducted in a single country. Prior research has shown that culture plays a role in technology adoption. Further research should investigate the role of mindlessness/mindfulness in other countries. Another limitation of this study is that it is not assessed which characteristics are most important in the decision taking: those pointing to mindless decision making or those pointing to mindful decision making. Further research is needed to reveal the relation between mindlessness, the size of the perceived 'requirement from the environment' to move on and the internal risks the company is willing to bear. Problems in the financial industry recently revealed that managers take big risks in an attempt to gain huge profits and that they get big bonuses for doing so. Mindlessness was stimulated. Mindlessly pursuing some opportunity that *may* be there is dangerous, especially if it is not decently investigated whether that opportunity is attainable for your specific company. Further research is needed on the right balance between mindlessness and mindfulness. This could lower the number of IT project failures and improve the image of the IT proficiency.

7 Conclusions

This Workshop paper presents the first results of research in progress from a survey conducted among 122 Chinese companies about drivers for RFID adoption. The paper considers drivers that could be related to both, mindful and mindless decision making. The promise to reach higher efficiency seems to be the most important driver for mindful RFID adoption decisions. The early implementers were more driven to adoption by the promise of higher efficiency, better supply chain monitoring and better collaboration than late implementers. The survey also indicates that late adopters show more mindless behavior than early adopters. Those early adopters also show signs of mindless decision making. Companies are motivated to invest in RFID technology if they observe others are implementing it. Our preliminary results point out that all implementers make the implementation decision part mindfully, part mindlessly.

References

1. Shih, D.H., Chiu, Y.W., Chang, S.I., Yen, D.C.: An Empirical Study of Factors Affecting RFID's Adoption in Taiwan. Journal of Global Information Management 16(2), 58–80, 23 (2008)
2. Angeles, R.: RFID Technologies: Supply-chain applications and implementation issue. Information Systems Management 22(1), 51–65, 15 (2005)
3. Junko, Y.: RFID. Electronic Engineering Times, 44 (2008)
4. Masset, M.: Analyse sectorielle RFID, le marché du Tag RFID (2005)

5. Swanson, E.B., Ramiller, N.C.: Innovating mindfully with Information Technology. MIS Quarterly 28(4), 553–583 (2004)
6. Field, A.: RFID's impact still spreading. Journal of Commerce 9(16), 22–23 (2008)
7. Fish Lynn, A., Forrest Wayne, C.: A Worldwide Look at RFID. Supply Chain Management Review 11(3), 48–55 (2007)
8. Fosso Wamba, S., Lefebvre, L.A., Lefebvre, E.: Integrating RFID technology and EPC network into a B2B retail supply chain : a step toward intelligent business processes. Journal of Technology Management & Innovation 2(2) (2007)
9. Wolf, A.: Best Buy Goes RFID Route. Consumer Electronics 19(22), 24 (2004)
10. Mccrea, B.: Plotting your RFID roadmap. Logistics Management 46(3), 42–44 (2007)
11. Loebbecke, C., Huyskens, C.: A Competitive Perspective on Standard-Making: Kaufhof's RFID Project in Fashion Retailing. Electronic Markets 18(1), 30–38 (2008)
12. Wailgum, T.: China Emerges as Largest RFID Market. CIO 21(13), 14 (2008)
13. RFIDMarket Projections 2008 to 2018, IDTechEx, `http://www.idtechex.com`
14. Ngai, E.W.T., Moon, K.K.L., Riggins, F.J., Yi, C.Y.: RFID research: An academic literature review (1995–2005) and future research directions. International Journal of Production Economics 112(2), 510–520, 11 (2008)
15. Kern, C.: Radio-frequency-identification for security and media circulation in libraries. The Electronic Library 22(4), 317–324 (2004)
16. Harrop, P., Crotch-Harvey, T.: RFID for Healthcare and Pharmaceuticals 2008-2018. IDTechEx (2008)
17. Xiao, N., Crotch-Harvey, T., Harrop, P., Das, R.: RFID in China 2008-2018, Complete coverage of RFID in the World's fastest growing economy. ID TechEx (2008)
18. Coyle, K.: Management of RFID in libraries. The Journal of Academic Librarianship 31(5), 486–489 (2005)
19. Feig, N.: Getting Personal. Bank Systems & Technology 44(6), 50 (2007)
20. Raghu, D., Harrop, P.: RFID Forecasts, Players & Opportunities 2008-2018, Complete RFID analysis and forecasts 2008-2018. ID TechEx (2008)
21. Octopus Card, `http://www.octopuscards.com`
22. Macmillan-Davies, C.: RFID tracks Australian military shipments. Mobile Radio Technology 25(6), 22 (2007)
23. Solis, W.M.: Defence Logistics: More Efficient Use of Active RFID Tags Could Potentially Avoid Millions in Unnecessary Purchases. GAO Reports 13, 1–13 (2006)
24. Davis, F.D.: Perceived usefulness, perceived ease of use, and user acceptance of information technology. MIS Quarterly 13(3), 319–340 (1989)

Managing Supply Uncertainty with an Information Market

Zhiling Guo[1], Fang Fang[2], and Andrew B. Whinston[3]

[1] Department of Information Systems, University of Maryland, Baltimore County
zguo@umbc.edu
[2] College of Business Administration, California State University at San Marcos
fangfang@csusm.edu
[3] McCombs School of Business, The University of Texas at Austin
abw@uts.cc.utexas.edu

Abstract. We propose a market-based information aggregation mechanism to manage the supply side uncertainty in the supply chain. In our analytical model, a simple supply chain consists of a group of retailers who order a homogeneous product from two suppliers. The two suppliers differ in their ability to fulfill orders – one always delivers orders and the other fulfills orders probabilistically. We model the supply chain decisions as a Stackelberg game where the supplier who has uncertain reliability decides a wholesale price before the retailers who independently receive signals about the supplier's reliability determine their sourcing strategies. We then propose an information market to trade binary contracts with payoffs contingent on the supplier's true reliability. Using a simple uniform demand distribution, we demonstrate that the market-based information aggregation mechanism improves the overall supply chain efficiency.

Keywords: Information market, Supply chain, Uncertainty, Game theory.

1 Introduction

Information market, also known as prediction market, is a powerful information acquisition mechanism to elicit and aggregate information from a variety of sources. For years, public prediction markets have been used for politics (Iowa Electronic Market), video game (simExchange) or movie box-office (Hollywood Stock Exchange) sales. Prediction markets focusing on economic statistics such as employment rates, retail sales, industrial production, and private sector returns have been launched by Goldman Sachs, Deutsche Bank, and the Chicago Mercantile Exchange. Economic Derivatives and Hedgestreet are two prediction markets that offer trading of innovative futures contracts.

In addition to predicting public events and macroeconomic indicators, many leading companies have experimented with internal prediction markets to forecast corporate events. For example, Google has designed quite a few internal markets to provide estimates by collecting intelligence from the wisdom of employees. These

R. Sharman, T.S. Raghu, and H.R. Rao (Eds.): WEB 2009, LNBIP 52, pp. 80–95, 2010.

markets are designed to forecast both demand for its own products, such as Gmail, as well as the performance of competitive products, such as the Apple iPhone. It is also well known that Hewlett Packard (HP) is among the first businesses to strategically deploy prediction markets. McAdams and Malone [7] proposed an internal futures market to allow plant managers learn information about which products are most profitable from sales people. Usually predictions about possible future events can be designed as tradable contracts whose payoffs depend on the future realization of certain events. Prices of these contracts can be interpreted as a market-generated forecast of uncertain future events.

Guo et al. [4] extend the internal, corporate use of prediction market to an external, supply chain environment. They propose a macro prediction market to manage the systematic demand risk in a supply chain. Fang et al. [3] discussed alternative market mechanisms to separate the information flow from the physical product flow in supply chain optimization. They demonstrate the potential of using properly designed market mechanisms to yield accurate demand forecasts among supply chain partners. They suggest that market mechanisms outperform other traditional methods of demand forecasting in several aspects. When being asked to back up predictions with real money, the performance-dependent reward mechanism well aligns supply chain partners' incentives to share useful information with the goal of improving overall forecast accuracy. Additionally, market mechanisms aggregate useful demand-related information from both within and outside the supply chain. The ability to crowd-sourcing the forecast information contributes to improved forecast accuracy and better business planning.

Though promising, the integration of prediction market with supply chain optimization and business decision making is still in an early stage. Prior work has demonstrated the usefulness of prediction market in supply chain demand forecasting. In this paper, we try to extend the scope of supply chain applications to manage supply side uncertainty. For example, a retailer may run a prediction market in its procurement team about the future delivery of a key component. If the same market can be opened to other retailers who are interested in knowing the reliability of the component supplier, the collective forecasting outcome in the large supply network could outperform that in the internal market.

Supply side uncertainty is a well recognized problem in the supply chain literature [1]. It is quite common in the semiconductor industry that the production process has yield variations. With random yield, firms often receive a random portion of the order placed with a supplier. In other cases, supply uncertainty is binary in nature. An order placed with a supplier either arrives in full or not at all. Natural disasters and equipment failures are common reasons to cause such supply disruption. To better manage uncertain yield, firms usually source from two or more suppliers. Operational issues of quantity allocation between competing suppliers and its effects on the inventory policies have practical significance. Additionally, supply chain partners have asymmetric information about the supplier's reliability. Yang et al. [10] adopts a mechanism design approach to characterize the optimal menu of contracts. Tomlin [8] studies sourcing strategies when a firm can update its forecast of a supplier's yield distribution. A central question addressed in the literature is how uncertainty about a supplier's reliability influences a firm's optimal sourcing and inventory decisions. In general, it is shown that reducing such uncertainty can improve supply chain efficiency.

This study aims to explore the potential of using an information market mechanism to crowd-source a supplier's reliability forecast in a supply chain setting. The paper is organized as follows. We present a simple supply chain game theoretical model in Section 2. The supply chain information structure and our information market mechanism design are discussed in Section 3. Using a simple example based on uniform demand distribution in Section 4, we demonstrate the benefit of market-based information aggregation in improving the overall supply chain profit. We conclude our paper with future research directions in Section 5.

2 The Base Model

In this section, we consider a stylized model in which a retailer determines a sourcing strategy from two potential suppliers to satisfy an uncertain market demand. We investigate how the supplier's reliability uncertainty and pricing decision influence the sourcing strategy used by the retailer to mitigate the supply risk. In the next section, we extend our model to a supply network of N retailers.

We assume that the two suppliers differ in their ability to fulfill orders. Supplier 1 guarantees delivery of orders from the retailer so she is always reliable. Supplier 2 delivers orders with probability θ. We interpret θ as the reliability measure of supplier 2. In case that supplier 2 fails to deliver, she pays the retailer a non-delivery penalty cost (compensation cost) c per unit. To simplify our analysis, we assume supplier 1's wholesale price v is exogenously given. We model the supply chain as a Stackelberg game where supplier 2 determines a wholesale price w, and the retailer decides the order quantity pair (Q, q), where Q and q represent the retailer's order quantities from supplier 2 and supplier 1, respectively. Moreover, the retailer only pays supplier 2 for the quantity that she actually delivers.

The retailer sells the product at an exogenous retail price r. We assume the market demand is random with density $f(x)$ and cumulative distribution function $F(x)$ on the interval $[\underline{x}, \overline{x}]$. Demand not filled in a period is lost. Suppose the lost sales cost is h per unit. Inventory left over at the end of the period is salvaged at the value of g per unit. We further assume supplier 2's unit production cost is c_s regardless of whether it is successful or not. Without loss of generality, we assume $v > h > c_s$, $v > g$, $r > v$, $w > h \geq c$, $r > w > g$. Note that these conditions do not put additional constraints to our model, but are used to avoid discussion of trivial cases. A complete list of notations is provided in the Appendix.

2.1 The Retailer's Sourcing Strategy

To mitigate the supply risk, the retailer has to determine her sourcing strategy based on her belief about supplier 2's reliability and announced wholesale price. Denote $\tilde{\theta}$ as the retailer's belief about the supplier's reliability. It may or may not be the same as supplier 2's true reliability θ, as shown later in Section 3.

Define $w_1 = \frac{v-(1-\tilde{\theta})(r+h-c)}{\tilde{\theta}}$ and $w_2 = v + \frac{c(1-\tilde{\theta})}{\tilde{\theta}}$. We have the following results about the retailer's optimal sourcing strategy and order quantities.

Proposition 1: *Given supplier 2's wholesale price w, the retailer's sourcing strategy can be characterized by:*

1. If $w \le w_1$, the retailer single sources from supplier 2 with order quantity determined by

$$Q^* = F^{-1}\left[\frac{\tilde{\theta}(r+h-w)+(1-\tilde{\theta})c}{\tilde{\theta}(r+h-g)}\right] \tag{1}$$

2. If $w_1 < w \le w_2$, the retailer dual source from both supplies with order quantities determined by

$$q^* = F^{-1}\left[\frac{r+h-v-\tilde{\theta}(r+h-w)-(1-\tilde{\theta})c}{(1-\tilde{\theta})(r+h-g)}\right] \tag{2}$$

$$Q^* = F^{-1}\left[\frac{\tilde{\theta}(r+h-w)+(1-\tilde{\theta})c}{\tilde{\theta}(r+h-g)}\right] - q^* \tag{3}$$

3. If $w > w_2$, the retailer single sources from supplier 1with order quantity determined by

$$q^* = F^{-1}\left[\frac{r+h-v}{r+h-g}\right] \tag{4}$$

The following figure illustrates the effect of wholesale price on sourcing strategies using a uniform demand distribution with parameter values chosen according to Table 1 in Section 4. Under other types of demand distribution such as the normal demand distribution, the shape may not be piecewise linear. But the qualitative insights remain the same.

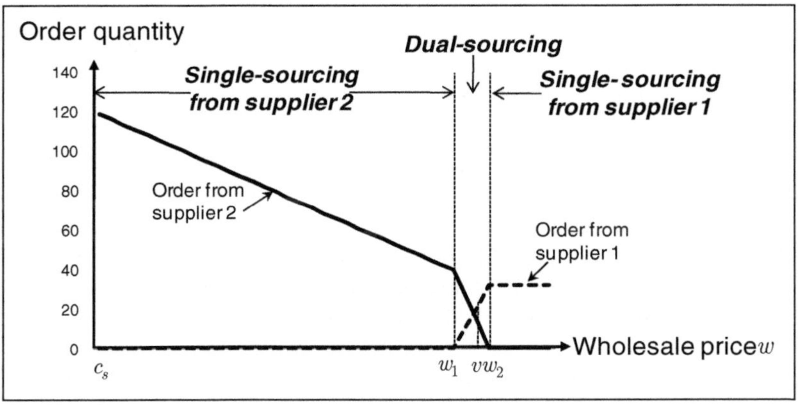

Fig. 1. Effect of Wholesale Price on Sourcing Strategies

We see that the retailer's order quantity from supplier 2 decreases as supplier 2's wholesale price increases. In addition, the total order quantity decreases in supplier 2's wholesale price as well. Not surprisingly, when supplier 2's wholesale price is significantly lower than supplier 1's, the retailer is interested in ordering from supplier 2 due to the lower price discount. Note that when $w = v$, the retailer would order more from supplier 1 than that from supplier 2. This is because, all else equal, supplier 2 is less reliable than supplier 1 so supplier 1 is more attractive. On the other hand, due to the compensation supplier 2 agrees to pay in case of delivery failure, it is equivalent that supplier 2 signs an option contract with the retailer. Supplier 2 pays c as a premium to elicit order from the retailer. The option contract is exercised at strike price $w - c$ if supplier 2 delivers the order, and the option contract is not exercised if supplier 2 fails to deliver the order. This flexible contract attracts the retailer to partially order from supplier 2 as a secondary souring channel even under the case that supplier 2's wholesale price is greater than or equal to supplier 1's.

2.2 Supplier 2's Pricing Game

Given the retailer's sourcing strategy characterized in Proposition 1, supplier 2's problem is to choose the wholesale price w to maximize the expected profit. The optimization problem can be expressed as:

$$\underset{w}{Max}\ \pi\left(Q^*, w\right) = \left[\theta w - (1-\theta)c - c_s\right]Q^* \tag{5}$$

Differentiating the supplier's objective function, we have

$$\frac{\partial \pi\left(Q^*, w\right)}{\partial w} = \theta Q^* + \left[\theta w - (1-\theta)c - c_s\right]\frac{\partial Q^*}{\partial w} = 0 \tag{6}$$

If the retailer sources solely from supplier 2, then under the condition $w \leq w_1$, differentiating Q^* from (1) we have $\frac{\partial Q^*}{\partial w} = -\frac{1}{(r+h-g)f\left(Q^*\right)}$. Substituting $\frac{\partial Q^*}{\partial w}$ into (6) we derive the optimality condition for the supplier's pricing game under the single-sourcing strategy.

If the retailer sources from both suppliers, then under the condition $w_1 < w \leq w_2$, differentiating Q^* from (3) yields $\frac{\partial Q^*}{\partial w} = -\frac{1}{(r+h-g)f\left(q^*+Q^*\right)} + \frac{\bar{\theta}}{\left(1-\bar{\theta}\right)(r+h-g)f\left(q^*\right)}$. Substituting $\frac{\partial Q^*}{\partial w}$ into (6) we derive the optimality condition for the supplier's pricing game under single-sourcing.

We assume that demand distribution has an increasing generalized failure rate (IGFR). Lariviere and Porteus [6] showed that if the demand distribution is IGFR with a finite mean, the supplier's problem is pseudo-concave. Therefore, we can characterize the equilibrium in the following proposition.

Proposition 2: *Let the pair* $\left(w^*, Q^*\right)$ *be the solution to the following system of equations:*

$$\theta Q^* - \frac{\theta w^* - (1-\theta)c - c_s}{(r+h-g)f\left(Q^*\right)} = 0 \tag{7}$$

$$F\left(Q^*\right) = \frac{\tilde{\theta}\left(r+h-w^*\right)+\left(1-\tilde{\theta}\right)c}{\tilde{\theta}(r+h-g)} \tag{8}$$

If $w^* \le w_1$ *, then* $\left(w^*, Q^*\right)$ *constitutes a Stackelberg equilibrium of the inventory game in which the retailer chooses a single-sourcing strategy. Otherwise, let the triple* $\left(w^{**}, q^{**}, Q^{**}\right)$ *be the solution to the following system of equations:*

$$\theta Q^{**} + \left(\theta w^{**} - (1-\theta)c - c_s\right)\left[-\frac{1}{(r+h-g)f\left(q^{**}+Q^{**}\right)} + \frac{\tilde{\theta}}{\left(1-\tilde{\theta}\right)(r+h-g)f\left(q^{**}\right)}\right] = 0 \tag{9}$$

$$Q^{**} = F^{-1}\left[\frac{\tilde{\theta}\left(r+h-w^{**}\right)+\left(1-\tilde{\theta}\right)c}{\tilde{\theta}(r+h-g)}\right] - q^{**} \tag{10}$$

$$q^{**} = F^{-1}\left[\frac{r+h-v-\tilde{\theta}\left(r+h-w^{**}\right)-\left(1-\tilde{\theta}\right)c}{\left(1-\tilde{\theta}\right)(r+h-g)}\right] \tag{11}$$

If $w_1 < w \le w_2$*, then the pair* $\left(w^{**}, Q^{**}\right)$ *constitutes a Stackelberg equilibrium of the inventory game in which the retailer chooses a dual-sourcing strategy. Otherwise, supplier 2 prices* $w^{***} = w_1$ *, and the retailer is indifferent between the single-sourcing and dual-sourcing strategies.*

3 The Information Structure

In this section, we extend our Stackelberg supply chain game to a supply chain network of N retailers. We assume the retailers only differ in their ability to observe signals about supplier 2's true reliability. For simplicity, we assume that the true reliability θ is unknown but can take two possible values: θ_L and θ_H , where $\theta_L < \theta_H$.

Before ordering, we assume each retailer obtains a signal s correlated to the supplier 2's reliability θ . We further assume that s takes two possible values: 0 and 1. One can consider receiving a signal 1 or 0 as receiving good news or bad news. Denote the total number of retailers who receive signal $s = 1$ is α and the total number of retailers who receive signal $s = 0$ is β . So $\alpha + \beta = N$.

Assume that $P\left(s = 1 \mid \theta = \theta_H\right) = P\left(s = 0 \mid \theta = \theta_L\right) = \lambda > 1/2$. That is, a retailer is more likely to receive a piece of good (bad) news when the true reliability $\theta = \theta_H$ ($\theta = \theta_L$). In addition, we assume that the prior belief that $P\left(\theta = \theta_H\right) = p$. In the following, we characterize the belief update under different supply chain information structures.

3.1 Decentralized Information Framework

For those retailers who receive $s = 1$, the posterior belief of $\tilde{\theta}$ will be updated as $\tilde{\theta}_h$, where:

$$P\left(\theta = \theta_H \mid s = 1\right) = \frac{p\lambda}{p\lambda + (1-p)(1-\lambda)}$$

$$\tilde{\theta}_h \triangleq E\left(\theta \mid s = 1\right) = \theta_L + \frac{p\lambda\left(\theta_H - \theta_L\right)}{p\lambda + (1-p)(1-\lambda)} \tag{12}$$

For those retailers who receive $s = 0$, the posterior belief of $\tilde{\theta}$ will be updated as $\tilde{\theta}_\ell$, where:

$$P\left(\theta = \theta_H \mid s = 0\right) = \frac{p(1-\lambda)}{p(1-\lambda) + (1-p)\lambda}$$

$$\tilde{\theta}_\ell \triangleq E\left(\theta \mid s = 0\right) = \theta_L + \frac{p(1-\lambda)\left(\theta_H - \theta_L\right)}{p(1-\lambda) + (1-p)\lambda} \tag{13}$$

Based on the posterior belief $\tilde{\theta}_j$, for $j = h, \ell$, the order quantities will have the same expression as described in Proposition 1 by simply substituting $\tilde{\theta}$ with $\tilde{\theta}_j$, depending on the received signals. Since we assume two types of signals, for given supplier 2's wholesale price, the order quantities are of two types. Denote Q_h^* and Q_ℓ^* as the order quantities when retailers receive signal 1 and 0, respectively. The total order quantity to supplier 2 will be $\alpha Q_h^* + \beta Q_\ell^*$. Accordingly, the total order quantities to supplier 1 will be $\alpha q_h^* + \beta q_\ell^*$.

3.1.1 Effect of Perceived Reliability on Sourcing Strategies

Based on different signals received, the retailer's sourcing strategies are described as follows.

Proposition 3: *Based on the received signal $s = 1$ or 0 and the perceived reliability (i.e., the corresponding posterior belief $\tilde{\theta}_j$, for $j = h, \ell$), the retailer's sourcing strategies are characterized by:*

1. *If $w < v$, the retailer dual source from both suppliers if $\tilde{\theta}_j < \overline{\theta}$, where $\overline{\theta} = \frac{r+h-c-v}{r+h-c-w}$; otherwise, the retailer will single source from supplier 2.*
2. *If $w > v$, the retailer dual source from both suppliers if $\tilde{\theta}_j \leq \underline{\theta}$, where $\underline{\theta} = \frac{c}{c+w-v}$; otherwise, the retailer will single source from supplier 1.*

The following figure illustrates how the sourcing strategy is affected by both the perceived reliability and the wholesale price. Again, the figure is plotted based on a uniform demand distribution with parameter values chosen according to Table 1 in Section 4.

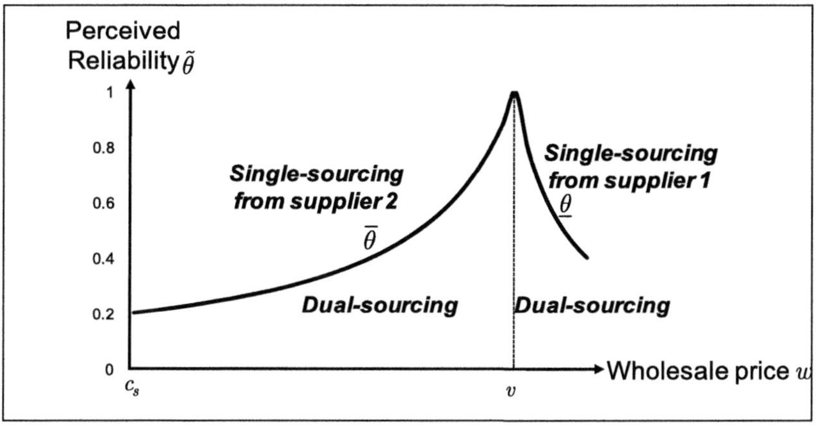

Fig. 2. Effect of Perceived Reliability on Sourcing Strategies

In Figure 2, $\overline{\theta}$ and $\underline{\theta}$ represent the threshold levels where the retailer changes her sourcing strategy. When supplier 2's wholesale price is lower than supplier 1's, retailers whose perceived reliability is above the curve would prefer a single-sourcing strategy. In this case, retailers prefer lower price, more reliable supplier. In contrast, when supplier 2's wholesale price is higher than supplier 1's, retailers whose perceived reliability is lower than the curve would be interested in ordering from supplier 2. This is due to the expected compensation from supplier 2.

For any given perceived reliability, we can draw a parallel line to cross over the threshold curve. We can see that the wholesale price range for dual-sourcing decreases as the retailer's perceived reliability increases. This implies that a dual sourcing strategy is more likely used by a retailer if the supply base is more differentiated.

3.1.2 Supplier 2's Incentive for Information Disclosure

In order to analyze supplier 2's incentive for information disclosure, we first characterize the effect of the perceived reliability on the retailer's order quantity. Figure 3 illustrates such effect.

In Figure 3, we denote the wholesale price corresponding to $\overline{\theta}$ and $\underline{\theta}$ as $\overline{w}$ and $\underline{w}$ respectively. We further use subscripts *H*, *L*, *N* to denote the scenarios where the perceived reliabilities are High ($s = 1$), Low ($s = 0$), or No information (under the prior probability). The No information case is equivalent to no information update so the prior belief is used to determine order quantity.

Corresponding to Figures 1 & 2, the kinks occur when the retailer changes from single-sourcing to dual-sourcing strategy. We see that, if the retailer single sources from supplier 2, then the order quantity decreases in the perceived reliability. If the retailer sources from both suppliers, then the order quantity for supplier 2 decreases faster when the perceived reliability is high than that when the perceived reliability is low as supplier 2's wholesale price increases. Additionally, when supplier 2's wholesale price is greater than supplier 1's, the retailer's order quantity for supplier 2 decreases in the perceived reliability.

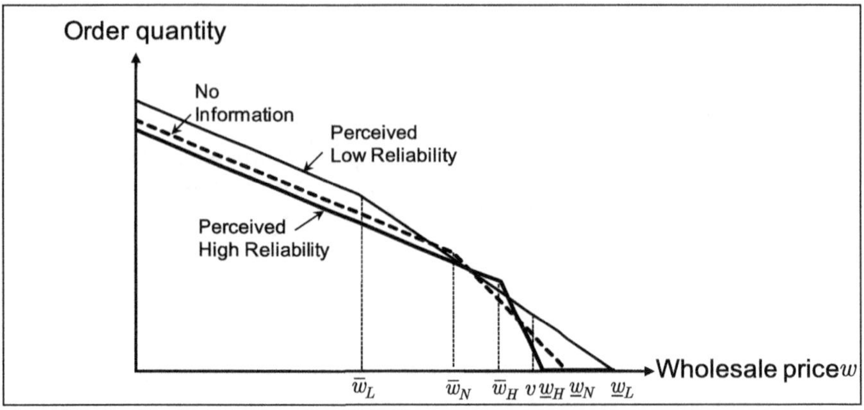

Fig. 3. Effect of Perceived Reliability on Order Quantity

Based on this observation, we can analyze the supplier's incentive for information disclosure as follows.

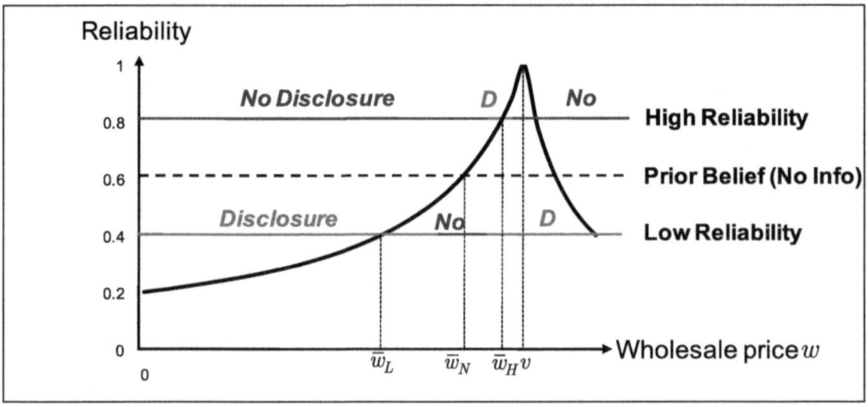

Fig. 4. Supplier 2's Incentive for Information Disclosure

From Figure 4, it is clear that a high reliability supplier has no incentive to disclose her reliability information most of the time. A high reliability supplier is only willing to disclose her reliability information when she decides to price around $\overline{w}_H$. In contrast, a low reliability supplier has incentive to disclose its reliability information most of the time. A low reliability supplier would not disclose its reliability when she decides to price around $\overline{w}_N$. In general, incentives for information sharing are not well aligned in this supply chain game. Supplier 2 cannot credibly signal her type to the retailers, and the retailers have no means to better forecast supplier 2's reliability. In the following section, we propose a market-based information aggregation mechanism to align retailers' incentives for information sharing.

3.2 Market-Based Collaborative Forecasting

We propose an information market to elicit and aggregate the retailers' private signals. Presumably the aggregate signals could yield a more reliable forecast of supplier 2's reliability, closer to the true reliability θ . Additionally, the market mechanism should provide adequate incentive for the retailers to "tell the truth." For this purpose, we design two binary contracts: the "High_Reliability" contract pays off \$1 if the future realized reliability is θ_H and \$0 if $\theta = \theta_L$; the "Low_Reliability" pays off \$1 if the future realized reliability is θ_L and \$0 if $\theta = \theta_H$. Similar types of binary contracts have been used in IEM trading, among others.

Based on their observed signals, the retailers decide which types of contract to trade in the market. According to [9], the equilibrium market prices will efficiently aggregate all the initially dispersed information and can be interpreted as the probabilities (or market beliefs) about supplier 2's reliability. Denote such equilibrium prices for the contracts "High_Reliability" and "Low_Reliability" as ϕ_H^* and ϕ_L^* . We can derive that:

$$\begin{cases} \phi_H^* \triangleq P(\theta = \theta_H \mid \alpha, \beta) = \frac{p\lambda^\alpha (1-\lambda)^\beta}{p\lambda^\alpha (1-\lambda)^\beta + (1-p)(1-\lambda)^\alpha \lambda^\beta} \\ \phi_L^* \triangleq P(\theta = \theta_L \mid \alpha, \beta) = \frac{p(1-\lambda)^\alpha \lambda^\beta}{p(1-\lambda)^\alpha \lambda^\beta + (1-p)\lambda^\alpha (1-\lambda)^\beta} \end{cases} \tag{14}$$

Therefore, the market-based belief (expected reliability) is expressed as

$$\tilde{\theta}^m \triangleq E(\theta \mid \alpha, \beta) = \phi_H^* \theta_H + \phi_L^* \theta_L \tag{15}$$

which is known to all retailers and supplier 2. Based on the aggregated information, the total order quantity is $NQ^*\left(\tilde{\theta}^m\right)$. One can justify that $\tilde{\theta}^m \to \theta$ when $N \to \infty$. So the market prediction of θ will be reliable and close to true value when the number of market participants is large.

4 An Illustration with Uniform Demand

Assume that the uncertain demand is characterized by a uniform distribution. The density function is expressed as:

$$f(x) = \begin{cases} 1/A & \text{if } 0 \le x \le A \\ 0 & \text{otherwise} \end{cases} \tag{16}$$

So, $F(x) = \frac{x}{A}$, for $0 \le x \le A$. We can easily verify that supplier 2's objective function is strictly concave. So a unique equilibrium solution exists. In this numerical example, we set $A = 100$.

We assume that the supplier 2's reliability is either high or low with equal probabilities. So $p = 0.5$. Since supplier 2 cannot creditably signal her true type (high or low), retailers use our market mechanism to aggregate information and form a collaborative forecast of supplier 2's reliability. We further assume there are 10 retailers. All parameter values are summarized in Table 1.

Table 1. Summary of Parameter Values

Parameter Interpretation	Parameter Value
True probability of supplier 2	$\theta_H = 0.8$ or $\theta_L = 0.4$
Number of retailers	$N = 10$
Demand distribution	$A = 100$
Unit retail price	$r = 1$
Unit opportunity cost of lost sales	$h = 0.1$
Unit salvage cost of overstock	$g = 0.15$
Unit production cost of supplier 2	$c_s = 0.05$
Unit compensation cost from supplier 2	$c = \{0.05, 0.06, 0.07, 0.08, 0.09, 0.1\}$
Supplier 1's wholesale price	$v = \{0.6, 0.7, 0.8, 0.9\}$
Prior probability	$p = 0.5$
Conditional probability	$P(s = 1 \mid \theta = \theta_H) = P(s = 0 \mid \theta = \theta_L) = \lambda = 0.75$

To demonstrate the benefit of market-based information sharing, we use the decentralized supply chain information structure as benchmark. In the decentralized supply chain, each retailer independently receives a private signal 1 or 0, which is observable by neither the other retailers nor supplier 2. Retailers who receive signals valued 1 and 0 would update their beliefs about supplier 2's reliability as $\tilde{\theta}_h = 0.7$ and $\tilde{\theta}_\ell = 0.5$, respectively. Based on this updated belief, retailers determine their order strategies and best response order quantities corresponding to supplier 2's wholesale price.

Supplier 2 does not have information about the retailers' signals. However, she knows that retailers' signal distribution follows a binomial distribution, contingent on its reliability. The probability mass function with N = 10 and $P(s = 1 \mid \theta = \theta_H) = P(s = 0 \mid \theta = \theta_L) = \lambda$ can be characterized by the following binomial distribution:

$$\Pr(\alpha = k) = \binom{N}{k} \lambda^k (1 - \lambda)^{N-k} \tag{17}$$

where $k = 0, 1, \ldots, 10$. According to this probability distribution, supplier 2 can fully anticipate the expected retailers' orders. Supplier 2 then determines a wholesale price w^{d*} that maximizes her expected profit.

Under the market-based information aggregation, the market efficiently aggregates all available information and the final equilibrium market prices are observed by both the supplier and the retailers. Correspondingly, the market belief $\tilde{\theta}^m$ is formed and is known to all supply chain members. Supplier 2 can fully anticipate the retailers'

Table 2. Supply Chain Profits under Market-Based (M) and Decentralized (D) Inforamtion Structure

v	c	Retailers (Aggregated)						Supplier 2				Supplier 1		Chain		
		TQ^d	TQ^m	Tq^d	Tq^m	PR^d	PR^m	w^d	w^m	$P2^d$	$P2^m$	$P1^d$	$P1^m$	PC^d	PC^m	Eff. Improvement
0.9	0.00	530.00	534.11	0.00	0.00	163.34	163.32	0.600	0.593	31.78	32.59	0.00	0.00	195.11	195.91	0.41%
	0.02	528.20	533.85	0.00	0.00	163.44	163.34	0.613	0.610	31.71	32.58	0.00	0.00	195.14	195.92	0.40%
	0.04	525.86	533.56	0.00	0.00	163.56	163.36	0.629	0.627	31.37	32.55	0.00	0.00	194.93	195.91	0.50%
	0.06	524.59	533.25	0.00	0.00	163.71	163.39	0.645	0.644	31.30	32.54	0.00	0.00	195.01	195.93	0.47%
	0.08	522.78	532.98	0.00	0.00	163.89	163.43	0.661	0.661	31.06	32.47	0.00	0.00	194.95	195.90	0.49%
	0.1	521.50	532.60	0.00	0.00	164.09	163.47	0.676	0.679	30.88	32.41	0.00	0.00	194.97	195.87	0.46%
0.8	0.00	617.76	571.73	2.76	32.77	158.13	154.33	0.511	0.526	58.02	49.66	2.07	24.58	218.22	228.57	4.74%
	0.02	618.98	571.84	1.32	32.75	158.62	154.35	0.525	0.543	58.53	49.75	0.99	24.56	218.14	228.67	4.83%
	0.04	619.55	571.43	0.00	32.94	159.15	154.37	0.540	0.560	58.73	49.73	0.00	24.71	217.87	228.81	5.02%
	0.06	613.53	571.09	0.00	33.14	159.63	154.40	0.560	0.577	56.32	49.73	0.00	24.85	215.95	228.98	6.04%
	0.08	606.60	570.93	0.39	33.19	160.01	154.43	0.581	0.594	53.85	49.69	0.30	24.89	214.15	229.01	6.94%
	0.1	596.90	570.53	1.97	33.39	160.31	154.47	0.603	0.611	51.05	49.65	1.48	25.04	212.84	229.16	7.67%
0.7	0.00	580.00	540.52	82.11	99.44	138.12	142.63	0.471	0.492	73.86	65.32	53.37	64.64	265.35	272.58	2.73%
	0.02	577.54	540.42	82.24	99.47	138.67	142.64	0.488	0.509	73.85	65.32	53.45	64.66	265.98	272.62	2.50%
	0.04	575.08	540.20	82.37	99.58	139.26	142.66	0.504	0.526	73.77	65.34	53.54	64.73	266.56	272.73	2.31%
	0.06	571.69	539.60	82.89	99.92	139.89	142.68	0.521	0.543	73.50	65.34	53.88	64.95	267.27	272.97	2.13%
	0.08	568.57	538.94	83.16	100.27	140.56	142.71	0.538	0.560	73.01	65.28	54.05	65.18	267.63	273.17	2.07%
	0.1	566.11	537.97	83.29	100.78	141.28	142.75	0.555	0.578	72.69	65.21	54.14	65.51	268.11	273.47	2.00%
0.6	0.00	600.70	552.19	150.88	173.40	114.88	126.06	0.386	0.411	121.75	111.10	82.98	95.37	319.62	332.52	4.04%
	0.02	613.98	551.65	144.21	173.71	115.26	126.08	0.394	0.428	123.29	111.19	79.32	95.54	317.86	332.81	4.70%
	0.04	619.02	550.95	142.11	174.10	115.51	126.11	0.406	0.445	124.31	111.23	78.16	95.75	317.98	333.09	4.75%
	0.06	613.84	550.38	146.01	174.37	115.75	126.17	0.421	0.462	125.17	111.25	80.30	95.91	321.23	333.32	3.76%
	0.08	607.87	550.15	150.18	174.55	116.13	126.22	0.437	0.479	125.55	111.32	82.60	96.00	324.27	333.54	2.86%
	0.1	602.56	549.38	154.21	174.92	116.47	126.30	0.453	0.497	126.02	111.27	84.82	96.21	327.31	333.78	1.98%

orders based on $\tilde{\theta}^m$. Supplier 2 then determines a wholesale price w^{m^*} that maximizes her expected profit. This optimal wholesale price w^{m^*} can be adjusted according to the actual number of retailers who receives high/low signals.

Table 2 reports expected values of the supply chain game outcome under both the decentralized and market-based information structure. We use superscript d and m to denote the decentralized, no information sharing case and the market-based, collaborative forecasting case side by side. We report the wholesale price w and the expected aggregated order quantities TQ and Tq from all the retailers to supplier 1 and supplier 2, respectively. We also present supplier 1, supplier 2, and retailers' expected profits, as well as the total supply chain profit (denoted as PS1, PS2, and PC). We then perform sensitivity analysis based on two key parameters: the compensation *c* and supplier 1's wholesale price v.

We see that, under all cases, the expected supply chain efficiency increases under the market-based collaborative forecasting framework in comparison with the decentralized framework. The last column in Table 2 presents the percentage improvement of the total supply chain profit. We measure the total supply chain profit as the sum of profits from all supply chain members including all retailers, supplier 1 and supplier 2. We measure the supply chain efficiency improvement as the ratio of the supply chain profit difference between the market-based framework and the decentralized framework to the decentralized supply chain profit, i.e., $(PC^m-PC^d)/PC^d$.

We further observe that the degree of supply chain efficiency improvement varies when v and *c* changes. Interestingly, the improvement is the highest when v values around 0.8. At this value, supplier 2 manipulates the wholesale price in the decentralized framework so that all the retailers single source from her in most of the cases. However, in the market-based framework, the market information aggregation helps reveal supplier 2's true type to all the retailers so it greatly reduce the room for supplier 2 to manipulate the market. As a result, the retailers choose to dual source from both suppliers in most of the cases. Since supplier 2's reliability is either 0.8 or 0.4 with equal probability, from the supply chain perspective, it is more beneficial if retailers order from the perfectly reliable supplier 1. This is because all price related parameters such as the wholesale price and compensation cost only affect the division of profit among supply chain members rather than the total supply chain profit. Sourcing from the more reliable supplier 1 can eliminate the supply chain inefficiency caused by lost sales opportunity due to the less reliable supplier's inability to fulfill orders. In the case that v = 0.8, we observe significantly higher order quantity $(Tq^m - Tq^d)$ from supplier 1. Hence the supply chain efficiency improves the most.

Another interesting observation is that increasing the compensation value *c* may or may not improve the degree of supply chain efficiency. When v is relatively high (e.g. v =0.8 or 0.9), the degree of improvement increases as *c* increases. However, when v is relatively low (e.g. v =0.6), the degree of improvement moves towards the other direction. This result is not too surprising. Even though supplier 2 agrees a fixed compensation to retailers in the case of non-delivery, she can adjust the wholesale price to incorporate the effect of compensation on her profitability. Hence an increase of compensation may not always make supplier 2 more attractive, but depend on how supplier 2 is actually adjusting the wholesale price. This intuition is confirmed with the observation that the higher compensation, the higher the average wholesale price. When v is relatively high, supplier 1 is less competitive in comparison with supplier

2. So supplier 2 can offer a relatively high compensation but effectively adjust the wholesale price upwards and still attract retailers to single source from her. As a result, supplier 2's profits increase and retailers' profits decrease as c increases (as seen when v = 0.9). On the other hand, when v is relatively low, supplier 1 becomes very competitive in comparison with supplier 2. Supplier 2 cannot increase the wholesale price aggressively when the compensation is high. Although supplier 2 would not worse off when she offers higher compensation, retailers benefit from the competition between the two suppliers and their profits increase (as seen when v = 0.6).

5 Concluding Remarks

An extensive body of work in the literature has shown that information market is a promising mechanism to effectively predict uncertain outcomes [2, 9]. However, existing applications of such markets have been limited to predict public events such as presidential election or internal corporate use such as the prediction of future sales. We aim to explore the potential application of information markets in a broader decision making environment including the management of supply side uncertainty in the supply chain.

In this paper, we demonstrate the benefit of a market-based information aggregation mechanism in improving the overall supply chain efficiency. We choose the uniform demand distribution as a simple illustration. In fact, similar qualitative insights can be extended to other demand distributions. In addition to fully analyze the game structure in equilibrium analysis, future work should formally characterize conditions under which the information market improves supply chain performance.

To better coordinate the supply chain and manage the supply-side uncertainty, we assume a compensation scheme is offered by supplier 2 as a form of risk sharing contract. However, we assume the unit compensation is predetermined and the supplier only needs to decide the wholesale price. Other forms of coordination contracts, including the options contract, could be studied in future work. Please refer to [5] for more general discussion on the distribution function and the coordination mechanisms.

Although we propose to trade simple binary contracts in this research, we expect more sophisticated trading contracts such as those with continuous payoffs could also be considered in future market mechanism design. Moreover, dynamic models might be an alternative modeling tool to study repeated interactions and market dynamics in multi-period supply chain coordination. We leave all these interesting explorations to future research.

References

1. Anupindi, R., Akella, R.: Diversification under Supply Uncertainty. Management Science 39(8), 944–963 (1993)
2. Berg, J.E., Rietz, T.A.: Prediction Markets as Decision Support Systems. Information Systems Frontiers 5(1), 79–93 (2003)

3. Fang, F., Guo, Z., Whinston, A.B.: Collective Outsourcing to Market (COM): A Market-Based Framework for Information Supply Chain Outsourcing. Journal of the Association for Information Systems 9(4), 98–118 (2008)
4. Guo, Z., Fang, F., Whinston, A.B.: Supply Chain Information Sharing in a Macro Prediction Market. Decision Support Systems 42(3), 1944–1958 (2006)
5. Guo, Z., Fang, F., Whinston, A.B.: A Market-Based Information Aggregation Mechanism to Manage Yield Uncertainty in Supply Chain. Working paper (2010)
6. Lariviere, M.A., Porteus, E.L.: Selling to the Newsvendor: An Analysis of Price-Only Contracts. Manufacturing Service Oper. Management 3(4), 293–305 (2001)
7. McAdams, D., Malone, T.: Internal Markets for Supply Chain Capacity Allocation. MIT Working paper (2005)
8. Tomlin, B.: Impact of Supply Learning When Suppliers Are Unreliable. Manufacturing Service Oper. Management 11(2), 192–209 (2009)
9. Wolfers, J., Zitzewitz, E.: Prediction Markets. Journal of Economic Perspectives 18(2), 107–127 (2004)
10. Yang, Z., Aydin, G., Babich, V., Beil, D.: Supply Disruptions, Asymmetric Information, and a Backup Production Option. Management Science 55(2), 192–209 (2009)

Appendix

Table 3. Table of Notations

Uncertainty	
θ	Supplier 2's true reliability, $\theta = \theta_H$ or θ_L
$\tilde{\theta}$	The retailer's belief about supplier 2's reliability
$x \in [\underline{x}, \overline{x}]$	Random demand with lower bound $\underline{x}$ and upper bound $\overline{x}$
$f(x)$	Probability density function of demand
$F(x)$	Cumulative density function of demand
Supply Chain Parameters	
$i = 1, \ldots N$	N retailers
v	Unit wholesale price charged by supplier 1
w	Unit wholesale price charged by supplier 2
q	The retailer's order from supplier 1
Q	The retailer's order from supplier 2
c	Supplier 2's unit compensation cost in case of non-delivery
c_s	Supplier 2's unit production cost
r	The retailer's unit retail price
h	Unit lost sales cost
g	Unit salvage value
Information Structure	
D	Denote decentralized information structure
M	Denote market-based information structure
$P(\theta = \theta_H) = p$	Prior belief that supplier 2's reliability is high
$P(\theta = \theta_L) = 1 - p$	Prior belief that supplier 2's reliability is low

Table 3. *(continued)*

$s = \{1,0\}$	The value of binary signal
α	Number of retailers who receive $s = 1$
β	Number of retailers who receive $s = 0$, $\alpha + \beta = N$
$P(s = 1 \mid \theta = \theta_H) = \lambda$	Conditional probability, $P(s = 0 \mid \theta = \theta_H) = 1 - \lambda$, $\lambda > 1/2$
$P(s = 0 \mid \theta = \theta_L) = \lambda$	Conditional probability, $P(s = 1 \mid \theta = \theta_L) = 1 - \lambda$, $\lambda > 1/2$
$\tilde{\theta}_h$ ($\tilde{\theta}_\ell$)	The retailer's perceived reliability if she receives signal $s = 1$ ($s = 0$)
$\tilde{\theta}^m$	Updated market belief based on market prices
ϕ_H^* (ϕ_L^*)	Equilibrium market prices for contracts "High_Reliability" ("Low_Reliability")
Threshold Values	
w_1	Wholesale price threshold value below which the retailer single-sourcing from supplier 2
w_2	Wholesale price threshold value above which the retailer single-sourcing from supplier 1
$\overline{\theta}$	Reliability threshold value above which the retailer single-sourcing from supplier 2
$\underline{\theta}$	Reliability threshold value above which the retailer single-sourcing from supplier 1
$\overline{w}$	Wholesale price threshold value corresponding to $\overline{\theta}$
$\underline{w}$	Wholesale price threshold value corresponding to $\underline{\theta}$

Remanufacturing with RFID Item-Level Information

Wei Zhou[1,3] and Selwyn Piramuthu[2,3]

[1] Information Systems and Technologies, ESCP Europe, 75543 Paris cedex 11, France
[2] Information Systems and Operations Management, University of Florida, FL 32611, USA
[3] RFID European Lab, Paris, France
{wzhou@escpeurope.eu,selwyn@ufl.edu}

Abstract. RFID technology has been widely utilized throughout supply chains across a wide spectrum of industries. However, its potential in recycling/remanufacturing has not received much attention in information systems literature. We consider RFID tags and their applications from a recycling/remanufacturing perspective and propose a novel framework to assist such process based on item-level information visibility and instantaneous tracking/tracing ability enabled by RFID tags.

Keywords: RFID, remanufacturing, reverse logistics, item-level information, closed-loop manufacturing.

1 Introduction

In recent years, Product Remanufacturing Management (PRM) and closed-loop manufacturing have gained increased attention from academic researchers and practitioners alike. The process of remanufacturing include the collection of defective (due to manufacturing) and end-of-life goods as well as manufacturing byproducts and re-engineering of products back to new or as-new or refurbished condition. Although remanufacturing is not new, it is still largely undervalued with respect to its economic, environmental and social benefits as well as from a strategic business perspective.

Due to its inherent properties and the need to integrate the remanufacturing processes with the regular manufacturing plan, product remanufacturing management has been faced by challenges that arise mostly as a result of uncertainty from a supply chain perspective. For instance, uncertainty from the market, inventory, processing time and materials recovered has a direct impact on the manufacturing plan. As a result, the complex tasks in a remanufacturing process normally are significantly different from those in a traditional manufacturing setup. Rather than tackle a part of the problem, we find it more beneficial to optimize the remanufacturing process as a whole, which makes RFID technology an ideal candidate for this purpose.

Being able to reveal item-level product information in a way that is fully automatic and instantaneous, radio frequency identification (RFID) technology not only provides a vitally important tool for supply chain management but also makes it a natural fit to optimize the product remanufacturing process. RFID is a tracking system that

R. Sharman, T.S. Raghu, and H.R. Rao (Eds.): WEB 2009, LNBIP 52, pp. 96–104, 2010.

uses tags (silicon chips implanted in a product or its packaging) to transmit information to a wireless receiver. The tag contains relevant product information at an item-level (Raza, Bradshaw, and Hague 1999; Shepard 2005; Zhou 2009). Unlike bar code that provides categorical-level information, RFID technology facilitates distinguishing individual products by assigning a unique electronic product code (EPC) to each of them. Unlike bar codes, which need to be seen to be scanned, RFID tags do not require direct line-of-sight for data transmission, making it possible to simultaneously read several tags as a batch.

Motivated by RFID's unprecedented characteristics for auto identification, we propose a framework to utilize RFID item-level information for product remanufacturing based on an adaptive knowledge-based system. We consider product remanufacturing process from a heuristic perspective with the goal of (1) reducing both environmental and economical waste, (2) improving manufacturing quality to decrease the rate of defects, (3) improving the efficiency of remanufacturing process, (4) facilitating product design and (5) enhancing Customer Relationship Management (CRM).

Because of the complexity of both tasks and data in the remanufacturing process, an adaptive learning system is chosen to assist the process. Given the nature of remanufacturing, it is essential for the system to be adaptive to facilitate the need to be flexible in dealing with disparate scenarios that are endemic to this domain. A knowledge-based adaptive system learns to proactively aid in generating appropriate strategies for any remanufacturing scenario that it is bound to encounter. While its performance may not be good at first during the learning stage, it gradually builds up its knowledge-base to incorporate the different kinds of defects it is likely to encounter in remanufacturing and the best possible solutions to address these shortcomings.

As a part of sustainable economy, remanufacturing process sometimes is called as closed loop recycling system. We consider products that have manufacturing defects with some missing or defective component, end-of-life used products that have some salvageable component parts in them and manufacturing byproduct into considerations. Remanufactured items are put on the market either as new or as refurbished. Most manufacturers treat remanufactured items that came from unused defective products as new and treat those from short-life products as refurbished.

Remanufacturing provides a closed loop environment where the amount of wastage is reduced. A side effect of this process is the availability of knowledge that help improve product quality by identifying problems in the manufacturing process by careful evaluation of returned products. Clearly, these problems do not necessarily result in dead on arrival (DOA) products. Instead, returned products (i.e., products found to be defective after being used for a short time period) contain very useful information both for quality management and for effective remanufacturing process. There are situations where the primary goal in manufacturing a product is not its long quality life-span. For instance, the marketing strategy might dictate the product life span to be set at a certain (relatively short) time for compulsory replacement. The proposed framework can be easily adjusted to learn and adapt to this scenario.

The remainder of this paper is organized as follows. We begin with literature review in Section 2. We present the dynamic remanufacturing framework in Section 3. We include several numerical examples to illustrate the presented model and its effectiveness. Section 4 concludes the paper with a brief discussion on the insights garnered and their implications.

2 Literature Review

Remanufacturing, reverse logistics, and recovery operations have been studied by researchers for at least during the past decade. For example, Goggin (1998) attempted to consider industrial practices to develop a theory on product recovery. Goggin (1998) developed typologies and models for product recovery operations based on typologies of manufacturing chains. Although remanufacturing, reverse logistics, and recovery operations have similar goals that attempt to address issues and constraints that are generally associated with reducing waste and effective use of products that are not perfect, they are not the same.

Rogers and Tibben-Lembke (1998) define reverse logistics as the process of planning, implementing, and controlling the efficient, cost effective flow of raw materials, in-process inventory, finished goods and related information from the point of consumption to the point of origin for the purpose of recapturing value or proper disposal." Other researchers have considered several facets of reverse logistics. For example, Fleischmann (2001) considers network design, inventory management, and production scheduling to develop models for optimizing each of those core operations. De Brito (2004) develops a framework for reverse logistics theory.

Product disassembly, a core area under product recovery management, is defined as an ecological approach that allows reusable, non-recyclable, and hazardous subassemblies to be selectively separated from recyclable ones (Seliger et al., 2001). According to Das, et al., (2000), key objectives of disassembly include (i) the recovery of valuable and reusable parts or subassemblies, (ii) product separation to facilitate the downstream material recovery process, (iii) the removal of hazardous or toxic materials, (iv) to remanufacture the product for another useful life, and (v) to destroy the proprietary parts of sub-assemblies. Given the importance of product recovery, several researchers have studied this problem in greater detail including Desai and Mital (2003), Feldmann and Scheller (1994), Gupta and McLean (1996), Lambert (2003). The interested reader is referred to these literature and the references therein.

3 Framework and Model

In general, product remanufacturing processes utilize end of life products, components, and materials with a purpose to recover as much of the economic (and ecological) value as possible, thereby reducing the ultimate quantities of waste. While the cost of remanufacturing also plays as one of the decision role for the management, how to improve efficiency and to reduce operational cost has become an eminent problem. We will investigate in this section the potential of utilizing RFID enabled adaptive learning system in remanufacturing process design.

3.1 Traditional View

Traditionally, remanufacturing starts from a normal manufacturing process, which produces a certain number of qualified products, a small portion of defective products (in some industry, such as plasma panel manufacturing, its number can be very significant), and some byproducts, Figure 1. The defective products, of which defects could be caused by various issues, are immediately put in the remanufacturing process that would try to recover value from these products. The end of life (EOL) products can be collected through different channel, such as consumer-retailer-manufacturer, consumer-manufacturer, consumer-third-party-manufacturer (Savaskan,Bhattacharya, and Van Wassenhove 2004). Both the defective and EOL products are diagnosed by technicians to identify the faulty components for further decisions.

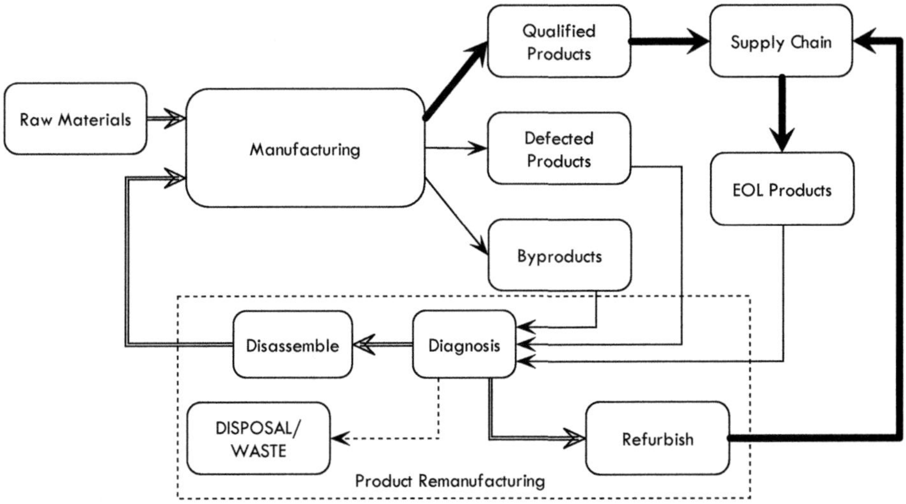

Fig. 1. Traditional product remanufacturing process

After collection, the products would go through several recovering procedures, which are usually implemented for remanufacturing that may include repairing and reusing, refurbishing, manufacturing, cannibalization and recycling (Thierry et al. 1995). The purpose of repairing and reusing is to fix used products to working order, which usually renders lower quality of the new products. Manufacturing using components from used/defective product is to bring used products up to quality standards that are as rigorous as those for new products by completely disassembling the products to the component level, accompanied by extensive inspection and replacement of broken/outdated parts. Refurbishing generally is characterized by first disassembling the product down to a preset module level, followed by inspection and replacement of broken modules. While discarding most of the components of a used/defective product, the procedure of cannibalization selects a small number of reusable parts and modules, which are usually of high value, from the used/defective products and uses these components/modules in manufacturing, repairing/reusing and refurbishing. Through separation processes, recycling involves collecting materials from used products, which are reused in the manufacturing of either the original or other products that shared the same materials.

Before Defective/EOL products can be restored for market, diagnosis and disassembly are usually performed and the operations of disassembly bring much uncertainty on planning, such as material resource planning, inventory management, shop floor control, production scheduling etc. After disassembly, parts are assessed as to their remanufacturability, within which those acceptable parts are then routed to the necessary operations. Parts not meeting minimum remanufacturing standards are disposed.

3.2 RFID Enabled Framework

Figure 2 illustrates the proposed product remanufacturing process with RFID and adaptive self-learning system, where we utilize artificial intelligence generated knowledge to assist selecting proper raw materials, configuring the normal manufacturing process and facilitating the diagnosis process. Integration of CRM and remanufacturing strategy (considering consumers' preference and perception on new, remanufactured, or refurbished products) could assist decision maker to gain insightful knowledge of the market and thus help establish the right market and manufacturing strategy.

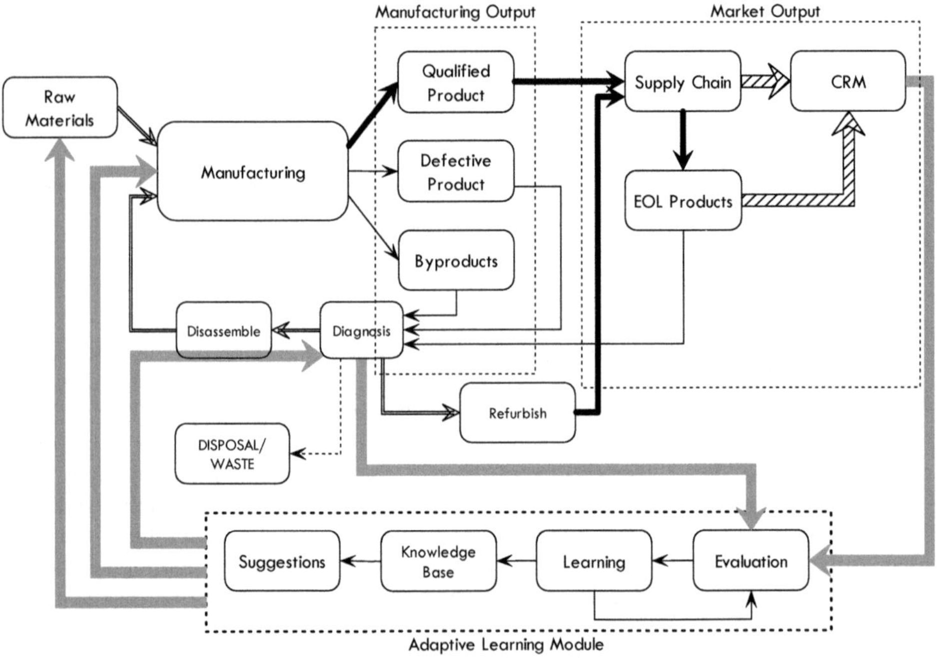

Fig. 2. Product remanufacturing process with RFID and adaptive self-learning system

Figure 3 illustrates a single manufacturing session with two sequential manufacturing processes. Raw materials are input at check point 1 in batch and are processed through P1 and P2. At check point 2, relevant characteristics of the products are measured and defective products are identified for further re-processing. Without RFID, all items are treated the same in throughout the manufacturing session and technicians would adjust the manufacturing configurations of both P1 and P2 based on information collected from check point 1 and check point 2, such that

Config(P1,P2)~F(ch1, ch2). With RFID real time item level information, we are now able to identify every single item at any time t, the associated characteristics of this item and possibly its ambient conditions. With refined continual information on individual parts throughout the session, the technician is able to fine tune the manufacturing processes for better quality, thus reducing the rate of producing defective products such that $Config(P1,P2)\sim F(ch1, ch2, ch_{RFID}(t))$.

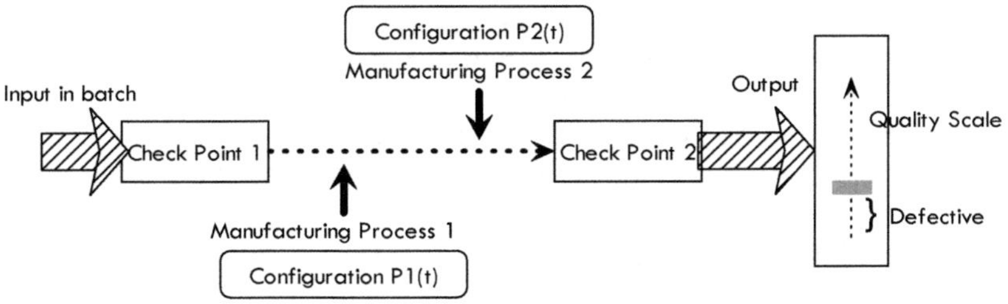

Fig. 3. Single manufacturing session with two sequential manufacturing processes

3.3 Adaptive Learning Module

The Adaptive Learning module is at the core of the proposed framework in facilitating the system to learn to adapt to dynamically changing environments. A majority of items that pass through the remanufacturing, reverse logistics and disassembly processes have disparate set of requirements depending on the number of component parts they have and the various ways in which these components can be compromised. This necessitates the system to possess the expertise to deal with the situation or at the least to gracefully (i.e., not break down in a brittle manner when faced with an entirely new situation) handle the situation based on partially similar situations it has encountered in the past.

The Adaptive Learning Module comprises four sub-components including the one for Learning, which learns necessary knowledge from products that have been remanufactured, disassembled or participated in reverse logistics earlier, Knowledge-base that contains knowledge obtained through learning, Evaluation for evaluating the resulting (e.g., remanufactured) product, and Suggestions for recommending the best possible course of action to take. These components act in consort to facilitate and accomplish the process of improving the performance of the system with time and experience as it recommends appropriate courses of action and learns of the resulting outcome.

Specifically, the Learning sub-component learns explicit and implicit patterns that are present in the domain (here, remanufacturing, disassembly, or reverse logistics) by using example scenarios that cover representative cases. The learned knowledge is then stored in the knowledge-base for later use when a similar pattern is witnessed in the system. Based on the instantaneous snap-shot of the system and any existing associated knowledge in the knowledge-base, the system suggests the best course of action. And, once this suggested course of action is implemented, the system waits to obtain more information on the outcome, which is then used to reinforce existing knowledge in the knowledge-base or learn new knowledge which can then be incrementally learned and incorporated in the knowledge-base. The Evaluation sub-component ensures and maintains the quality and completeness of the knowledge-base by enabling continual learning on the part of the Learning module by identifying existing deficiencies in the knowledge-base

The general steps that are involved in the proposed process can be summarized as follows:

1. Set evaluations interval (T)
2. Set initial values for raw material selection (R)
3. Set initial values for manufacturing parameters setting (P)
4. Repeat steps 5-11 until time T
5. Manufacturing begins. Specify local time (t). Set local-time=0.
6. If Reman(current configuration R) >> Reman(previous configuration R), go to step 8.
7. If local-time < t, go to step 6
8. Learning
9. If expected improvement(Δ(configuration)) > pre-determined threshold, go to 11
10. Else, go to step 4
11. Performance evaluation and Learning

3.4 Results and Analysis

We illustrate the benefits of implementing RFID-enabled real-time system in the context of manufacturing / remanufacturing by a numerical example. Consider a manufacturing session that consists of two manufacturing processes, as shown in Figure 3. After the raw materials are processed, there is a check point at the end of the manufacturing session that measures the characteristics of output products. However, depending on the process, we assume that there is no check point during the session. We consider the configuration of the first manufacturing configuration ($cnfg_1$) to be normalized and set to 10, which is subject to certain variance during the manufacturing process. The variance can be caused by uncertainties from external or internal sources so that at any given time point $cnfg_1$ can be 10.2, 9.9, etc., which is subject to a random distribution. While it is the same for the second manufacturing configuration, $cnfg_2$ that is set to 5, without real-time item-level tracing and tracking ability, the actual manufacturing information for the product is indeed missing. The general performance results of each individual manufacturing process as well as the quality characteristics of products at the check points, however, are available.

We consider the product quality at check point 2 as a direct result of the manufacturing configuration at the two processes, $Q(cnfg_1, cnfg_2)$. Without RFID information visibility, the quality of the output products can only be described by their aggregate statistical characteristics. Table 1 lists a set of sample numerical data for 12 products that go through the manufacturing session with two processes. Without RFID, while the only information available is the quality measurement at the check point, where the manufacturing configurations of processes 1 and 2 of each individual item are missing. With RFID real-time item-level information, we are able to obtain the following manufacturing history data for each product.

After analysis using the above data, we are able to identify certain patterns in the manufacturing session. For instance, product #3, 4, and 10's quality are below average, while historical data for those products show that both configurations 1 and 2 are below their pre-set levels which are 10 and 5 respectively. With these information and observation, we may conclude by saying that lower configuration on both manufacturing processes would result in a low quality product.

With RFID-generated information visibility and post-data-processing, we are able to obtain two possible benefits: 1. improve the manufacturing process, and 2. pinpoint possible quality issues related to individual defective products by considering its historical manufacturing data. Without RFID tracking and tracing ability, the information is based on statistical description at an aggregate level that deprives the ability to refine the manufacturing and remanufacturing process at an item level.

Table 1. Manufacturing history & quality data with two manufacturing processes

ID	$cnfg_1$	$Cnfg_2$	Quality
1	10.1	5.2	8.5/10
2	9.8	5.1	9.4/10
3	9.5	4.7	6.5/10
4	10.4	5.2	6.5/10
5	10.0	4.9	9.8/10
6	10.1	5.1	9.0/10
7	9.7	4.7	8.0/10
8	9.8	5.2	8.5/10
9	10.0	5.0	9.9/10
10	9.9	4.4	5.5/10
11	9.9	5.1	9.0/10
12	10.2	5.0	9.0/10

4 Discussion

We considered one of the problems faced by manufacturers with respect to dynamically adjusting manufacturing/remanufacturing process using a knowledge-based system framework. This process can be automated and operationalized in a seamless fashion through RFID-embedded component tags on individual parts. These RFID identified manufacturing parts also enable the quality manager to continually adjust manufacturing parameters at the item-level as is deemed necessary. We illustrated the proposed knowledge-based framework using heuristics. Preliminary results indicate that the manufacturer would benefited by such a framework and setup using RFID-generated information.

References

1. Das, S.K., Yedlarajiah, P., Narendra, R.: An approach for estimating the end-of-life product disassembly effort and cost. International Journal of Production Research 38(3), 657–673 (2000)
2. Desai, A., Mital, A.: Review of literature on disassembly algorithms and design for disassembly guidelines for product design. International Journal of Industrial Engineering: Theory Applications and Practice 10(3), 244–255 (2003)
3. de Brito, M.P.: Managing reverse logistics or reversing logistics management. PhD Dissertation, Erasmus University (2004)
4. de Brito, M.P., Parlikad, A.K.: Closed-Loop Supply Chain Management and Networked RFID - a Research Note (2005)
5. Feldmann, K., Scheller, H.: Disassembly of electronic products, pp. 81–86. IEEE, Piscataway (1994)
6. Goggin, K.: Modeling end-of-life product recovery, PhD Dissertation, National University of Ireland (1998)
7. Gupta, S.M., McLean, C.R.: Disassembly of products. Computers & Industrial Engineering 31(1-2), 225–228 (1996)
8. Lambert, A.J.D.: Disassembly sequencing: A survey. International Journal of Production Research 41(16), 3721–3759 (2003)
9. Thierry, M.C., Salomon, M., van Nunen, J.A.E.E., Van Wassenhove, L.N.: Strategic issues in product recovery management. California Management Review 37(2), 114–135 (1995)
10. Tibben-Lembke, R.S., Rogers, D.S.: Differences between forward and reverse logistics in a retail environment. Supply Chain Management 7(5) (2002)
11. Seliger, G., Keil, T., Rebafka, U., Stenzel, A.: Flexible disassembly tools, pp. 30–35. Institute of Electrical and Electronics Engineers Inc., Denver (2001)
12. Piramuthu, S.: Knowledge-based framework for automated dynamic supply chain configuration. European Journal of Operational Research 165(1), 219–230 (2006)
13. Wei, Z.: RFID and item-level information visibility. European Journal of Operational Research 198(1), 252–258 (2009)

Producer-Intermediary Relationships in the Long Tail

Robert J. Kauffman, T.S. Raghu, and Matt Sopha

W.P. Carey School of Business, Arizona State University, Tempe, AZ
{rkauffman,raghu.santanam,msopha}@asu.edu

Abstract. The role of intermediaries in long tail markets is different from those in traditional markets, due mainly to the heterogeneous nature of the buyers, the sellers and the products that comprise these markets. We propose a theory-based framework that identifies different kinds of long tail intermediaries who provide services to producers of digital goods. We also identify a set of unique descriptors for these process intermediaries that make them vital to long tail producers, and the factors that bring them together.

Keywords: Intermediation, long tail, process facilitation, middle range theory.

1 Introduction

The rise of the Internet and digital markets has also made *the long tail* of consumer demand and producer supply possible [5]. What makes the long tail unique is the behavior exhibited by the population of long tail producers. Producers in the long tail exhibit needs that are different from those of larger mainstream market producers. Long tail markets also feature *intermediaries*, who exist when there are benefits on both sides of the middleman that can be margined in excess of the cost of the intermediary's services [9][10]. Intermediated markets are needed when there are a large number of producers or when markets have many heterogeneous products and none of them have very large demand [2][3]. Given this, it is worthwhile to examine how the functions of intermediaries have been transformed to meet the needs of this idiosyncratic market space. The long tail market literature has yet to address the nature and evolution of producer-intermediary relationships, and the processes related to these interactions.

The key research questions we address are: What types of intermediaries are involved in facilitating the delivery of digital goods in the long tail? What factors drive a producer's choice of intermediary and the intermediary's decision to transact goods in the long tail? And what processes do intermediaries support that match the unique requirements of the long tail?

2 Theory and Methods

Long tail theory proposes a significant market comprised of millions of items that were previously relegated to specialty retailers [1][6]. They are dependent on mitigating

R. Sharman, T.S. Raghu, and H.R. Rao (Eds.): WEB 2009, LNBIP 52, pp. 105–108, 2010.

consumer search costs and increasing confidence about the quality of the product and the security of the seller in the eyes of the buyer.

It is difficult for any single intermediary to adequately fulfill the needs of all buyers and sellers in long tail markets [4]. As such, very different types of intermediaries have emerged in long tail markets. Given the lack of research on intermediary types in long tail markets, we develop a framework that matches producer types to intermediary types that is rooted in the processes that are of greatest value in the market. The approach that we use to develop our framework follows the tenets of *middle range theory* development [7][9].

The first component of our framework is the three basic types of producers in the long tail. They each possess their own preferred form of process support that they expect from process intermediaries in the long tail [8]. *Potential superstars* are driven by the need to have their products legally protected, achieve adequate and substantial financial returns, be sold via reputable and well-connected entities, and be readily accessible to buyers. *Independents* seek only adequate fit with their desired customer base and rapid access via distribution channels that they deem acceptable. *Indifferents* require similar functionality as independents and potential superstars. The key differentiators are the scope of their market entry and penetration, their lack of concern for financial returns beyond simple return on investment, and the intensity and awareness of the independent spirit of the customer base.

The second component of our framework is an intermediary typology that is based on the needs of producers and the demands of the market. *Direct retailers*, representing digital storefronts for long tail products, have to offer robust and effective search functions. They also require strong and safe transaction processing and delivery systems. *Distributors* serve fewer buyer needs, but are essential to producers who require access to more diverse markets than can be offered by other intermediaries. As they also assist with brand creation, they must offer significant protection for the intellectual property of digital goods producers. *Classifieds* are intermediaries that offer rapid access for consumer bases, represented by robust search methods. Finally, *scouts* are intermediaries that elevate producers from the long tail to larger, more profitable markets. Table 1 presents the relationship alignment between the producer and intermediary types.

Table 1. Producer-Intermediary Alignment in the Long Tail

PRODUCER TYPE	DIRECT RETAILERS	DISTRIBUTORS	CLASSIFIEDS	SCOUTS
Potential Superstars	X	X		X
Indifferents	X		X	
Independents			X	

Potential superstars, seeking profit, exposure, and access to larger, deeper markets would do well to align early with distributors. They also can simultaneously offer a small portion of their product selection to be sold via direct retailers, to permit consumers to sample them. Once the potential superstar producer has effectively saturated the customer segments in the long tail, it is time to seek out scout intermediaries to attempt entry into the wider commercial markets. Independents will benefit most by effectively leveraging the processes offered by classified intermediaries. Finally, indifferent producers, like the independents, will be concerned with the development of their products. They will retain a desire for financial gain and minor profit, and will leverage the networks of classified intermediaries, while offering their products via networks of direct retailer intermediaries.

The usefulness of the alignment framework becomes apparent when the long tail market of independent music is analyzed. For example, Coldplay, an independent music group formed in 1996 fits in as a "potential superstar" producer. Coldplay successfully leveraged Napster as a "direct retailer" initially and then signed with a "scout intermediary," Fierce Panda Records. Similarly, the Hybrid Ice music group, formed in 1969, can be identified as an "independent" producer. Hybrid Ice has relied mainly on bulletin board systems and weblogs to distribute its music (i.e., classifieds). We find similar types of evolution of intermediary-producer relationships over time among many other independent music bands. We believe that similar patterns of alignment can be observed in other long tail market settings such as the book publishing and independent movie markets.

3 Intended Contributions

A major implication of the long tail process intermediation framework is that producers can seek relationships with multiple types of intermediaries. Similarly, it is possible for intermediaries to provide process support for multiple types of producers.

The framework characterizes the producer-intermediary relationships and clarifies the alignment of interests for the relevant players. A key implication of our analysis is that intermediary-producer mappings are potentially fluid. While long tail markets are traditionally viewed as being composed of a large variety of different products, producer objectives may still create opportunities for segmentation of long tail markets. This insight is important for a variety of intermediary organizations in developing strategies for targeting end-customers and producers.

The production of value from intermediation is not a one-shot deal. Instead, the value that a long tail intermediary can provide to producers and consumers will be based on how its functionality changes in the face of market competition and technological changes over time. The essence of such change is being able to morph or transform the contents of the intermediation processes that are offered. We acknowledge that more work is needed to develop testable hypotheses in this area. We are currently exploring different options to extend this analysis in that direction.

References

1. Anderson, C.: The Long Tail: Why the Future of Business is Selling Less of More. Hyperion, New York (2006)
2. Bakos, J.: The Emerging Landscape for Retail E-commerce. J. Econ. Persp. 15(1), 69–80 (2001)
3. Bailey, J., Bakos, J.: An Exploratory Study of the Emerging Role of Electronic Intermediaries. Intl. J. Elec. Comm. 5(3), 7–20 (1997)
4. Biglaiser, G.: Middlemen as Experts. RAND J. Econ. 24(2), 212–223 (1993)

5. Brynjolfsson, E., Hu, Y., Smith, M.: From Niches to Riches: Anatomy of the Long Tail. Sloan Mgmt. Rev. 47(4), 67–71 (2006)
6. Elberse, A., Oberholzer-Gee, F.: Superstars and Underdogs: An Examination of the Long Tail Phenomenon in Video Sales. Working paper 07-120, Harvard Business School, Boston (2007)
7. Gregor, G.: The nature of theory in information systems. MIS Qtrly. 30(3), 611–642 (2006)
8. Kambil, A., van Heck, E.: Reengineering the Dutch Flower Auctions: A Framework for Analyzing Exchange Organizations. Info. Sys. Res. 9(1), 1–19 (1998)
9. Merton, R.K.: Social Theory Social Structure. Free Press, New York (1968)
10. Spulber, D.: Market Microstructure, Intermediaries and the Theory of the Firm. Cambridge University Press, New York (1999)

Avoiding Demand Amplification Phenomenon via Hi-tech Application: A What-If Supply Chain Analysis

Elena Ciancimino and Salvatore Cannella

Faculty of Engineering, University of Palermo
viale delle Scienze, Parco d'Orleans,
90128 Palermo, Italy
{eciancimino,cannella}@unipa.it

Abstract. The well-known deleterious effect of the amplification of variance of order rates in multi-echelon systems, commonly known as demand amplification phenomenon or bullwhip effect, still presents new challenges and continues to fascinate the operations management community. Recently this research field is focusing on the study of robustness of bullwhip avoidance techniques under uncertainty, as environmental conditions often determine variations in processes, with regards to production and delivery lead time, and variations in the parameters of the decision policies. This work aims at quantifying the efficacy of bullwhip dampening techniques and at verifying this efficacy against variations in the business context. The original value of the research consists in showing that the bullwhip dampening efficacy, provided by hi-tech applications and practices of supply chain collaborations, persists when operational parameters vary within a certain range.

Keywords: bullwhip effect; supply chain collaboration; inventory management; differential equation model, simulation.

1 Introduction

As reported by Schmenner [1], the deleterious effect of the amplification of variance of order rates in multi-echelon systems, commonly known as demand amplification phenomenon, was recognized as early as 1919 in the supply chain of Procter and Gamble. Seventy-eight years later Lee, Padmanabhan and Whang [2, 3] published two of the most popular papers based on a study of the well-known company, coining the term "bullwhip effect" to indicate the phenomenon where the variance of the demand signal increases as the demand signal flows up the supply chain. Today the problem still presents new challenges and continues to fascinate the operations research community [4].

In the last period, while the existence of bullwhip phenomenon has been widely confirmed, the discussion has shifted from strategies aimed at preventing the bullwhip effect to collaboration in the supply chain through collaborative planning, information sharing and VMI and other strategies [5] To contribute to the bullwhip avoidance literature, a robust what-if analysis focused on hi-tech applications and practices of supply chain collaboration is presented. This work aims at quantifying the efficacy of bullwhip dampening techniques and at verifying this efficacy against variations in the business context and at verifying this efficacy against variations in the business

R. Sharman, T.S. Raghu, and H.R. Rao (Eds.): WEB 2009, LNBIP 52, pp. 109–121, 2010.

context. In the real world, environmental conditions often determine variations in processes, with regards to production and delivery lead time, and variations in the parameters of the decision policies. Shared real-time point-of-sales information, sales forecasts, inventory order policies and inventory reports to support multi-tiers integration decision rules represent the key element to achieve the bullwhip dampening ability regardless of the operational parameters.

The research methodology consists of analytical modelling, continuous simulation, and design of experiment. First, systems of nonlinear ordinary difference equations are used to model supply chain [6]. Equations are solved by Vensim software that uses Euler integration as default simulation method. This tool evaluates the system state every constant time interval (Δt), then the new system state is recorded and statistics collected [7]. Finally nine experiments are presented, obtained by varying three parameters of the model with Latin square design [8]. For each scenario two process performance assessments are calculated for every echelon, the Order Rate Variance Ratio and the Inventory Variance Ratio, and a customer service metric, the Fill Rate.

The article is organized as follows. Section 2 reports a literature review on recent bullwhip effect solutions obtained by innovative supply chain operation practices. The simulation model, the adopted nomenclature and the related set of equations are explained in section 3. Section 4 presents the bullwhip metrics and the analysis of simulation data. Section 5 presents discussions and suggestions for future research.

2 Literature Review

Supply chain instability, bullwhip effect and the influence of inventory level on demand have attracted the attention of researchers and practitioners in different fields of management science. In the last bullwhip investigation phase, the researchers in the field of demand amplification phenomena have deeply investigated the development of collaboration among partners in the supply chain and innovative information technologies solutions, both with empirical studies of real cases, analytical methods and what-if simulation. Among the contributions to bullwhip field are those by Chen et al. [9], Disney and Towill [10], Dejonckheere et al. [11], Chatfield et al. [12], Gonçalves et al. [13], Villegas and Smith [14], Ouyang [15], Boute et al. [16], Jakšič and Rusjan [17] and Duc et al. [18].

Chen et al. [6] investigate the bullwhip problem in a multi-echelon supply chain with information sharing using stochastic approaches. They show the benefit of information sharing for the Order-up-to policies based on exponential smoothing forecast in an enriched scenario and propose an analytical metric to quantify the bullwhip effect.

Disney and Towill [7] present an analytic solution to the bullwhip problem for the DE-APIOBPCS (Deziel and Eilon Automatic Pipeline Inventory and Order Based Production Control System) order policy. They show that the way to minimise the bullwhip problem with this policy is increasing the average age of forecasts, and reducing the rate at which inventory and WIP correction are accounted for in the production/distribution-ordering algorithm.

Dejonckheere et al. [8] examine with control theory approach two supply chain information scenarios for Order-up-to and APIOBPCS replenishment policies. They quantify the benefit of sharing end customer demand forecasting by analytically demonstrating the relevant dampening of demand amplification along the tiers.

Chatfield et al. [9] present a k-stage serial supply chain model to determine Order-up-to levels and order quantities for each stage. Using a simulation model, they perform a set of experiments that employ factors related to lead-time variation, information quality, and information sharing to conclude that information sharing reduces total variance amplification and stage (node to node) variance amplification. Furthermore, their results show that information sharing protects a supply chain against "cascading failures", the effect that stockout at the upper echelons may have on multiple downstream nodes.

Gonçalves et al. [10] via system dynamics approach focus on the causes of oscillatory behaviour in capacity utilization at a semiconductor manufacturer of Intel Corporation and explore the role of endogenous customer demand in influencing the company's production and service level. They suggest that typical policy prescriptions of lean inventory and responsive utilization policies hold only when demand is assumed to be exogenous.

Villegas and Smith [12] show how an Automatic Planning System (APS) may be modified to better manage the trade-off between order and inventory oscillations. They state that in real supply chains APSs have introduced a new source of demand distortion, which is reflected as high variation in production order quantities as the desired inventory levels are maintained according to company policies. The problem is studied in a four echelon model that faces a seasonal predictable demand, using difference equation and mathematical optimisation models. The paper suggests ways in which the operating policies and the APS model can be modified to reduce the demand amplification phenomenon.

Ouyang [13], via frequency domain approach, presents a system control framework for analyzing the bullwhip effect in multi-echelon supply chains with information sharing. He derives robust analytical conditions to predict whether or not the bullwhip effect will arise without knowing the customer demand, and also develops exact formulae for the variance of the order stream at any level of a multi-stage chain knowing only the spectrum of the customer demand process. He shows a special case in which sharing customer demand information across the chain significantly reduces, but does not completely eliminates, the bullwhip effect.

Boute et al. [14] present a model with two-echelon supply chain: a single retailer holds a finished goods inventory to meet an i.i.d. customer demand, and a single manufacturer produces the retailer's replenishment orders on a make-to-order basis. They show that, by including the impact of the order decision on lead times, the order pattern can be smoothed to a considerable extent without increasing stock levels and avoiding bullwhip effect.

Jakšič and Rusjan [15] demonstrate through transfer function method that demand forecasting with simple exponential smoothing effectively lowers the variability of orders over demand, and thus decreases the probability of the bullwhip effect occurring.

Duc et al. [16] quantify the impact of the bullwhip effect as the phenomenon in which information on demand is distorted as moving up for a simple two-stage supply chain with one supplier and one retailer. Assuming that the retailer employs a base stock inventory policy, and that the demand forecast is performed via a mixed autoregressive-moving average model ARMA(1,1), they investigate the effects of the autoregressive coefficient, the moving average parameter, and the lead time on the bullwhip effect. They report two significant properties of the bullwhip effect: (1) the bullwhip effect does not always exist, but its existence depends on the values of autoregressive and moving average coefficients of the ARMA model; (2) the bullwhip effect does not always increase when the lead time increases.

As showed, the literature advocates that policies that stimulate information sharing and coordination are solutions to supply chain instability, stockholding, and poor customer care. Supply chain connectivity, cooperation and coordination within the production/distribution network are indispensable to avoid bullwhip effect. In the next section we present a multi-echelon model structure able to inhibit the bullwhip effect.

3 The Bullwhip Avoidance Model

The multi-tier structure is composed by four serially-linked business entities $i=\{1,2,3,4\}$, whose order policies are based on the integrated data on marketplace

Table 1. Notation

Wip_t^i	work in progress (includes incoming transit units) at echelon i at time t.
Inv_t^i	inventory of goods at echelon i at time t.
DO_t^i	units finally delivered at echelon i at time t.
Th_t^i	throughput at echelon i at time t.
d_t	market demand at time t.
$\hat{d}_t$	customer demand forecast at time t.
R_t^i	order quantity at echelon i at time t.
Bl_{t-1}^i	existing backlog of orders at echelon i at time t.
$VirtInv_t^i$	virtual inventory at echelon i at time t.
$VirtWip_t^i$	virtual work in progress at echelon i at time t.
$TVirtWip_t^i$	target virtual work in progress at echelon i at time t.
$TVirtInv_t^i$	target virtual inventory at echelon i at time t.
$\sigma_{R^i}^2$	variance of order quantity rate at echelon i
σ_d^2	variance of customer demand.
$\sigma_{Inv^i}^2$	variance of inventory at echelon i.
μ_{R^i}	mean value of order quantity at echelon i.
μ_d	mean value of market demand.
α	forecast smoothing factor.
T_p^i	physical production/distribution lead time (incoming transit time from supplier plus the production lead time).
T_c^i	cover time for the inventory control.
T_y^i	smoothing inventory parameter.
T_w^i	smoothing work in progress parameter

demand, tiers' inventory and work in progress. Echelon number four (retailer) accesses sale forecasts and point-of-sales data; its order policy is based on this information and on its inventory and work in progress reports. Echelon number one (manufacturer) gains data from the whole network: real-time sales forecast, and global item positions along the chain.

In the real business world the information structure of our model can be associated to a data-driven decision support system provided by a cyber communication platform that releases continuous feedback on the multi-echelon item flow data (Fig.1).

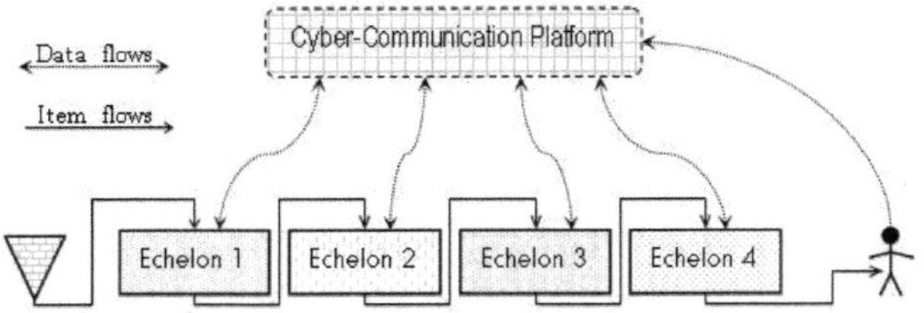

Fig. 1. Multi-tier Structure

The mathematical formalism of the model is reported in the following. The generic echelon's position is represented by index i. Echelon i=1 stands for the manufacturer and i=4 for the final customer.

The system is modelled under the following assumptions:

a) K-stage production-distribution serial system. Each echelon in the system has a single successor and a single predecessor.
b) Unconstrained production-distribution capacity. No quantity limitations in production, buffering and transport are considered.
c) Single product. Aggregate production plans are assumed.
d) Non negative condition of order quantity. Products delivered can not be returned to the supplier.
e) Backlog allowed. Orders not fulfilled in time are backlogged so that inventory remains a positive or null value.
f) Uncapacitated raw material supply condition. Orders from echelon i=1 (producer) are always entirely fulfilled in time.
g) Market demand is visible to all echelons. All echelons adopt the exponential smoothing rule to forecast demand.
h) A generic echelon receives information about order quantity from the downstream adjacent echelon, on the up-to-date market demand and on cover time factors, lead times, inventory levels, and work in progress levels W_j from all downstream echelons
i) Lead times and safety stock factors are equal for all echelons:

The mathematical formalism of the business network is as follows.

$$Wip_t^i = Wip_{t-1}^i + DO_t^{i-1} - Th_t^i \,. \tag{1}$$

$$Inv_t^i = Inv_{t-1}^i + Th_t^i - DO_t^i \,. \tag{2}$$

$$Bl_t^i = Bl_{t-1}^i + R_t^{i+1} - DO_t^i \cdot \tag{3}$$

$$DO_t^i = MIN(R_t^{i+1} + Bl_{t-1}^i ; Inv_{t-1}^i + Th_t^i) \cdot \tag{4}$$

$$Th_t^i = DO_{t-T_p}^{i-1} \cdot \tag{5}$$

$$\hat{d}_t = \alpha d_{t-1} + (1-\alpha)\hat{d}_{t-1} ; \ 0 < \alpha \leq 1 . \tag{6}$$

$$VirtWip_t^i = \sum_{j=i}^{4} Wip_t^j \cdot \tag{7}$$

$$VirtInv_t^i = \sum_{j=i}^{4} Inv_t^j \cdot \tag{8}$$

$$TVirtWip_t^i = \hat{d}_t \sum_{j=i}^{4} T_p^j \cdot \tag{9}$$

$$TVirtInv_t^i = \hat{d}_t \sum_{j=i}^{4} T_c^j \cdot \tag{10}$$

$$R_t^i = \hat{d}_t + \frac{1}{T_w^i}(TVirtWip_t^i - VirtWip_t^i) + \frac{1}{T_y^i}(TVirtInv_t^i - VirtInv_t^i) ; \ R_t^i \geq 0, \forall i . \tag{11}$$

Equations (1), (2) and (3) represent the state variables of the model. Work in progress and Inventory describe physical flows of items in downstream direction, while Backlog is representative of service level for each tier [19]. Equation (4) expresses the dynamic of delivered orders, allowing backlog as stated in assumption (e) [20]. Eq. (5) represents the production/delivery lead time delay, represented by the parameter T_p. Eq. (6) models the exponential smoothing formula to forecast demand [21], where d_{t-1} stands for the end customer demand and α is the smoothing parameter. The market demand forecast equation is shared by all the echelons.

Equation (7) is obtained by orders-in-the-pipeline at stage *i* plus the work in progress of downstream echelons. Equation (8) for an individual echelon is the sum of the Inventory at stage i and Inventory of subsequent echelons. Target Virtual Wip (9) and Target Virtual Inventory (10) are two further elements supporting data warehouse for the replenishment rule [22], generated by two operational parameters and the forecasted demand. Equation (11) models the order rule investigated in this work. It is a well-known variant of an Order-Up-To replenishment rule, namely APIOBPCS [23], largely utilized in industry and studied by academics [24]. This replenishment rule implies that at every time the ordered quantity is equal to the forecasted demand, plus a fraction of the discrepancy Target Virtual Wip and actual Virtual Wip ($1/T_w$), plus a fraction of the gap between virtual and actual Inventory ($1/T_y$). The peculiar feature of this order rule lies on taking into account pipeline feedback in the inventory policy and including smoothing parameters to gradually restore wip and inventory desired level.

4 Bullwhip Metrics and Design of Experiments

We set up nine different experiments, obtained by varying three parameters of the model:

(i) *The forecast smoothing factor* α. This value represents the weighting factor of the exponential smoothing rule. The value of α is between 0 and 1. The higher the value of α, the greater is the weight placed on the more recent demand levels. The lower the α value the greater is the weight given to demand history in forecasting future demand.

(ii) *The physical production/distribution lead time* T_p. This parameter represents the incoming transit time at echelon *i* from supplier plus the production lead time.

(iii) *The smoothing inventory parameter* (T_y=T_w). T_y is representative of the discrepancy between actual inventory and target inventory levels, which is equal to the smoothing work in progress parameter T_w, representative of the discrepancy between actual WIP and target WIP levels. This peculiar design (T_y=T_w) was investigated by Deziel and Eilon [25], and it is largely demonstrated in literature [26] that it lies well within the stable regime with extremely well behaved dynamic response.

We use a 3x3 Latin square design, in which each variable has three levels. Each factor varies between a maximum level and a minimum level, and it also assumes an average value. The chosen design is balanced and orthogonal. Design of experiments is used to check whether the estimated effects of changing the inputs of the simulation models agree with the experts' qualitative knowledge about the system [8, 27].

The 3x3 Latin square used to design the experiment and the variables' levels are shown in Table 2. Cardinal numbers from 1 to 3 stand for the levels of α, Roman

Table 2. Experimental design and factors' levels

	T_p		
α	I	II	III
1	A	B	C
2	B	C	A
3	C	A	B

α	T_p	T_w=T_y
1/6	1	2
1/3	2	3
2/3	3	4

numbers for the levels of T_p, capital letters for the levels of the order policy smoothing parameters T_w and T_y.

For each scenario we calculate two process performance assessments for every echelon: the Order Rate Variance Ratio (12) proposed by Chen et al. [9] with the Disney and Towill variation [28], the Inventory Variance Ratio (13) proposed by Disney and Towill [29], and the Fill Rate (14) as customer service metric [30]

$$ORVrRatio = \sigma_{R^i}^2 / \sigma_d^2 . \tag{12}$$

$$InvVrRatio = \sigma_{Inv^i}^2 / \sigma_d^2 . \tag{13}$$

$$FillRate_t = \left(DO_t^{retailer} / d_t \right) 100 . \tag{14}$$

The Order Rate Variance (OR Vr) Ratio metric is a smart and concise quantification of the order rate instability. The theoretical value of (12) is equal to 1 in case of absolute absence of demand amplification. When demand is amplified along the chain, the values of the Order Rate Variance Ratio show a geometrical or exponential trend in upstream direction.

The Inventory Variance (Inv Vr) Ratio is a supplementary measure of multi-echelon system instability obtained by comparing the inventory variance magnitude to the variance of the market demand. Equation (13) permits to explore the impact of the deleterious consequences caused by demand amplification and, at the same time, it offers additional value to investigate the effect of order policies on inventory levels. A geometrical or exponential increase of this metric is representative of the transmission of inventory instability along the network, caused by information distortion and unsynchronized decision planning between the trading partners.

The Fill Rate is defined as the percentage of orders delivered 'on time', that is, no later than the delivery day requested by the customer. Equation (14) is calculated as the fraction of demand immediately filled from the stock on hand.

5 Supply Chain Performance Analysis

In continuous time domain we simulate the dynamics of the information-integrated structure and the response of the system for a step increase in final demand. The model runs are for a total of 100 time units, with a time step equal to 0.25; the demand signal from marketplace changes from 100 items per time unit to 200 items/time unit in the tenth simulation period.

Table 3 reports the values for the OR Vr Ratio and for the Inv Vr Ratio in the nine scenarios, measured in each echelon.

Table 3. Bullwhip Magnitudes Outcome

	Echelon 4			Echelon 3	
	OR Vr Ratio	Inv Vr Ratio		OR Vr Ratio	Inv Vr Ratio
1°Set	2,98	20,96		6,54	17,90
2°set	1,49	19,98		2,54	18,33
3°set	1,50	19,62		2,51	17,74
4°set	1,69	29,23		3,11	27,58
5°set	1,91	30,11		3,54	25,85
6°set	7,17	38,87		15,84	26,50
7°set	2,01	37,54		4,01	38,93
8°set	10,39	49,86		22,49	38,56
9°set	6,34	46,56		13,01	33,50

	Echelon 2			Echelon 1	
	OR Vr Ratio	Inv Vr Ratio		OR Vr ratio	Inv Vr Ratio
1°Set	7,59	14,67		5,34	14,23
2°set	3,32	16,55		3,55	15,78
3°set	3,38	15,73		3,76	14,92
4°set	3,68	25,66		3,17	23,57
5°set	4,29	23,16		3,79	21,87
6°set	16,58	21,82		7,09	20,92
7°set	4,68	33,49		3,39	28,03
8°set	22,07	33,03		6,51	27,39
9°set	615,73	30,89		7,47	26,89

The output indicates that when adopting a collaborative planning supply chain practice there is no geometric increase of the bullwhip with the level in the chain [11]. The value of the two reported metrics clearly indicates that demand amplification magnitude does not get massive at higher nodes in the system. Furthermore, in our experiments the variance of inventory decreases along the chain in upstream direction, regardless of the parameter setting. Note that for the first echelon's (manufacturer) no production lead time is considered.

The analysis of two process metrics shows that the bullwhip effect is dampened when the lead time is reduced, and when the smoothing inventory and work in progress parameters increase [29]. Furthermore, Inv Vr Ratio always decreases when analysing the structure from the retailer to the first echelon. Despite the similar behaviour along the nine sets, there is a considerable difference among the scenarios grouped by lead time: as the lead time increases the value of Inv Vr Ratio becomes higher. An additional significant outcome, in contrast with the result presented by Duc. et al. [18], consists in the reduction of the lead time, which is closely related to the global performance of the supply chain as it induces demand amplification avoidance, inventory stability and better satisfaction of the actual marketplace demand.

Analysing the Fill Rate (FR) in each scenario enables to get an insight on the properties of the proposed model in terms of customer satisfaction. The FR is reflective of the network's ability to meet the market demand: when all orders are fulfilled in time, the FR at time t is equal to 100%. For every set in the first ten periods the market demand is satisfied no later than the delivery day requested by the customer. For the step increase in demand, a variation in the Fill Rate occurs.

We report in Figure 2 the values of the FR from period 5 until it gets stable to 100%. Diagrams are grouped by lead time.

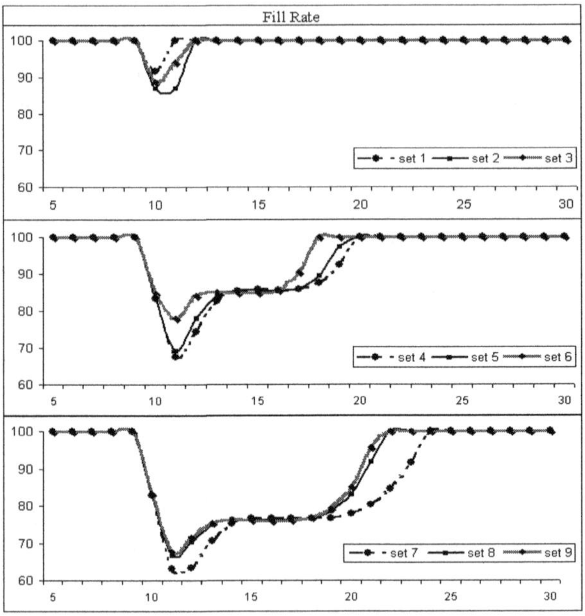

Fig. 2. Fill Rates

The values of FR confirm the observation brought forth by the OR Vr Ratio and Inv Vr Ratio metrics. It is important to underline that a global metric high performance, measuring the effectiveness of the entire production/distribution network, implies also local improvement for each node. Among the nine simulated set, only the last group (T_p=3) presents a weak customer satisfaction metric. Nonetheless, even the worst scenario outperforms a non-collaborative traditional ordering structure [19, 27]. Moreover, the FR measures confirm the importance of lead time reduction, not only in terms of demand amplification and inventory stability, but also with regards to customer satisfaction.

6 Conclusion

In 2006 Geary, Disney and Towill [32] presented the most recent historical review on the demand amplification problem, in which they identify the ten major causes of bullwhip and discuss on the expected future impact of the famous phenomenon. They suggest that a way forward to systematically remove all avoidable causes of uncertainty is to re-engineer the supply chain. This requires the effective application of business systems engineering principles involving technical, cultural, organisational, and financial aspects of the project.

This work presented an operational and technical re-engineering of serially-linked supply chain to avoid the demand amplification phenomena. We have performed a robust what-if analysis focused on hi-tech applications and practices of supply chain collaboration. The supply chain business entities adopt a replenishment rule and order fulfilling decisions supported by a data-driven decision support system provided by a cyber communication platform that makes available constant feedback data on marketplace demand, tiers' inventory and work in progress.

To perform our what-if analysis we have set up a difference equations system implemented through a Vensim tool. The simulation provides an assessment of the dynamics of the structure and the response of the information-integrated system to demand variations in terms of bullwhip effect.

Furthermore a Latin square design of experiment approach is adopted for both quantifying the benefits resulting from coordination, connectivity and cooperation through information technology-enabled business practices and demonstrating the robustness of such practices across a reasonably wide range of scenarios, characterised by different values of the forecast smoothing factor, the physical production/distribution lead time, the smoothing inventory and work-in-process parameters.

We have shown that the e-business technology infrastructure allows making real-time decisions on the basis of marketplace demand variations: shared real-time point-of-sales information, sales forecasts, inventory order policies and inventory provide a win-win business operational strategy to avoid bullwhip effect. We quantified the value of information technologies and supply chain collaboration practices to improve production/distribution network competitiveness, and furthermore we verified that competitiveness against variations in the structure setting.

The original value of this research consists in having shown that the bullwhip dampening efficacy, provided by hi-tech applications and practices of supply chain collaborations, persists when operational parameters vary within a certain range.

Finally, another relevant outcome coming from the present work is the close correlation between lead time reduction, inventory instability, customer satisfaction and bullwhip effect avoidance: the supply chain global performance improves when information or materials delay decrease.

Future research will involve testing the efficacy of hi-tech applications and practices of supply chain collaboration under several real supply chain conditions as production plant constraints and interruptions.

References

1. Schmenner, R.W.: Looking ahead by looking back: swift, even flow in the history of manufacturing. Production and Operations Management 10, 87–96 (2001)
2. Lee, H.L., Padmanabhan, V., Whang, S.: Information distortion in a supply chain: the bullwhip effect. Management Science 43, 546–558 (1997)
3. Lee, H.L., Padmanabhan, V., Whang, S.: The Bullwhip effect in supply chains. Sloan Management Review 38, 93–102 (1997)

4. Cannella, S., Ciancimino, E.: On the Bullwhip Avoidance Phase: Supply Chain Collaboration and Order Smoothing. International Journal of Production Research 44(22), 6739–6776 (2010)
5. Holweg, M., Disney, S.M.: The Evolving Frontiers of the Bullwhip Problem. In: Proceedings of the Conference EurOMA: Operations and Global Competitiveness, Budapest, Hungary, June 19-22, pp. 777–716 (2005)
6. Riddalls, C.E., Bennett, S., Tipi, N.S.: Modelling the dynamics of supply chains. International Journal of Systems Science 31, 969–976 (2000)
7. Sterman, J.: Business Dynamics: Systems Thinking and Modelling for a Complex World. McGraw-Hill, New York (2000)
8. Cannella, S., Ciancimino, E.: Supply Chain Modelling and Analysis: an Application of Latin Square to a Repeated Coupling of Non Linear Differential Equations. International Journal of Logistics Systems and Management (in press)
9. Chen, F., Drezner, Z., Ryan, J.K., Simchi-Levi, D.: Quantifying the bullwhip effect in a simple Supply Chain: the impact of forecasting, lead-times and information. Management Science 46, 436–443 (2000)
10. Disney, S.M., Towill, D.R.: A discrete transfer function model to determine the dynamic stability of a vendor managed inventory supply chain. International Journal of Production Research 40, 179–204 (2002)
11. Dejonckheere, J., Disney, S.M., Lambrecht, M.R., Towill, D.R.: The impact of information enrichment on the bullwhip effect in Supply Chains: A control engineering perspective. European Journal of Operational Research 153, 727–750 (2004)
12. Chatfield, D.C., Kim, J.G., Harrison, T.P., Hayya, J.C.: The bullwhip effect - Impact of stochastic lead time, information quality, and information sharing: A simulation study. Production and Operations Management 13, 340–353 (2004)
13. Gonçalves, P., Hines, J., Sterman, J.: The impact of endogenous demand on push-pull production system. System Dynamics Review 21, 187–216 (2005)
14. Villegas, F.A., Smith, N.R.: Supply chain dynamics: Analysis of inventory vs. order oscillations trade-off. International Journal of Production Research 44, 1037–1054 (2006)
15. Ouyang, Y.: The effect of information sharing on supply chain stability and the bullwhip effect. European Journal of Operational Research 182, 1107–1121 (2007)
16. Boute, R.N., Disney, S.M., Lambrecht, M.R., Van Houdt, B.: An integrated production and inventory model to dampen upstream demand variability in the supply chain. European Journal of Operational Research 178, 121–142 (2007)
17. Jakšič, M., Rusjan, B.: The effect of replenishment policies on the bullwhip effect: a transfer function approach. European Journal of Operational Research 184, 946–961 (2008)
18. Duc, T.T.H., Luong, H.T., Kim, Y.-D.: A measure of bullwhip effect in supply chains with a mixed autoregressive-moving average demand process. European Journal of Operational Research 187, 243–256 (2008)
19. Ciancimino, E., Cannella, S.: Modelling the bullwhip effect dampening practices in a limited capacity production network. In: Yang, J., et al. (eds.) UNISCON 2009. LNBIP, vol. 20, pp. 475–486. Springer, Heidelberg (2009)
20. Cannella, S., Ciancimino, E.: Up-to-date Supply Chain Management: the Coordinated (S,R). In: Dangelmaier, W., et al. (eds.) IHNS 2010. LNBIP, vol. 46, pp. 175–185. Springer, Heidelberg (2010)
21. Makridakis, S., Wheelwright, S.C., McGee, V.E.: Forecasting. Methods and applications. John Wiley & Sons, West Sussex (1998)
22. Cannella, S., Ciancimino, E., Márquez, A.C.: Capacity constrained supply chains: A simulation study. International Journal of Simulation and Process Modelling 4, 139–147 (2008)

23. John, S., Naim, M.M., Towill, D.R.: Dynamic analysis of a WIP compensated decision support system. International Journal of Management Systems Design 1, 283–297 (1994)
24. Wikner, J., Naim, M.M., Rudberg, M.: Exploiting the order book for mass customized manufacturing control system with capacity limitations. IEEE Transactions on Engineering Management 54, 145–155 (2007)
25. Deziel, D.P., Eilon, S.: A linear production: inventory control rule. The Production Engineer 43, 93–104 (1967)
26. Disney, S.M., Towill, D.R.: A methodology for benchmarking replenishment-induced bullwhip'. Supply Chain Management: An International Journal 11, 160–168 (2006)
27. Kleijnen, J.P.C.: An overview of the design and analysis of simulation experiments for sensitivity analysis. European Journal of Operations Research 164, 287–300 (2005)
28. Disney, S.M., Towill, D.R.: effect of vendor managed inventory (VMI) dynamics on the Bullwhip Effect in supply chains. International Journal of Production Economics 85, 199–215 (2003)
29. Disney, S.M., Towill, D.R.: On the bullwhip and inventory variance produced by an ordering policy. Omega, the International Journal of Management Science 31, 157–167 (2003)
30. Kleijnen, J.P.C., Smits, M.T.: Performance metrics in supply chain management. The Journal of Operational Research Society 54, 507–514 (2003)
31. Ovalle, O.R., Marquez, A.C.: The effectiveness of using e-collaboration tools in the supply chain: An assessment study with system dynamics. Journal of Purchasing and Supply Management 9, 151–163 (2003)
32. Geary, S., Disney, S.M., Towill, D.R.: On bullwhip in supply chains - historical review, present practice and expected future impact. International Journal of Production Economics 101(1), 2–18 (2006)

The Role of SOA for BPO Intention – Proposing a Research Model

Daniel Beimborn, Nils Joachim, and Frank Schlosser

University of Bamberg, Department for Information Systems and Services,
Feldkirchenstr. 21, 96045 Bamberg, Germany
{daniel.beimborn,nils.joachim,frank.schlosser}@uni-bamberg.de

Abstract. How does the availability of an Service-Oriented Architecture (SOA) within a firm affect the potential of and intention for outsourcing business activities? Since one of the promises of SOA is to modularize the IT representation of business processes, it should facilitate business process outsourcing (BPO) in terms of buying the provision of single business functionalities. In this paper, we develop a conceptual research model that theorizes the relationship between SOA and BPO intention.

Keywords: Service-oriented architecture (SOA), business process outsourcing (BPO), business flexibility, modularity, standards, research model development.

1 Introduction

With the spread of the Internet and the opportunities information technology gives to all firms, most of them are engaged in e-Business nowadays. However, for many companies, e-Business does not belong to the core competencies as it merely constitutes an additional channel for doing business with trading partners and customers. Consequently, business process outsourcing (BPO) provides an attractive course of action in order to help firms exploit the potential benefits of e-Business while, at the same time, not letting get the core competencies out-of-focus. But, in the scientific literature, BPO has not been investigated intensively in the past [1]. Considering the nature of e-Business starting with its parts of highly repetitive and standardizable activities (e.g., Electronic Bill Presentment and Payment (EBPP), product inquiries, acknowledgments of receipt), there are several aspects that open the field for outsourcing such activities to an external service provider. One step further, e-Business is about "running the entire business through Internet technologies" [2], reasoning the need for cooperation with other firms to ensure high-quality business processes, giving Internet and Web technologies a central role in gluing services [2]. Looking at the results of studies that investigated various facets of BPO, it has been shown that besides a couple of benefits (e.g., cost advantages and quality improvement) being associated with BPO, a noteworthy number of risks (e.g., performance losses or problems, strategic lock-ins) exist. Both benefits and risks do influence the intention to outsource business processes. In this paper, we will propose a research model to highlight the role of information technology and its effects on BPO intention by affecting BPO benefits and risks as perceived by the firm, and BPO

R. Sharman, T.S. Raghu, and H.R. Rao (Eds.): WEB 2009, LNBIP 52, pp. 122–136, 2010.

flexibility. This is an area largely neglected in prior research. In particular, we expect the actual degree of Service-Oriented Architecture (SOA) adoption within a firm, SOA's characteristics, and distinct environmental factors related to SOA to have a significant impact on a firm's BPO intention, and thus, its willingness to leverage a larger amount of the potential made possible through BPO. Finally, a higher use of BPO and exploitation of its possibilities can then serve as a means to doing better in e-Business activities, especially for those companies which have their core business in non-IT and see e-Business processes as secondary processes within their value chain.

The remainder of this paper is structured as follows: the next section introduces the research domains of BPO and SOA. Subsequently, the third and main section presents our research model which relates the degree of SOA adoption and the related characteristics to the BPO potentials and thus to a firm's intention to outsource business activities.

2 Basics

2.1 Business Process Outsourcing (BPO)

BPO represents the delegation of a particular business activity or an overall business process, including the related supporting services [3], to an external provider, and may also cover the IT that facilitates the business processes, but – in contrast to IT outsourcing or software outsourcing – it is not about serving the IT functions or running the software applications rather than about delivering a business process result. Often, BPO is more closely defined as the outsourcing of IT-intensive processes since IT enables the inter-organizational integration of business processes and thus ensures straight-through processing across firm boundaries [4, 5]. The provider takes over the complete business task and is free in how to implement and to execute it while the outsourcing firm only receives the process outcome [6]. While BPO of many information-intensive processes (e.g., HR administration, procurement, payments or securities processing in banks, accounts payable and receivable in non-banks etc.) shows potentially high benefits from both a cost and a strategic perspective, many areas still show rather low rates of adoption, compared to IT outsourcing (cf. e.g., TPI outsourcing index at www.tpi.net).

Most research on BPO draws on the IT outsourcing research strand. Usually, research works follow the established (IT) outsourcing models and empirically identify determinants and inhibitors of BPO adoption [3, 7], determine the outcomes of BPO [8], or investigate the role of BPO success factors [9], such as effective control and governance structures [10, 11], effective sourcing mechanisms [12], and client firm-internal BPO readiness [13].

Only a few articles have focused on the role of IT for successful BPO. This is particularly interesting as Davenport [14] emphasizes that standard interfaces between information systems, which support the business processes, allow easier outsourcing of business activities. In addition, Abramovsky and Griffith [15] conclude – based on their empirical study – that organizations, which use more IT, outsource more services. Therefore, we investigate the influence of SOA on BPO intention.

2.2 Service-Oriented Architectures (SOA) – Background and Design Principles

Both practitioners and researchers offer different interpretations regarding Service-Oriented Architectures (SOA), which vary from a purely technical focus to a holistic focus covering IT and business. According to Krafzig et al. [16] "a Service-Oriented Architecture (SOA) is a software architecture that is based on the key concepts of an application frontend, service, service repository, and service bus". In contrast to this IT driven perspective, Bieberstein et al. [17] define SOA with respect to both IT and business as “framework for integrating business processes and supporting IT infrastructure as secure, standardized components - services - that can be reused and combined to address changing business priorities”. Incorporating business processes and workflows into the service-oriented IT perspective results in a so-called Service-Oriented Enterprise (SOE) [18].

On the IT layer, service-orientation is associated with common design principles, i.e., reusable logic is divided into services, services share a formal contract, are loosely coupled, composable, autonomous, stateless, discoverable and abstract from underlying logic [17, 19, 20]. Using such modular services, which are based on standardized interfaces and are independent from programming platforms, offer an organization the opportunity to flexibly orchestrate and re-use services in different business processes or even to offer services to third parties and thus acting as a service provider [21]. Thus, a service-oriented IT provides the foundation for the long-demanded flexibilization of firm borders where dynamic configuration of business processes from business activities [22], regardless of being located outside or inside an organization, takes place [16].

While most of the literature explores the technical aspects of SOA, in recent years researchers increasingly investigate the organizational impact of SOA, e.g. conceptualizing models explaining the adoption of SOA [23], showing potential business benefits of SOA from case studies [e.g. 24, 25] or empirically evaluating specific benefits of SOA, such as organizational integration [22] or information sharing in supply chains [26]. However, to the best of our knowledge no one has developed a research model, which investigates the impact of SOA on the intention to outsource business activities, before.

3 Model Development

Our paper tackles the question whether and how the availability of an SOA in a firm affects (e.g., enables, facilitates, or inhibits) this firm’s BPO activities. Therefore, we develop a research model that links SOA to the drivers of the intention to outsource business processes (i.e., “BPO intention”).

3.1 BPO Intention and Determinants

The intention to outsource business activities (“BPO intention”) represents the final dependent variable to be explained by our model. Drawing on the theory of reasoned action [27], Gewald et al. [3, 7] define BPO intention as the responsible managers’ expression of support for outsourcing of particular business processes. As the theory of reasoned action postulates, intention is driven by a positive attitude towards the action (BPO, for instance), and itself will (frequently, but not always) lead to the actual action. Since selective outsourcing of single services, based on an SOA, is still not very common in the industry, BPO intention can be used as an adequate proxy for BPO activities. Moreover, the link from intention to action is affected by a multitude of further contingencies (such as management characteristics, budget constraints, firm characteristics etc.) [27] which might dilute the theoretical, causal role of SOA as an BPO enabler in an empirical examination.

BPO intention is driven by some basic determinants which have frequently been examined in the outsourcing literature. *Anticipated benefits* will increase BPO intention while *anticipated risks* and problems will decrease it. Even though there are other explanations for and against outsourcing (such as institutional pressures [28], imitation/bandwagon effects [29, 30], or fundamental in-house governance problems and weak management [31]), our research will be restricted to benefits and risks, and furthermore focus on those facets that are theoretically related with SOA, i.e., that themselves are in a certain way affected by SOA.

The identification of benefits from outsourcing represents the oldest research question in the outsourcing research strand. Loh and Venkatraman [32] argued in one of the very first models of outsourcing determinants that the bad cost structure and bad performance of a firm will drive its outsourcing activities. Over the subsequent two decades, cost advantages, in particular, have consistently shown to be the predominant outsourcing decision determinant [33-35]. Cost advantages can result from economies of scale (i.e., bundled processing volumes lead to lower marginal processing costs) [36, 37], economies of skill (higher competencies and learning effects allow the vendor to have superior cost structures) [28, 38], or economies of scope (vendors can utilize their resources to produce different outputs for different clients). A side effect stems from cost variabilization, where the vendor charges the client based on a pay-per-use rule and thus transforms the client's fixed costs into variable costs [39]. On the downside, outsourcing causes transaction costs (for negotiation, contracting, transition, provider monitoring, and relationship management [40] which can be substantial and do often lead to situations where outsourcing is not beneficial from a financial perspective [33].

Beside the cost effect, organizations outsource processes in order to receive a higher level of quality [3]. Vendors have specialized on particular business activities and cannot only deliver them at lower costs but often at higher quality, as well. For example, higher volumes justify a higher degree of automation which might reduce error rates. Consequently, outsourcing grants access to specialized superior resources (technology, process skills, management knowledge, etc.) [41-44].

From a strategic perspective, a firm can more effectively focus on its core competencies by outsourcing all non-core activities [45]. Thus, the management can focus on sustaining and improving the firm´s core competencies [46-48], following the very fundamental economic principle of specialization and division of work. Consequently, the firm is more flexible from a strategic perspective in order to react to changing market demands [46, 49, 50].

Table 1. Perceived Benefits of BPO

Dimension	Definition	Description
Cost advantages	Reduction in overall costs = production costs + transaction costs (including costs for migration, negotiation etc.)	Cost advantages result from economies of scale, skill, and scope. The vendor is proposed to produce the same service at a lower price. Nevertheless, cost advantages have to incorporate additional costs that are caused by outsourcing (for negotiation, contracting, migration, provider monitoring, and relationship management).
Quality improvement	Improving quality of service by tasking a provider that has superior capabilities	Outsourcing tasks to a vendor, which is specialized on performing these particular tasks, will lead to quality improvements for the outsourcer, which does not have such superior capabilities necessary for performing these tasks. Moreover, outsourcing can trigger the redesign of existing processes and thus further improve the quality.
Focus on core competencies and strategic flexibility	Focus own management on the firm's core competencies in order to gain productivity and to sustain the firm's competitiveness	If the firm's management gets unburdened by outsourcing tasks that are not within the firm's set of core competencies, the firm gets more agile in the market and the management can focus on maintaining and improving existing core competencies but also on developing new ones. The development of sustainable core competencies is essential for a firm's survival and competitive advantage in the market; therefore outsourcing from a strategic perspective helps the management to stay focused and to support its long-term survivability.

According to Gewald and Dibbern [3], we propose:

Proposition 1: The higher the perceived benefits in terms of cost advantages, quality improvements, core competence focus, and strategic flexibility improvements, the higher is the intention to outsource business processes.

Besides the benefits described above, BPO is also related with various risks. Many scholars have identified and classified particular dimensions of risks and risk drivers in regard to outsourcing [31, 51-53]. Based on the perceived risk framework of Cunningham [54], Gewald et al. [3] tested a research model which links particular types of perceived risks being relevant in BPO arrangements to the intention to outsource business processes. They defined perceived BPO risks as the potential loss in the pursuit of a desired outcome of outsourcing business processes and they distinguished between performance, financial, strategic, and psychosocial risks (p. 250). Their empirical analysis found the first three dimensions to be highly relevant in determining the BPO intention. We draw on their findings and propose financial risk, performance risk, and strategic risk, in particular, to (negatively) influence the intention to outsource business processes. The dimensions are described in detail in Table 2.

Table 2. Perceived Risks in BPO, based on Gewald and Dibbern as well as Gewald et al. [3, 7]

Dimension	Definition	Description
Financial risk	The risk that the actual costs may exceed the planned/budgeted costs of the outsourcing engagement.	Costs may exceed the budget due to various issues [31]. Contracting and transition of services can be more expensive than anticipated, incomplete contracts might require renegotiations during the ongoing relationship, or internal management of monitoring the vendor and maintaining the relationship lead to more effort than expected.
Performance risk	The risk that the service provided by the outsourcing vendor will not be delivered as expected by the client.	Performance risk can be caused by overdrawn expectations on the client side, incomplete contracts that insufficiently document the duties and service levels the vendor has to fulfill, or simply by lacking capabilities and resources on the client side. Adverse selection of incompetent vendors and moral hazard in the ongoing relationship are typical reasons for performance risk.
Strategic risk	The risk that the client firm will lose its ability to react flexibly and unconstrained to changing market conditions.	Strategic risk often is rooted in the client's loss of competencies because everything was outsourced [31, 48]. Another important and related problem is the lock-in to a particular vendor's services, i.e., limited or no possibilities to backsource the service or to change the providers. These can be caused by prohibitively high switching costs, caused, e.g., by the technological infrastructure) or by a too low number of valid alternatives (no superior provider in the market).

Proposition 2: The lower the perceived risks in terms of financial risk, performance risk, and strategic risk, the higher the intention to outsource business processes.

An important issue when deciding upon outsourcing is the flexibility of the outsourcing engagement. If outsourcing is complex and difficult, there might be several technical, organizational, and contractual inhibitors which do not allow for subsequent adaptations of the engagement, e.g., to changing processing volumes or new requirements. Tan and Sia [55] define sourcing flexibility as the flexibility to change, extend, or reduce the BPO arrangement and to change service providers. It may not be confused with strategic business flexibility, which represents a desired outcome (cf. above). Tan and Sia provide a framework to conceptualize sourcing flexibility, consisting of four dimensions: *robustness* and *modifiability* of the outsourcing relationship, extensibility about *new capabilities*, as well as *ease of exit*. Those are described in the following table.

Table 3. Sourcing flexibility, based on Tan and Sia [55]

Dimension	Definition	Description
Robustness	Variability of service capacity	The ability of an outsourcing relationship to allow operational changes exceeding projected capacity on existing service delivery, e.g., service volume fluctuation, variations in standard user requests, urgent or special case processing, and exception handling
Modifiability	Alteration of service attributes	The ability of an outsourcing relationship to allow alternation of attributes of its existing services in addressing changing business requirements, e.g., new configuration setup, alternation of processing workflow or business rules, new reporting requirements, and reference data updates.
New capability	Addition of innovative capability	The ability of an outsourcing relationship to allow the addition of entirely new services to address radical changes or shifts in business paradigms, e.g., new government regulations, technological revamps, functional breakthroughs, and process inovations.
Ease of exit	Switch to another vendor or insourcing	The ability of an outsourcing relationship to allow transfer of services to other vendors, or to be brought in-house, e.g., premature termination, vendor instability, or pricing disagreement or dispute.

The more flexible an outsourcing arrangement is in terms of these four dimensions, the lower might be the outsourcing risks and the more likely the benefits can be realized[1].

Proposition 3: The higher the sourcing flexibility in terms of robustness, modifiability, new capability, and ease of exit, the higher the intention to outsource business processes. This impact is mediated by outsourcing benefits and outsourcing risks.

3.2 How SOA Affects BPO Determinants

This paper focuses on how SOA influences BPO. Consequently, this section will draw on the relationship between SOA and the BPO determinants, identified as BPO benefits, BPO risks, and sourcing flexibility in the previous section.

We propose that an SOA can facilitate the achievement of economies of scale, scope, and skill. By implementing an SOA, a business process is divided into single business activities which are implemented by services. Due to their modularity, these services can be executed quite independently – which supports the economic principle of labor division which in turn represents the base for achieving cost advantages from production economies. Granular division of work creates potentials for higher processing volumes by merging tasks from different business processes (and multiple client firms) [59], leading to economies of scale. Further, services possess standardized

[1] Unfortunately, there is not much literature evidence about the relationship between sourcing flexibility and (anticipated) sourcing success or its antecedents [55]. Nevertheless, we draw on the common view that flexibility basically is a good thing [56-58], although being aware that there might be counter-arguments as well.

interfaces and thus can be recombined differently in different contexts [21, 60]. Thus, economies of scope can be achieved, as well.

Reduction of software and system redundancy by an SOA reduces maintenance costs [24]. These cost savings may be even stronger if delegating the service operations to a service provider. Similarly, re-use will reduce development costs and re-use is more likely if capabilities of various vendors are considered [60]. Thus, the necessity to (re-)develop a service might decrease both for the client and for the vendor.

Economies of skill and quality improvements will be achieved more easily because modularity allows for modular sourcing. Thus, single business activities can be outsourced to those firms that are core competent in providing them [61]. Similarly, technological independence, modularity, and autonomy of the services allow the provider to offer his specialized resources with lower efforts [59].

From a transaction cost perspective, SOA allows for an easier transition of services and change of vendors since services (if they exhibit loose coupling and standardized interfaces) can be more easily extracted from and integrated into IT systems [16, 62]. Thus, the transition costs, which are a major part of the transaction costs, are lower. Moreover, SOA enables easier and more detailed activity-based performance monitoring [63, 64]. This allows the client to get easier direct and real-time access to the performance data generated by the service provider, and thus, reduces monitoring costs.

From a strategic perspective, vom Brocke and Lindner [61] argue that SOA facilitates a firm's strategy to refocus on core competencies, without outsourcing whole business processes but only selected tasks. Thus, the firm can more dedicatedly define its core competencies on a level of single activities. A side effect would be that those core activities identified can also be offered to other firms (i.e., the outsourcing firm itself acts as a service provider for core activities while itself outsourcing the remainder) [22].

Proposition 4: If a firm has an SOA in place, it will perceive higher BPO benefits regarding those business processes running on the SOA.

SOA leads to a modularization of business processes and a subsequent standardization of activities since the objective is to re-use them in different processes. Therefore, each service in an SOA consists – despite other artifacts – of a service contract, which "provides an informal specification of the purpose, functionality, constraints, and usage of the service" [16]. Thus, service contracts help to define clear and concise semantics on the functionality and performance of the services. Moreover, business process standards increase performance [14, 65], allow for easier outsourcing and transparency and thus reduce the risk of misunderstandings about the service to be delivered between the parties (reducing performance risk) [14]. Further, the joint use of process standards and technical standards regarding the communication protocols and service descriptions reduces the threat of a lock-in in a particular vendor's service portfolio (reducing strategic risk). Service modularity and using standardized technologies also makes migration costs more controllable because the functionalities can be easier unhinged from the outsourcer's infrastructure and integrated into the vendor's infrastructure [66] (reducing financial risk). Moreover, modular and standardized services lead to a higher number of comparable service offerings from different potential partners [63], which also reduces the strategic risk [66]. An SOA offers the opportunity to multi-source, i.e., outsource different functionalities to different service providers. Despite the possibility to balance the three dimensions of BPO risks by multi-sourcing, this can nevertheless also have *negative* consequences by increasing the performance risk since the orchestration involves multiple parties with shared responsibilities. Thus, the potentials for technical coordination problems and also for moral hazard may increase.

Proposition 5: If a firm has an SOA in place, it will perceive lower BPO risks regarding those business processes running on the SOA.

SOA directly increases the flexibility and adaptability of an organization's IT infrastructure [62]. Correspondingly, Schulte et al. [67] and Heutschi [68] show empirically that SOA enables firms to more flexibly change business processes.

In the following, we argue that SOA directly contributes to each of the four sourcing flexibility dimensions specified by Tan and Sia (cf. Table 3). SOA allows for splitting business processes into modular activities which are connected by interfaces and interact via standardized communication and messaging protocols [60, 69]. This feature directly transforms to a higher degree of *modifiability*, in contrast to traditional software applications which cover business functions without service-oriented interfaces or whole business processes [69]. Loose coupling and an adequate, i.e., business activity-oriented, level of service granularity allow for easily adapting business processes since changes often only need to be implemented very locally in single services without affecting the overall implementation of the business process [16].

The same argumentation holds for the sourcing flexibility dimension of *new capability*. Adding new capabilities requires the integration of new services and interfaces but, if the SOA is well designed, does not cause changes in the overall system [66]. Moreover, the reusability of functionalities allows for quicker creation of new capabilities by orchestrating existing services with those that actually need to be newly developed [70]. Obviously, it is again important that the SOA is well designed and that standard protocols and service descriptions are used.

A well designed SOA consists of loosely coupled services, which can be altered more easily than point-to-point connections [69]. In addition, web services, as one important potential implementation platform for realizing an SOA, are platform independent and rely on standardized interfaces. Therefore in a BPO context, a service requestor can switch more easily from one service provider to another; thus, SOA facilitates the exchange of vendors (*ease of exit*) [16].

Regarding *robustness*, SOA exhibits properties particularly relevant to meet this requirement. First, loose coupling leads to a robust reaction to errors and failure of other services. Services are relatively independent within their runtime environment. If a service fails, the registry can provide a substitute and the ESB can dynamically bind the new service into the process [71]. Second, the ESB itself increases robustness: on the one hand, services can be multiply registered and the ESB can provide load balancing based on these redundancies. Second, the use of multiple ESBs, controlled by a master-ESB, is possible and increases the robustness in terms of performance, reliability, and avoidance of overload [71].

Proposition 6: If a firm has an SOA in place, sourcing flexibility in terms of robustness, modifiability, new capability, and ease of exit will be higher.

3.3 SOA Characteristics as Moderators

The impact of SOA on the BPO determinants (perceived benefits, perceived risks, and sourcing flexibility) is moderated by particular SOA characteristics, namely SOA design principles and use of SOA standards, implemented by the outsourcing firm. The argumentation already emphasized that an SOA has to be successfully designed in order to contribute to the perceived BPO benefits, sourcing flexibility and to the reduction of perceived risks. Therefore, a firm can leverage SOA's impact on these BPO determinants by following certain design principles and using mature standards. In the following, we discuss those attributes which are particularly relevant in the BPO context.

SOA design principles: SOA implementation reference guidelines request an SOA to consist of modular (i.e., loose coupling, abstraction from underlying logic and sharing of formal contracts), stateless, and autonomous services [17, 19, 20]. Further, SOA architects have to choose an adequate level of service granularity that matches with the business activities and optimizes the trade-off between inter-service communication and intra-service standardizability. Consequently, following the SOA design principles will allow for an easier replacement of services from the own infrastructure by services offered by the vendor. Thus, migration costs will be reduced (increased perceived benefits) and perceived performance risks will be lower.

Use of SOA standards: Basically, SOA is purely an architectural paradigm which does not specify the use of any technology or standard. Nevertheless, there have emerged several technological paradigms being typically used to implement an SOA at the technical level, headmost the XML Web Services family of standards (SOAP, WSDL etc.). SOA can only lead to advantages in BPO if both the vendor and the client follow (the same) certain technical standards [66].

Proposition M1: The impact of a firm's SOA on the perceived BPO benefits is moderated by its particular characteristics (in terms of SOA design principles and appropriate granularity) and the use of standards.

Proposition M2: The impact of a firm's SOA on the perceived BPO risks is moderated by its particular characteristics (in terms of SOA design principles and appropriate granularity) and the use of standards.

Proposition M3: The impact of a firm's SOA on the sourcing flexibility is moderated by its particular characteristics (in terms of SOA design principles and appropriate granularity) and the use of standards.

3.4 Environment as Determinant of SOA-Based BPO Determinants

Generally, the availability of potential vendors ("supplier presence") increases the perceived benefits and reduces the perceived risks of BPO. Ang and Straub [33] argue that competition among multiple vendors leads to decreasing opportunistic behavior and thus to a reduction in transaction costs. Moreover, SOA lowers the barriers-to-entry since it will be easier to offer a product/service to a broad customer base if well established open standards, e.g., Web Services, are in place. Therefore, multiple vendors available in the market decrease the strategic risk of lock-in. Consequently, in SOA-based BPO we can argue that the more vendors offer similar services, the higher the perceived benefits and the lower the perceived risks are [62]. Obviously, the argumentations from above will only hold if the vendor offers his BPO services based on the SOA paradigm and uses compatible technologies and standards. Krafzig et al. [16] comment: "A major obstacle that can jeopardize the positive effect of constantly choosing the cheapest supplier is the inability of IT to support these changes within reasonable time and costs. An SOA solves a couple of issues that are related to a supplier change. Most importantly, an SOA provides an easy-to-use integration infrastructure that reduces the efforts of both business partners."

Proposition 7: The availability of SOA-based BPO offerings affects the perceived BPO benefits and risks.

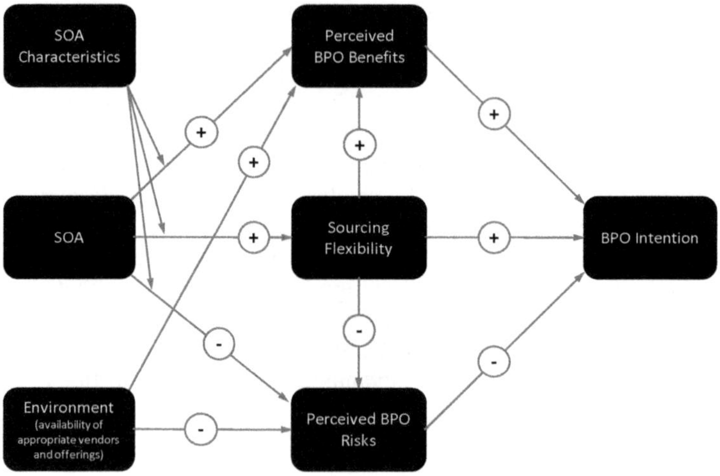

Fig. 1. Research model

4 Conclusion and Outlook

In this paper, we have presented a research model in order to explain how the existence of an SOA within a firm influences the perceived benefits and risks of business process outsourcing, and thus, the intention to outsource distinct business processes. Our model distinguishes between the degree of SOA being in place in a firm, environmental factors, and SOA characteristics, which we propose to moderate the effect of SOA on perceived BPO benefits and risks, and sourcing flexibility. In general, we expect firms that already have implemented an SOA or are within the SOA implementation process to show a significantly higher BPO intention compared to firms that have not adopted SOA.

By our research, we aim at extending previous investigations on the drivers and inhibitors of BPO intention by revealing the role of IT, in particular SOA, giving insights into the effects that SOA may have in a BPO context. Thus, by linking two different strands of research together, being (1) the question for the business impact of SOA and (2) the quest for IT-related BPO success factors, we aim at contributing to both of them and uncovering new findings from the proposed interdependencies.

References

1. Rouse, A.C., Corbitt, B.: IT-supported Business Process Outsourcing (BPO): the good, the bad, and the ugly. In: Proceedings of the 8th Pacific-Asia Conference on Information Systems (PACIS), Shanghai (2004)
2. Umar, A.: IT Infrastructure to Enable Next Generation Enterprises. Information Systems Frontiers 7(3), 217–256 (2005)
3. Gewald, H., Dibbern, J.: Risks and Benefits of Business Process Outsourcing: A Study of Transaction Services in the German Banking Industry. Information & Management 46(4), 249–257 (2009)
4. Pfannenstein, L.L., Ray, J.T.: Offshore outsourcing: current and future effects on American IT industry. Information Systems Management 21(4), 72–80 (2004)
5. Dayasindhu, N.: Information technology enabled process outsourcing and reengineering: case study of a mortgage bank. In: 10th Americas Conference on Information Systems (AMCIS), New York, NY (2004)
6. Braun, M.: Vom IT- zum Business Process Outsourcing. Bankmagazin. 53(2), 22 (2004)
7. Gewald, H., Wüllenweber, K., Weitzel, T.: The Influence of Perceived Risks on Banking Managers' Intention to Outsource Business Processes - A Study of the German Banking and Finance Industry. Journal of Electronic Commerce Research 7(2), 78–96 (2006)
8. Willcocks, L.P., Hindle, J., Feeny, D.F., Lacity, M.C.: IT and business process outsourcing: the knowledge potential. Information Systems Management 21(4), 7–15 (2004)
9. Wüllenweber, K., Beimborn, D., Weitzel, T., König, W.: The Impact of Process Standardization on BPO Success. Information Systems Frontiers 10(2), 211–224 (2008)
10. Kim, G.-m., Kim, S.-Y.: Exploratory Study on Effective Control Structure in Global Business Process Sourcing. Information Resource Management Journal 21(3), 101–118 (2008)
11. Mani, D., Barua, A., Whinston, A.B.: Successfully governing business process outsourcing relationships. MIS Quarterly Executive 5(1), 15–29 (2006)
12. Tanriverdi, H., Konana, P., Ge, L.: The Choice of Sourcing Mechanisms for Business Processes. Information Systems Research 18(3), 280–299 (2007)
13. Martin, S., Beimborn, D., Parikh, M.A., Weitzel, T.: Organizational Readiness for Business Process Outsourcing: A Model of Determinants and Impact on Outsourcing Success. In: 41st Hawaii International Conference on System Sciences (HICSS-41), Waikoloa, Hawaii (2008)
14. Davenport, T.H.: The coming commoditization of processes. Harvard Business Review 83(6), 100–108 (2005)
15. Abramovsky, L., Griffith, R.: Outsourcing and Offshoring of Business Services: How Important is ICT? Journal of the European Economic Association 4(2/3), 594–601 (2006)
16. Krafzig, D., Banke, K., Slama, D.: Enterprise SOA: Service-oriented Architecture Best Practices. Prentice Hall, Upper Saddle River (2005)
17. Bieberstein, N., Bose, S., Fiammante, M., Jones, K., Shah, R.: Service-Oriented Architecture (SOA) Compass: Business Value, Planning, and Enterprise Roadmap. IBM Press, Upper Saddle River (2005)
18. Demirkan, H., Goul, M.: AMCIS 2006 Panel Summary: Towards the Service Oriented Enterprise Vision: Bridging Industry and Academics. Communications of the Association for Information Systems 18(1), 546–556 (2006)
19. Erl, T.: Service-Oriented Architecture: A Field Guide to Integrating XML and Web Services. Prentice Hall, Upper Saddle River (2004)

20. Keen, M., Acharya, A., Bishop, S., Hopkins, A., Milinski, S., Nott, C., Robinson, R., Adams, J., Verschueren, P.: Patterns: Implementing an SOA Using an Enterprise Service Bus. IBM Redbooks (2004)
21. Zhao, J., Tanniru, M., Zhang, L.-J.: Services computing as the foundation of enterprise agility: Overview of recent advances and introduction to the special issue. Information Systems Frontiers 9(1), 1–8 (2007)
22. Oh, L.-B., Leong, Y.-X., Teo, H.-H., Ravichandran, T.: Service-oriented Architecture and Organizational Integration: An Empirical Study of IT-Enabled Sustained Competitive Advantage. In: Proceedings of the 28th International Conference on Information Systems, Montreal, QC, Canada (2007)
23. Beimborn, D., Joachim, N., Weitzel, T.: Drivers and Inhibitors of SOA Business Value – Conceptualizing a Research Model. In: Proceedings of the 14th Americas Conference on Information Systems, Toronto, ON, Canada (2008)
24. Yoon, T., Carter, P.E.: Investigating the Antecedents and Benefits of SOA Implementation: A Multi-Case Study Approach. In: Proceedings of the 13th Americas Conference on Information Systems, pp. 1–11. Colorado State University, Keystone (2007)
25. Baskerville, R., Cavallari, M., Hjort-Madsen, K., Pries-Heje, J., Sorrentino, M., Virili, F.: Extensible Architectures: The Strategic Value of Service-Oriented Architecture in Banking. In: Proceedings of the 13th European Conference on Information Systems, Regensburg, Germany (2005)
26. Kumar, S., Dakshinamoorthy, V., Krishnan, M.S.: SOA and Information Sharing in Supply Chain: "How" Information is Shared Matters! In: Proceedings of the 28th International Conference on Information Systems, Montreal, QC, Canada (2007)
27. Ajzen, I., Fishbein, M.: Understanding attitudes and predicting social behaviour. Prentice-Hall, Englewood Cliffs (1980)
28. Ang, S., Cummings, L.: Strategic response to institutional influence on information systems outsourcing. Organization Science 8(3), 235–256 (1997)
29. Hu, Q., Saunders, C.S., Gebelt, M.: Research report: diffusion of information systems outsourcing: a reevaluation of influence sources. Information Systems Research 8(3), 288–301 (1997)
30. Loh, L., Venkatraman, N.: Diffusion of IT outsourcing: influence sources and the Kodak effect. Information Systems Research 3(4), 334–358 (1992)
31. Earl, M.J.: The risks of outsourcing IT. Sloan Management Review 37(3), 26–32 (1996)
32. Loh, L., Venkatraman, N.: Determinants of information technology outsourcing: a cross-sectional analysis. Journal of Management Information Systems 9(1), 7–24 (1992)
33. Ang, S., Straub, D.W.: Production and transaction economies and IS outsourcing: a study of the U.S. banking industry. MIS Quarterly 22(4), 535–552 (1998)
34. Lacity, M.C., Willcocks, L.P.: An empirical investigation of information technology sourcing practices: lessons from experience. MIS Quarterly 22(3), 363–408 (1998)
35. Dibbern, J., Goles, T., Hirschheim, R., Jayatilaka, B.: Information systems outsourcing: a survey and analysis of the literature. The DATA BASE for Advantages in Information Systems 35(4), 6–102 (2004)
36. Aubert, B.A., Patry, M., Rivard, S.: A Framework for Information Technology Outsourcing Risk Management. The DATA BASE for Advances in Information Systems 36(4), 9–28 (2005)
37. Kakabadse, A., Kakabadse, N.: Trends in outsourcing. European Management Journal 20(2), 189–198 (2002)

38. Lammers, M.: Make, buy or share - Combining resource based view, transaction cost economics and production economies to a sourcing framework. Wirtschaftsinformatik 46(3), 204–212 (2004)
39. Lacity, M.C., Willcocks, L.P.: Interpreting information technology sourcing decisions from a transaction cost perspective: findings and critique. Accounting, Management and Information Technologies 5(3/4), 203–244 (1995)
40. Cheon, M.J., Grover, V., Teng, J.T.C.: Theoretical perspectives on the outsourcing of information systems. Journal of Information Technology 10(4), 209–219 (1995)
41. Apte, U.M., Sobol, M.G., Hanaoka, S., Shimada, T.: IS outsourcing practices in the USA, Japan, and Finland: a comparative study. Journal of Information Technology 12(4), 289–304 (1997)
42. Clark, T.D.J., Zmud, R.W., McGray, G.E.: The outsourcing of information services: transforming the nature of business in the information industry. Journal of Information Technology 10(4), 221–237 (1995)
43. Huber, R.L.: How Continental Bank outsourced its crown jewels. Harvard Business Review 71(1), 121–129 (1993)
44. Saunders, C.S., Gebelt, M., Hu, Q.: Achieving success in information systems outsourcing. California Management Review 39(2), 63–79 (1997)
45. Grover, V., Cheon, M.J., Teng, J.T.C.: The effect of service quality and partnership on the outsourcing of information systems functions. Journal of Management Information Systems 12(4), 89–116 (1996)
46. Slaughter, S., Ang, S.: Employment outsourcing in information systems. Communications of the ACM 39(7), 47–54 (1996)
47. Smith, M., Mitra, S., Narasimhan, S.: Information systems outsourcing: a study of pre-event firm characteristics. Journal of Management Information Systems 15(2), 61–93 (1998)
48. Quinn, J.B., Hilmer, F.G.: Strategic outsourcing. Sloan Management Review 35(4), 43–55 (1994)
49. Franke, J., Wüllenweber, K.: The Impact of Potential Flexibility Gains and Losses on the Intention to Outsource Business Processes In: 14th European Conference on Information Systems (ECIS), Göteborg (2006)
50. Young-Ybarra, C., Wiersema, M.: Strategic Flexibility in Information Technology Alliances: the Influence of Transaction Cost Economics and Social Exchange Theory. Organization Science 10(4), 439–459 (1999)
51. Aubert, B.A., Dussault, S., Rivard, S., Patry, M.: Managing the Risk of IT Outsourcing. In: 32nd Hawaii International Conference on System Sciences (HICSS-32). IEEE Computer Society, Wailea (1999)
52. Aubert, B.A., Patry, M., Rivard, S.: Assessing the Risk of IT Outsourcing. In: 31st Hawaii International Conference on System Sciences (HICSS). IEEE Computer Society, Honolulu(1998)
53. Bahli, B., Rivard, S.: Validating measures of information technology outsourcing risk factors. Omega 33(2), 175–187 (2004)
54. Cunningham, S.M.: The Major Dimensions of Perceived Risk. In: Cox, D.F. (ed.) The Major Dimensions of Perceived Risk, Risk Taking and Information Handling in Consumer Behaviour, pp. 82–108. Harvard University Press, Boston (1967)
55. Tan, C., Sia, S.K.: Managing Flexibility in Outsourcing. Journal of the Association for Information Systems 7(4), 179–206 (2006)
56. McFarlan, F., Nolan, R.: How to manage an IT outsourcing alliance. Sloan Management Review 36(2), 9–23 (1995)

57. Avison, D., Powell, P., Keen, P., Klein, J., Ward, S.: Addressing the Need for Flexibility in Information Systems. Journal of Management Information Systems 7(2), 43–60 (1995)
58. Lacity, M.C., Willcocks, L.P.: Global Information Technology Outsourcing: In Search of Business Advantage. John Wiley & Sons, Chichester (2001)
59. Goolsby, K.: New Impacts on Outsourcing in 2009. Outsourcing Journal (November 2008)
60. Lim, B., Wen, H.J.: Web Services: An Analysis of the Technology, its Benefits, and Implementation Difficulties. Information Systems Management 20(2), 49–49 (2003)
61. vom Brocke, J., Lindner, M.A.: Service Portfolio Measurement: A Framework for Evaluating the Financial Consequences of Out-tasking Decisions. In: 2nd International Conference on Service-Oriented Computing (ICSOC), New York (2004)
62. Benazeer, M.S., Verelst, J., van Grembergen, W., Mannaert, H.: Aligning Technology with Business - An Analysis of the Impact of SOA on Outsourcing. Journal of Theoretical and Applied Information Technology 4(3), 244–252 (2008)
63. vom Brocke, J., Sonnenberg, C.: Serviceorientiertes Prozesscontrolling - Unternehmensindividuelle Wirtschaftlichkeitsrechnungen zur Nutzung serviceorientierter Architekturen bei der Prozessgestaltung. In: Nissen, V., Petsch, M., Schorscht, H. (eds.) Service-orientierte Architekturen - Chancen und Herausforderungen bei der Flexibilisierung und Integration von Unternehmensprozessen, pp. 185–204. Gabler, Wiesbaden (2008)
64. Müller, J., Jostock, F., Götze, J., Müller, P.: Workflow Monitoring in Service-orientierten Architekturen. In: Nissen, V., Petsch, M., Schorscht, H. (eds.) Service-orientierte Architekturen - Chancen und Herausforderungen bei der Flexibilisierung und Integration von Unternehmensprozessen, pp. 185–204. Gabler, Wiesbaden (2008)
65. Münstermann, B., Joachim, N., Beimborn, D.: An Empirical Evaluation of the Impact of Process Standardization on Process Performance and Flexibility. In: 15th Americas Conference on Information Systems (AMCIS), San Francisco (2009)
66. Ren, M., Lyytinen, K.: Building Enterprise Architecture Agility and Sustenance with SOA. Communications of the AIS 22, 75–86 (2008)
67. Schulte, S., Repp, N., Eckert, J., Berbner, R., Blanckenburg, K.v.: General Requirements of Banks on IT Architectures and the SOA Paradigm. In: Veit, D.J., Weitzel, T., Kundisch, D., Weinhardt, C., Rabhi, F.A., Rajola, F. (eds.) Financecom 2007. LNBIP, vol. 4, pp. 66–80. Springer, Heidelberg (2008)
68. Heutschi, R.: Serviceorientierte Architektur - Architekturprinzipien und Umsetzung in die Praxis (2007)
69. Papazoglou, M.P., Heuvel, W.-J.v.d.: Service Oriented Architectures: Approaches, Technologies and Research Issues. The VLDB Journal 16, 389–415 (2007)
70. Bieberstein, N., Bose, S., Walker, L., Lynch, A.: Impact of Service-Oriented Architecture on Enterprise Systems, Organizational Structures, and Individuals. IBM Systems Journal 44(4), 691–708 (2005)
71. Siedersleben, J.: SOA Revisited: Komponentenorientierung bei Systemlandschaften. Wirtschaftsinformatik 49(Special Issue), 110–117 (2007)

Analyzing Processes behind Web Service Standards Development

Karthikeyan Umapathy[1], Sandeep Purao[2], and John W. Bagby[2]

[1] School of Computing, University of North Florida, Jacksonville, FL-32224, USA
[2] College of IST, Penn State University, University Park, PA-16802, USA
k.umapathy@unf.edu, spurao@ist.psu.edu, jbagby@ist.psu.edu

Abstract. Anticipatory standards such as Web service standards are artifacts 'designed' by consortium-based standards development organizations. Intricate processes followed to develop anticipatory standards are not well-understood. Recently, the D-S-N model was developed to explain these processes, and suggested that these processes contain cycles of design (D), sense-making (S), and negotiation (N) activities. In this paper, we provide an initial report of a case study that empirically analyzes archival documents of SOAP standard development. Our findings reveal that the D-S-N model is applicable to the Web service standardization process followed at W3C but this model provides only partial explanation of the process, and that design and sense-making are the core activities of the process. Our findings also show that participants spent most of their time discussing technical issues and identifying action items to be performed, large organizations dominated the process, and negotiation is the least frequent activity.

Keywords: E-Business Standards, Standardization Processes, Anticipatory Standards, SOAP, W3C.

1 Introduction

Web service standards, like most Information and Communication Technology (ICT) standards are known as anticipatory standards, i.e. standards that contain substantial design components developed before widespread acceptance of the technology [1]. Anticipatory standards are expensive, time-consuming, and complex to craft. Nowadays, with increasing demand for newer ICT standards, they are developed by consortium-based Standards Development Organizations (SDOs) such as World Wide Web Consortium (W3C) rather than traditional SDOs such as American National Standards Institute (ANSI) [2].

In contrast to traditional SDOs where standards are developed as products of legislative and regulative processes [3], consortium-based SDOs use an open and consensus oriented process to design standards. In the consortium-based SDO process, consortium and other members, who even though are competitors, cooperate with each other to design mutually acceptable standards [4]. However, because these members may have different goals and interests, it might result in a compromised

R. Sharman, T.S. Raghu, and H.R. Rao (Eds.): WEB 2009, LNBIP 52, pp. 137–146, 2010.

standard that may be ineffective, inelegant, or not responsive to its core concerns [5]. Nevertheless, standardization processes followed to develop anticipatory standards continue to be severely under-researched [1] and our understanding of exactly how these processes are carried out is highly inadequate.

One model that has been recently used to understand standardization processes is the Design, Sense-making, and Negotiation model (D-S-N) [6]. The D-S-N model considers standardization as a recursive process of designing a technical artifact, making sense of others and of the environment, and negotiating the potential differences and reaching a consensus in spite of conflicting interests [6]. The D-S-N model provides a generic, overarching framework and some insights regarding what kinds of activities are performed during the processes. However, it does not provide in-depth details on what roles the participants play, and what design, sense-making, and negotiation activities are performed by participants during standardization processes. In addition, empirical research regarding these perspectives is limited. Thus, our research objective is to conduct empirically grounded analysis on standardization processes followed at W3C and to apply the D-S-N model to identify different design, sense-making and negotiation activities performed by participants.

In this paper, we focus on a specific subset of Web service standard, Simple Object Access Protocol (SOAP) 1.2 [7] to understand how the standards are being developed at W3C. Publicly available W3C documents on SOAP standard were analyzed to identify different activities performed by participants and whether the standardization process is consistent with the D-S-N model. In this paper, we report initial findings of this on-going and exploratory research.

2 D-S-N Model

The D-S-N model provides a "dynamic process model of standardization" by combining three different theoretical threads: Design (D), Sense-making (S), and Negotiation (N) [6]. The first thread, *Design* is primarily drawn from works of Simon [8] to term the events within the standardization process where standards are crafted [1]. The model suggests that during design, participants perform activities such as proposing, implementing, and evaluating design alternatives ranging from simple elements to complex overarching standards architecture. The second thread, *Sense-making* is primary drawn from works of Weick [9] to term the events within the standardization process where participants respond to observed and imagined changes that are occurring to standards [1]. The model suggests that during sense-making, participants are trying to make sense of alternative design options, processes, or other participants. The third thread, *Negotiation* is primary drawn from works of Latour [10] to term the events within the standardization process where participants are reconciling design solutions with other participants regarding their interests [1]. The model suggests that during negotiation, participants interact with each other to resolve differences and come to an agreement with respect to the divisions of labor and the standards. The essence of the D-S-N model is that standardization processes involves cycles and recursion of design, sense-making, and negotiation activities. The study by Virili [11] provides early evidence of the applicability of the D-S-N model to the processes of standards development. However, that research lacks a systematic and empirical treatment of the model to understand how the underlying standards development processes unfold.

3 Research Methodology

In this research, we used a case study approach [12] to investigate anticipatory standardization processes. We selected Web service standards developed at the W3C as the domain because they have many standards with substantial design components. The specific standard used for this investigation is Simple Object Access Protocol (SOAP) 1.2 [7].

We employed content analysis techniques to examine the standardization processes that underlie the development of SOAP [13]. Content analysis allows us to make categorical inferences on large volumes of textual data in a systematic and replicable manner [14]. Content analysis was performed on documents that were publicly available on the W3C website, primarily including transcripts of the meetings (either face-to-face meetings or telephone meetings) that were related to development of SOAP 1.2 standard. Drawing on the content analysis techniques, we read through these documents and examined each passage without any preconceived notion to identify trends and patterns of activities within standardization processes.

The content analysis was conducted by a research team, in which some members conducted the initial coding, whereas the other members questioned, examined, and ultimately corroborated the interpretations suggested by them. There were two important elements of the analysis: text fragments and categorical inferences. A text fragment was usually a text segment related to a significant event or activity performed by participants. A categorical inference was the label conveying the meaning attached to the identified text fragment. The analysis was supported by Atlas.Ti, a content analysis software [15], which allowed the research team to manage documents and record categorical inferences obtained from specific text fragments in the documents.

To maximize the consistency of the interpretation of text fragments in the documents, the analysis was initially performed independently by two researchers on the same set of documents. The results from both researchers were compared to ensure that they had established a shared understanding of which text fragments to be identified, and what meanings to be assigned. Shared understanding among researchers was measured using inter-coder reliability measures provided by Neuendorf [16]. After three iterations (for each iteration, three randomly selected documents were used for analysis), satisfactory inter-coder reliability of 81% was achieved. Inter-coder reliability above 70% is considered to be sufficient for exploratory studies [17].

Based on this shared understanding, the researchers developed a set of syntactic and semantic rules to carry on additional analysis. These rules ensured that interpretations of texts by different researchers were consistent. After establishing these rules, the two researchers independently performed content analysis on additional documents. For this case study, above described exploratory and emergent process was used to obtain categorical inferences that provided ontology of purposeful activities performed by participants in the processes of developing SOAP standard. The results reported in this paper were obtained based on analysis of all relevant documents (a total of 120) that were archived during the process of developing SOAP 1.2 standard, which began on September 13, 2000 and ended on June 24, 2003.

4 Data Analysis

The analysis revealed 95 purposeful activities performed by participants when developing SOAP standard. Top five major activity categories were: (i) discussing technical issues, (ii) identifying action items to be performed, (iii) reaching consensus, (iv) suggesting alternative design options against to a proposed solution, and (v) resolving design issues.

Discussing technical issues was the most frequent activity during the standardization process of SOAP, indicating that participants spent most of their time interacting with others to collectively craft the standard. Other high-frequency activities such as identifying action items to be performed, suggesting alternative design options, and resolving issues indicate that the core of the standardization processes were design activities where participants actively utilized their experiences and cognitive abilities. These activities echo Simon's notion of design as a problem solving and decision making activity primarily to create an innovative technological product—by "finding occasions for making a decision, finding possible courses of action, choosing among courses of action, and evaluating past actions" (pg. 40) [18]. High frequency of reaching consensus activity indicates that participants actively interpreted entities under consideration, and over time they either transformed or changed their frames of thinking about the standard. Table 1 provides a list of top ten activities for developing SOAP standard along with the frequency count for those activities and the corresponding association to the D-S-N model.

Certain activities such as identifying action items to be performed, suggesting alternative design options, proposing design solutions, and raising issue with design solutions were further analyzed to examine the types of participating members, i.e., whether participating members were large organizations, small organizations, W3C employee, or Chair of the working group. Table 2 provides tabulation of frequency counts for above activities based on types of participating members. From the table 2, it can be observed that members of large organizations dominated SOAP standard development. This domination may be occurring because of their ability to invest on research activities outside the standards development to propose innovative design

Table 1. Ten most frequent standardization activities

Activity	DSN Element	Frequency Count
Discussions on technical issues	D	802
Identifying action items to be performed	D	801
Reaching consensus	S	539
Suggesting alternative design solutions	D	314
Resolving issues	D	259
Chairperson of the committee performing his/ her duties	N/A	240
Proposing design solutions	D	246
Raising issue with design solutions	S	246
Participants expressing their opinions through voting process	N/A	115
Discussions on issues related to W3C standardization process	N	132

Table 2. Activity categorization based on type of participating members

	Frequency Count
Identifying action items to be performed	
Large Organizations	339
Small Organizations	131
Chair	95
W3C employee	60
Draft Editors	109
Unassigned	67
Suggesting alternative design solutions in against to proposed solution	
Large Organizations	197
Small Organizations	68
Chair	47
W3C employee	2
Proposing design solutions	
Large Organizations	167
Small Organizations	36
Chair	34
W3C employee	9
Raising issue with design solutions	
Large Organizations	176
Small Organizations	37
Chair	26
W3C employee	7

solutions. Another interesting observation is that in the SOAP standard development, Chair of the working group played a major role. This observation indicates importance of leadership for managing standardization process.

Analysis of the SOAP standards development indicates large organization members cooperated more often with other large organization members than with small organization members to solve an issue. Analysis also indicates that members of large organizations more often expressed their concerns during the process, expressed their interests with standards, expressed confusion over topic under discussion, rejected suggested designs, and volunteered to perform action items than any other type of participating members. Interestingly, analysis indicates that W3C employees more often expressed their frustration with the standardization process than any other type of participating members.

5 Analyzing Using the D-S-N Model

Standardization activities that emerged from the content analysis of the archival documents of SOAP standard development were mapped against the Design (D), Sense-making (S), and Negotiation (N) constructs of the D-S-N model. Mapping was performed based on the meaning assigned to activities inferred during content analysis and description of the constructs provided in the D-S-N model. In order to obtain consistent mapping, each researcher of this study independently performed mapping for all 95 inferred activities. Each activity was mapped to the closest category it resembles while avoiding force fitting an activity into either of the categories. For activities with contradicting mappings, researchers engaged in discussion until collective agreement was reached. Application of the D-S-N model to the inferred activities revealed that not all activities can be mapped to D-S-N constructs. Therefore, those activities were mapped as not applicable (N/A). Most of those activities were related to aspects of managing and regulating the process. Table 1 shows examples of these mappings for the top ten frequent activities.

Application of the D-S-N model constructs indicated that out of 95 activities—37 were Design (D) activities, 33 were Sense-making (S) activities, only 9 were Negotiation (N) activities, and rest of the 16 were non-DSN activities. This analysis indicates that the D-S-N model is applicable to the standardization process followed by W3C for developing SOAP standard, even though it does not provide a comprehensive view of the standardization process. However, given that there is lack of theoretical frameworks to explain anticipatory standardization processes, the finding that the D-S-N model can partially explain anticipatory standardization processes is a promising sign. Analysis also indicates that design and sense-making were the core activities of standardization process.

Further analysis was performed by tallying frequency count of activities based on their mapping to D, S, N, and non-DSN constructs. Figure 1 provides pie chart depiction of frequency count for D-S-N model constructs. The analysis indicates that design is at the heart of the standardization process, which is not a surprising finding because SOAP is an anticipatory standard. Analysis also indicates that sense-making activities is the second most frequent activity, followed by non-DSN activities and then by negotiation activities. Negotiation activities are the least frequent among all of the inferred activity is a surprising finding given that most of the participants are competing with each other in their marketplace. This finding suggests either that

Fig. 1. Frequency total for the D-S-N model constructs

Table 3. Five most frequent activities for each of the D-S-N model elements

	Frequency Count
Top five design activities	
Discussions on technical issues	802
Identifying action items to be performed by a large organization	339
Resolving issues	259
Suggesting alternative design solutions by a large organization	197
Proposing design solutions by a large organization	167
Top five sense-making activities	
Reaching consensus	539
Raising issue with design solutions by a large organization	176
Large organization participant expressing their concerns and confusion	52
Discussions between a large and a small organization participants on design solutions	52
Participants expressing disagreement	51
Top five negotiation activities	
Discussions on issues related to W3C standardization process	132
Volunteering to perform an activity by a large organization	44
Discussions on sociopolitical issues	25
Volunteering to perform an activity by a small organization	7
Volunteering to perform an activity by W3C	3
Top five non-DSN activities	
Chairperson of the committee performing his/ her duties	240
Regulating discussions among participants	132
Participants expressing their opinions through voting process	115
Participants intentionally decide to procrastinate discussion on an issue	67
Participant responsible for an issue performing his/ her duties	32

participants might present their design solutions in a way that is not opposite to other participants' interests in a significant manner, or that negotiation is held outside the realm of documented standards development processes or that participants did not have any relevant proprietary implementation or make large investments towards it.

One of the major limitations of the D-S-N model is that it does not provide detailed guidance on what activities are involved with design, sense-making, and negotiation that can take place during the standardization processes [19]. Our empirical analysis not only identified 95 inferred activities, but also mapped these activities into the D-S-N model. Table 3 below provides a list of top five design, sense-making, negotiation, and non-DSN activities, identified from analysis of SOAP standardization processes.

Our analysis of SOAP standard development process indicates that most frequent design activities are discussing issues, identifying issues, resolving issues, proposing solutions, and suggesting alternative solutions in opposition to existing solutions. These design activities are quite similar to Simon's [8] notion of design as goal oriented activity involving identifying courses of actions, developing solutions, and evaluating alternative solutions. Most frequent sense-making activities are reaching consensus among participants and critiquing proposed solutions. These sense-making activities reflect Wieck's [9] notion of sense-making as participants utilizing their experience and frame of reference to critic alternative solutions and those who developed solutions respond to critics to establish a shared understanding. Most frequent negotiation activities include volunteering to develop solutions and discussions on standardization process and sociopolitical issues. These negotiation activities are close to Latour's [10] notion of establishing socio-technical network as participants formulating normative framework for conducting standardization processes, participants positioning themselves as part of the network by volunteering to perform certain activities, and participants questioning other participant's intentions. Most frequent non-DSN activities are chairperson of the process exercising his/her role, regulating standardization process, and participants expressing opinions through a voting process. These non-DSN activities indicate that standardization processes needs to be regulated, so that processes are steered towards development of the intended standard. These non-DSN activities are not design activities as they do not deal with any technical issues, are not sense-making activities as they do not deal with interpretation or reaching shared understanding, and are not negotiation activities as they do not deal with negotiating participant's identities or establishing norms followed within the standardization process.

6 Discussion

In this paper, we have described initial findings of an empirical analysis on a standardization process followed at W3C, more specifically the development of SOAP 1.2 standard. Analysis reveals that design activities are the core of processes. The application of inferred standardization activities from the empirical analysis against the D-S-N model constructs indicates that this model explains most aspects of the process other than those activities related to managing and regulating the development process. Analysis suggests that apart from design, sense-making, and negotiation aspects, there is also regulation aspect that needs to be considered for understanding standardization processes. As a part of future work, we intend to extend the D-S-N model to incorporate regulation aspects of standardization process.

Analysis on standardization activities indicates that participants spend most of their time discussing technical issues, identifying action items to be performed, and engaging to reach consensus. Analysis based on mapping between activities and the D-S-N model demonstrates that most frequent design activities are similar to Simon's notion of design activities such as identifying new course of actions, proposing solutions and suggesting other alternative solutions. Analysis based on the mapping demonstrates that most frequent sense-making activities are similar to Wieck's notion of sense-making activities such as critiquing alternative solutions and establishing shared understanding around viable solutions. Analysis based on the mapping demonstrates that negotiation activities are similar to Latour's notion of negotiation activities such as positioning oneself in the network and questioning other intentions and relationship within the process. Our analysis of most frequent activities, therefore, indicates that the D-S-N model is a relevant and appropriate model to examine standardization processes. We argue that findings reported in this paper demonstrate that the D-S-N model has potential to explain and provide insights into anticipatory standardization processes.

Analysis based on the mapping also indicated that negotiation is the least frequent activity. Lack of significant negotiation activities is quite surprising given that most participating organizations are competing with each other in the market space. We conducted analysis on meeting minutes that were made publically accessible after being reviewed by W3C and participating members. During standardization process, participants can use a private mailing list for conducting asynchronous discussion, which is not accessible to public. Therefore, it is possible that some form of negotiation is taking place in these private avenues. Further exploration, perhaps using ethnography methodology, can help to gain better insights into negotiation aspects of standardization process. The analysis on standardization activities also suggests that large organizations dominate the process. Domination of process by large organizations also requires further investigation on whether W3C policies have some inherent barrier for small organizations to participate or it is just mere a fact that organizations need a considerable amount of prior investment to make effective contributions.

Processes followed to develop anticipatory standards are considered as a black box due to our lack of understanding on dynamics of these processes. The main contribution of this paper is advancing our understanding on these processes by identifying emerging set of activities performed by participants during standards development. Further investigation of these activities can help us in understanding dynamics of standardization processes. Empirical investigation described in this study can be used to study processes followed to develop other anticipatory standards. Such studies would provide us in-depth understanding of standardization processes and its activities. As a part of future work, we plan to conduct similar analysis on other W3C standards to examine the validity and applicability of our findings, in order to gain an in-depth understanding of standardization processes followed at W3C. We also intend to identify recurring patterns of activities within standardization processes to investigate how recursive process of D-S-N constructs lead to development of anticipatory standards. Currently standardization processes are conducted with minimal technological support, developing adequate tool support to ensure that standardization processes yield effective standards would require in-depth understanding of standardization processes and its activities.

References

1. Lyytinen, K., Keil, T., Fomin, V.: A Framework to Build Process Theories of Anticipatory Information and Communication Technology (ICT) Standardizing. International Journal of IT Standards and Standardization Research 6, 1–38 (2008)
2. Hill, J.L.: ICT standardization: changing the world for a better tomorrow. Standardization and Innovation in Information Technology, 21–23 (2003)
3. Weiss, M., Cargill, C.: Consortia in the Standards Development Process. Journal of the American Society for Information Science (JASIS) 43 (1992)
4. Kretschmer, T., Muehlfeld, K.: Co-opetition in Standard-Setting: The Case of the Compact Disc. NET Institute Working Paper No. 04-14 (2004)

5. Purao, S., Bagby, J., Umapathy, K.: Standardizing Web Services: Overcoming 'Design by Committee'. In: Zhang, L.-J., Hofmann, P. (eds.) IEEE Congress on Services - Part I, pp. 223–230. IEEE Computer Society, Hawaii (2008)
6. Fomin, V., Keil, T., Lyytinen, K.: Theorizing about Standardization: Integrating Fragments of Process Theory in Light of Telecommunication Standardization Wars. Sprouts: Working Papers on Information Environments. Systems and Organizations 3 (2003)
7. W3C-XMLWG: XML Protocol Working Group. Vol. 2006. W3C (2000)
8. Simon, H.A.: The Sciences of the Artificial. The MIT Press, Cambridge (1996)
9. Weick, K.E.: Sensemaking in Organizations. Sage Publications, Thousand Oaks (1995)
10. Latour, B.: Where are the Missing Masses? The Sociology of a Few Mundane Artifacts. In: Bijker, W., Law, J. (eds.) Shaping Technology/Building Society: Studies in Sociotechnical Change, pp. 225–258. MIT Press, Cambridge (1992)
11. Virili, F.: Design, Sense-Making And Negotiation Activitie. In: The "Web Services" Standardization Process. MIS Quarterly Special Issue Workshop on Standard Making: A Critical Research Frontier for Information Systems (2003)
12. Yin, R.K.: Case Study Research: Design and Methods. Sage Publications, Thousand Oaks (2003)
13. Krippendorff, K.: Content Analysis: An Introduction to Its Methodology. Sage Publications, Inc., Thousand Oaks (2003)
14. Stemler, S.: An overview of content analysis. Practical Assessment, Research & Evaluation 7 (2001)
15. ATLAS.ti: ATLAS.ti. Scientific Software Development GmbH, Berlin, Germany (2005)
16. Neuendorf, K.A.: The Content Analysis Guidebook. Sage Publications, Inc., Thousand Oaks (2001)
17. Lombard, M., Snyder-Duch, J., Bracken, C.C.: Content Analysis in Mass Communication: Assessment and Reporting of Intercoder Reliability. Human Communication Research 28, 587–604 (2002)
18. Simon, H.A.: The New Science of Management Decision. Prentice Hall PTR, Englewood Cliffs (1977)
19. Choi, B., Raghu, T.S., Vinze, A., Dooley, K.J.: Process Model for e-Business Standards Development: A Case of ebXML Standards. IEEE Transactions on Engineering Management 56, 448–467 (2009)

A Model-Based Software Architecture to Support Decentral Product Development Processes

Patrick D. Stiefel and Jörg P. Müller

Clausthal University of Technology, Department of Informatics, 38678 Clausthal-Zellerfeld, Germany
{patrick.stiefel,joerg.mueller}@tu-clausthal.de

Abstract. The cross-organizational, collaborative product development needs adaptive and open platforms for integration that scale well and provide an intelligent environment especially in regard to definition and design. Based on these requirements our research focuses on how decentral information technology can further the processes especially needed for collaborative product development (CPD). We therefore follow a model driven development (MDD) approach, but it is still an open research question how requirements for that approach in a decentral development process should be reconciled with the potential of decentralized IT systems (especially in P2P environments). This paper presents methods and models which have been hardly taken into consideration by existing centralized collaborative systems. We aim to provide the basics for the next generation of loosely coupled collaborative systems for cross-organizational CPD.

Keywords: Decentral and collaborative product development (CPD), Peer-To-Peer(P2P)-based collaboration, model driven development (MDD) of decentral organized information systems, loosely coupled collaboration platform.

1 Introduction

Collaboration platforms are a modern approach to support cross-organizational knowledge processing in product engineering. The resulting cooperative product data management networks not only support worldwide access to all data concerning the product life cycle but also contribute to the-long term challenges of digital product engineering processes.

According to projections of [1] there is going to be a revolution in key industries within the automobile economy. Increasing pressure in cost and innovation is expected to force manufactures into a "productivity squeeze". This is expected be the third industry changing revolution after the assembly line introduced by Henry Ford and the introduction of Lean Production by Toyota. Key changes affect the structure of products in general, the in-house production depth, relocation of innovation and revenue drivers leading to moving away from OEM based production models towards system suppliers massively influencing the end product.

Collaborative product development (CPD) is the most important part of this development. It can be divided into synchronous ("same time – different place") and

R. Sharman, T.S. Raghu, and H.R. Rao (Eds.): WEB 2009, LNBIP 52, pp. 147–159, 2010.

asynchronous ("different time – different place") collaboration. The first mode is mainly used upon real-time communication or data transmission while the latter focuses on workflow management [2]. During multi party cross-organizational engineering projects CPD platforms provide an added value at definition and execution stages, as the main motivation is usually to combine distributed core competencies in design, production, and process know-how. CPD platforms that we are talking about focus on design-by-feature technologies that are mainly used in product design and development. These systems provide distributive and collaboration-enabling support for global design collaboration. One of its major challenges is to share large data volume design models and design changes among a working team efficiently [3].

Based on these requirements our research focuses on developing decentral information technologies to support CPD processes ([4],[6]). A result is the Product Collaboration Platform (PCP). The PCP is an experimental peer-to-peer(P2P)-based software platform to support decentral organized product development processes. We follow a model driven development (MDD) approach to design information systems for decentral and collaborative product development (DeCoP). Based on Computation Independent Models (CIM) we develop in an iterative process different abstraction of IT models: starting from IT architecture models (platform independent models, PIM) over platform specific models (PSM) to concrete software artifacts.

It is still an open research question how requirements for a MDD approach in a decentral development process should be reconciled with the potential of decentralized IT systems (especially in P2P environments). This paper presents methods and models which have been hardly taken into consideration by existing centralized collaborative systems. We propose approaches at different levels of MDD, which can be used to generate decentral architecture models and in the end software artifacts – automated on some levels. We aim to provide the basics for the next generation of loosely coupled collaborative systems for cross-organizational product development.

Section 2 of this paper deals with fundamentals of DeCoP. In Section 3 we discuss the current state-of-the-art of model driven engineering and the specific requirements during the processes of the MDD approach for the development of decentralized collaboration platforms. Section 4 presents models of the different MDD levels and section 5 concludes with an evaluation of the presented approach with view to real world scenarios.

2 Background

There are actually four buzzwords used as descriptors for what people need to do to work together: ***Communication, Coordination, Cooperation*** and ***Collaboration.*** People tend to use these words interchangeably.

According to the 3C model of Teufel et al. ***communication*** describes the way on how information (especially human experiences) is transferred in organizations [7]. Without ***coordination*** different units create overlap, redundancy and/ or separation. Unlike *communication*, *coordination* looks to inform each unit or part of the whole as to how and when it must act to achieve efficiency in the group. What's still missing is a connection between inputs and outcome to tell about the consequence dependent on context. ***Cooperation*** is the strongest style of teamwork among groups and needs a strong compliance of targets: the group as a whole needs to be in charge of the result ("get with the group").

Collaboration is distinct from each of the C words mentioned before. Unlike *communication* it is not about exchanging information, it is about using information to create something new. Unlike *coordination*, it has a desire for spontaneity not structural harmony. And unlike *cooperation*, it allows disagreement, dissent and even conflict. *Collaborations* are established to solve problems, to develop new understandings and to design new products. The following steps are needed to create *collaboration*: Define the challenge (achievement point), define the collaborators, create a space (blackboard/ shared screen), allow the time and harness the result like a prototype e.g. ([8],[9]).

Our research describes different shapes of *collaboration* dealing with the challenges of cross-organizational product engineering aiming to facilitate the engineering of a product model proposal which satisfies the requirements set out by all parties involved in said process. A *product model* is defined as "[...] a general product structure for a certain individual product. It contains information on an individual product, recorded and arranged to (a corresponding) *product information model*. For example, the individual product units', product models or product structures for two similar but customized products might differ, even though the products are alike at a generic, product information model level" [10].

According to Lindemann business processes in cross-organizational product engineering reflect a certain development process and work with a specific product model shape [11]:

- ***Target model:*** gathering, structuring and documenting of desired system properties.
- ***Problem model:*** to improve the understanding of problems and challenges of the product in regard to existing or future properties (i.e. strain, feasibility, material characteristics).
- ***Development model:*** to aid in the specifications regarding the structure and the geometric and material condition of the product to be developed.
- ***Verification model:*** compilation and analysis of essential properties which matter for the evaluation with view to expected quality and requirements.

Each DeCoP process describes a distributed solution of a given product engineering problem (***specification***). Our approach, as shown in Figure 1 is based on the Distributed Problem Solving paradigm solving paradigm developed for multi-agent systems ([12],[13]). The DeCoP process provides a synthesis of the distributed partial solutions of the participants (***proposals***) to an overall solution satisfying the initial requirements of the initiator.

Nowadays decentral organization of distributed systems is a known paradigm for managing global and dynamic networks [14]. A decentral architecture based on P2P technology provides the needed flexible and scalable approach for a collaborative product engineering platforms:

- Support of ad-hoc interconnections of world-wide distributed partners that usually did not cooperate in the past.
- Efficient distribution of product models among participating engineers either for load balancing reasons or for the reasons of task distribution resulting in exploitation of net locality to facilitate lower latency.

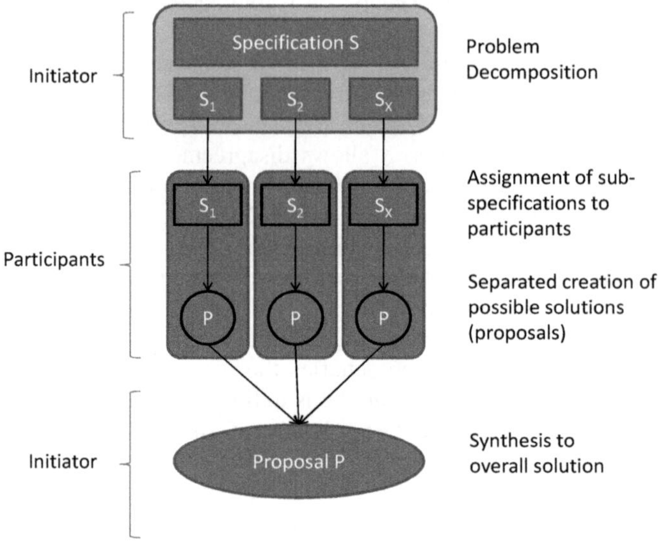

Fig. 1. Decentral and Collaborative Product Development (DeCoP)

3 Model-Driven Decentral and Collaborative Product Development

The definition of models on different levels of abstraction and therefore the modeling of different aspects is one of the main ideas of MDD [15]. CIM describes the functionalities of the collaborative platform on the functional level and is expressed in a language suitable for the audience (i.e. engineers). It is meant to facilitate the collaboration among the stakeholders (i.e. software developers and engineers) in the DeCoP. In our research we ended up with the Business Process Modelling Notation (BMPN) after starting off with Aris Event-driven Process Chains (EPC). BPMN is a notation for business processes as well as technical models (i.e. loops, exception handling, and transactions). Workflows expressed in BPMN get interpreted and executed with the process engine of a Business Process Management System (BPMS). Business Process Diagrams (BPDs) provide a visual representation of BPMN models.

The platform concept in MDD characterizes a closed software component or technology with access through interfaces. Accessing components need not to know about the implementation of concrete platform functionalities. The platform provides technical services that are necessary to provide an expected software behavior. In correlation to platform the concept of a *Platform Independent Model (PIM)* is used. A PIM is a model for the functionalities of components which is independent of the platform. The *Platform Specific Model (PSM)* in contrast knows about services compositions, DRM, and overlay specifications. The PSM and its services enable the PIM on the platform.

3.1 Concept

MMD concepts are already applied in the field of product lifecycle management. Néjib et. al present case studies about its application to develop software applications that ensure the interoperability between given heterogeneous information systems [5]. As shown in Figure 2, we follow this top-down idea and start with functional descriptions of DeCoP business processes on CIM level to end up in decentral architectures at PSM level [6]. Our architecture approaches are described in three PSM layers: a SOA framework, a Decentral Resource Management (DRM) layer and a specific P2P overlay.

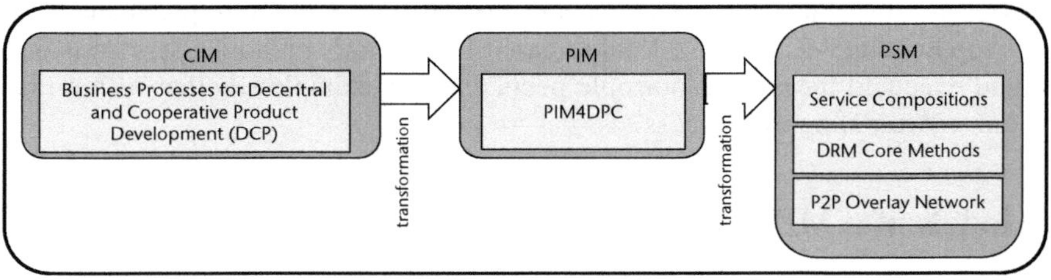

Fig. 2. MDD process for DeCoP

The DRM is an abstraction layer of specific P2P overlay functions especially enhanced for decentral product model handling (publish, search, subscribe, notify). Generic collaborative services are based on these DRM core methods (i.e. the management of a product model structure). They are part of the service layer and get executed from local service engines.

3.2 Requirements

During the model generation at MDD process we were made aware that – for decentral organized information systems – all layers of the model deal with requirements concerning the network topology. We provide two examples in the *CIM layer* to illustrate our findings: First a goal of cooperation could be to facilitate a design for the product structure based on a *development model*. Second could be a CIM workflow dealing with the exchange of ideas aiming to find valid states for the *target model*. Both business processes differ – independent from being decentral – on how they make use of generic product development processes to represent a DeCoP process. In the first case several participants work on isolated partial problems and send their results to an initiator. The initiator reviews the results, comes to a conclusion, and decides on how to proceed (cp BPD at Figure 3, left hand). The second example does not really deal with a centrally managed process as there are several initiators involved working on several iterative produced results in a parallel manner. Both collaborative scenarios are decentrally organized collaborations but with totally different requirements for their participants in regard to their level of trust concerning their contributions to the product models (cp Section 4.1). During the model transformation the requirements influence an outcome of the models in the *PIM layer*.

Decentralism becomes more of an issue once we descend down to the architecture in the *PIM*. It develops more towards questions regarding the requirements resulting from the mappings in CIM and how those affect specific properties of the P2P overlay. The decision whether a structured or hybrid approach is made during that stage (independent from how it is going to be implemented later). In addition how roles are going to be assigned to which peers during the collaboration process and how these roles lead to the meeting of specific requirements set for those roles and task in question. It results in specific architectures and services (cp Section 4.4).

Based on the architecture and services in the PIM layer the *PSM* implements corresponding service oriented architectures (SOA) and specific P2P overlay implementations to match the requirements of the DRM layer. As the PIM describes how the processes are distributed the PSM maps needed Service Choreographies and Compositions (cp Section 4.2 and 4.3). It takes care of the details on how a service is distributed and executed through responsible peers and for example whether or not there is someone coordinating the process?

4 Models of a MDD Process

4.1 DeCoP Business Processes at CIM Layer

A basic business process of DeCoP is shown in the BPD on the left hand in Figure 3. Creating a specification starts with the thoughts of the initiator leading to an initial idea about a possible shape and properties ending up in a first sketch of a development model and parameters called *specification*. Corresponding to that artifact a data element *proposal* is getting published by a participant. The initiator receives and checks the proposal. Product model collaborations derived from the basic business process have the following dimensions: Product Model(PM-)Distribution, Hierarchy, and Iteration. Figure 3 (right hand) illustrates the introduced dimensions of the product development scenarios introduced in this paper. E.g., a simple scenario is the combination: no iterations/ central model repository / no hierarchy.

PM-Distribution: The BPD explicitly assigns specifications and proposals to their respective owners. The initiator decides how the data is distributed among participants in the engineering process – trust can be one of the criteria. There are three different strategies: central, hybrid, and decentral PM-Storage.

In case of a *central PM-Storage* one single peer stores the specification and the corresponding proposals, default peer is the initiator. The BPD reflects this with an assignment of the artifacts *specification* and *proposal* to the initiator´s pool (cp Figure 3, left hand). In addition Figure 4 shows on the left hand the case of a cooperative network with central PM-Storage. The notation Vz(Ty).x next to the product models reflects the state of the element as version x of proposal z made by participant y.

In case of a *hybrid PM-Storage* all participants organize the storage themselves. Accordingly the BPD shows the artifact specification at the initiator and the proposals at the corresponding participants. The option to distribute proposals over several participants remains. That would result in a collaboration of a subset among the participants which would be the case when partial results from other peers are needed to submit a proposal (cp Figure 4, right hand).

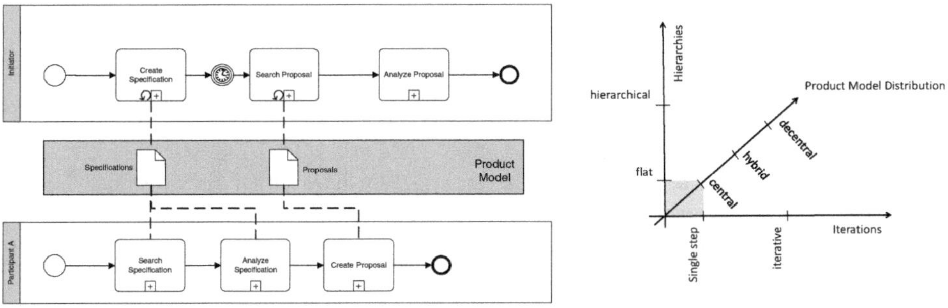

Fig. 3. DeCoP basic business process, designed as BPD (left hand) and DeCoP Dimensions (right hand)

In case of decentral PM-Storage the specifications and proposals get stored "arbitrarily" at peers in the network (decentral method). For that reason neither specification nor proposals get assigned to a specific pool in the BPD.

Hierarchies: A participant has the option to further split and distribute the given sub-problem from the initiator to participants of his choice (i.e. in a separate network). A BPD illustrates this with a set of sub specifications following the earlier mentioned notation. In general there is no limit for additional participants or hierarchy level s. Hierarchies are possible in all PM-Storage options.

Iterations: Collaboration processes without iterations are unlikely in reality. In the decentral development of a product model, numerous iterations should be needed in reality. For instance an initiator notices the need for an update to his specification after receiving the first proposals. The option to request an update to specific proposals exists as well. For that reason two new processes get introduced ("update specification" and "update proposal").

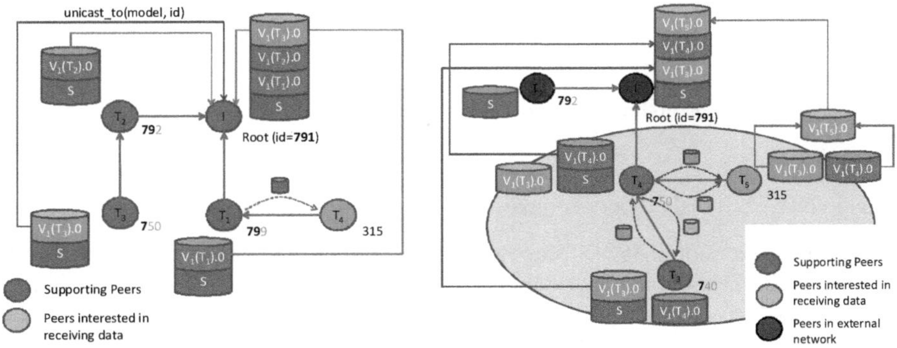

Fig. 4. Product Model Distributions: Central PM-Storage (left hand) and hybrid PM-Storage (right hand)

4.2 DeCoP Architecture Styles

According to Roser we distinguish between three archetypes of architectures for the execution of cross-organizational business processes: brokerless, central broker, and decentral broker architecture [16].

Brokerless architecture: The brokerless architecture uses either message passing between services or observer services on a virtual product model to establish a certain level of control flow logic. The needed interaction between nodes can be achieved with choreography while a peer's local task services (TS) are simply orchestrated [16].

Central broker architecture: A central broker runs a controller service (CS) to achieve the needed control flow logic of the collaborative business process. The idea is following the paradigm of an orchestration.

Decentral broker architecture: The central controller service is split among peers acting as controller service over a subset of the network. These peers run a service to distribute information to achieve the same orchestration and control flow logic as if there were a central broker.

The choice of one of these archetypes depends on the concrete service distribution. The distribution describes which roles (initiator/participant) provide services and who is allowed to use them. This decision is directly related to the product model distribution set by the developer of the business process (cp section 4.1). Which strategy is going to be used during the collaboration is decided during runtime and is based on the participating users and the trust among them.

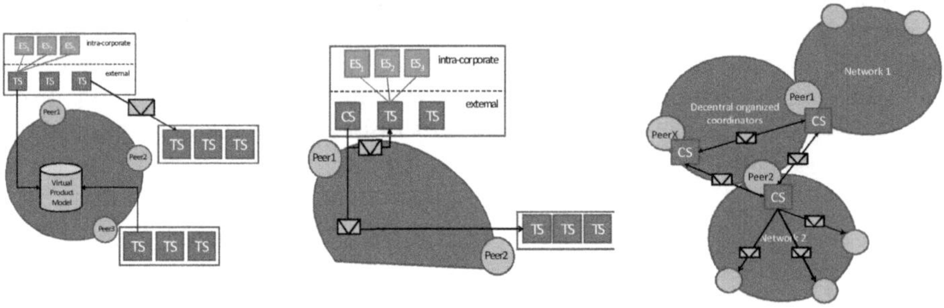

Fig. 5. Archetypes of architectures for the execution of DeCoP business processes (Roser 2008)

It has to be distinguished between the following *Service-Distributions*:

1. In case of a central PM-Storage on a fixed set of nodes the *brokerless architecture* is the best choice. Every node in the network ends up with all collaboration services (= *central availability of the services*).
2. In case of a hybrid PM-Storage all proposals get stored on nodes of a trusted subset of the network. Peers in a team are therefore able to share services among them. The *central broker architecture* is a good fit. The initiator assumes the role as CS and the TS roles are assumed by selected participants (= *hybrid availability of services*).

3. In case of decentral PM-Storage (i.e. load balancing) product models can be "arbitrarily" distributed among the nodes. In this case *decentral broker architecture* provides a good fit. The CS uses P2P technologies i.e. DHT technologies of structured P2P networks *(= decentral availability of services*).

4.3 Platform-Specific Models for DeCoP (PSM4DeCoP)

As part of our research we started with basic modeling and evaluations of the brokerless architecture in the PSM (cp Figure 6). Each peer has a set of functional services which is developed locally through a participant. For instance the service "Create Specification" could result in the creation of a specification with data extracted through a product data management system (i.e. Teamcenter Engineering, TCE). In addition there are a number of technical services like "Publish", "Search", "Subscribe", and "Notify" which – according to the architecture model – are implemented the same way in all peers [4]. A workflow is assigned to each development partner and includes a plan for the local services to make sure the business process is executable.

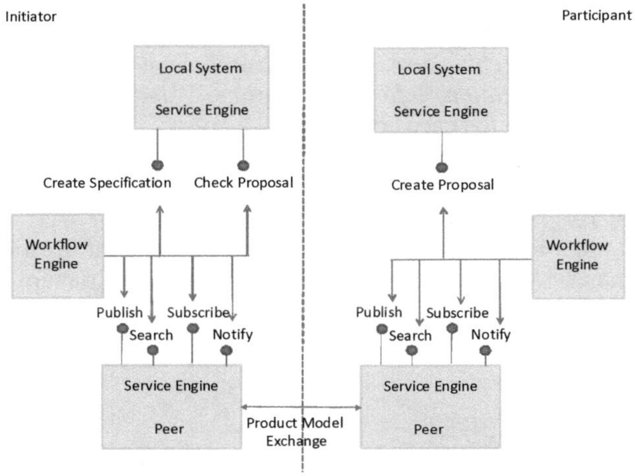

Fig. 6. Model of a brokerless architecture for DeCoP

4.4 Platform Independent Model for DeCoP (PIM4DeCoP)

Sections 4.1-4.3 show that the models at CIM, PIM and PSM level are not static. Some parameters reflect this and are needed to set up for a top-down approach based on the business process designer on the one hand and for a bottom-up approach based on the IT expert on the other hand. We give an example for the top-down approach: the business process designer creates the following two scenarios for DeCoP (A and B) and sets the parameters for the given dimensions in Table 1.

Table 1. DeCoP dimensions

DeCoP Dimension	Development Models	Target Models
Maximum number of participants (including sub initiators)	100 (10)	1000 (1)
Number of specifications	10	1000
Number of proposals per specification and participant (Iterations)	10	100
Permitted collaboration-independent sub-developments	Yes	No
Participant behavior	Confidential product models/ cooperation only with initiator	Non-confidential PM/ Cooperative behavior

The challenge for PIM4DeCoP is based on the evaluation of adjusted parameters (cp Table 1) to make an automated transformation and to come up with a recommendation for the architecture (cp section 4.2). We would expect the following: DeCoP scenario A should end up in a *brokerless architecture* while scenario B is a candidate for a *decentral broker architecture*. PIM4DeCoP´s metamodel describes the following four aspects: *organization, information, process, and overlay* (cp Figure 7; the model was simplified due to space constraints).

The *organization´s metamodel* describes the collaboration structure among the *actors*. Actors can only take over *processes* they are suited for according to their *privileges*, they were assigned to over their *team role*.

The *information´s metamodel* contains all the necessary information for the product development. An *InformationObject(IO)* represents the structure and design of a

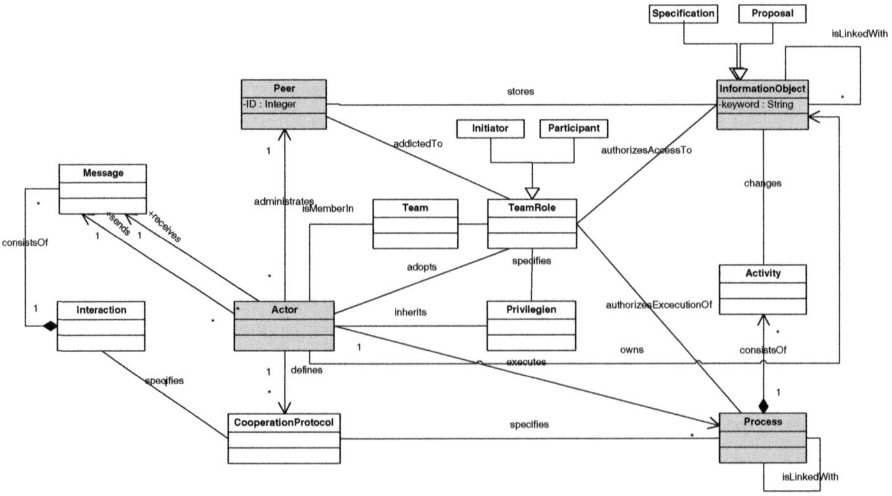

Fig. 7. PIM4DeCoP metamodel

product model and connections between *specifications* and corresponding *proposals*. Each *IO* gets assigned to an *actor* based on its *TeamRole* and is stored on an associated *peer*.

The *process´s metamodel* maps *activities* in a graph to represent collaborative business processes. *Activites* are assigned to *actors* and correspond to specific *IOs*. Several *activities* result in a collaborative business *process* which is further specified by a *CollaborationProtocol*.

The *overlay´s metamodel* is one source of information for the identification of a P2P overlay in the PSM. Core components of the metamodel are *peers* and their corresponding *actors* and *IOs*.

5 Evaluation and Summary

Our paper indicates how to develop a platform for DeCoP with the aid of existing MDD process models. We introduced approaches to the different levels of abstraction. We are going to focus on two aspects for our concluding evaluation of the MDD approach:

1. To what extent is the model driven process suited for our approach of developing a decentral organized collaboration platform. Therefore we are going to focus on the final product quality to measure whether the introduced models in the CIM, PIM, and PSM layer suffice. The quality is measured based on two criteria: a) acts the software as expected by the modelers and b) are the models flexible enough to support a decentral infrastructure?
2. How well do the introduced processes do in the decentral environment when compared to traditional client server collaborative platforms?

Aspect 1a: Tests and simulations based on our implemented prototypes indicate whether the software produces the expected results of the modeler. The following criteria help to determine that:

- Was the goal of the collaboration achieved? If it was not, is the business process correctly designed?
- Does the achieved product model distribution match the model?
- If all workflows are correct: Does the achieved collaboration course match the expected process?

Aspect 1b: It is difficult to answer whether the models are flexible enough for the decentral case or not. The resulting dynamic of the system has to be taken into account during design time as the success of the collaboration at run time depends on the level of model details. Because peers act autonomous it cannot be said whether a peer is available all the time which makes it kind of difficult to make deterministic assumptions during design time.

The dynamic system behavior – characteristic of a P2P network – has to be taken into account during all modeling stages of the MDD. Generally we account that by generating independent model parts at all MDD levels – This could for example be a self-contained local part of a cooperative business process or an adapted local workflow part executed by a single peer. The interaction between several separated activities is realized through the product model itself. Therefore we normally talk about model-centric processes. Furthermore we model dynamic system behavior with expected behavior at PIM (Quality of Service, QoS). This allows us to select relevant P2P overlay structures one the one hand and to optimize needed workflows and service distributions on the other hand. The following OoS parameters are relevant:

- Availability of local product models
  - Definition of groups which replicate each other´s data
  - Inheritance of roles within teams
  - Queuing theory for buffering data during temporary non availability
- Scalability
  - Efficient product model storage in the network matching the dependencies of the company structure in the DeCoP
  - Content-delivery strategies / data chunks for large files
- Search
  - Efficient search for peers and product models (i.e. wildcards, exact match, range queries) independent of the amount of peers in the network
- Trustworthiness
  - Private key infrastructures for sensitive product models
  - Possibility for keyword-based subnets

Metrics allow the evaluation on how good an implementation of the overlay is fulfilling the QoS requirements. Metrics measure adaptivity (scalability/ stability/ flexibility), efficiency, validity and trustworthiness (reliability/ security) [18].

Aspect 2: In the end the acceptance of DeCoP in companies depends on a lot of elements which have to be taken into account during the development. The following paragraph mentions a few of them.

Comparing the P2P approach to the traditional client-/server approach reveals advantages in regard to scalability, flexibility, data storage, and response time. Even though all of these advantages never lead to a P2P based implementation of a collaboration platforms used in companies. After we presented our prototype to companies the feedback provided us with two main reasons why this was neglected so far:

- The product engineers are afraid of losing the control of their product data and
- Companies are not sufficiently aware of the need to disclose their processes for more efficient collaboration.

We claim that the MDD approach introduced in this paper should help to overcome these obstacles. We have to create an awareness among users that the behavior (and its consequences) of the actors already needs to be taken into account during design time. It is part of our concept to have designers of decentral organized, cross-organizational cooperative product development processes to model business processes on CIM level in their well known environment (i.e. BPDs). This would allow designers to work on their CMP processes without the need to take care of the IT level decisions and get a concrete P2P network supporting the process.

References

1. Frise, P.R.: Integrating design and manufacturing processes in automotive suppliers. In: Bramley, A., NcMahon, C., Coutellier, D., Brissaud, D. (eds.) Advances in Integrated Design and Manufacturing in Mechanical Engineering, Pages, pp. 227–242. Springer, Netherlands (2005)
2. Li, W.D., Qiu, Z.M.: State-of-the-Art Technologies and Methodologies for Collaborative Product Development Systems. International Journal of Production Research 44(13), 2525–2559 (2006)
3. Li, W.D., Ong, S.K., Nee, A.Y.C.: Integrative and Collaborative Product Development Environment. In: Technologies and Implementations. World Scientific Publishing Co. Pte. Ltd., Singapore (2006)
4. Stiefel, P.D., Müller, J.P.: ICT interoperability challenges in decentral, cross-enterprise product engineering. In: Gonçalves Ricardo, J., et al. (eds.) Enterprise Interoperability II: New Challenges and Approaches, pp. 171–182. Springer, London (2007)
5. Néjib, M., Hanène, C., Yacine, O., Frédéric, N., Abdelaziz, B.: Model-Driven Architecture to enhance interoperability between product applications. In: Proceedings of the 5th International Conference on Product Lifecycle Management, Seoul, Korea,
6. Stiefel, P.D., Müller, J.P.: Realizing dynamic product collaboration processes in a model-driven framework: Case study and lessons learnt. In: Thoben, K.-D., Pawar, K.S., Gonçalves, R. (eds.) 14th International Conference on Concurrent Enterprising, Lisbon, Portugal, June 23-25 (2008)
7. Teufel, S., Sauter, C., Mühlherr, T.: Computerunterstützung für die Gruppenarbeit, Oldenbourg (1995)
8. Schrage, M.: The New Technologies of Collaboration, p. 140. Random House, NY (1990)
9. Winer, M., Ray, K.: Collaboration Handbook: Creating, Sustaining, and Enjoying the Journey, Fieldstone Alliance, 1st edn. (1994)
10. Saaksvuori, A., Immonen, A.: Product Lifecycle Management, p. 22. Springer, Heidelberg (2005)
11. Lindemann, U.: Methodische Entwicklung technischer Produkte. In: Methoden flexibel und situationsgerecht anwenden. bearb. Aufl, vol. 2. Springer, Berlin (2007)
12. Müller, J.P.: The Design of Intelligent Agents. LNCS, vol. 1177. Springer, Heidelberg (1996)
13. Smith, R.G.: Frameworks for Cooperation in Distributed Problem Solving. IEEE Transactions on Systems, Man, and Cybernetic 11, 61–70 (1981)
14. Stäber: Service layer components for decentralized applications. Dissertation, TU Clausthal (2008)
15. Miller, J., Mukerji, J.: MDA Guide Version 1.0.1 OMG (2003), http://www.omg.org/cgi-bin/doc?omg/03-06-01
16. Roser: Designing and Enacting Cross-Organizational Business Processes, Dissertation, University of Augsburg (2008)
17. Erl, T.: Service-oriented architecture. Concepts, technology, and design. 5th print. Prentice-Hall, Upper Saddle River (2006)
18. QuaP2P: Reports of the QuaP2P research group established by the German Research Society DFG for the "Improvement of the Quality of Peer-to-Peer Systems by Systematically Researching Quality Features and Their Interdependencies" (FOR 733) (2009), http://www.quap2p.tu-darmstadt.de/

The Value of IT-Enabled Business Process Standardization from the Real Options Perspective

Qizhi Dai, Robert J. Kauffman, and Bin Wang

Drexel University, Arizona State University, University of Texas Pan America
qd24@drexel.edu, rkauffman@asu.edu, binwang@utpa.edu

Abstract. IT-enabled business processes support firm agility, and business process standardization has become an essential part of IT architecture. Business process standardization value partly comes from the real options such projects enable. Drawing from research on real options and IT value, we propose that business process standardization initiatives create real options. We further propose that the value of such IT-enabled real options increases with market volatility, and differs between primary and support business processes. We collected data from the Lexis-Nexis, Compustat and CRSP databases to explore some of these issues. We offer a number of empirical findings: (1) IT-enabled business process standardization enhances firm growth potential; (2) the option value of such initiatives is higher when market volatility is higher; and (3) primary business process standardization projects yield greater option value.

Keywords: Business processes, IT value, real options, standardization, valuation, volatility.

1 Introduction

Information technology (IT) enables businesses to cut costs, improve productivity, and supports competitive advantage through improving or transforming business processes. However, the high risk and failure rate associated with IT projects, together with the downturn of the economy since 2000, resulted in increasing pressure on firms relative to IT investment decisions. So investors cautiously interpret signals about firms' strategic investments in IT. As business processes are one basic unit for implementing IT, the value of IT–enabled business process improvement has become an important topic for information systems (IS) research [12]. However, to date, no research has examined how IT value develops from the standardization of different types of business processes. We fill this gap by examining the business value of IT-enabled business process standardization initiatives through the lens of real options. We ask: Do such investments present firms with real options? How does *real options theory* inform us on the business value of IT projects that standardize business processes? We focus on the main elements of our theoretical perspective here, and offer a brief overview of our empirical results.

R. Sharman, T.S. Raghu, and H.R. Rao (Eds.): WEB 2009, LNBIP 52, pp. 160–165, 2010.

2 Relevant Literature in IT Value Research

Researchers have examined the business value of IT at multiple levels. At the firm level, researchers have used large samples of firm-level IT capital investment and productivity data shows that IT improves firm productivity, firm valuation, and consumer welfare. Internal organizational resources such as technology readiness, financial resources, and technological capabilities affect the payoffs associated with IT investments [13]. IT investments have been shown to improve business processes and firm capabilities. Firms also can obtain higher returns on their investments when they transform business processes while implementing IT. The payoff of IT investments depends on the type of processes affected and related organizational resources. IT investments that improve primary business processes lead to higher and quicker payoffs compared with IT investments in support business processes [7].

Another stream in IT value research is the impact of IT investments on a firm's market valuation such as abnormal stock returns and Tobin's *q*. Investors react positively to investment announcements in IT [4], IT infrastructure [2], and innovative or transformational IT [3], while the results are mixed for e-commerce initiatives [6]. Factors such as uncertainty, firm diversification and growth prospects, the strategic role of IT, and alignment between IT and industry innovativeness affect the abnormal returns associated with IT investment announcements.

Investments in IT also can be viewed as *operating options*, wherein a firm acquires the right but not the obligation to subsequently invest in related projects. The cost associated with the initial IT investment (e.g., a pilot test or the first phase of a multi-stage IT project) is the price of the option. By paying this price, a firm acquires flexibility to carry out follow-on projects if the first phase is successful, or to cancel or defer additional investments otherwise. This flexibility is valuable when there is a high degree of uncertainty related to the IT, firm, competition or the marketplace [1]. Because of the complexity and high failure rate of IT projects, uncertainty is always high, although it typically gets worked out over time. Researchers have used options thinking to analyze IT investment decisions, especially investments in infrastructure. Another issue that is often studied is the relationship between IT project risks and the option value of IT investments. The option value of IT platform investments is argued to be affected by *technology strategy, organizational learning, innovation bandwagons,* and *technology adaptation* [5]. Uncertainty in the costs and payoffs of an IT project are also incorporated into decision-making on IT investments [11].

3 The Business Value of Business Process Standardization

The integration of IT and business processes has been a key issue for senior managers who wish to achieve successful implementation of IT. One approach to IT-enabled business process change is to adopt standardized procedures for the execution of business functions. Business processes can be standardized in a firm so the same function is performed the same way across different units and locations. Process standards can be based on external standards or defined by the firm. An example is standards for procurement processes to interact with suppliers using XML.

IT-enabled business processes offer real options that enable organizational agility by increasing firms' sensing and responding ability [10]. With standardized business processes, firms can reduce the effort to monitor and collect information on the performance of the business function, because similar tasks will be carried out in the same manner and data will be processed in the same way. They can discover differences in daily operations of the processes and functions in a timely manner, enhancing the firm's ability to sense changes in its internal operations and external environment. They can also respond to changes swiftly because formulating and implementing strategies should take less time with standardized business processes that facilitate smooth communications and coordination.

IT platforms also offer future growth opportunities – *growth options* – that allow firms to build additional applications or expand their businesses when such needs arise and the environment is favorable. In particular, standardizing business processes with IT is an effort that involves constructing a technology platform as part of the organizational IT architecture. This will set the firm up for effective growth in the future, and make the firm more adaptable to changes. Any effort in IT standardization is conducive to better integration of applications and data, which can lead to better process integration and higher firm performance down the road [9]. So, we assert:

- **Hypothesis 1 (The Real Option Hypothesis).** *IT projects involving business process standardization bear real options.*

The option value of such initiatives is affected by the benefits of potential future opportunities and market volatility. Option value increases with *market volatility* because the option holder has the flexibility and the capability to exploit future opportunities that generate additional business value, while avoiding unfavorable investments. When business processes are standardized, firms gain the flexibility to modify or use related IT applications and business processes that they have already established, if they are needed in the future. Systems flexibility includes capabilities in upgrading, expanding and developing new applications when the benefits become available. Such flexibility makes it more efficient to reuse existing business processes, or to simply wait and do nothing more – or even abandon the project. This is the essence of considering the impacts of environmental volatility. So we assert:

- **Hypothesis 2 (The Market Volatility Hypothesis).** *When market volatility is higher, IT projects that involve business process standardization generate higher business value for the firm.*

In addition to market volatility, the benefits of IT initiatives are influenced by the characteristics of the business process. For example, Tallon et al. [12] point out that IT projects vary in their business process emphases and hence their impacts on firm value. In the strategy literature, business processes are categorized into two types: primary and support. *Primary business processes* are made up of value activities that directly transform inputs into final products, or logistics related to shipping in raw materials and delivering the final products to customers. *Support business processes* support primary processes and their influence on core business operations is indirect. Standardizing primary business processes exerts a direct impact on how the firm delivers value or positions itself in the market by changing the performance of its major value activities. Standardizing support business processes will have a less direct impact, and should result in leverage for tactical improvements, not strategic ones. Moreover, as a platform for future projects, standardized primary business processes will enable new business initiatives related to the organization's core value activities that will have higher strategic importance. From the real options perspective, an IT project will have a higher option value when it can create more competitive or strategic advantages. So standardization of primary business processes bears a higher option value than standardization of support business processes. This leads us to state:

- **Hypothesis 3 (The Primary Business Process Standardization Hypothesis)** *IT projects that involve primary business process standardization will generate higher business value than those for support business process standardization.*

4 Empirical Study and Primary Findings

We retrieved Lexis-Nexis announcements on business process standardization projects from 1996 to 2005 – altogether 243 announcements. Two authors encoded the two types of business processes standardizations: *primary* and *support*. Our inter-rater reliability ratio was 91%, and we resolved differences through discussion. We next compiled a group of firms that did not make announcements on business process standardization projects during our sampling period. For each firm that announced a standardization project in our sample, we selected one firm in the same industry that owned total assets in the range of 70% to 130% of total assets of the original firm in the year when the announcement was made. We then collected firm annual performance data from the Compustat and CRSP databases. After removing observations with missing data, we identified 98 sample observations and 59 comparison firms.

We computed Tobin's q and ROA as measures for firm financial performance to capture the business value of IT-enabled business process standardization. We used weighted least squares regression to test our hypotheses. The dependent variables are *Tobin's q* and *ROA*. The independent variables are the market volatility, primary business process (1 if the project involved primary business process standardization, 0 otherwise), support business process (1 if the project involved support business process standardization, 0 otherwise). The control variables are firm size measured by ln(total assets), and an industry dummy (1 if the firm is in IT industry, 0 otherwise). We also included two interaction terms: volatility × primary business process, and volatility × support business process. This model was estimated with data in the years when announcements were made and again with data in the second years after the announcements.

Our estimation results show that firms with primary business process standardization initiatives had comparable *Tobin's q* and *ROA* estimates in the year of the announcement. Two years later, the impact became positive. Firms with support business process standardization initiatives had lower values for *Tobin's q* and *ROA* than the comparison firms in the year when they announced their projects. Two years later, those firms' performance approximated the comparison group. These results offer support for the Real Options Hypothesis (H1).

Next, we used changes in *Tobin's q* and *ROA* in two years after announcements as dependent variables to estimate the effects of market volatility and business process types. The estimation results show that the interaction term between volatility and primary business process has significant positive effects on changes in *Tobin's q*, indicating that, when market volatility rises, firm performance increases also as a result of primary business process standardization. This supports the Market Volatility Hypothesis (H2). When it comes to the Primary Business Process Standardization

Hypothesis (H3), a significant positive coefficient on *PrimaryProcess* indicates that firms with primary business process standardization projects achieved higher changes in *Tobin's q* values than those with support business process standardization projects in two years. Thus the results appear to support H3 as well.

5 Conclusion

In this study, we applied real options theory to examining the value of IT-enabled business process standardization initiatives. We argued that such initiatives create real options by offering flexibility and agility in responding to changes in the future. We also proposed that the option value of IT-enabled business process standardization is higher when the market volatility is higher, and when primary business processes are standardized.

This research provides some useful implications for IS research. First, it contributes to the literature on IT value, particularly the research stream on real option-based valuation. Our work presents an empirical study on IT value that is based on option theory. The findings support arguments for the impacts of market volatility, based on rigorous modeling and estimation work. Second, this research contributes to the literature on business process management. IT-enabled business process redesign has been of interest to interdisciplinary researchers in IS, operations, supply chain management and accounting since the middle of 1990s due to its profound impacts on business performance. More recently, business process redesign has evolved into business process management, and standardized business processes have become an essential part of the IT practices within the modern firm. Research on the value of business process management mostly has used case study methods though. Our work with empirical data complements this existing body of knowledge. More importantly, we have demonstrated empirical evidence that business process standardization creates real options, which are convertible to business value when managers take future actions that unlock their potential for additional firm growth.

References

1. Benaroch, M.: Managing IT Investment Risk: A Real Options Perspective. J. Mgmt. Info. Sys. 19(2), 43–84 (2002)
2. Chatterjee, D., Pacini, C., Sambamurthy, V.: The Shareholder Wealth and Trading Volume Effects of IT Infrastructure Investments. J. Mgmt. Info. Sys. 19(2), 7–42 (2002)
3. Dehning, B., Richardson, V.J., Zmud, R.W.: The Value Relevance of Announcements of Transformational IT Investments. MIS Qtrly. 27(4), 637–656 (2003)
4. Dos Santos, B.L., Peffers, K., Mauer, D.C.: The Impact of IT Investment Announcements on the Market Value of the Firm. Info. Sys. Res. 4(1), 1–23 (1993)
5. Fichman, R.G.: Real Options and IT Platform Adoption: Implications for Theory and Practice. Info. Sys. Res. 15(2), 132–154 (2004)
6. Im, K.S., Dow, K.E., Grover, V.: A Reexamination of IT Investment and the Market Value of the Firm: An Event Study Methodology. Info. Sys. Res. 12(1), 103–117 (2001)
7. Menon, N.M., Yaylacicegi, U., Cezar, A.: Differential Effects of the Two Types of Information Systems: A Hospital-Based Study. J. Mgmt. Info. Sys. 26(1), 297–316 (2009)

8. Oh, W., Pinsonneault, A.: On the Assessment of the Strategic Value of IT: Conceptual and Analytical Approaches. MIS Qtrly. 31(2), 239–265 (2007)
9. Rai, A., Patnayakuni, R., Seth, N.: Firm Performance Impacts of Digitally Enabled Supply Chain Integration Capabilities. MIS Qtrly. 30(2), 225–246 (2006)
10. Sambamurthy, V., Bharadwaj, A., Grover, V.: Shaping Agility through Digital Options: Reconceptualizing the Role of IT in Contemporary Firms. MIS Qtrly. 27(2), 237–263 (2003)
11. Schwartz, E.S., Zozaya-Gorostiza, C.: Investment under Uncertainty in IT: Acquisition and Development Projects. Mgmt. Sci. 49(1), 57–70 (2003)
12. Tallon, P.P., Kraemer, K.L., Gurbaxani, V.: Executives' Perceptions of the Business Value of IT: A Process-Oriented Approach. J. Mgmt. Info. Sys. 16(4), 145–173 (2000)
13. Zhu, K.: The Complementarity of IT Infrastructure E-Commerce Capability: A Resource-Based Assessment of Their Business Value. J. Mgmt. Info. Sys. 21(1), 167–202 (2004)

Privacy and E-Authentication: The Dangers of Self-disclosure in Social Networks

Divakaran Liginlal[1] and Lara Khansa[2]

[1] Carnegie Mellon University at Qatar, Information Systems Program, PO Box 24866 Doha, Qatar
[2] Virginia Polytechnic and State University, Pamplin College of Business, 2062 Pamplin Hall (0235), Blacksburg, VA 24060, USA
liginlal@cmu.edu, larak@vt.edu

Abstract. We propose a Bayesian model of privacy in e-authentication and develop associated entropy-based metrics. A major contribution of this work is the application of weighted entropy to characterize the user's privacy preferences. Further, we model the effects of side information on privacy and relate it to self-disclosure on Internet web sites and social networks. Specifically, our empirical study of Internet users' information disclosure habits within social networks along with the theoretical results provide insights into building a regulatory framework to address privacy concerns in e-authentication.

Keywords: Privacy metrics, authentication, Bayesian, weighted entropy, social network.

1 Introduction

The act of establishing confidence in the claimed identity of a user, device, or another entity in an information or communication system is called authentication [3]. Knowledge-based authentication (KBA) is an economic method of authenticating users for on-line transactions that occur on an infrequent basis, with the potential of providing reasonably secure authentication [13, 17]. KBA consists of matching one or more pieces of information (also called factoids) provided by an individual (claimant) against information sources associated with the claimant for the purpose of verifying his/her identity. The participants of a KBA scheme include individuals or other organizations asserting identity, relying parties, and verifiers [3]. Relying parties make use of an identity credential or assertion of identity to decide what actions need to be taken in a given application context. Often they use verifiers or trusted verification services to gain confidence in the identity assertion.

The term KBA has conventionally been used [13] in the context of e-government to encompass those systems relying on proprietary sources of claimant information that do not require prior registration by the user. However, systems that use cognitive passwords [12], otherwise known as recognition-oriented KBA [7], also fall under the umbrella of KBA. With the advent of Federal Financial Institutions Examination Counsel's (FFIEC) regulations mandating strong authentication for financial transactions,

R. Sharman, T.S. Raghu, and H.R. Rao (Eds.): WEB 2009, LNBIP 52, pp. 166–176, 2010.

e-banking systems have widely incorporated KBA as a secondary authentication method, for applications such as password resets. KBA systems rely on an effective matching of a claimant's real time responses to challenge questions against the identity attribute values supplied by trusted sources. A suitable matching function would need to take into consideration the effect of an attacker correctly guessing a response (guessability metric) and the ability of a genuine user to recall and enter the correct response (memorability). Chen and Liginlal [5] provide a comprehensive literature review of KBA and a discussion of KBA metrics and model selection from a security perspective. Our objective in this paper is to address the issue of privacy in KBA.

Information privacy is defined by Westin [26] as "the ability of individuals, groups, or institutions to determine for themselves when, how, and to what extent information about them is communicated and the subsequent uses of such information." Privacy considerations in authentication have attracted researchers' attention only recently [24]. In the context of authentication, three types of privacy issues arise [20]: (1) Decisional privacy aims to prevent interference with decisions about self and family; (2) Information privacy is the individual's right to control access to and dissemination of personal information; and (3) Communication privacy deals with the confidentiality of the individual's communications. Often communication privacy is bundled with information privacy.

2 A Bayesian View of Privacy in E-Authentication

A recent definition of KBA metrics [7] follows a frequentist approach to estimating the guessability of a set of statistically independent factoids. A Bayesian approach to modeling KBA, on the other hand, confers the ability to incorporate subjective probabilities or beliefs about attacker strategies. Further, the use of conditional probabilities helps to model parameters such as guessability and memorability of factoids, while also considering factoid dependencies.

Fig. 1 shows a Bayesian network [21] model of KBA (BN-KBA). BN-KBA is a directed acyclic graph representing a probabilistic model, with each node representing a random variable that can take on two or more possible values. The arrows indicate the existence of direct effects between linked variables. The associated conditional probabilities embody the strength of these influences. The hypothesis variable 'Authentication' assumes a state from {true, false} and the evidence variables $\{e_1, e_2, \ldots, e_7\}$ take states from {correct, wrong}. The values of the evidence variable correspond to whether or not factoid values are entered correctly. Associated with each node is a probability distribution to be specified in advance. The conditional probabilities $P(e_i = \text{correct} \mid \text{Authentication} = \text{true})$ represent the likelihood of a genuine user recalling and entering the evidence correctly, or in other words the memorability associated with the factoid. Similarly, $P(e_i = \text{correct} \mid \text{Authentication} = \text{false})$ represents the likelihood of an imposter guessing the value of the evidence correctly or, in other words, the guessability of the associated factoid. The nodes representing external knowledge sources such as the Social Security Administration (SSA), the Credit Bureaus (CB), and the Internal Revenue Service (IRS) take the states {trusted, untrusted} with associated probabilities denoting their trustworthiness.

In Fig. 1, we also depict the actual factoid variables taking on states corresponding to all possible values for a factoid in a specific KBA domain. We treat these factoid variables as hidden nodes, which are actually needed only for parameter estimation and factoid selection. Once we have selected a set of factoids, we can absorb the effect of the states of the knowledge sources and the factoid variables and perform the authentication step with only the evidence and hypothesis variables. The major strength of BN-KBA is that probabilistic inference can be made directly from the conditional probabilities. Thus, the posterior P(Authentication = true | e), where e is the set of all evidence variables, computed by applying Bayes' rule, determines the level of assurance one may gain from the authentication process. We refer the reader to [5] for details about parameter estimation and factoid selection for BN-KBA.

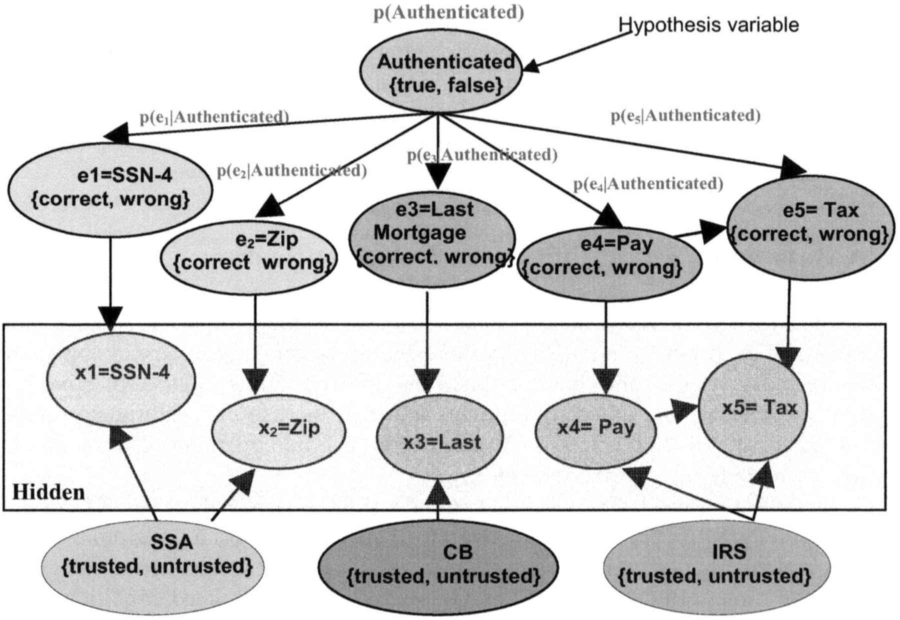

Fig. 1. A model of BN-KBA depicting the factoid variables and knowledge sources

2.1 Entropy Reduction in BN-KBA

The privacy characteristic of KBA is better understood by examining the nature of data embedded in the factoids. The factoids may be classified based on whether they are static or dynamic, and personal or not personal. Examples of static factoids are one's mother's maiden name and date of birth. Dynamic factoids, such as credit card balances, last paycheck amount, and last mortgage paid, exhibit the most dependencies. Another classification of factoids is based on whether they are personal or not personal. Personal factoids, such as favorite color or movie, are in general unique to a person. Examples of nonpersonal factoids are cell phone number and home address. For e-government applications, proprietary databases such as the social security administration (SSA), credit bureau (CB), and the internal revenue service (IRS) serve as reference sources for verifying the response to user challenges. In general, data from such sources are either static or dynamic. One may also add data sourced directly from individuals, also referred to as personal entropy [10]. These require the user's prior registration with either the relying party or a verifier.

To better understand the privacy implications of KBA, one needs to also dissect the attacker strategies (See [3] for details). We consider, for the purpose of our discussion, a rational attacker, who knows all probable factoid values involved in a KBA domain deduced from public information about databases or through insider information or other attacks. The attacker may try out each value with equal probability, or the attacker knows the probability distribution of the factoid values and exploits that knowledge in the attack, or the attacker tries out the most probable values. If an attack is successful, the recovery from the disclosure of static information, whether personal or not personal, is often very hard to achieve. Also, if an imposter successfully authenticates as a genuine user, this would lead to access to transaction logs and other profile information of the user and ultimately identity theft.

Bayesian conceptualization of privacy. We consider an n-factoid vector **x**. Each univariate x_i in **x** follows a discrete probability distribution $p(x_i)$. Privacy metrics can be developed by considering the distribution of values in x_i, the attacker strategy, i.e., the information at the attacker's disposal, and the disutility [23] for the owner of the identity (id) for each x_i. Our assumption is that disutility can help factor in a user's assessment of the likelihood of a privacy breach that will be damaging to an individual in one form or another, i.e., reputation, financial, social, and legal.

Information entropy is a measure of the uncertainty associated with a random variable. The Bayesian Network in Fig. 1 may be considered as an information channel. When the factoid variables, denoted by the nodes marked x_1 to x_5, are instantiated with their corresponding values, information flows to remove the uncertainty associated with the hypothesis variable. This entropy reduction forms the basis for an authentication decision.

2.2 Privacy Metric for KBA

For our analysis, we adopt Shannon entropy that measures the average information content in a random variable [8].

Definition 1. Given a random variable x with an associated probability distribution $\{p_j\}_{j=1,\ldots,k}$ satisfying $p_j \geq 0_{j=1,\ldots,k}$ and $\sum p_j = 1$, Shannon entropy (or ordinary information entropy), is defined by,

$$H(x) = -c\sum_{x} p(x)\log[p(x)] \,, \quad (1)$$

where c is a positive constant, usually set equal to unity. The result is expressed in bits if the logarithm is to the base 2, and the notation H(p) is often used in place of H(x).

The joint entropy H(x, y) of a pair of discrete random variables with joint distribution p(x,y) is defined as,

$$H(x,y) = -\sum_{x}\sum_{y} p(x,y)\log p(x,y) \ , \tag{2}$$

Let $(x_1,x_2, \ldots, x_n)$ be drawn according to $p(x_1,x_2, \ldots, x_n)$. The Shannon entropy $H(x_1,x_2, \ldots, x_n)$ is defined as the sum of the individual Shannon entropies, if the x_i's are statistically independent. Otherwise, by applying the chain rule for entropy, one may express the joint entropy as a sum of the conditional entropies, i.e.,

$$H(x_1, x_2, \ldots, x_n) = \sum_{i=1}^{n} H(x_i \mid x_{i-1}, \ldots, x_1) \ , \tag{3}$$

This leads to the following definitions of KBA privacy metrics $£_{KBA}$ at the domain level and $£_{KBA,\, id}$ at the identity level.

Definition 2 (Domain-level KBA privacy). In order to define domain-level KBA privacy ($£_{KBA}$), we consider the average amount of private information available about KBA users with respect to a selected set of factoids. We quantify $£_{KBA}$ by the Shannon entropy, of the selected n-factoid vector $\mathbf{x} = \{x_1 \ldots x_n\}$, i.e.,

$$£_{KBA} = H(p_x) \ , \tag{4}$$

If the factoids are independent, $£_{KBA}$ is the sum of the individual entropies of the factoids in **x**. It is important to note that dependencies only reduce the uncertainty associated with a factoid, thus leading to the notion of maximal privacy.

Given that privacy is a term more often associated with an individual's control over his/her personal information, it will be more appropriate to also define KBA privacy at the identity level. Each individual may have preferences about what factoids to be used in an authentication session, partly based on an estimate of the likelihood of a privacy breach. The concept of weighted Shannon entropy [1] provides a way of incorporating the disutilities, associated with user preferences.

Definition 3. Given a disutility vector $\{d_j\}_{j = 1, \ldots, k}$ satisfying $\{d_j \geq 0\}_{j = 1, \ldots, k}$ associated with each event indexed by j in the discrete probability distribution p_j, the weighted Shannon entropy [11] is defined by,

$$Hw(x) = -c\sum_{x} d_j p(x)\log[p(x)] \ , \tag{5}$$

Weighted entropy has been applied to a variety of contexts, including pattern recognition and econometric modeling [16]. For a factoid x_i, assume the jth value is associated with an individual id. Let id assign a disutility d_j to the factoid. Then the weighted information associated with the factoid instance j is $I_d(d_j, p_{xij}) = -kw_j \log p_{xij}$ [1]. This weighted information measure also helps quantify the notion of personal entropy associated with an individual's factoid.

Consider a disutility vector $d_j = \{d_{1j} \ldots d_{nj}\}$, $\{d_{ij} \geq 0\}_{j=1 \ldots n}$ associated with a factoid vector $x = \{x_1 \ldots x_n\}$ for an individual user identified by id. Let $\chi_j = \{ \chi_{1j}, \ldots, \chi_{nj}\}$ represent the instance level values for id.

Definition 4 (Identity-level KBA privacy). In order to define identity-level KBA privacy ($£_{KBA,id}$), we consider the amount of private information available about a specific KBA user denoted by id, with respect to a selected set of factoids. $£_{KBA,id}$ under factoid independence (maximal privacy) can be quantified as the sum of the weighted information of the factoid instances as follows,

$$£_{KBA,id} = \sum_i £_{i,id} = -k \sum_i d_{ij} \log[p(x_i = \chi_{ij})] \,, \tag{6}$$

Although we implicitly assume that the factoids are independent, the actual amount of privacy reduction due to the dependencies is determined by the mutual information across all the factoids.

We now show that the definition of KBA domain-level privacy is meaningful to our discussion of privacy and captures in essence the privacy expectation of KBA users considered as a whole.

Theorem 1. If users' privacy preferences are invariant across all identities and neutral across all factoids, $£_{KBA}$ is upper bounded by the expected value of $£_{KBA,\,id}$, aggregated over all identities.

Proof. If users' privacy preferences are invariant across all identities, their disutility vectors are the same, given a set of factoids. In addition, if users are neutral in their privacy preferences across all selected factoids, the disutility vector can be represented as di = {c, …, c}, where $c \geq 0$ is a constant. Under this condition, the expected value becomes,

$$\begin{aligned} E_{id}(£_{KBA,id}) &= E_{id}\left(\sum_i £_{i,id}\right) = -k_1 \sum_i \sum_j p(x_i = \chi_{ij}) \log[p(x_i = \chi_{ij})] \\ &= -k_1 \sum_i H(p(x_i)) = -k_1 \sum_i p(x_i) \log(p(x_i)) \end{aligned} \,, \tag{7}$$

where $k_1 = kc$. In the definition of entropy it is customary to set the scaling value $k_1 = 1$. Thus, $£_{KBA} = H(p_x) \leq \sum_i H(p(x_i)) = -k_1 \sum_i p(x_i) \log(p(x_i)) = E_{id}(£_{KBA,id})$. This concludes the proof.

3 Side Information and Its Influence on Privacy

The term side information is used in a variety of contexts such as in communication systems [22], financial markets [4, 15], and cryptography [2] to mean auxiliary information that is correlated to a significant variable of interest in a stochastic process.

3.1 Modeling Side Information in KBA

In the case of KBA, strategic knowledge about a KBA domain, or about specific identities gleaned from various sources, constitutes information that a potential adversary may exploit. Electronic sources of side information include home pages, web search engines, email archives, social networking sites, and people search provider services. Inference attacks on identities, based on profile information publicly available about individuals, constitute a rich source of data given the proliferation of personal home pages and social networking sites [6, 14]. For the following discussion, we assume that side information is modeled as a random variable u_i correlated with a factoid x_i.

Definition 5. The expected privacy leak due to side information is equal to the amount of mutual information I(xi,ui) [8] in xi and ui.

Theorem 2. Side information reduces domain-level KBA privacy.

Proof. The proof follows from the definition of mutual information $I(x_i,u_i) = H(x_i) - H(x_i|u_i) \geq 0$.

Theorem 3. KBA privacy reduction in a factoid x_i due to side information u_i is upper bounded by $H(u_i)$.

Proof. The proof follows from a basic property of mutual information, i.e., $I(x_i,u_i) \leq H(u_i)$.

3.2 The Link to Information Disclosure

Information disclosure on a variety of Internet sites inflates the dangers of reduced privacy (and security) for knowledge-based authentication. Weighted entropy metrics allow the KBA designer to incorporate a user's preferences based on his/her estimates of the likelihood of a privacy breach at design time. The definition of these measures does not take into account the fact that a user is often unaware of auxiliary information that exists about a particular factoid due to self-disclosure or disclosure by others both online and in other social contexts. The uncertainty representing such auxiliary information is factored into the attacker strategies in the form of the guessability metric, which has relevance during a KBA challenge-response session. On the other hand, for factoid selection it will be useful to study online sources of side information that may be exploited to initiate identity-level attacks. Common examples are personal home pages, blogs, chat rooms, and social networks.

One may come up with three approaches to filtering identity-related information on the web. The first approach is one in which a user agent searches the web to find matching profiles and checks whether the selected factoids have already been disclosed. Involving the user interactively helps enhance the accuracy of the results. Such filtering methods could plausibly use ontology-based search tools such as Google's APIs. The second approach is targeted at social networks to harvest user profiles based on community interests and to infer side information about users. Chen and Liginlal [6] apply state-of-the-art statistical machine learning techniques to fit a classification model to textual data collected from MySpace and use the learned classifier to predict critical personal attributes, e.g., hobbies, salary, and occupation, of previously unseen user examples.

In this paper, we discuss an approach based on a user agent deployed to search small worlds [19] formed in popular social networks around communities conforming to the specialized interests of a KBA user. We present results from our small world experiments on MySpace and Friendster to study the dangers of self-disclosure and ways of estimating the prior probabilities associated with side information.

3.3 The Dangers of Self Disclosure

Watts et al. [25] present a model that offers an explanation of social network searchability in terms of recognizable personal identities, i.e., sets of characteristics measured along a number of social dimensions. They demonstrate that their model can account for Milgram's [19] experimental findings that short paths of average size 6 exist between individuals in a large social network and that ordinary people are able to find these short paths.

We used the following methodology to build small worlds within a social network.

1. Repeat steps (i) through (iv) N times
   - (i) Randomly (or through profile matching) select a user from the network, such that the selected user has about 150 immediate friends and has not been picked in an earlier step. The number 150 conforms to the Dunbar number which is a theorized cognitive limit to the number of individuals, with whom any one person can maintain stable social relationships [9]. Save the profile of the selected user.
   - (ii) Randomly select the user's network of immediate friends from individuals whose settings are not private, who have a significant number (10% of the Dunbar number) of immediate friends, and who were not chosen in an earlier step. Save the profile of the selected friends.
   - (iii) Repeat (recursively) step ii up to five hops for each selected friend, i.e. six interconnected friends from the root user in step i. This means that if the network cannot go to 6 levels we abandon our attempt and repeat the entire sequence i-iii.
   - (iv) Parse the saved profiles of users constructed in steps i-iii. Create frequency counts corresponding to information disclosure trends for each attribute of interest to us from a KBA perspective.
2. Average the frequency counts of each attribute over all small worlds.
3. Repeat the entire experiment in steps 1 and 2, choosing new seeds for the random number generator used for sampling. Accumulate the information disclosure statistics and average over all experiments.

3.4 Results of Empirical Study

Table 1 shows the results of our experiments. We built in each experiment an average of 22 small worlds with N=100. The average number of users sampled in each experiment was 10,112 for MySpace and 9,871 for Friendster, out of which we found that nearly 31% users for MySpace and 29% users for Friendster had either restricted privacy settings or number of friends not displayed. The results from the publicly searchable space clearly point to the dangers of information revelation within social networks.

First, we test the hypothesis that self disclosure habits of individuals in small worlds are invariant across the two social networks. We instrumentalize the test by

Table 1. Average frequency count of factoids disclosed in small worlds in MySpace and Friendster

Factoid	MySpace Frequency Count %	Friendster Frequency Count %
Favorite Music	50.04	47.24
Favorite Movie	43.31	44.78
Favorite TV Show	38.73	40.53
Favorite Book	36.54	34.14
Favorite Sport	0.13	0.24
Favorite Color	0.41	0.72
Street grown up	0.00	0.01
Pet's name	0.01	0.03
Model of first car	0.04	0.02
Zipcode	0.00	0.01
High School Mascot	0.00	0.00

comparing the frequency count of factoid values disclosed in the two networks under consideration. The null hypothesis that the difference across both networks is insignificant could not be rejected (t-value = 0.014; p-value > 0.1).

The four attributes that are directly searchable are favorite music, favorite movie, favorite TV show, and favorite book. A large percentage of users revealed this information. Confidence in the trustworthiness of this information is high because we ensured in our sampling that each user had a significant number of friends in their immediate network and they were part of a small world that emanated from a user with at least 150 friends and extended five hops in diameter. We parsed the other fields such as "Interests" and "About Me" searching for information related to favorite sport, favorite color, street in which a user grew up, pet's name, model of first car, zipcode, and high school mascot. The results were not as significant as in the case of the directly searchable attributes. This could be partially attributed to the limitations of our search method although, we attempted to manually cross-validate our findings while using variations in the search tokens used. Regardless, the findings show that favorite sport, favorite color, pet's name, and model of first car were also disclosed by a small percentage of users.

3.5 Implications of the Study

The theoretical and empirical results from this research provide several useful guidelines for building a regulatory framework encompassing the three important stakeholders in an authentication process.

From the perspective of the relying party there is an implicit assumption in authentication that 'user consent' has been given for acquisition and storage of verifying data and its 'fair' usage. This assumption is fraught with dangers. Regulations mandating strong authentication need to specifically ensure that 'user consent' for acquiring and using personal data for the purposes of authentication doesn't necessarily entail loss of control by the user, resulting in privacy breaches with lifelong implications.

Regulations need to emphasize the need for proactive risk assessment in the context of authentication, selection of a risk minimization method possibly limiting the amount of personal information the user is required to provide, and raising the level of awareness for administrators of authentication systems in the privacy implications. Verifiers and third party credential services need to be strictly regulated in terms of the safeguards for database protection. There is a need for federal privacy laws not only to complement state laws but also to provide stiffer sanctions for breach. The individual's control must necessarily extend to these services who may have acquired personal data from multiple sources, often without the knowledge of the owner. The individual must also have a say in what attributes can be provided to verifiers and must be able to revoke or withdraw the data. It is obvious that this is very challenging to implement practically.

Most KBA implementations require users to enter their personal information at registration time. There must, thus, be sufficient scrutiny in the manner in which factoids are acquired from personal entropy sources. Such acquisition must be orchestrated through a trusted and secure process totally within the control of the individual. In fact, instead of actual factoid data, weak keys generated from such data should be acquired and only such keys ought to be used in a challenge-response authentication [18]. Enhancing user awareness through user education must necessarily be a role played by relying parties and verifiers. While the concern of the KBA designer is to gain high levels of assurance in authentication, the user must be empowered to safeguard as well as track the dissemination of his/her private information. The KBA system may collude with the user to deploy privacy agents routinely on the web to mine websites and social networks and glean information about possible privacy breaches. Such agents must be deployed under user control so that the user has the option to trust the agent with sensitive personal information for the purpose of profile matching.

4 Conclusion and Future Research

In this paper, we considered a Bayesian view of privacy in KBA whereby privacy is quantified in terms of the information required to remove uncertainty about the hypothesis variable relative to an authentication session. This provides the basis for a definition of domain-level and identity-level KBA privacy metrics relying on information-theoretical concepts. A major contribution of our research work is the application of weighted entropy concepts that allow the incorporation of personal privacy preferences of a KBA user into the factoid selection process. Finally, we reported the study of social networking sites to show how user profiling and collaborative filtering methods can be applied to study the impact of side information on identity-level KBA security and privacy.

The empirical study reported in the paper is only meant to provide evidence of the drawbacks of side information. The important question we investigated relates to how much people really value privacy over security. This is the fundamental theme of this paper tackled from a rather theoretical perspective. An empirical study designed to differentiate between perceived and actual disclosure behavior will be useful to understand the implications of user participation in online services on KBA security and privacy. The models and metrics discussed in the context of KBA can be extended easily to multifactor authentication. Since Shannon entropy only facilitates the study of average-case effects of side information, it will be interesting to pursue alternate entropy formulations of KBA privacy. Finally, defining a unified framework for usability, privacy, and security in KBA is an important extension of this research.

References

1. Belis, M., Guiasu, S.: Quantitative-Qualitative Measure of Information in Cybernetic Systems. IEEE Transactions on Information Theory 14, 593–594 (1968)
2. Bennett, C.H., Brassard, G., Crépeau, C., Maurer, U.M.: Generalized Privacy Amplification. IEEE Transactions on Information Theory 41, 1915–1923 (1995)
3. Burr, W.E., Dodson, D.F., Polk, W.T.: Electronic Authentication Guideline: Recommendations of the National Institute of Standards and Technology. NIST Special Publication 800-63 Version 1.0.2, National Institute of Standards and Technology, NIST (2006)
4. Caroline, H.: Comparison of Insiders' Optimal Strategies Depending on the Type of Side-Information. Stochastic Processes and their Applications 115, 1603–1627 (2005)
5. Chen, Y., Liginlal, D.: Bayesian Networks for Knowledge-Based Authentication. IEEE Transactions on Knowledge and Data Engineering 19, 695–710 (2007)
6. Chen, Y., Liginlal, D.: Information Disclosure on the Internet-A Machine Learning Perspective. Working Paper, University of Wisconsin-Madison (2008)
7. Chokhani, S.: Knowledge Based Authentication (KBA) Metrics. In: KBA Symposium-Knowledge Based Authentication: Is It Quantifiable?, Gaithersburg, MD (2004)
8. Cover, T., Thomas, J.: Elements of Information Theory. Wiley, Chichester (2006)
9. Dunbar, R.I.M.: Neocortex Size as a Constraint on Group Size in Primates. Journal of Human Evolution 20, 469–493 (1992)
10. Ellison, C., Hall, C., Milbert, R., Schneier, B.: Protecting Secret Keys with Personal Entropy. Future Generation Computer Systems 16, 311–318 (2000)
11. Guiasu, S.: Weighted Entropy. Reports on Mathematical Physics 2, 165–179 (1971)
12. Haga, W.J., Zviran, M.: Cognitive passwords: from theory to practice. Data Processing and Communications Security 3, 19–23 (1989)
13. Hastings, N.E., Dodson, D.F.: Quantifying Assurance of Knowledge Based Authentication. In: 3rd European Conference on Information Warfare and Security, ECIW 2004 (2004)
14. He, J., Chu, W.W., Liu, Z.: Inferring Privacy Information from Social Networks. In: Mehrotra, S., Zeng, D.D., Chen, H., Thuraisingham, B., Wang, F.-Y. (eds.) ISI 2006. LNCS, vol. 3975, pp. 154–165. Springer, Heidelberg (2006)
15. Hillairet, C.: Comparison of Insiders' Optimal Strategies Depending on the Type of Side-Information. Stochastic Processes and their Applications 114, 1603–1627 (2005)
16. Karmeshu, J.: Entropy Measures, Maximum Entropy Principle and Emerging Applications. Springer, Heidelberg (2003)
17. Lawler, B.: Models of Knowledge Based Authentication (KBA). In: KBA Symposium-Knowledge Based Authentication: Is It Quantifiable?, Gaithersburg, MD (2004)
18. Lowry, S.: Challenge & Response within E-Authentication Framework. In: KBA Symposium-Knowledge Based Authentication: Is It Quantifiable?, Gaithersburg, MD (2004)
19. Milgram, S.: The Small-World Problem. Psychology Today 1, 61–67 (1967)
20. Millett, L.I., Holden, H.S.: Authentication and its Privacy Effects. IEEE Internet Computing 6, 54–58 (2003)
21. Pearl, J.: Probabilistic Reasoning in Intelligence Systems. Morgan, San Maleo (1988)
22. Shannon, C.E.: Channels with Side Information at the Transmitter. IBM J. Res. Develop, 289–293 (1958)
23. Theil, H.: Disutility as a Probability. Management Science 20, 109–116 (1980)
24. US National Research Council. Who Goes There? Authentication through the Lens of Privacy. Nat'l Academy Press, Washington (2003)
25. Watts, D.J., Dodds, P.S., Newman, M.E.J.: Identity and Search in Social Networks. Science 296, 1302–1305 (2002)
26. Westin, A.: Privacy and Freedom. Atheneum, New York (1967)

An Exploration of the Search for Information Security

Jingguo Wang[1], Nan Xiao[2], and H.R. Rao[2]

[1] The University of Texas at Arlington
jwang@uta.edu
[2] University at Buffalo
{nanxiao,mgmtrao}@buffalo.edu

Abstract. People use search engines to seek information. This study investigates the motives that drive the search for information security knowledge via a search engine. We empirically examine the effects of network attacks and vulnerability disclosures on the frequency of search for information security knowledge. . We find that network attacks of current day and one day prior significantly impact the search, while vulnerability disclosure does not significantly affect the search.

Keywords: Information Security, Information Search Behavior, Network Attacks, Vulnerability Disclosures.

1 Introduction

Search engines have become the primary, powerful, and convenient tool for users to find relevant information from huge amounts of online information sources. Millions of individuals regularly use modern search engines for topics ranging from news to healthcare. More than 80% internet users use search engines as their starting point of web surfing [1].

The study empirically investigates the effects of network attacks and vulnerability disclosures on the frequency of search for information security knowledge. Online search for information security knowledge can be treated as a step users take towards the protection of their computer systems. Similar to the role information search plays in health care, search for information security knowledge can reduce users' anxiety, increase feelings of self-efficacy, and improve the effectiveness of protection [2].

2 Drivers of the Search for Information Security

2.1 Network Attacks

While computer technology and internet connections have fundamentally changed the way of life, various attacks over networks pose severe threats. A computer/network breach may cause serious losses, including loss of confidential data and system failure. Users' behavior of search for information security knowledge can be affected by network attacks directly or indirectly. Those users whose systems have been

R. Sharman, T.S. Raghu, and H.R. Rao (Eds.): WEB 2009, LNBIP 52, pp. 177–180, 2010.

infected by viruses or compromised by a hacker will have to take prompt actions to identify and diagnose problems, recover the system, and mitigate the damage.

Increased perceived risk or threat could trigger users' protection behaviors [3-5]. To avoid or minimize their losses, users will actively seek approaches to protect their systems when perceiving the immediate attack threats is high. Protecting the system from attack needs sufficient knowledge and proper tools; however, most individuals, including some professionals, lack such knowledge and technology solutions to protect them against these attacks [6]. They may rely on search engines to find related solutions or suggestions once faced with the attacks.

Therefore, we consider that when network attacks increase, in order to prevent the afflictions and reduce the damages associated with the attacks, users will be actively engaged in seeking information security related knowledge via search engines. Network attacks can be measured from two dimensions: intensity and prevalence. The intensity of network attacks refers to the average number of attacks arriving at a computer in a unit time. High-intense attacks increase the possibility of a system being breached. The prevalence of network attacks refers to the number of computer systems targeted by the attacks. Since some computers may not be properly protected, a more prevalent attack is more likely to affect a larger number of computer users.

2.2 Vulnerability Disclosures

A vulnerability is a technical flaw or weakness in the design, implementation, or operation and management that can be exploited to violate a system's security policies [7]. Most of vulnerabilities originate from software vendors' design flaws. The vulnerabilities pose potential risks to users, and such risks are realized when they are exploited by network attacks.

Vulnerability disclosures may have limited impacts on users' search for information security knowledge due to the following four reasons. First, the communication channel used by vulnerability disclosures limits the information dissemination to general public. While some websites send vulnerability information to users by emails, this service is usually limited to subscribers. Second, most of vulnerability announcements contain many technical terms. Hence, for ordinary users, it is not straightforward to know how these vulnerabilities could affect their systems. The lack of capability could reduce the motivation of search for information security knowledge[8]. Third, as suggested by protection motivation theory, response cost, which refers to any cost associated with taking protection actions, will reduce the possibility of response [9]. Fourth, Vulnerabilities, unlike network attacks, do not cause immediate damages until they are exploited. Consequently, users may be less motivated in seeking for information security knowledge when vulnerabilities are disclosed. As we can see, the effects of vulnerability disclosures are unclear on user search behaviors.

3 Data and Measurements

We collected data from three sources. First, we derive the frequency of search for information security knowledge using a search log from AOL Research [10]. The search log includes about 658,000 users over a three-month period from March 01 to May 31, 2006. We use keyword matching to identify the queries that were intended to seek for information security related topic.

Second, we collected the measurements for network attacks via DShield (www.DShield.org). DShield is a community-based collaborative firewall/intrusion detection log correlation system (see, e.g., wikipedia.org). We derived two measurements of network attacks, intensity and prevalence, based on the DShield reports on Daily Survival Time and those on Daily Data Volume (Submissions/Day) respectively. The measurement of network attacks is calculated based on daily reports of survival time for five different categories of ports: Windows specific ports (e.g. File sharing) (denoted as I_t-*WIN*, t=1,...92), Unix specific ports (e.g. dns, ssh) (I_t-*UNI*), ports which are used (and vulnerable) by applications on various operating systems (I_t-*APP*), ports used by P2P software(I_t-*P2P*), and ports that are commonly used by backdoors(I_t-*BCK*). Our second measurement, the prevalence of network attacks, was derived based on the reports of daily data volume (Submissions/Day). We used a normalized daily number of targets (i.e., daily number of targets divided by daily number of the reports) (denoted as P_t , t=1,...92) as our measurement of the prevalence of network attacks.

Third, we collected vulnerability disclosures from National Vulnerability Database (NVD) (see, http://nvd.nist.gov/). For each vulnerability, the database has the date when it was initially published and a CVSS (Common Vulnerability Scoring System, http://www.first.org/cvss/cvss-guide.html) base score ranging from 0 to 10. We counted the daily number of vulnerabilities in CVSS severity high (denoted as H_t), medium (M_t), low (L_t) respectively in order to examine the possible different impacts they might have.

4 Results and Conclusion

We conducted a dynamic regression analysis[11]. Our findings suggest that both intensity and prevalence of network attacks on current day and one day prior significantly positively impact the frequency of search for information security knowledge. Users actively acquire information security related knowledge when they are experiencing attacks. This finding is consistent with health care literature which finds that the spread of biological virus is correlated with the frequency of patients' search. This result reveals that people present similar behavior patterns in both physical and cyber world when they are facing threats.

We did not find significant relationship between vulnerability disclosures and search for information security knowledge. While vulnerability disclosures may accelerate patch release and make information security professionals take proactive protection actions, they do not lead common users to seek more information security knowledge. The limited reactions of common users to vulnerability disclosures can be due to different reasons, such as dissemination channel and the technical nature of the announcements. Further users may not perceive vulnerabilities as immediate threats as network attacks, and be less motivated to search [4].

Acknowledgments. The research of the third author is supported in part by NSF under grant 0916612 and by Sogang Business School's World Class University Project (R31-20002) funded by Korea Research Foundation.

References

1. Jansen, B.J.: The Comparative Effectiveness of Sponsored and Nonsponsored Links for Web E-commerce Queries. ACM Transactions on the Web 1(1), 3-es (2007)
2. Ybarra, M.L., Sumanb, M.: Help seeking behavior and the Internet: A national survey. International Journal of Medical Informatics 75(1), 29–41 (2006)
3. Kumar, N., Mohan, K., Holowczak, R.: Locking the door but leaving the computer vulnerable: Factors inhibiting home users' adoption of software firewalls. Decision Support Systems 46(1), 254–264 (2008)
4. Liang, H., Xue, Y.: Avoidance of Information Technology Threats: A Theoretical Perspective. MIS Quarterly 33(1), 71–90 (2009)
5. Ng, B.-Y., Kankanhalli, A., Xu, Y.C.: Studying users' computer security behavior: A health belief perspective. Decision Support Systems 46(4), 815–825 (2009)
6. Furnell, S.M., Jusoh, A., Katsabas, D.: The challenges of understanding and using security: A survey of end-users. Computers & Security 25(1), 27–35 (2006)
7. Png, I., Wang, C., Wang, Q.: The Deterrent and Displacement Effects of Information Security Enforcement: International Evidence. Journal of Management Information Systems 25(2), 125–144 (2008)
8. Rogers, R.W.: A protection motivation theory of fear appeals and attitude change. Journal of Psychology 91(1), 93–114 (1975)
9. Floyd, D.L., Prentice-Dunn, S., Rogers, R.W.: A Meta-Analysis of Research on Protection Motivation Theory. Journal of Applied Social Psychology 30(2), 407–429 (2000)
10. Pass, G., Chowdhury, A., Torgeson, C.: A Picture of Search. In: the First International Conference on Scalable Information Systems (INFOSCALE 2006), Hong Kong (2006)
11. Pankratz, A.: Forecasting with Dynamic Regression Models. John Wiley & Sons, New York (1991)

On the Two Factors Affecting Information Systems Success in the Extreme Event Context

Insu Park[1], R. Sharman[2], H. Raghav Rao[2], and S. Upadhyaya[3]

[1] Management and Information Systems, Montclair State University, NJ 07043
[2] Management Science and Systems, SUNY Buffalo, NY 14260
[3] Computer Science and Engineering, SUNY Buffalo, NY 14260

Abstract. This study examines the impact of perceived risk and organizational resilience on information systems success process in the context of hospitals. The research model was tested with the data collected from three of the hospitals in the Western New York area that were affected by a major snowstorm that was labeled as a federal disaster. The analysis and results appear. Theoretical and practical implications of this study and future research directions are discussed.

Keywords: perceived risk, organizational resilience, information systems success, system quality, information quality.

1 Introduction

The purpose of this study is twofold. First, we identify the effect of perceived risks and resilience on effectiveness of hospital information systems. We also examine whether information and system quality, which are antecedents of information systems, mitigate the perceived risk and enhance organizational resilience. In particular, we argue that perceived risk decreases the information systems effectiveness in the following ways: (a) perceived risk influences the system users' perception and belief levels regarding resilience, and (b) perceived risk decreases users' confidence in using the information systems by transforming the negative effect of risk to the perception of organization resilience.

We propose the following information systems qualities: system quality, information quality. This paper focuses on the proposed constructs that reduce risks and increase resilience in the extreme events context.

Based on the preceding statements, a research model is proposed that aims to understand and prescribe how resilience and perceived risk affect the information systems success model. In this model, information systems effectiveness is determined by information quality and systems quality [1-3].

R. Sharman, T.S. Raghu, and H.R. Rao (Eds.): WEB 2009, LNBIP 52, pp. 181–185, 2010.

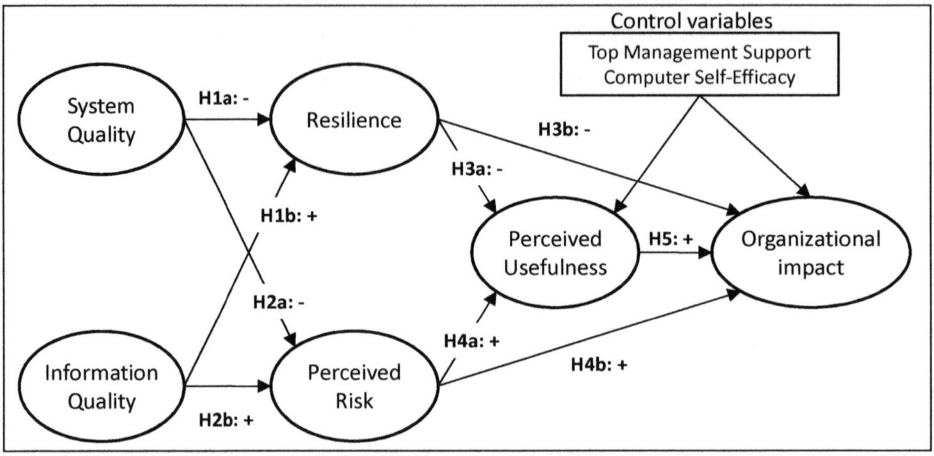

Fig. 1. Conceptual Model

2 Hypothesis Development

As first step, we hypotheses the information and systems qualities. Important aspects of information systems serve not only to encourage user access of systems with ease, but also to have good quality output to promote confidence in the business continuity of the organization. Specifically, system users are likely to be particularly attentive to the quality of information on the organization systems; because the quality of information should aid their performance and help those making good decisions. As users perceive that their information systems present quality information, they should gain confidence that the organization is interested in maintaining resilient information systems. Therefore, to the extent that users perceive that the information system presents reliable information and high service quality, they are more likely to have confidence that the organization itself is reliable.

Similarly, a high level of information systems quality in the organization will increase users' confidence that their information systems infrastructure is strong. This experience of systems quality will then increase users' confidence that the organization keep performance of information systems high. As a result, perceived organization resilience is likely to be increased because of such a belief. That is, as users' perception of information systems quality increases, these users might tend to believe that the hospital information systems encourage employees work performance by providing ease of use (i.e., systems quality) and good quality of output (i.e., information quality). Such a belief, in turn, may positively affect organization resilience.

As second step, we hypotheses the effects of two factors in terms of extreme events: perceived risk and organizational resilience. Perceived risk is likely to be reduced because of such perceived quality. That is, as employees' perception of information and system quality increases, these employees will possibly believe that their information systems offer ''implicit'' promises in that they will work to fix any problem that occurs.

Such a belief, in turn, may lessen their perceived risk. Previous research findings conducted in the physical environment show perceived quality can reduce perceived risk [4-5]. The relationship between perceived risk and perceived usefulness in organization has not received much attention in literature. Individuals tend to use or not use information systems to the extent they believe it will help them perform their job better. Perceived risk may minimize effectiveness of information systems by reducing high confidence and expectations toward their information systems' capabilities and discouraging them to positively use the system. In a disaster context, organizations' employees who perceive high risk are likely to engage in a conservative evaluation of their individual and organizational performances and, in turn, internal risk will reduce the hospital information systems effectiveness.

The term, 'resilience' has been widely used in various fields including ecology, psychology, economics, business, and applied critical infrastructure [See, 6, 7-8]. In disaster contexts, resilience refers to the capacity of an entity or system to maintain and renew itself particularly in the presence of stressors, or the ability or capacity of a system to absorb or cushion against damage or loss [9]. At an individual level, employees' *organizational resilience* is defined as a person's belief that their organization has a relatively stable trait characterized by the ability to bounce back from negative experience and by flexible adaptation to the emergency contexts.

This study argues that the impact of information systems on performance would be lower if an employee does not believe that their organization has the resilience to handle unexpected events. Thus, individuals will be more likely to perceive high organizational impact when they believe such their information systems to be able to confer positive values.

3 Analysis and Results

As third step, this study analyzed and tested nine hypotheses. First, system quality has a significant positive impact on organizational resilience and negative impact on perceived risk. However, information quality has no significant impacts on both organizational resilience and perceived risk. Therefore, hypotheses for the effect of system quality, H1a and H2a, were strongly supported. Second, organizational resilience has no significant impact on perceived usefulness but organizational impact. Perceived risk has a significant negative impact on both perceived usefulness and organizational impact. These findings support H3b, H4a, and H4b. Third, perceived usefulness positively influences organization impact, thereby validating H5. Table 1 shows summary results of hypothesis test.

Overall, in the results based on the statistical analysis using Partial Least Square, this study shows important implications and contributions to information systems success research. First, this study demonstrates the importance of including contextual measures (i.e., perceived risk and organizational resilience) in the middle of the process when studying the information systems success process. Consistent with the past research, this study shows that systems qualities positively influenced organizational

Table 1. Summary of Hypothesis Testing Results

Hypothesis	Descriptions	Support
H1a	The greater the perceived system quality, the higher organization resilience will be perceived by hospital information system users.	Yes
H1b	The greater the perceived information quality, the higher organization resilience will be perceived by hospital information system users.	No
H2a	The greater the perceived system quality, the less risk will be perceived by hospital information system users.	Yes
H2b	The greater the perceived information quality, the less risk will be perceived by hospital information system users.	No
H3a	Organizational Resilience will positively affects perceived usefulness.	No
H3b	Organizational Resilience will positively affects organizational impact.	Yes
H4a	Perceived risk is negatively related to perceived usefulness.	Yes
H4b	Internal risks will negatively affect organizational impact.	Yes
H5a	H5: perceived usefulness is positively related to organizational impact.	Yes

resilience and perceived usefulness and mitigated the effect of perceived risk, but information quality affected only perceived usefulness. Our study highlights the importance of including individual beliefs as intermediaries in this research. More specifically, we showed that perceived risk and organizational resilience can work to increase and decrease perceived usefulness and organizational impact. In addition, our findings help shift out and provide initial insights into the relative effects of two contextual predictors on the information system success. By integrating the effects of risks and resilience in a model, which are often described as different sides of the same coin, we identify contextual predictors (i.e. perceived risk and organizational resilience) of perceived usefulness and organizational impact in information systems success.

4 Conclusion

In sum, this study on the roles of perceived risks and resilience for information systems effectiveness in extreme events contexts opens up rich and exciting opportunities for theoretical extensions to the present model and practical development of the effect of information systems on organizational performance. Despite theoretical and practical limitations, this study represents an initial step in developing a better understanding of perceived risks, resilience, and information assurance regarding information effectiveness, and it provides feasible suggestions for further investigation. This study encourages researchers to seek out further insights into the effect of organizational resilience in various structural, as well as disaster contexts, as future research progresses.

References

1. Seddon, P.B.: A respecification and extension of the DeLone and McLean model of IS success. Information Systems Research 8, 240 (1997)
2. DeLone, W.H., McLean, E.R.: Information Systems Success: The Quest for the Dependent Variable. Information Systems Research 3, 60–95 (1992)
3. Rai, A., et al.: Assessing the validity of IS success models: An empirical test and theoretical analysis. Information Systems Research 13, 50 (2002)
4. Barki, H., et al.: Toward an assessment of software development risk. Journal of Management Information Systems 10, 203 (1993)
5. Jiang, J.J., et al.: Information system success as impacted by risks and development strategies. IEEE Transactions on Engineering Management 48, 46 (2001)
6. Masten, A.S., Reed, M.-G.J.: Resilience in development. In: Synder, C.R., Lopez, S.J. (eds.) Handbook of positive psychology, pp. 74–88. Oxford University Press, New York (2002)
7. Adger, W.N.: Social and ecological resilience: Are they related? Progress in Human Geography 24, 347–364 (2000)
8. Holling, C.S.: Resilience and stability of ecological systems. Annual Review of Ecology and Systematics 4, 1–23 (1973)
9. Rose, A.: Defining and measuring economic resilience to disasters. Disaster Prevention and Management 13, 307 (2004)

Mobile Application Market: A Mobile Network Operators' Perspective*

Adrian Holzer[1] and Jan Ondrus[2]

[1] Polytechnique de Montréal, Université de Montréal, Canada
[2] ESSEC Business School, Paris, France
adrian.holzer@unil.ch, ondrus@essec.fr

Abstract. The mobile telecommunication market has recently been shaken by the arrival of new actors, such as Apple and Google. As a consequence, the relatively well-established mobile network operators (MNO) have to rethink their position in the market if they want to participate in the growth of mobile telecommunication revenues. Mobile applications and services are being seen as great opportunity of new revenue sources. However, with the current market structure, MNOs do not hold a privileged position compared to mobile platforms providers such as Apple with iTunes. In this paper, we assess whether or not there is still space in the mobile application market for MNOs. In order to do so, we examine different roles in the mobile application value chain and determine how MNOs can position themselves in this turbulent new market. Our analysis shows that MNOs will have to focus on their core business as network provider and establish alliances with platform providers.

Keywords: Mobile network operators, mobile application development.

1 Introduction

Despite their essential role in the mobile telecommunication market, mobile network operators (MNOs) are facing major challenges for their future positioning. They have heavily invested to build a reliable and fast mobile network infrastructure. Indeed, their investments have greatly enhanced mobile communication and data transmission. Since competition on voice and data transmission rate is fierce, MNOs have to find new ways to secure and increase revenues for the long term. As their revenues tend to erode year after year, it seems that diversification of activities is key for sustainability. MNOs have already started to find other business opportunities in their industry. As such, MNOs have set the objective to become service integrators, which would provide mobile value-added services to different segments of consumers. Their privileged relationship with end-users and mobile application providers seems to make MNOs suitable intermediaries. In line with this objective, they initiated the launches of mobile portals based on WAP technology (e.g. Vodaphone Live, Orange World). So far, their initiatives as service integrator have not been as successful as hoped.

* This research is partially funded by the Swiss National Science Foundation under grant PBLAP2-127668/1.

R. Sharman, T.S. Raghu, and H.R. Rao (Eds.): WEB 2009, LNBIP 52, pp. 186–191, 2010.

Recent developments in the mobile application market have strongly shaken incumbent MNOs. During many years, the development of mobile services was mostly controlled and managed by MNOs, phone manufacturers, and mobile application and content providers. Recently, this has changed with the arrival of new mobile phones and platforms such as the iPhone. More than ever, such devices can run rich standalone applications as well as distributed client-server applications that access information via web gateways. The constant improvement of hardware related to mobile computing (e.g., small chips with better computing power, larger wireless network bandwidth) enhances general capabilities of mobile devices. The evolution of devices opens new avenues for future mobile application and service development.

Traditionally, in the mobile application industry, there are several actors intervening along the value chain [1, 2, 3, 4, 5, 6, 7]. Each actor has its own importance and role. The current trends indicate that the market structure and value chain are evolving into value networks [5, 8]. Roles are changed, combined and exchanged. Some lost control on the device (i.e., MNOs), some got new revenues streams (i.e., portal providers), and some became more seamlessly integrated into the platforms (e.g., financial institutions, content providers).

For long, MNOs have locked down and controlled the market while slowly developing and securing their value proposition (i.e., walled garden strategy). In many cases, they usually took commission fees exceeding 50% on value-added services and applications sold through them. These high fees were not very encouraging for mobile application developers and thus somehow hindered the emergence of this market. With the arrival of more aggressive platform providers, MNOs were not able to keep their privileged position as they have been rather slow in adapting to the new rules of the market. After investing heavily in their UMTS infrastructure, MNOs have struggled in making money in the mobile application area. Therefore, end-users were mostly using 3G networks for basic services such as emails, limited web browsing, and multimedia messaging (MMS) [9].

The current mobile development market is dominated by five big platform providers, i.e., companies that offer an operating system (OS) and development tools to enable the creation of high level applications, namely: Nokia with its Symbian OS (52.4%, percentages represent worldwide smartphone sales by OS in 2008). RIM with its Blackberry OS (16.6%), Microsoft with its Windows CE OS family (11.8%), Apple with its iPhone OS (8.2%), and LiMo Foundation with its Linux Mobile operating system (8.1%) [10]. Furthermore, Google recently launched its Android operating system and is expected to rapidly become part of the big players in the industry.

In this paper, we examine the roles of MNOs in the current mobile application market in light of two different elements of the value network (i.e., network & financial infrastructure and mobile application portals). The objective is to clarify the market structure and help us to study the trends and the position of the different stakeholders in relation with MNOs. While we describe the market, we also assess the potential opportunities for MNOs to evolve. As each context is different, we focus our research effort on Western and developed countries in which platforms such as the iPhone and Android phones were launched. Our research does not apply to countries which have a different market structure (e.g., Japanese and South Korean markets).

2 Roles for MNOs

In the current practices, mobile applications are published on an application portal and can be downloaded unto the consumer's mobile device through a network infrastructure. The consumer will in turn pay the application using a financial network. This process involves several key actors playing different roles. First, mobile device manufacturers and operating system (OS) providers support mobile applications and provide tools to ease their development process, i.e., software development kits (SDKs). Second, developers create applications and services. Third, application portals act as application shopping centers for consumers. In order for consumers to make their purchase, a network operator is needed in order to allow data transfers between mobile devices and distant application portals or the Internet. Finally, a financial institution is needed to take care of the billing and payment processes.

Hereafter, we assess the position of MNOs when it comes to fill two roles on this value chain. First, we investigate the MNOs core business, which is providing network infrastructure with payment facilities. Second, we investigate how MNOs can compete on the application portal market.

2.1 MNOs as Network and Financial Infrastructure

Providing network and financial infrastructure in order to bill network traffic is the core business of MNOs. However, their position has been shaken over the last few years with the introduction of new technology and fierce competitors.

In the early 21st century, MNOs in Europe used to enjoy a comfortable role as sole communication providers between mobile devices and mobile portals and Internet in general via GPRS or UMTS technology. Even though the market for telecommunication had been opened up for competition, prices did not drop radically. Furthermore, MNOs also enjoyed a unique relationship with consumer through their monthly bills. This relationship was used for billing early mobile services. For example by sending a premium text message, one would receive simple information (e.g., train schedule, sports results, traffic alerts) through a text message reply. Early mobile payment experiments also relied on the relationship with MNOs. A consumer could purchase items from a vending machine by sending a text message and get charged on the monthly bill. This privileged position allowed MNOs to charge large fees on transferred data and payments. Unfortunately, these initiatives did not really drive much innovation nor enhanced user's adoption of data-intensive services.

In the current market, network and financial infrastructures have become much more competitive with the introduction of the mobile internet using telecommunication networks or WiFi. Direct access to the Internet allows bypassing the MNOs' controls to access mobile services. Furthermore, the emergence of online accounts such as the ones from the iTunes store (i.e., storage of the credit card information), allowed merchants to directly charge their consumers without having to pay fees to MNOs. As a result, the position of MNOs to bill consumers for value-added services has been weakened.

2.2 MNOs as Application Portal Providers

In order to facilitate the distribution of applications from developers to consumers, an application portal can be created. These revenues of these portals come from taking a fee on every application sold. Currently, this fee represents 30% in portals such as the Apple AppStore, Google Android Market and Nokia OVI. Portals are two-sided structures which need to leverage on two parties (i.e., developers and consumers) to increase their revenues [11, 12, 13]. In other words, if they offer enough attractive applications, they will attract more consumers, which in turn will stimulate the development of more applications, and so forth. This positive feedback loop increases the number of transactions and therefore increases the portal's revenue.

Prior to the introduction of Apple AppStore and more recently Google Android Market, mobile applications for a given device or operating system were not located on a main central portal. Developers would usually distribute their applications through several third-party portals in addition to their own website. One downside of such a decentralized distribution strategy is that the great variety of portals does not provide a comprehensive overview of existing applications. Therefore, it does not facilitate access to the applications. In the past, mobile services or digital content such as ringtones and news could be obtained through MNOs or other content providers via a premium text message.

Unfortunately, MNOs are not in a very comfortable position to compete as portal providers. Furthermore, the current market tends towards portal centralization in order to attract and regroup more developers and more consumers and thus leverage on positive network effects, which are essential in two-sided markets. Chances are that this trend will put MNOs in an even worse position as bystanders.

3 Discussion and Future Work

The emergence of newcomers in the mobile application industry has increased the pressure on voice and data prices, which remain a major revenue stream for MNOs. Furthermore, MNOs tend to lose their privileged relationship with end-users as platforms providers control most of the mobile application purchase process. As their long reign in the walled-garden model as middlemen is coming to an end, other revenue streams should be considered. This loss of control on the value network should be taken into account with the indirect consequences of portal centralization and increased pressure on prices.

The emergence of more sophisticated mobile phones and usage of advanced mobile services increases consumers' need to subscribe to more expensive data plans. In the short term, the ARPU will increase. However, MNOs cannot hope that this situation last long without a battle on data plan prices. Their long term revenues will drop if they do not find another way to sustain or create additional revenue streams.

A risk is that MNOs become transmission pipes that do not capture any value of transactions made using their infrastructure. They would be in the same position as most Internet Service Providers (ISP). On their side, ISP tried to counter-attack by becoming content providers while providing triple-play services (i.e., phone, TV, internet).

However the trend towards portal centralization combined with the pressure on price could actually be an opportunity for MNOs. Until recently, it took expert users to download and install third-party applications. It usually involved an internet search, a credit card payment, and the use a personal computer to transfer a file via Bluetooth to the mobile phone. Now it has become a "one-click" operation directly executable on the mobile device. MNOs can benefit from this purchase facilitation as their users will naturally increase their demand for advanced mobile services. This will also create opportunities for MNOs to supply some application through the platform integrators. Furthermore, the trend towards cheaper data communication encourages consumers to consume more advanced mobile services, such as downloading applications, browsing the Internet, emailing photos, watching TV and sharing videos. MNOs could create more sophisticated pricing for data plans in order to satisfy their consumers to avoid high churn.

This is a major opportunity for MNOs to continue to provide network infrastructure and services and closely work with other actors in order to enhance user experiences by providing more integrated and consistent services and applications (e.g., visual voice mail, teleconference).

Future research will try to identify the exact reasons of the late success of mobile applications, which had been announced as potentially successful many years ago. The nature of these reasons could support a better understanding of how MNOs could take advantage of future developments in the mobile application industry. As the topic is quite new and evolving in a day-to-day basis, we hope that our research will open new paths of research in the mobile application market and motivate other researchers to investigate further the evolution of this market.

References

1. Adrian, B.: Overview of the Mobile Payments Market 2002 – 2007, Gartner (2002)
2. Ballon, P., Walravens, N., Spedalieri, A., Venezia, C.: The Reconfiguration of Mobile Service Provision: Towards Platform Business Models. In: Proceedings of ICIN 2008 (2008)
3. Barnes, S.J.: The Mobile Commerce Value Chain: Analysis and Future Developments. International Journal of Information Management 22(2), 91–108 (2002)
4. Buellingen, F., Woerter, M.: Development Perspectives, Firm Strategies and Applications in Mobile Commerce. Journal of Business Research 57(12), 1402–1408 (2004)
5. Funk, J.L.: The Emerging Value Network in the Mobile Phone Industry: The Case of Japan and its Implications for the Rest of the World. Telecommunications Policy 33(1-2), 4–18 (2009)
6. Maitland, C.F., Bauer, J.M., Westerveld, R.: The European Market for Mobile Data: Evolving Value Chains and Industry Structures. Telecommunications Policy 26(9-10), 485–504 (2002)
7. Tsalgatidou, A., Pitour, E.: Business Models and Transactions in Mobile Electronic Commerce: Requirements and Properties. Computer Networks 37(2), 221–236 (2001)
8. Peppard, J., Rylander, A.: From Value Chain to Value Network: Insights for Mobile Operators. European Management Journal 24(2-3), 128–141 (2006)
9. Walden, P., Han, S., Carlsson, C., Majlender, P.: The Sleeping Giant – A Longitudinal Study Surveying the Mobile Service Market in Finland. In: Proceedings of the Fifteenth European Conference on Information Systems, ECIS 2007 (2007)

10. Gartner, `http://www.gartner.com/it/page.jsp?id=910112` (accessed in June 2009)
11. Parker, G.G.: Two-sided Network Effects: A Theory of Information Product Design. Management Science 51(10), 1494–1504 (2005)
12. Rochet, J.-C., Tirole, J.: Platform Competition in Two-sided Markets. Journal of the European Economic Association 1(4), 990–1029 (2003)
13. Shapiro, C., Varian, H.R.: Information Rules: A Strategic Guide to the Network Economy. Harvard Business School Press, Boston (November 1998)

The Impact of Gender Differences on Response Strategy in e-Negotiation

Wan-Jung Lin, Chia-Hua Hu, and Hsiangchu Lai*

National Sun Yat-sen University, Kaohsiung 80424, Taiwan, R.O.C.
d934020008@student.nsysu.edu.tw, ookk36@gmail.com,
hclai@mail.nsysu.edu.tw

Abstract. Gender issues have been present in the traditional negotiation field for a long time, as it has become common for women to play key roles in business. However, few studies have investigated this issue in online situations. Since online negotiation is inevitable in the global business age and its context is different from that of a traditional face-to-face environment, it is valuable to have more understanding of the impact of gender differences on online negotiation. This study explores the impact of different gender dyads on how negotiators strategically respond to their counterparts' behavior from the dyadic interaction perspective. The adopted strategy clusters include (1) distributive information, (2) integrative information, (3) claiming value, and (4) creating value. The content analysis method was applied in order to translate all negotiation transcripts into quantitative data, i.e. behavior units. The resulting behavior units belonging to the four strategy clusters were mined to find the two-sequence dyadic behavioral patterns of each negotiation dyad and then of each gender composition group. Finally, these two-sequence behavioral patterns were categorized into three appropriate strategic behavioral sequences: (1) reciprocal sequence, (2) complementary sequence, and (3) structural sequence. The results indicate that negotiators' strategic responses to their counterparts were impacted by the genders of both the counterparts and the negotiators themselves. In general, negotiators in intra-gender dyads adopt more structural strategy and less reciprocal strategy than those in inter-gender dyads. No matter whether female or male, a negotiator will adapt his or her response strategy based on his or her counterpart's gender.

Keywords: Online negotiation, Gender difference, Gender dyad, Strategic behavior, Response strategy, Sequential pattern, Dyadic interaction.

1 Introduction

The rapid development of electronic commerce has made the Internet an important and unavoidable communication and transaction channel for businesses. With the increase in electronic commercial activity, the chance to engage in negotiation over the Internet, i.e. e-negotiations, is not only inevitable but is also increasing quickly, since e-negotiations allow companies to conquer the limitations of time zones and

* Corresponding author.

R. Sharman, T.S. Raghu, and H.R. Rao (Eds.): WEB 2009, LNBIP 52, pp. 192–205, 2010.

geographical locations [1]. With new communication and computer technologies, negotiations conducted over the Internet are more common and popular [2].

In addition, it is becoming more and more common for women to play important roles in business and in the public arena. This indicates that more women will be involved in e-negotiation. Researchers argue that men and women have different social norms for conversational interaction, to the extent that they even form "distinct speech communities" [3]. Compared with men, women tend to be more collaboration-oriented. As the Internet becomes the major medium of communication, its lack of interpersonal cues, social cues, and physical attractiveness will change communication behavior [4]. For example, the difficulty of presenting social cues creates equal online negotiation circumstances for both genders [5]. Therefore, it is worthwhile to investigate the impact of gender differences on e-negotiation behavior in order to increase the chance of success in the context of e-negotiation. However, few researches have investigated the gender issue in e-negotiation. Stuhlmacher et al. [6] reviewed 43 studies and explored gender differences by comparing face-to-face negotiation with online negotiation via meta-research methods. However, this research examined gender differences but ignored the essential dyadic interactions in e-negotiation. The absence of the dyadic aspect hinders the revelation of the impact of gender on negotiation, since negotiation is a dynamic process of interactions between two negotiators. Koeszegi et al. [7] noticed the dyadic characteristics of negotiation and compared the gender differences between different gender compositions: a male-only group, a female-only group, and a mixed-gender group. However, they only investigated the frequencies of individual negotiators' behavior types rather than the dyadic interactions among different gender compositions.

Based on the above discussions, we can see that understanding the gender influence from the perspective of dyadic interaction is more valuable than understanding it from the viewpoint of individual behavior. The results should contribute to both individual- and organizational-level e-negotiation because the individual negotiator often negotiates on behalf of his or her affiliation. Therefore, the purpose of this study is to explore gender differences in e-negotiation by examining the strategic behavioral sequence from a dyadic perspective.

2 Negotiation, Media and Gender

2.1 Electronic Negotiation

E-negotiation is a negotiation process that includes information exchange via electronic media [8]. As e-negotiation becomes popular, the difference in communication media is being considered a major factor affecting the negotiation process and results [9]. Poole [10] found that electronic negotiation could facilitate negotiation without the limitations of time and space, support directional comments, and help negotiators focus on negotiation tasks. However, it could also increase a negotiators' feeling of anonymity and reduce abnormal socio-emotional communication due to the lack of interpersonal cues, social cues, and physical attractiveness. Several studies have concluded that different media really influence negotiation processes and results, including decision-making quality, communication satisfaction, and task effectiveness and efficiency [4, 11-13].

2.2 Gender Differences in Negotiation

Socio-linguistic researchers argue that men and women have different social norms for conversational interaction, to such an extent that they even form "distinct speech communities" [3]. Men tend to be competitive, focus on social hierarchy, assert independence, and seek respect. On the contrary, women tend to be network-oriented, create intimacy, and highlight cooperation [3, 14].

When negotiation is conducted online, the different negotiation channels might lead men or women to change their communication styles because the online communication medium may have many fewer interpersonal, social, and physical cues than traditional face-to-face context. Koeszegi [7] found that women in e-negotiation tend to disclose more information about personal interests and needs and to show more yielding behavior, while men tend to be more persuasive and competitive. Stuhlmacher [6] also found that women are more hostile in electronic negotiation than in face-to-face negotiation. This might result from the fact that the environment of electronic negotiation can allow women to ignore status cues and can reduce the pressure of the obedience norm. E-negotiation may also allow women to focus on negotiation tasks rather than the maintenance of relationships.

2.3 Interaction between Gender Composition of Negotiation Dyads

Negotiation is a series of social interactions and communications that involves two or more participants [15]. Since gender differences affect negotiation behavior, it is expected that the negotiation process will be impacted by the gender composition of a negotiation dyad. When a negotiator knows his or her counterpart's gender, he or she might develop expectations and beliefs about that counterpart based on gender stereotypes. Since negotiation is a process of interactions between negotiator and counterpart, such gender stereotypes would affect both the negotiator's and counterpart's behaviors [16]. In a mixed-gender group discussion in a face-to-face environment, men generally like to present themselves and are more talkative. When communication channel shifts to online, women viewed computer-mediated communication more favorably than men because the online environment may increase women's opportunities to "have their say" without being shut out of active roles by dominant men within a group decision [17].

Prior research has found that in a problem-solving discussion within a mixed-gender group in a face-to-face environment, men proposed the first suggestion for a solution five times as often as women did. However, when the same group discussed problems via a computer-mediated medium, women were often the first to suggest a solution, doing so as often as the men [18]. This result implies that when there is not enough information about a counterpart, there can be no gender differences in expectations and perceptions. When they learned their partners' gender, women were perceived as more cooperative and less exploitative than men [19]. Koeszegi et al. [7] also found that men will display more integrative and sensitive behaviors when negotiating with women, while they become more contributive to current issues when negotiating with other men. Based on the above discussion, we can infer that gender differences still exist in the e-negotiation context and could result from the synergistic effect of the gender composition of negotiation dyads and the selected communication media.

2.4 Negotiation Behavior, Sequence, and Strategy

Strategy is a systematic plan of action presented by a behavioral sequence. A strategy decision will have an impact on negotiation behavior, hence the outcomes [20]. Typically, negotiation behaviors can be classified into two types: distributive and integrative strategies. The former means that a negotiator's goal is to maximize his or her interests. In contrast, the goal of the latter strategy is to maximize mutual joint gain [21, 22]. Further, Weingart et al. [23] explored negotiation strategy through two dimensions: strategy orientation and strategy function. Strategy orientation includes distributive and integrative strategies, while strategy function involves information and action. Based on these two dimensions, there are four negotiation strategies: (1) distributive information, (2) integrative information, (3) claiming value, and (4) creating value (Table 1).

Table 1. Four Types of Negotiation Strategies

Strategy Function	Strategy Orientation	
	Distributive	Integrative
Information	Distributive Information ● Positions ● Facts	Integrative Information ● Priorities ● Needs ● Interests
Action	Claiming Value ● Substantiation ● Threats ● Power Use ● Bottom-Line ● Single-Issue Offer	Creating Value ● Packaging ● Tradeoffs ● Creative Solutions ● Multi-Issue Offers

Source: [23, 24]

Table 2. Examples of Strategic Behavioral Sequences

Initial Behavior	Type of Strategic Behavioral Sequence		
	Reciprocal	Complementary	Structural
Integrative Information (InfoI)	InfoI→InfoI	InfoI→Create	InfoI→Claim InfoI→InfoD
Creating Value (Create)	Create→Creat	Create→InfoI	Create→InfoD Create→Claim
Distributive Information (InfoD)	InfoD→InfoD	InfoD→Claim	InfoD→Create InfoD→InfoI
Claiming Value (Claim)	Claim→Claim	Claim→InfoD	Claim→InfoI Claim→Create

Source: [25]

As shown above, negotiation is a dynamic process of continually intertwined interactions between the involved negotiators. These interactions, i.e., actions and associated responses, form the sequences of negotiation behaviors [25]. These sequences result in the negotiation process and outcome [26]. Further, prior research has identified three types of strategic behavioral sequences based on whether or not negotiators are moving in synchronization. These are (1) reciprocal sequences, (2) complementary sequences, and (3) structural sequences [25, 27, 28]. A reciprocal sequence indicates that a negotiator responds to a counterpart's integrative or distributive behaviors with exactly the same type of behavior. A complementary sequence is when a negotiator replies to an integrative or distributive behavior with a different but functionally similar behavior. Finally, a structural sequence is when a negotiator reacts to a counterpart's behavior with a very different behavior belonging to a different strategy cluster. Table 2 shows an example of this phenomenon.

3 Research Model

The purpose of this study is to explore the gender differences in e-negotiation. Because the negotiation process can be viewed as a series of actions and reactions that are highly interdependent, it is important to examine the strategic behavioral sequence from a dyadic perspective. A dyadic sequence examination can provide more sophisticated findings than an examination of an individual's behavior because the strategic behavioral sequence presents the causal relation between a negotiator's action and an associated counterpart's reaction. A negotiation dyad could be women only, men only, or women and men. Prior research has found gender differences in e-negotiation. However, such studies have examined either individual behavior only or the frequency of dyadic behavior, rather than the dyadic behavioral sequence. This study explores gender differences by examining whether or not the dyadic behavioral sequence will be impacted by the gender composition of negotiation dyads. We adopted three types of strategic behavioral sequences: (1) reciprocal sequence, (2) complementary sequence, and (3) structural sequence [25]. The research model is shown in Fig. 1.

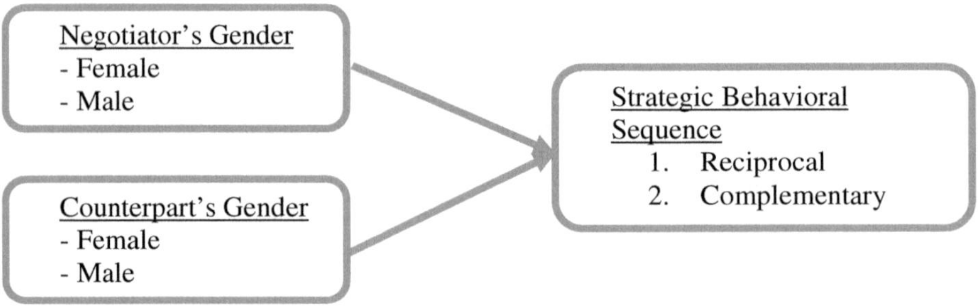

Fig. 1. Research Model

4 Research Methodology

4.1 Data Collection

The data was collected by the Inspire system, an e-negotiation system that has been operational since 1996. From the numerous samples we selected 60 pairs (120 negotiators) of negotiations based on the research model. All negotiators belonged to three different gender compositions: female-only (women in an intra-gender group), male-only (men in an intra-gender group) and mixed-gender. Each composition had 20 dyads. Female-only and male-only dyads form intra-gender groups, while mixed-gender dyads form inter-gender groups. In order to avoid the interference of cultural differences, all selected subjects were from Western countries. However, due to limited data, this research only chose subjects from some representative Western countries (Austria, Germany, the U.S., and Canada).

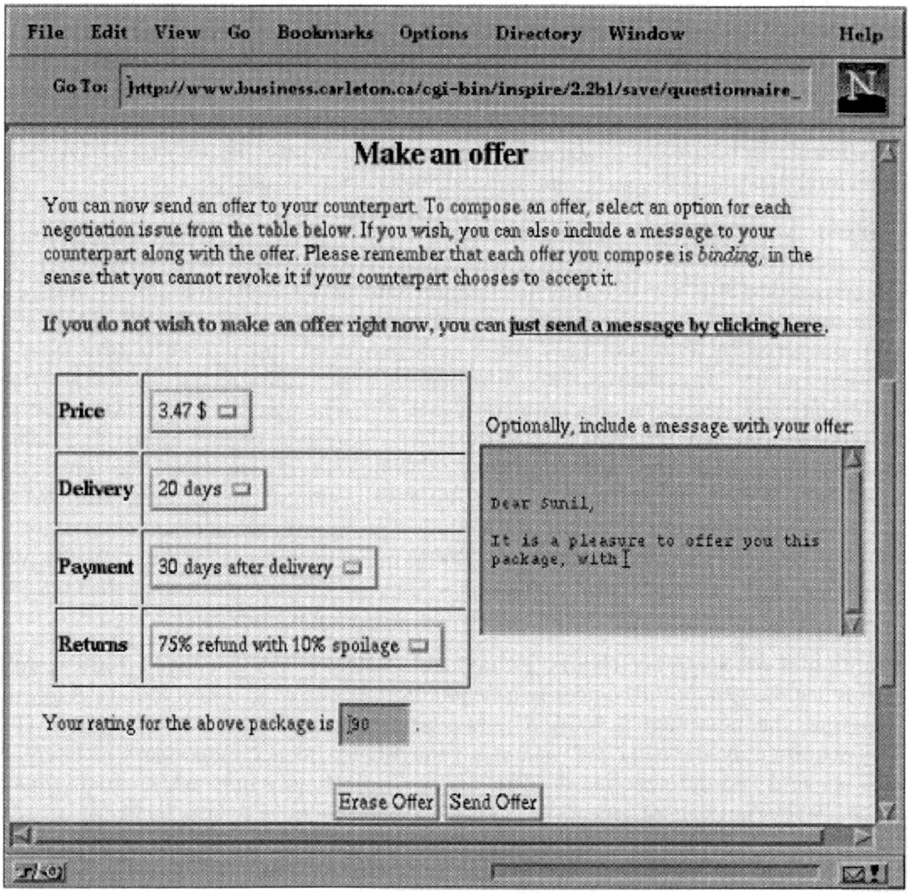

Source: [29]

Fig. 2. Inspire System Interface

The negotiation scenario, role-play, and utility design were the same for all subjects. The only difference was the gender composition of the negotiation dyads of different groups. The negotiation case dealt with the purchasing of bicycle parts, an interaction between a buyer and a seller. The deal included four issues: price, delivery, payment, and returns. All subjects were allowed to negotiate for three weeks. In order to simulate the real world, they had full freedom to reveal or hide their own gender background and could terminate the negotiation at any time. Fig. 2 shows the Inspire interface for submitting offers and messages.

4.2 Data Transfer Process

A great benefit of e-negotiation is that the negotiation process can be completely collected. The main purpose of this research is to study the dyadic sequences of the strategic behavior of different gender compositions. Therefore, the negotiation transcripts of all selected subjects are the data source for this research. Three major analyses were applied to these transcripts, step by step: (1) content analysis – to translate the qualitative messages of each negotiator into quantitative behavioral units; (2) mining of two-sequence dyadic behavioral patterns – to find the two-sequence dyadic behavioral pattern of each negotiation dyad and then of each gender composition group; (3) strategic behavioral sequence identification – identify the two-sequence dyadic behavioral patterns into appropriate strategic behavioral sequences.

Content Analysis. Two critical issues of content analysis when translating the negotiation transcripts into quantitative behavioral units are unitization and categorization [30]. We adopted the thought unit as the behavior unit to unitize all transcripts. Regarding categorization, the nine major categories adopted in this study were proposed by Weingart [23] and Koeszegi [7]: (1) integrative information, (2) creating value, (3) distributive information, (4) claiming value, (5) private communication, (6) communication protocol, (7) text-specific units, (8) procedural communication, and (9) push to closure. There were two coders to conduct content analysis throughout the whole process. Throughout the process, the inter-coder reliabilities of unit segmentation, coding reliability, and coding outlines were checked and modified iteratively. For unit segmentation reliability, we adopted Guetzkow's U reliability test [31] and the result (U = 0.0009) indicates high reliability [32, 33]. With Cohen's Kappa, coding reliability (Cohen's Kappa = 0.90) is also higher than 0.8 [34]. Finally, there are nine major behavioral categories with 60 sub-categories.

Mining of Two-Sequence Dyadic Behavioral Patterns. The essence of this research is to examine the gender differences in e-negotiation from a dyadic interaction perspective. Therefore, the next step is to find a two-sequence dyadic behavioral pattern. Here, "two-sequence dyadic behavior" means a behavioral sequence including a counterpart's behavior unit and the negotiator's own responding behavior unit, while "two-sequence dyadic behavioral pattern" means a significant two-sequence dyadic behavior of which the frequency is higher than a threshold. Since each negotiation dyad may have a very different length of transcripts, we adopted two steps to mine the two-sequence dyadic behavioral pattern. The first is to find the pattern within each negotiation dyad and the second is to find the pattern within a particular gender composition group. The threshold of a two-sequence dyadic behavioral pattern within a negotiation dyad is the average frequency of the two-sequence dyadic behavior type, i.e. the total two-sequence dyadic behavioral units of a negotiation dyad divided by the number of two-sequence dyadic behavior types. For the threshold of a two-sequence dyadic behavioral pattern within a particular gender composition group, we adopted 0.3 as a support rate. This means that the two-sequence dyadic behavioral patterns should be found in more than 30% of the negotiation dyads of a particular gender-composition group.

Identifying Strategic Behavioral Sequences. Since we examine gender differences from a strategic dyadic interaction perspective, only the two-sequence dyadic behavioral patterns in which both sequential behaviors belong to the four strategic categories were targeted for analysis. The four strategic categories are integrative information, creating value, distributive information, and claiming value. The final step of data transfer is to identify the two-sequence dyadic behavioral patterns into appropriate strategic behavioral sequences. The three strategic behavioral sequences—reciprocal sequence, complementary sequence, and structural sequence—are borrowed from prior research [35].

5 Data Analysis and Discussion

After translating the negotiation transcripts into strategic behavioral sequences, statistical analyses were performed based on the following levels of group division of all subjects: (1) whole group; (2) intra-gender vs. inter-gender groups; (3) women vs. men in inter-gender and intra-gender groups.

5.1 Whole Group

Table 3 summarizes the communication rate of three strategic behavioral sequences of the whole group. Here, the communication rate of each strategic behavioral sequence type is the average percentage of total two-sequence strategic behaviors that belong to that type and are significant patterns. It indicates the level of popularity of the strategic behavioral sequence of the target group. The data in Table 3 shows that negotiators in the whole group are most likely to present the reciprocal sequence (5.90%), then the structural sequence (4.92%) and the complementary sequence (3.18%). Although this result roughly shows the idea of a negotiator's strategic response, it does not provide information about negotiation behavior in different gender compositions.

Table 3. The Communication Rate of Strategic Behavioral Sequences of Whole Groups

Reciprocal		Complementary		Structural	
Type	Communication Rate	Type	Communication Rate	Type	Communication Rate
1→1	4.78%	1→2	2.20%	1→3	1.31%
2→2	0.00%	2→1	0.98%	3→1	0.99%
3→3	1.12%	3→4	0.00%	2→4	0.00%
4→4	0.00%	4→3	0.00%	4→2	0.00%
				2→3	0.00%
				3→2	1.79%
				1→4	0.83%
				4→1	0.00%
Total	5.90%	Total	3.18%	Total	4.92%

Note:

(1) A→B represents a dyadic strategic sequence where A is counterpart's behavior and B is the negotiator's responding behavior.

(2) 1: Integrative Information; 2: Creating Value; 3: Distributive Information; 4: Claiming Value.

5.2 Intra-gender Group vs. Inter-gender Group

In order to examine the gender impact, we divided the whole sample into two groups: intra-gender and inter-gender. Table 4 shows the frequency of each strategic behavioral sequence. If a two-sequence dyadic behavior type could not pass the threshold in the mining process, it was classified as "other" in order to correctly reflect the proportion of all dyadic behaviors. A Chi-square independence test was applied to see if there was a connection between gender composition and strategic behavioral sequence. The result shows that strategic behavioral sequences are affected by intra- and inter-gender compositions in e-negotiation (Chi-square = 417.224; $df = 3$; $p = 0.00$). The post-hoc test result (Fig. 3) shows that the reciprocal and structural sequences are significantly different between intra- and inter-gender groups, but the complementary sequence is not. In summary, in e-negotiation, inter-gender dyads are more likely to respond with reciprocal strategies, while intra-gender dyads are more likely to respond with structural strategies.

Table 4. Two-Sequence Strategic Behavioral Pattern of Intra- and Inter-Gender Groups

		Gender Composition			
		Intra		Inter	
		Frequency	Column N %	Frequency	Column N %
Strategic Behavioral Sequence	Reciprocal	1035	4.8%	752	7.5%
	Complementary	768	3.5%	369	3.7%
	Structural	1507	6.9%	193	1.9%
	Other	18460	84.8%	8738	86.9%

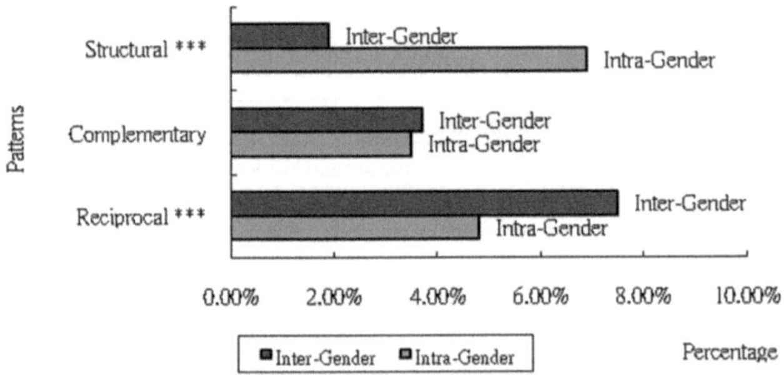

Note:

***means the strategic sequence is significantly different between the two groups (p<0.05)

Fig. 3. Comparisons of Proportions of Intra- and Inter-Gender Groups

5.3 Women vs. Men in Intra-gender and Inter-gender Groups

Women in Intra-Gender and Inter-Gender Groups: Female-Female Group vs. Male-Female Group. Table 5 shows the strategic behavioral sequences of female-female and male-female groups. Again, a Chi-square independence test was applied in order to examine the impact of a counterpart's gender on a female negotiator's strategic response behavior. The result shows that there is a significant difference in women's response to different gender counterparts (Chi-square = 84.340; $df = 3$; $p = 0.00$). Fig. 4 presents the post-hoc result. It reveals that female negotiators response to male counterparts with more reciprocal strategies and respond to female counterparts with more complementary and structural strategies.

Table 5. Two-Sequence Strategic Behavioral Pattern of Female-Female and Male-Female Groups

		Gender Group			
		Female-Female		Male-Female	
		Frequency	Column N %	Frequency	Column N %
Strategic Behavioral Sequence	Reciprocal	701	6.0%	372	7.7%
	Complementary	555	4.8%	133	2.7%
	Structural	931	8.0%	250	5.2%
	Other	9497	81.3%	4094	84.4%

Note:

A-B means that B responds to A's strategic behavior, so Male-Female means a female negotiator responds to a male counterpart's strategic behavior and so on.

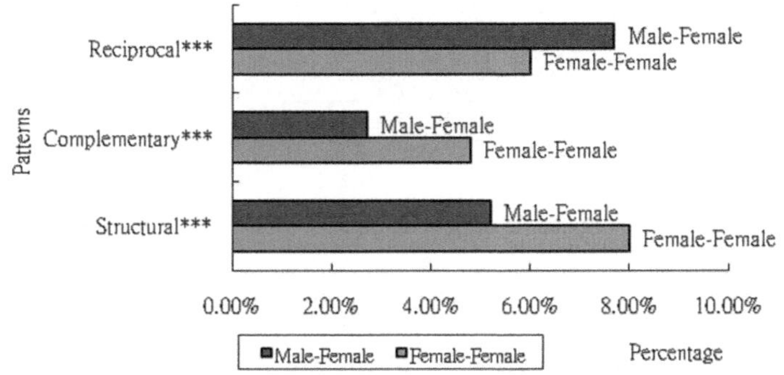

Note:

(1) ***means the strategic sequence is significantly different between the two groups ($p<0.05$)

(2) A-B means that B responds to A's strategic behavior, so Male-Female means a female negotiator responds to a male counterpart's strategic behavior and so on.

Fig. 4. Comparisons of Proportions of Male-Female and Female-Female Groups

Men in Intra-Gender and Inter-Gender Groups: Male-Male Groups vs. Female-Male Groups. After examining how female negotiators respond to different gender counterparts, we also examined whether or not male negotiators respond differently to male and female counterparts. A Chi-square independence test was applied, and Table 6 shows that there is a significant difference when male negotiators respond to different gender counterparts (Chi-square = 24.432; $df = 3$; $p = 0.00$). Fig. 5 shows the post-hoc result. It indicates that male negotiators respond with more reciprocal strategies to female counterparts and with more structural strategies to male counterparts.

Table 6. Two-Sequence Strategic Behavioral Pattern of Male-Male and Female-Male Groups

		Gender Group			
		Male-Male		Female-Male	
		Frequency	Column N %	Frequency	Column N %
Strategic Behavioral Sequence	Reciprocal	522	5.2%	315	6.1%
	Complementary	369	3.7%	223	4.3%
	Structural	551	5.5%	205	3.9%
	Other	8644	85.7%	4460	85.7%

Note:
A-B means that B responds to A's strategic behavior, so Female-Male means a male negotiator responds to a female counterpart's strategic behavior and so on.

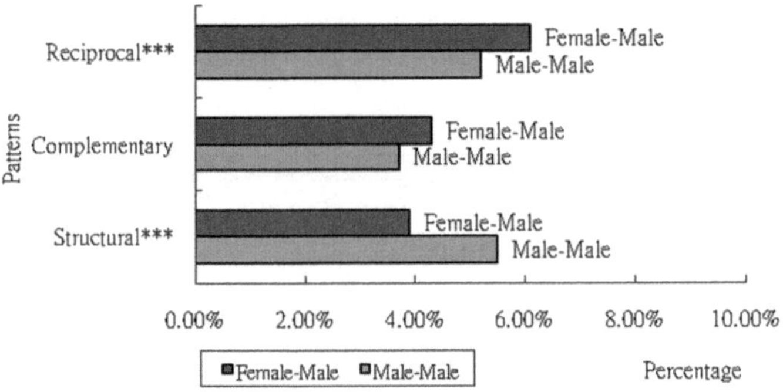

Note:
(1)***means the strategic sequence is significantly different between the two groups (p<0.05).
(2)A-B means that B responds to A's strategic behavior, so Female-Male means that a male negotiator responds to a female counterpart's strategic behavior and so on.

Fig. 5. Comparisons of Proportions of Male-Male and Female-Male Groups

5.4 Discussion

We draw the following findings from the analyses:

1. In general, negotiators present more reciprocal strategy than structural strategy or complementary strategy from the dyadic interaction strategy perspective.
2. Comparing intra-gender with inter-gender compositions, negotiators in intra-gender dyads present more structural strategy but less reciprocal strategy than those in inter-gender dyads.

3. When women negotiate with different gender counterparts, they adopt more structural and complementary strategies, but they use less reciprocal strategy with female counterparts than with male counterparts.
4. When men negotiate with different gender counterparts, they adopt more structural strategy but less reciprocal strategy with male counterparts than with female counterparts. There is no significant difference in terms of complementary strategy.

Since the negotiations were done via the Internet only, we cannot know whether the differences stem only from the gender issue or from both the gender issue and the communication media. However, since e-negotiation has become popular and might sometimes be an inevitable choice, these findings could help us to find possible response strategies in an e-negotiation context based on the counterparts' gender.

6 Conclusions and Future Research

This study explores the impact of gender composition on how negotiators strategically respond to their counterparts' strategy from the dyadic interaction perspective. The research data are based on negotiation transcripts rather than on a questionnaire. All of the transcripts were translated into quantitative data. The results indicate that negotiators' strategic responses to their counterparts were impacted by the genders of both the counterparts and the negotiators themselves. In general, negotiators in intra-gender dyads adopt more structural strategy and less reciprocal strategy than in inter-gender dyads. No matter whether male or female, a negotiator will adapt his or her response strategy based on his or her counterpart's gender background.

Since there are more and more available communication media such as video, audio, and combinations thereof, in the future, it will be worthwhile to investigate the impact of media on negotiation behavior. In addition to examining dyadic strategic response behavior, the ways in which that behavior affects the negotiation outcome will be a valuable issue to study in the future. We believe that the research findings will benefit individual negotiators as well as organizations.

Acknowledgements. This research was partially supported by the National Science Council (grant number 96-2416-H-110-013-MY2) and the "Aim for the Top University Plan" of National Sun Yat-sen University and the Ministry of Education, Taiwan, R.O.C.

References

1. Jain, B.A., Solomon, J.S.: The effect of task complexity and conflict handling styles on computer-supported negotiations. Information & Management 37(4), 161–168 (2000)
2. Kersten, G.E., Desmarais, P.: E-Negotiation System: Interaction of People and Technologies to Resolve Conflict. In: Unescap Third Annual Forum on Online Dispute Resolution, Melbourne, Australia (2004)
3. Coates, J.: Women, men and languages: Studies in language and linguistics. Longmen, London (1986)

4. Yuan, Y., Head, M., Du, M.: The Effects of Multimedia Communication on Web-Based Negotiation. Group Decision and Negotiation 12(2), 89–109 (2003)
5. Kiesler, S., Siegel, J., McGuire, T.W.: Social Psychological Aspects of Computer-Mediated Interaction. American Psychologist 39(10), 1123–1134 (1984)
6. Stuhlmacher, A.F., Citera, M., Willis, T.: Gender Differences in Virtual Negotiation: Theory and Research. Sex Roles 57(5), 329–339 (2007)
7. Koeszegi, S.T., Pesendorfer, E.M., Stolz, S.W.: Gender Salience in Electronic Negotiations. Electronic Markets 16(3), 173–185 (2006)
8. Bichler, M., Kersten, G., Strecker, S.: Towards a structured design of electronic negotiations. Group Decision and Negotiation 12(4), 311–335 (2003)
9. Bazerman, M.H., Curhan, J.R., Moore, D.A., Valley, K.L.: Negotiation. Annual Reviews 51(1), 279–314 (2000)
10. Poole, M.S., Shannon, D.L., DeSanctis, G.: Communication media and negotiation processes. In: Putnam, L.L., Rolloff, M.E. (eds.) Communication and Negotiation, pp. 46–66. Sage, Thousand Oaks (1992)
11. Kinney, S., Dennis, A.: Reevaluating media richness: cues, feedback, and task. In: The Annual Hawaii International Conference on System Sciences, pp. 21–30. IEEE Computer Society Press, Los Alamitos (1994)
12. Purdy, J.M., Nye, P., Balakrishnan, P.V.: The Impact of Communication Media on Negotiation Outcomes. The International Journal of Conflict Management 11(2), 162–187 (2000)
13. Bordia, P.: Face-to-Face Versus Computer-Mediated Communication: A Synthesis of the Experimental Literature. The Journal of Business Communication 34(1), 99–118 (1997)
14. Tannen, D.: You just don't understand: Women and men in conversation. Ballantine Books, New York (1990)
15. Kersten, G.E.: The science and engineering of e-negotiation: An introduction. In: The 36th Annual Hawaii International Conference on Systems Sciences, p. 27. IEEE Computer Society Press, Los Alamitos (2003)
16. Deaux, K., Major, B.: A social-psychological model of gender. In: Rhode, D. (ed.) Theoretical perspectives on sexual difference, pp. 81–91. Yale University Press, New haven (2000)
17. Hiltz, S.R., Johnson, K.: User satisfaction with computer-mediated communication systems. Management Science 36(6), 739–764 (1990)
18. McGuire, T.W., Kiesler, S., Siegel, J.: Group and computer-mediated discussion effects in risk decision making. Journal of Personality and Social Psychology 52(5), 917–930 (1987)
19. Matheson, K.: Social cues in computer-mediated negotiation: Gender makes a difference. Computers in Human Behavior 7(3), 137–145 (1991)
20. Carnevale, J.P., Pruitt, D.G.: Negotiation and Mediation. Annual Reviews Psychology 43(1), 1–531 (1992)
21. Walton, R.E., McKersie, R.B.: A behavioral theory of labor negotiations. McGraw-Hill, New York (1965)
22. Pruitt, D.G.: Strategic choice in negotiation. American Behavioral Scientist 27(2), 167 (1983)
23. Weingart, L.R., Brett, J.M., Olekalns, M., Smith, P.L.: Conflicting Social Motives in Negotiating Groups. American Psychological Association 93(6), 994–1010 (2007)
24. Olekalns, M., Brett, J.M., Weingart, L.R.: Phases, transitions and interruptions: Modeling processes in multi-party negotiations. International Journal of Conflict Management 14(3/4), 191–211 (2003)

25. Brett, J., Weingart, L., Olekalns, M.: Baubles, bangles, and beads: Modeling the evolution of negotiating groups over time. In: Blount, S., Mannix, B., Neale, M. (eds.) Research on Managing Groups and Teams, pp. 39–64. Elsevier Science, New York (2002)
26. Lai, H., Doong, H.S., Kao, C.C., Kersten, G.E.: Negotiators' Communication, Perception of Their Counterparts, and Performance in Dyadic E-negotiations. Group Decision and Negotiation 15(5), 429–447 (2006)
27. Donohue, W.A.: Analyzing negotiation tactics: Development of a negotiation interact system. Human Communication Research 7(3), 273–287 (1981)
28. Putnam, L.L., Jones, T.S.: Reciprocity in Negotiations: An Analysis of Bargaining Interaction. Communication Monographs 49(3), 171–191 (1982)
29. Kersten, G.E., Noronha, S.J.: WWW-based Negotiation Support: Design, Implementation, and Use. Decision Support Systems 25(2), 135–154 (1999)
30. Srnka, K., Koeszegi, S.: From Words to Numbers: How to Transform Qualitative Data into Meaningful Quantitative Results. Schmalenbach's Business Review 59(1), 29–57 (2007)
31. Holsti, O.R.: Content Analysis for the Social Sciences and Humanities. Addison-Wesley, Reading (1969)
32. Angelmar, R., Stern, L.W.: Development of A Content Analytic System for Analysis of Bargaining Communication in Marketing. Journal of Marketing Research 15(1), 93–102 (1978)
33. Graham, J.L.: The Influence of Culture on the Process of Business Negotiations: An Exploratory Study. Journal International Business Studies 16(1), 81–96 (1985)
34. Brennan, R.L., Prediger, D.J.: Coefficient Kappa: Some Uses, Misuses, and Alternatives. Educational and Psychological Measurement 41(3), 687–699 (1981)
35. Adair, W.L., Brett, J.M.: The negotiation dance: Time, culture, and behavioral sequences in negotiation. Organization Science 16(1), 33–51 (2005)

Determinants of Customer Loyalty for Social Networking Sites

Rui Gu, Lih-Bin Oh, and Kanliang Wang

School of Management, Xi'an Jiaotong University
28 Xianning Xilu, Xi'an, 710049 Shaanxi, P.R. China

Abstract. Although customer loyalty has been widely examined in various Internet contexts, the conceptualization and empirical validation of a customer loyalty model for social networking sites (SNSs) has not been addressed adequately. This study attempts to shed light on the determinants of customer loyalty for SNS. We propose a theoretical model comprising of perceived value, satisfaction, and consumer knowledge as antecedents of SNS customer loyalty. Theoretical and managerial implications together with suggestions for future research are discussed.

Keywords: customer loyalty, social networking sites, perceived value, user satisfaction, consumer knowledge.

1 Introduction

Social networking sites (SNSs) have emerged as one of the most popular Internet services over the recent years. SNSs allow users to construct a public or semi-public profile, articulate a list of other users, view and traverse their connections, and communicate with one another in their networks [1]. Since the first SNS SixDegrees.com was launched in 1997, we are witnessing the mushrooming of various types of SNSs, either based on shared interests (e.g., politics, literature) or focus on certain groups (e.g., college students, businessmen). In 2008, the total number of SNS users has grown by 25 percent worldwide [2].

The SNS scene has become very competitive. In the U.S., the top five SNSs Facebook.com, Myspace.com, Twitter.com, Flixster.com, and LinkedIn.com were reported to have 1191m, 810m, 54m, 53m, and 43m monthly visits, respectively in January 2009 [3]. Meanwhile, in China, the world's largest Internet market with 384m users [4], the popularity of SNS is also surging phenomenally. The number of Chinese SNS users is expected to achieve a growth rate of 67.8% and will reach 100m by the end of 2009 [5]. This figure is expected to hit 170m by 2011 while the potential revenue of SNSs in China would reach 1.7b Yuan in 2010 [6]. It was reported that there are at least more than 30 SNSs in China with sizeable user base [7]. The four leading Chinese domestic SNSs 51.com, Xiaonei.com, Chinaren.com, and Kaixin001.com were reported to have weekly independent visitors of 14m, 9.5m, 7m, and 3.5m, respectively [8]. Kaixin001 had more than 9m registered users by February 2009 and is one of the top 150 most-visited sites worldwide registering more than 60m hits a day [9].

R. Sharman, T.S. Raghu, and H.R. Rao (Eds.): WEB 2009, LNBIP 52, pp. 206–212, 2010.

However, it was found that the percentage increase of Chinese SNS users' browsing time varied greatly from less than 40 percent to more than 200 percent amongst different SNSs [10]. Similarly, U.S. Internet users spent five percent of online time on Facebook and only 2 percent on Myspace in January 2009 [11]. Considering the fact that there are so many competing SNS services, SNSs are facing the critical issue of customer loyalty. Hence, the challenge for SNSs is to be able to differentiate their services from other similar SNSs. They need to design services that users will find useful and valuable so as to increase website stickiness for user retention. In addition, it is also important for SNS operators to have a better appreciation of the factors that determine users' decision to remain with a certain SNS. Unfortunately, little research has been done on user repeat patronage behavior or customer loyalty for SNSs. Prior customer loyalty decision model derived in the context of e-commerce and other Internet services require a new examination considering the unique social capital building capabilities of SNS and the level of intense competition in the SNS market. Based on the research of customer value and knowledge, we propose a theoretical model to investigate the factors that influence SNS customer loyalty.

2 Conceptual Development

Figure 1 shows our proposed research model.

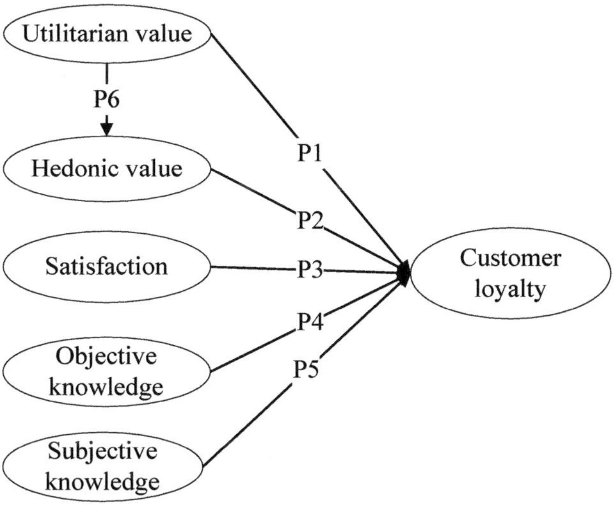

Fig. 1. Model of Customer Loyalty for Social Networking Sites

2.1 Perceived Value and Customer Loyalty

Customer loyalty is regarded as the relationship between the relative attitude toward an entity (brand/service/store/vendor) and repeat patronage behavior. It can be influenced by cognitive, affective, and conative factors [12] and is often suggested to express an intended behavior related to the service or the company [13]. Furthermore, it represents a deeply held commitment to rebuy or repatronize a preferred product/service consistently in the future, thereby causing repetitive same-brand or same brand-set purchasing, despite situational influences and marketing efforts having the potential to cause switching behavior [14]. One of the most important determinants of customer loyalty is the level of utilitarian and hedonic value that customers perceived.

Utilitarian value often arises from the conscious pursuit of an intended consequence [15] and is primarily instrumental, functional, and cognitive [16]. For example, savings, higher product quality, and improved convenience can be classified as utilitarian values [16, 17, 18]. Traditionally, marketers believed that market choices and consumer preferences were driven by utilitarian value [19]. In SNS context, utilitarian value mostly derives from the ability to interconnect with other users. For instance, users can upload their photos or interesting videos, post comments on each other's pages, blog, view each other's profiles, join virtual groups based on common interests, to realize their need of communicating with others. In addition, SNS users can find and reconnect with old friends, former classmates, or some relatives, as long as they are within the same SNS platform. As a tool of communication, SNS provides a larger pool of contacts available to their members and allow them to easily manage and maintain virtually unlimited number of contacts by just sending or accepting a request.

Conversely, *hedonic value* results from spontaneous responses that are more subjective and personal [15]. Hedonic values, such as entertainment, exploration, and self-expression [16, 17], are non-instrumental, experiential, and affective. They are derived more from fun and enjoyment than from task completion [18, 20]. SNSs offer many interesting and highly interactive applications that appeal to millions of Internet users. Users can indulge in many online applications that can provide them with a virtual realm to fulfill their needs for affinity and social needs. It has been found that both utilitarian and hedonic values can have a significant positive influence on both repatronage intentions and loyalty as well as preference towards Internet retailers [21, 22]. Thus, we propose that:

Proposition 1 (P1): The level of perceived utilitarian value is positively associated to the level of SNS customer loyalty.

Proposition 2 (P2): The level of perceived hedonic value is positively associated to the level of SNS customer loyalty.

2.2 Satisfaction and Customer Loyalty

Satisfaction is a consumer's post-purchase evaluation and affective response to the overall product or service experience [23]. A consumer's post-purchase response to a brand is believed to occur through a matching of expectations and perceived performance. The resulting satisfaction/dissatisfaction is considered to act as an antecedent to loyalty [12]. It has been widely suggested that satisfaction is a reliable predictor of repurchase intentions [24, 25, 26]. In addition, the relationship between customer satisfaction and purchase loyalty is nonlinear such that when satisfaction increases above a critical level, behavioral loyalty will increase dramatically [27]. In e-service context, customer satisfaction can have a strong positive influence on the loyalty [28]. This relationship was also established in different information systems (IS) contexts such as mobile commerce [29] and customer relationship management [30]. In the case of content-based service, it was found that satisfaction with the service provider will positively impact user loyalty [31]. Thus, we expect that:

Proposition 3 (P3): The level of satisfaction is positively associated to the level of SNS customer loyalty.

2.3 Customer Knowledge and Customer Loyalty

The level of consumer knowledge about alternative products and services can have an impact on the perception toward the present choice. Given higher payoffs and lower costs, knowledgeable consumers are more likely to search for new information prior to making a decision, and will expect their decision criteria to change as product knowledge increases [12, 32]. Additionally, expert consumers may seek a greater amount of information about particular product attributes simply because they are aware of the existence of those attributes or because they are more capable of formulating specific questions about them [32].

Consumer research has traditionally considered consumer knowledge to comprise of objective and subjective knowledge. *Objective knowledge* refers to accurate information about the product/service class stored in long-term memory, while *subjective knowledge* refers to people's perceptions of what or how much they know about a product/service class [33]. Higher levels of objective knowledge about alternative choice at initiation of pre-purchase search are associated with greater likelihood to defect by influencing evaluation of alternatives [34], which means less loyalty for incumbent choice. Besides, subjective knowledge about alternatives can also affect choice of search strategy. Specifically, people high in subjective knowledge are quick to rule out alternatives they believe to be inferior and prefer to avoid relying on dealer opinions [35]. It was suggested that more subjective knowledge leads to less perceived risk and can influence decision making by increasing the likelihood of searching for alternatives [36, 37]. Hence, customers with high levels of subjective knowledge about alternatives would be less likely to remain loyal to their present product or service [34]. Accordingly, we expect that the level of customer knowledge about SNS alternatives can affect customer loyalty for incumbent choice. Therefore, we propose that:

Proposition 4 (P4): The level of objective knowledge about alternative SNSs is negatively associated to the level of SNS customer loyalty for the incumbent SNS.

Proposition 5 (P5): The level of subjective knowledge about alternative SNSs is negatively associated to the level of SNS customer loyalty for the incumbent SNS.

2.4 Relationship between Utilitarian and Hedonic Value

Customer perceived utilitarian value has a significant positive effect on perceived hedonic value [38]. Consumers can gain self-esteem (a form of hedonic value) from utilitarian benefits like monetary promotions [16]. For SNS users, utilitarian value is reflected in the convenience of communicating with friends, time saving on managing friend contacts and the ease of sharing interesting videos or meaningful articles etc. These instrumental, functional benefits can bring users hedonic values such as self-expression, exploration, entertainment and enjoyment. Therefore, we propose that:

Proposition 6 (P6): The level of perceived utilitarian value is positively associated with the level of perceived hedonic value.

3 Implications and Future Research

With the rapid development of SNS worldwide, identifying the key determinants of customer loyalty and understanding their differentiated effects will become a priority for all companies aiming to deliver superior and more attractive services. In order to have a sustainable SNS business model, it is of paramount importance to ensure that customers will be attracted and remained attached to a specific SNS. Our proposed model can have some implications for SNS operators and managers. First, the proposed set of determinants can inform SNS companies the important aspects that they should pay attention to in the tensely-competitive SNS market. Second, it should also help SNS operators and managers to better understand users' behavior so as to provide a stronger basis for functionalities design. Third, user segmentation can also be done so that more targeted strategies can be implemented to cultivate customer loyalty.

This paper is a response to the lack of understanding of customer loyalty in the SNS context. Through synthesizing relevant research, our proposed SNS customer loyalty model offers some insights into the determinants of SNS user behavioral loyalty. The contributions of this model to Internet services customer loyalty research are twofold. First, it applied the traditional conceptualization of customer loyalty in a new SNS context that is different from other services examined in prior studies. Second, it can serve as a foundation for extensive empirical examination of customer perceived value, satisfaction, and customer knowledge about alternative services as antecedents of SNS user loyalty.

Researchers can apply the conceptual model to different contexts, e.g., different regions or cultures, to examine whether the relationships in the model are supported, and which factors in different contexts have more significant influence on customer loyalty. Since it is both managerially and theoretically important to be able to identify the factors that determine different type of users' decision to stay or switch among different SNSs, researchers can conduct empirical investigations by classifying users into stayers (those who have been using the same SNS since they first started) and switchers (those who have changed SNS), and then perform a comparative study between them. This can lead to interesting insights on customers' loyalty behavior and advance our understanding of the factors that determine SNS users' decision to stay or switch among different SNSs. Such research endeavors will certainly have immense potential to contribute substantially to the emerging IS literature on Web 2.0 and social media.

Acknowledgements

This research was partially supported by the National Natural Science Foundation of China (NSFC Grant No. 70890081) and the Chinese Ministry of Education New Faculty Grant (MOE Grant No. 20090201120037).

References

1. Boyd, D.M., Ellison, N.B.: Social network sites: Definition, history, and scholarship. Journal of Computer-Mediated Communication 13(1), 210–230 (2008)
2. ComScore, I., http://www.comscore.com/Press_Events/Press_Releases/2008/08/Social_Networking_World_Wide/language/eng-US
3. Kazeniac, A.: http://blog.compete.com/2009/02/09/facebook-myspace-twitter-social-network/
4. CNNIC, http://www.cnnic.cn/uploadfiles/pdf/2010/3/15/142705.pdf
5. CCID, C., http://www.ccidconsulting.com/en/insights/content.asp?Content_id=21144
6. iResearch, C.G., http://report.iresearch.cn/Reports/Charge/996.html#
7. Chinalabs.com, http://top.chinalabs.com/ciis_sort.aspx?Sort=0022
8. ChinaTechNews.com, http://www.chinatechnews.com/2009/04/24/9636-cr-nielsen-releases-ranking-list-of-chinese-sns-websites
9. Wang, S., http://www.chinatoday.com.cn/ctenglish/se/txt/2009-05/06/content_194150.htm
10. iResearch, C.G., http://news.iresearch.cn/viewpoints/98899.shtml
11. Prebluda, A., http://blog.compete.com/2009/02/26/facebook-myspace/
12. Dick, A.S., Basu, K.: Customer loyalty: toward an integrated conceptual framework. Journal of the Academy of Marketing Science 22(2), 99–113 (1994)
13. Andreassen, T.W., Lindestad, B.: Customer loyalty and complex services. International Journal of Service Industry Management 9(1), 7–23 (1998)
14. Oliver, R.L.: Whence consumer loyalty? Journal of Marketing 63(4), 33–44 (1999)
15. Babin, B.J., Darden, W.R., Griffin, M.: Work and or fun: measuring hedonic and utilitarian shopping value. Journal of Consumer Research 20(4), 644–656 (1994)
16. Chandon, P., Wansink, B., Laurent, G.: A benefit congruency framework of sales promotion effectiveness. Journal of Marketing 64(4), 65–81 (2000)
17. Ailawadi, K.L., Neslin, S.A., Gedenk, K.: Pursuing the value-conscious consumer: store brands versus national brand promotions. Journal of Marketing 65(1), 71–89 (2001)
18. Chaudhuri, A., Holbrook, M.B.: The chain of effects from brand trust and brand affect to brand performance: the role of brand loyalty. Journal of Marketing 65(2), 81–93 (2001)
19. Arnould, E.J., Price, L.L., Zinkhan, G.M.: Consumers. McGraw-Hill, New York (2002)
20. Hirschman, E.C., Holbrook, M.B.: Hedonic consumption: emerging concepts, methods and propositions. Journal of Marketing 46(3), 92–101 (1982)
21. Overby, J.W., Lee, E.J.: The effects of utilitarian and hedonic online shopping value on consumer preference and intentions. Journal of Business Research 59(10-11), 1160–1166 (2006)
22. Jones, M.A., Reynolds, K.E., Arnold, M.J.: Hedonic and utilitarian shopping value: Investigating differential effects on retail outcomes. Journal of Business Research 59(9), 974–981 (2006)
23. Oliver, R.L.: An investigation of the attribute basis of emotion and related affects in consumption: suggestions for a stage-specific satisfaction framework. Advances in Consumer Research 19(1), 237–244 (1992)

24. LaBarbera, P.A., Mazursky, D.: A longitudinal assessment of consumer satisfaction/dissatisfaction: the dynamic aspect of the cognitive process. Journal of Marketing Research 20(4), 393–404 (1983)
25. Bitner, M.J.: Evaluating service encounters: the effects of physical surroundings and employee responses. Journal of Marketing 54(2), 69–82 (1990)
26. Patterson, P.G., Spreng, R.A.: Modelling the relationship between perceived value, satisfaction and repurchase intentions in a business-to-business, services context: an empirical examination. International Journal of Service Industry Management 8(5), 414--434 (1997)
27. Oliva, T.A., Oliver, R.L., MacMillan, I.C.: A catastrophe model for developing service satisfaction strategies. Journal of Marketing 56, 83–95 (1992)
28. Luarn, P., Lin, H.H.: A customer loyalty model for e-service context. Journal of Electronic Commerce Research 4(4), 156–167 (2003)
29. Lin, H.H., Wang, Y.S.: An examination of the determinants of customer loyalty in mobile commerce contexts. Information & Management 43(3), 271–282 (2006)
30. Wang, Y., Lo, H.P., Chi, R., Yang, Y.: An integrated framework for customer value and customer-relationship-management performance: a customer-based perspective from China. Managing Service Quality 14(2/3), 169–182 (2004)
31. Gummerus, J., Liljander, V., Pura, M., van Riel, A.: Customer loyalty to content-based Web sites: the case of an online health-care service. Journal of Services Marketing 18(3), 175–186 (2004)
32. Alba, J.W., Hutchinson, J.W.: Dimensions of consumer expertise. Journal of Consumer Research 13(4), 411–454 (1987)
33. Park, C.W., Mothersbaugh, D.L., Feick, L.: Consumer knowledge assessment. Journal of Consumer Research 21(1), 71–82 (1994)
34. Capraro, A.J., Broniarczyk, S., Srivastava, R.K.: Factors influencing the likelihood of customer defection: the role of consumer knowledge. Journal of the Academy of Marketing Science 31(2), 164–175 (2003)
35. Brucks, M.: The effects of product class knowledge on information search behavior. Journal of Consumer Research 12(1), 1–16 (1985)
36. Moorman, C., Diehl, K., Brinberg, D., Kidwell, B.: Subjective knowledge, search locations, and consumer choice. Journal of Consumer Research 31(3), 673–680 (2004)
37. Moutinho, L., Davies, F., Curry, B.: The impact of gender on car buyer satisfaction and loyalty A neural network analysis. Journal of Retailing and Consumer Services 3(3), 135–144 (1996)
38. Babin, B.J., Babin, L.: Seeking something different? A model of schema typicality, consumer affect, purchase intentions and perceived shopping value. Journal of Business Research 54(2), 89–96 (2001)

Experimental Evaluation of Declining Buyout Price Models for Online Auctions

Roumen Vragov, Richard D. Shang, and Karl R. Lang

Baruch College, City University of New York
One Bernard Baruch Way, New York, NY 10010
{karl.lang,di.shang,roumen.vragov}@baruch.cuny.edu

Abstract. There is disagreement in the auction literature on the question of whether dynamic Buy-It-Now (BIN) prices can increase the efficiency of online auctions. We report results from an experimental study with economically motivated subjects that compares the standard online auction format currently used on eBay with a new auction format (Online Linear Dutch Auction - OLDA) that allows for dynamic BIN prices. We find no statistically significant differences between these two auction formats. We then compare our results with these of another study investigating OOBCA (Online One-time BIN-price Change Auction - another auction format that allows for dynamic BIN prices), which finds that OOBCA outperforms the standard online auction format. OLDA is more dynamic in nature than OOBCA yet OOBCA outperforms a generalized static online auction design in the laboratory while the OLDA does not. We discuss theoretical and practical implications of our findings.

Keywords: Internet auction design, auction performance, buyout price, dynamic auctions, experimental economics, electronic markets.

1 Introduction

In most conventional physical auctions, all buyers, their representatives, or both are usually present at the same place and time. Once the auction starts, the buyers submit bids according to the auction's rules. The outcome is determined relatively quickly (normally within a few minutes). By contrast, an online auction typically lasts longer and buyers arrive and bid at different times and of course from different locations. Evidently, online auctions should be designed as dynamic processes in which prices change to reflect the changing market conditions in near-real time, synchronously or asynchronously. This fact has already been recognized in the current literature (see [1], [2], [11], [23], [25]), but there is an unsettled debate in the auction literature about the effect that dynamic BIN prices can have on the operational efficiency of online auctions.

There are some studies which imply that dynamic prices should improve the efficiency of online auctions [12], [13], [14], [16], [24], [26], [27]. At the same time, in an important contribution to the literature, Gallien and Gupta [5] find that dynamic

R. Sharman, T.S. Raghu, and H.R. Rao (Eds.): WEB 2009, LNBIP 52, pp. 213–225, 2010.

Buy-It-Now (BIN)[1] prices are impractical, despite their theoretical appeal in terms of auction efficiency. They argue that because of their inherent complexity dynamic BIN prices are unlikely to produce any substantial advantage over simple, static BIN prices in real settings in the field. Gallien and Gupta also posit that current online auction models make too many simplifying assumptions to be able to make valid predictions about auction outcomes.

We share Gallien and Gupta's skepticism about the ability of restricted dynamic models to predict actual human behavior and auction outcomes, especially because previous theoretical models of dynamic auction designs have failed extensive laboratory tests (see [3]). In addition, there are many possible implementations of dynamic BIN prices that might impact auction outcomes in ways unexpected by theory. For example, more recently Vragov et al. [21] demonstrated in the laboratory that one specific implementation of a dynamic BIN price has the potential to increase sellers' revenues and the operational efficiency of online auctions without hurting buyers. They allowed sellers to change their BIN prices only once during the middle of the auction. We call this specific implementation of a dynamic BIN price an Online One-time BIN-price Change Auction (OOBCA).

In this paper, we conduct a laboratory test of another implementation similar to the one suggested by Wenyan and Bolivar [24]. We consider an auction design in which buyout prices decrease continuously during the auction in a linear fashion, and sellers decide the rate of change at the beginning of the auction. We call this auction the Online Linear Dutch auction (OLDA) to differentiate it from the Dutch auction that is used, for example, on eBay to sell multiple units of the same product simultaneously. OLDA is more dynamic than OOBCA because BIN prices changes occur more frequently, in this case, once every second for OLDA but only once per trading period in OOBCA. OLDA represents a closer approximation of the theoretical auction model presented in Gallien & Gupta [5] than OOBCA. We use our experimental design to implement a direct laboratory test of Gallien & Gupta's theoretical model, which puts us in position to compare our results with those of Vragov et al. [21] since we are using exactly the same experimental environment and parameters.

The specific research questions that we address in this paper are the following two:

1. *How does OLDA perform, compared to current static online auction designs?*
2. *How does OLDA perform, compared to OOBCA?*

To answer these questions we design an experiment using the methodology of experimental economics. We use auction efficiency, buyer and seller surplus, and auction website revenue as our criteria to evaluate auction performance. We find that OLDA does not significantly improve buyer surplus, seller surplus, or auction website revenues. This means that OLDA's performance in the laboratory justifies some of the concerns voiced by Gallien and Gupta. OLDA is more complex for buyers and sellers and there is not enough evidence to suggest that OLDA should be introduced in practice.

---

[1] The Buy-It-Now price in each auction is set by the seller. A buyer can accept the BIN price, usually any time during the auction, thus ending the auction, winning the auctioned item, and paying the BIN price.

We also compare OLDA to OOBCA and find that OOBCA outperforms OLDA in the laboratory. OOBCA also increases seller surplus compared to the static BIN price design. We conclude that the benefits of dynamic BIN prices depend on how the BIN prices are implemented and also that the frequency of price changes is not the only factor to consider. The importance of other factors such as auction complexity or the way information is exchanged between buyers and sellers need to be investigated in future theoretical models of auctions and experimental tests.

The contributions of our study are fourfold. (1) We present a scientific test of an important theoretical result from the controversial dynamic auction literature in the laboratory. (2) We provide some guidelines for future theoretical models of online auctions and future experimental test of online auction designs. (3) We introduce a novel dynamic online auction design, suggested by previous theoretical literature, and test its important properties in the laboratory. (4) We derive business implications for online auction managers by showing that dynamic pricing may or may not outperform conventional static pricing, depending on the specific implementation of the dynamic pricing mechanism, concluding that the specific implementation is critical for success in practice. The remainder of this paper is organized as follows. In the next section, we discuss related literature on the modelling of auctions. We then describe our hypotheses and the methodology issues. In the last three sections we present our results, we discuss our findings and limitations, and we conclude with some final remarks.

2 Background and Theoretical Perspective

Looking at online auctions as dynamic systems has been fairly recent. For example, Wang et al. [23] use differential equations to describe single-item one-sided online auctions on eBay. Other studies have explored the dynamic online auction model further by analyzing strategic bidder behavior in dynamic settings [2], [5], [11].

Gallien and Gupta [5] have been the first to explore theoretically a dynamic feature (a pre-announced continuous BIN price) in their theoretical auction design. The model they provide may be the most general one discussed in the extant literature, although the authors offer a mathematical description of only a small subset of equilibrium buyer strategies, because of analytical complexity. The authors use simulations to compare seller's revenue under three different option scenarios: static temporary BIN, static permanent BIN, and permanent dynamic BIN. For the last pricing option, which represents the dynamic case, the authors conclude that the potential revenue increase enabled by dynamic buyout pricing is small. They therefore reason that it does not sufficiently justify adoption in commercial real-world settings because of the complexity of its implementation and the potential for negative bidder reactions. Moreover, their model does not allow a closed–form solution for allocative efficiency and buyer surplus – important variables that need to be taken into consideration when a design recommendation is made.

The idea that dynamic pricing might be able to improve online auctions has origins in the previous auction literature. For example, one might think of online auctions as examples of two-sided markets wherein buyers and sellers meet to exchange items in real time. A long experimental research tradition dedicated to the study of the most dynamic market institution, the Continuous Double Auction (CDA), has shown that it is also the most efficient trading mechanism used in practice (see [13], [19]). The CDA is an extremely dynamic auction format because its bids and asks both arrive and are matched in real time. Transaction prices can change quickly if necessary. Dynamic buyout practices are also commonly observed in the financial markets—in upstairs block trading [6], [16]. In summary, the literature on dynamic buyout practices suggests that the more dynamic the auction, the more efficient the market.

Wenyan & Bolivar [24] discuss a declining price auction model, which is a combination of a Dutch, public, second-price format. Since, auction participants are not physically co-present at online auctions, the model has a starting BIN price when the auction begins (just as in traditional Dutch auctions), but then it deceases throughout the auction duration by means of an exponential optimal curve with a low price drop rate in the beginning of the auction and a high price drop rate towards the end of auction. The authors suggest that this auction model will speed up the auction duration, and that buyers have no incentive to bid at the very last moment as they do in the majority of current eBay auctions.

The first laboratory test related to dynamic BIN prices is reported in Vragov et al. [21]. There, the authors introduce a different implementation of dynamic BIN prices – a one-time price change in the middle of the trading period (OOBCA) and compare it to a standard online auction design with a permanent static BIN price. Contrary to Gallien and Gupta [5], they did find that OOBCA increases auction efficiency and revenue.

3 Research Hypotheses

From a theoretical perspective, it has been recognized that online auctions are clearly dynamic systems (see [1], [2], [11], [23]). Accordingly, optimal auction designs would likely require dynamic prices. There is both theoretical and experimental evidence for this claim (see [13], [14], [16], [19], [24]) — as we have already discussed above in our literature review. As one can clearly see there is an unresolved controversy in the dynamic auctions literature. However, it is still not clear whether dynamic BIN prices would benefit or hurt the operational efficiency of online auctions. Gallien and Gupta [5] use a theoretical model and simulations to show that dynamic BIN prices would not increase efficiency, but Vragov et al. [21] use laboratory experiments to show that dynamic BIN prices would increase seller revenue and also efficiency of online auctions. However, the way dynamic BIN prices are implemented under GG and Vragov et al. are different. Gallien and Gupta use a pre-announced continuous changing BIN price, and Vragov et al. use a previously unannounced one-time change in the BIN price in the middle of the auction. To investigate the reasons for these different results we implement the OLDA, that is, we design an experiment that mimics Gallien & Gupta's pricing method which allows us to directly test heir model in the laboratory. We use the result in Gallien and Gupta to formulate our central hypothesis (H1):

Hypothesis 1: Seller surplus under OLDA is not significantly different from seller surplus under current online auctions with static BIN.

While we do have some theoretical models of online auctions predicting the effect of dynamic BIN prices on sellers, there is a lack of theory on how dynamic prices might affect the other side of the market, the buyers. The dynamic models in the literature, such as, for example, the one presented in Gallien and Gupta [5] are too complex and incomplete to theoretically predict the effect of dynamic prices on buyer surplus. On the other hand, this can be easily studied in a laboratory setting because buyer surplus is directly measurable. And since the effects on all auction participants should be studied before any design is implemented, we address this question as well, although we cannot derive specific research hypotheses that are solidly grounded in theory.

Therefore, in the absence of theory for the buyer side, we develop the next two hypotheses as exploratory research hypotheses. Both have considerable significance for auction design and auction business practice. Their purpose is to investigate the effect of OLDA on buyers (H2) and to evaluate its overall market performance and efficiency (H3).

Hypothesis 2: Buyer surplus under the OLDA auction is not significantly different from buyer surplus under current online auctions with static BIN.

Hypothesis 3: Operational efficiency under the OLDA auction is not significantly different from operational efficiency under current online auctions with static BIN.

4 Auction Design and Experimental Treatments

The need of laboratory experiments in e-commerce research has also been recognized and discussed in Kauffman and Wood [8]. Under their methodological framework, laboratory experiments allow the researcher to study relevant phenomena with complicating environmental context-related conditions removed. Such experiments enable precise measurements of relevant effects while necessarily sacrificing some generality and realism. The methodology of experimental economics is suitable for our investigation, especially because in online auctions individual preferences are private and unobservable. Costs related to the value of time are likewise private and unobservable by other auction participants. Moreover, to the best of our knowledge, at the time of this writing there are no Internet auction sites that offer dynamic prices (including dynamic BIN options). In addition, most theoretical models of auction behavior do not explicitly or adequately incorporate behavioural effects. Thus, in accordance with Kagel [7] and Vragov [22], we conclude that experimental laboratory research is likely to produce new insights with respect to theory-building as well as reveal implications for the practical design and implementation of online auctions.

We followed the procedures established in Vragov et al. [21] as closely as possible to conduct the study. Eighty subjects were recruited randomly from the undergraduate student population at a large urban university in the U.S. The subjects were split into eight groups of ten participants each: five buyers and five sellers. The subjects were paid a ten-dollar show-up fee plus a performance-based payout that averaged about 25 dollars per person and session. Eight sessions, lasting about two hours each, were run. Each treatment was applied four times, with different participants. After the volunteer subjects came to the experimental laboratory, they were randomly assigned to the role of a buyer or seller. They read a set of online instructions and participated in a short simulation that explained the rules of the market and how to use the trading system developed for the experiment. Subjects were encouraged to raise questions, which were answered on an individual basis by one of three experimenters in the room. Typically it took about half an hour before everyone in the session had successfully completed the instruction module. The actual experiment took about another hour, starting with one practice round of five minutes (whose data was discarded), followed by ten consecutive experimental rounds of five minutes each. Prior to the experiments, a number of pilots were run as the researchers developed the electronic market design and trading system implementation.

Table 1. Value Draws for Bidders

Round	Value draws from highest to lowest	Round	Value draws from highest to lowest
1	78, 49, 31, 19, 9	6	57, 31, 30, 8, 6
2	98, 94, 49, 33, 25	7	68, 45, 35, 22, 15
3	90, 59, 45, 23, 13	8	84, 75, 31, 23, 14
4	96, 90, 51, 35, 31	9	84, 56, 16, 14, 11
5	93, 92, 87, 52, 5	10	87, 85, 78, 27, 22

Our experimental environment consists of five buyers and five sellers. Each seller has one unique product to sell and each buyer has an independent private value for each item sold in the market. This allows us to hold five auctions with up to five buyers in each, independently and simultaneously. The presence of as many as five buyers in an auction experiment is sufficient to stimulate competition and prevent buyer collusion [17]. We normalize direct product costs to zero. Each seller exhibits a private, linear time cost, expressing his or her individual time preferences and cost of delay. More specifically, seller time cost is modelled as a linear function in experimental time: $cis(t)= i{\times}t\,/100$ for all $i\in \{1,..,5\},\ 0\leq t\leq T$. This is in accord with previous auction experiments involving time costs (see [20]). In the experiments, all auctions are scheduled to run for five minutes of real time (i.e., 300 seconds). Time costs accrue as the auction unfolds; the quicker an item sells the less time cost is incurred by the seller. Each buyer in the experiment has a specific willingness to pay (WTP) for each product, whose value is randomly chosen between 0 and 100, with equal probability. All WTP value draws used in the experiment are shown in Table 1. Likewise, buyers are assigned linear time costs $cjb(t)= j{\times}t\,/100$ for all $j\in \{1,..,5\},\ 0\leq t\leq T$.

The experiment has two treatments. Across the two treatments, most parameters are the same. The only difference is that in the first treatment sellers are allowed to set a permanent BIN price at the beginning of the auction (static pricing treatment), while in the second treatment sellers are allowed to set an initial BIN price and a rate at which this price will linearly change during the auction (OLDA treatment).

Each experiment consists of one practice round and ten real rounds. In each round, the bidders' WTP, as given in Table 1, is scrambled so that every buyer has equal chance to be the highest WTP holder in a given round for a given auction. The sellers know the buyers' WTP distribution and can see their bids as they come in. The experiment begins with the random assignment to each bidder of his or her WTP values

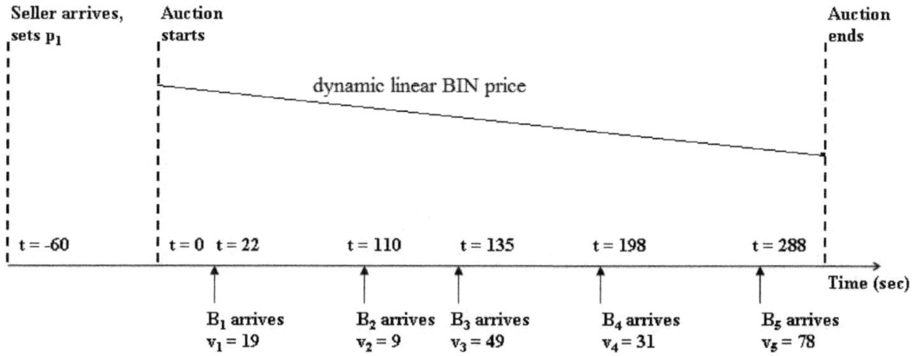

Fig. 1. An Example of Auction Arrival Times and Bidder Values in the OLDA Treatment

and time-cost function. Time costs are specified as a function of time expressed in cost accrued per second as the round progresses. Then sellers are given one minute to set their permanent (static case) or initial BIN prices and rate of decrease (OLDA treatment). Once the BIN price is set, buyers start arriving randomly in sequence at any time during the five-minute auctions. Each of the five sellers runs one, and only one, auction per round, trying to sell his respective unique items to any of the five potential buyers. The five sellers run their auctions concurrently. All five buyers have an interest in the five unique items offered by the sellers and may submit bids in any or all of the five parallel auctions. The WTP for an item varies across buyers and is given by an individual valuation V_i. Figure 1 depicts an illustration of the bidder arrival process.

The dynamic trajectories of some of the relevant variables in the chosen auction round are displayed in Figure 2. V_1 and V_2 show the time trajectories of the highest and second-highest WTP net of buyers' linear time costs. R_1 and R_2 show the time trajectories of seller's revenue if the auction price happens to be V_1 and V_2 net of seller's linear time cost, which is represented by the line C. The graph is based on the arrival times and values shown in Figure 1 In addition, seller's time cost is assumed to be \$0.01per second and buyer i's time cost is assumed to be $(i \times 0.01)$ per second for $i = 1, 2, 3, 4, 5$.

Once bidders arrive at an auction, they may either submit a bid or, if their current WTP is higher than the current buyout price, accept the buyout price. When a buyer accepts a buyout price, he terminates the auction immediately and collects his profit. Otherwise, bidders may increase their bids as often as they wish until the auction finishes at the predetermined closing time after 300 seconds. As soon as the auction starts and buyers may bid, time costs kick in and their WTPs are discounted and automatically updated on the buyer screen, according to the buyer's specific time-cost function. In the OLDA treatment, sellers set the rate at which their BIN price changes during the auction. If someone accepts a BIN price, the auction ends at once and the seller and buyers in this auction stop incurring time costs. If the BIN price is not accepted, the auction continues until its scheduled conclusion. At the end, the bidder with the highest bid wins the auction and pays his or her current bid.

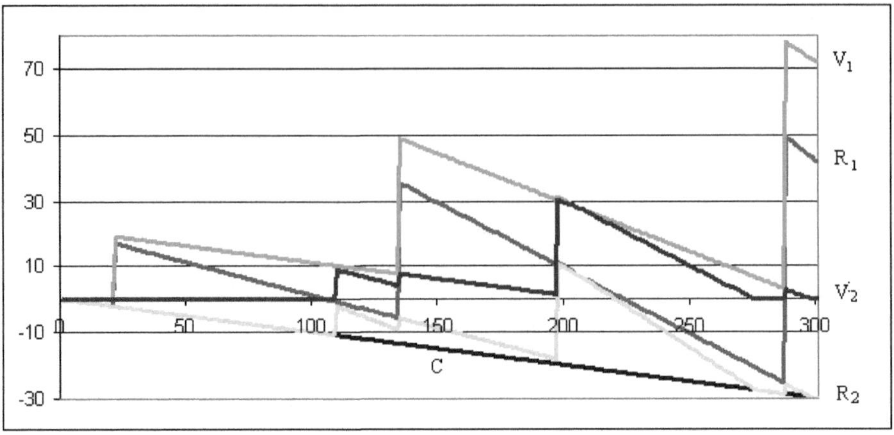

Fig. 2. The Impact of Time Costs on the Highest and Second-Highest Willingness to Pay and Potential Auction Revenue for the Example in Figure 1

At the end of every round, both seller and buyers accumulate profit.[2] They are paid accordingly at the end of the experiment, after completing ten rounds. A buyer's surplus is determined by adding up the profits from all the items she won in any of the fifty auction rounds in which she participated. Any won item contributes an amount of the WTP net transaction price to her total profits. Seller profits are equal to total revenue minus time cost, since the product costs have been normalized to zero. Obviously, time costs diminish profits for both buyers and sellers. Both buyers and sellers face a trade-off between getting the best possible price and selling or buying as quickly as possible and thus minimizing time costs. Performance-based payouts provide a strong incentive to subjects to do well in the auctions in terms of buying and selling at or near the right price point.

The total earnings in the experiment are the sum of the earnings in each round. These data can be used to evaluate how the OLDA auction performs compared to a standard current online auction with a static BIN price. The cash payouts to the subjects equal their total earnings from the experiment, converted to U.S. dollars by applying an exchange rate from experimental dollars to actual U.S. dollars, plus the additional ten-dollar show-up fee. This arrangement induces economically motivated behavior in the subjects.

5 Experimental Findings

The chief purpose of our study is to test the three hypotheses discussed in Section 3. More specifically, we compare the differences between our two experimental treatments, which represent two distinct BIN price policies: one static and the other

[2] For example if a seller with a time cost of \$0.05 per second chose a BIN of \$60 and that BIN was accepted after one second by a buyer then the seller will earn \$60-0.05=\$59.95 for this round. At the same time if this buyer's value was \$84 and his time cost was \$0.04 per second, then the buyer will earn \$84-60-0.04=\$23.96 for this round.

dynamic. Given the relatively small number of experimental sessions conducted (4 for each of the 2 treatments), the non-parametric Mann-Whitney U test adjusted for small samples is the most appropriate and powerful tool for detecting differences in auction efficiency and performance (see [10]). We next report our results.

Table 2. Seller Surplus Comparison across Treatments

Session	Mean Total Seller Surplus per Session	Mean Total Seller Surplus per Treatment	U-test p-value
Standard1	200.72		
Standard2	204.52		
Standard3	255.02	224.84	
Standard4	239.10		0.248
OLDA1	235		
OLDA2	244	248.65	
OLDA3	270.8		
OLDA4	244.8		

First we test our main hypothesis (H1), developed based on the theoretical prediction that dynamic BIN pricing will not significantly increase seller surplus when implemented in practice. Under H1, we expect that observed seller profits are drawn from the same distribution in the two treatments. Table 2 shows the mean total seller surplus (per round over all 4 sessions) for the two treatments. The difference between seller surplus in the two treatments is insignificant (p-value = 0.248, two-tailed test). Therefore the hypothesis is supported.

Now we test our second hypothesis, namely that buyer surplus is not different in the OLDA auction. Under that hypothesis, we again assume that our observations of buyer surplus in the two treatments follow the same distribution. Table 3 shows average buyer surplus across the two treatments.

As Table 3 shows, buyer surplus in the two treatments is not significantly different (p-value = 0.248, two-tailed test), which supports hypothesis H2.

Finally, we test our last hypothesis (H3), which states that the OLDA auction design does not improve total surplus. Table 4 shows that the total surplus treatment comparisons and the total surplus average in all four sessions of the two treatments.

Table 3. Comparison of Buyer Surplus Treatment Averages

Session	Mean Total Buyer Surplus per Session	Mean Total Buyer Surplus per Treatment	U-test p-value
Standard1	104.81		
Standard2	104.49	89.36	
Standard3	57.92		
Standard4	90.20		0.248
OLDA1	79		
OLDA2	88.9	75.03	
OLDA3	61.6		
OLDA4	70.6		

Table 4. Total Surplus Comparisons

Session	Mean Total Surplus per Session	Mean Total Surplus per Treatment	U-test p-value
Standard1	305.53		
Standard2	309.01	314.20	
Standard3	312.94		
Standard4	329.30		0.083
OLDA1	314		
OLDA2	332.9	323.68	
OLDA3	332.4		
OLDA4	315.4		

Table 5. Comparison of Seller Revenue Treatment Averages

Session	Mean Total Seller Revenue per Session	Mean Total Seller Revenue per Treatment	U-test p-value
Standard1	230.75		
Standard2	227.5	251.165	
Standard3	283.91		
Standard4	262.5		0.149
OLDA1	262.6		
OLDA2	269.1	274.4	
OLDA3	293		
OLDA4	272.9		

Realized surplus values in each session are statistically independent. Our test comparing the difference of the average surplus between the two treatments is insignificant (p-value = 0.083, two-tailed test). Thus, we accept H3.

It will be in the interest of auction market providers to know whether the OLDA auction design increases the revenue of the auction website, even though, as shown above, the proposed design does not improve surplus for either buyers or sellers. Table 5 shows that total seller revenue in OLDA design is not significantly different from the standard one. Since the market providers' revenue is most of the time from commissions based on sellers' revenue, our result suggests that the OLDA design will not significantly benefit market providers either.

6 Discussion

The results of our experiment confirm Gallien and Gupta's claim that implementing a pre-announced continuous dynamic BIN price in online auctions will not bring about higher profits to the sellers. Assuming some revenue-sharing arrangement between sellers and web site owners, OLDA does not result in higher revenues for the auction provider. In addition, the OLDA design does not significantly improve surplus.

To explain this result, let us compare OLDA to OOBCA. We use the results from our and Vragov et al. [21] to construct Table 6. We can see that OOBCA outperforms OLDA even though the BIN price changes only once under OOBCA. This suggests

Table 6. Comparison of OLDA and OOBCA Buyout Price Models

Auction Model	Seller Surplus	Buyer Surplus	Total Surplus	Seller Revenue
OOBCA	Significantly improved	No significant difference	Significantly improved	Significantly improved
OLDA	No significant difference	No significant difference	No significant difference	No significant difference

that the frequency of price changes is not the only factor that determines the effect of dynamic BIN prices on auction performance. There are other factors that might be more important. One of them might be the complexity of the dynamic setting, which might present individual decision-makers with a cognitive task that is too complex. Another possible explanation is that a pre-announced dynamic BIN price does not involve real bargaining between the seller and the buyer. If the supply and demand conditions change during the auction, or if the seller receives some new information during the auction, the seller cannot adjust the BIN price or the rate at which it changes. This lack of flexibility translates to only marginal and insignificant improvements over a one-time static BIN price. Both discussed factors should be included explicitly in future theoretical models of auctions and be tested in the laboratory in future experiments.

Let us conclude with pointing out some limitations. Our experiment tested a variety of value combinations and arrival times. However, there are still some gaps in the parameter space (for example affiliated values) and these gaps should be explored in future experiments. Duration times in real online auctions are also much longer than in our experiments and bidder values could be affiliated. Both of these differences could influence some of our results. The experiment does not consider implementation and usability costs. It is also possible that in a real-world setting, for example, buyers may resent such new features that might improve the auction at their expense.

7 Conclusion

Theoretical models of auctions that involve dynamic optimization techniques are based on too many unrealistic assumptions to reliably predict the effect of changes in auction design on important auction parameters. This renders current theory of dynamic auctions controversial and immature. Our study offers several contributions to this relatively new body of literature. We experimentally confirm for the first time an important theoretical prediction from dynamic auction theory reported by Gallien and Gupta [5] for the specific case of a pre-determined linearly-decreasing dynamic BIN price. We introduce a completely new dynamic online auction mechanism (OLDA) that has not been used before and evaluate its properties using the methods of experimental economics. We find that this new design is viable, although it does not generate significant increase in performance as compared to static online auction designs. By comparing OLDA and OOBCA, we derive important implications for future theoretical models of dynamic auctions and future laboratory experiments. We find that the benefits of dynamic BIN prices depend on how the BIN prices are implemented and also that the frequency of price changes is not the only factor to consider. The importance of other factors such as auction complexity or the way information is exchanged between buyers and sellers seem important and should be investigated further.

References

1. Ariely, D., Simonson, I.: Buying, Bidding, Playing, or Competing: Value Assessment and Decision Dynamics in Online Auctions. Journal of Consumer Psychology 13(1&2), 113–123 (2003)
2. Caldentey, R., Vulcano, G.: Online Auction and List Price Revenue Management. Management Science 53(5), 795–813 (2007)
3. Coppinger, V., Smith, V., Titus, J.: Incentives and Behavior in English, Dutch, and Sealed-Bid Auctions. Economic Inquiry 18(1), 1–22 (1980)
4. Durham, Y., Roelofs, M., Standifird, S.: eBay's Buy-It-Now function: Who, when and how? Topics in Economic Policy and Analysis 4(1), 1316 (2004)
5. Gallien, J., Gupta, S.: Temporary and Permanent Buyout Prices in Online Auctions. Management Science 53(5), 814–833 (2007)
6. Grossman, S.: The Information Role of Upstairs and Downstairs Markets. Journal of Business 65(4), 509–529 (1992)
7. Kagel, J.H.: Auctions: A Survey of Experimental Research. In: Kagel, J.H., Roth, A.E. (eds.) The Handbook of Experimental Economics, pp. 501–586. Princeton University Press, Princeton (1997)
8. Kauffman, R., Wood, C.: Research Strategies for E-Business: A Philosophy of Science View in the Age of the Internet. In: Kauffman, R., Tallon, P. (eds.) Economics, Information Systems, and Electronic Commerce: Empirical Research, September 30, M.E. Sharp, Inc., USA (2008)
9. Krishna, V.: Auction Theory. Academic Press, San Diego (2002)
10. Mann, H.B., Whitney, D.R.: On a test of whether one of two random variables is stochastically larger than the other. Annals of Mathematical Statistics 18(1), 50–60 (1947)
11. Mathews, T.: The Impact of Discounting on an Auction with a Buyout Option: a Theoretical Analysis Motivated by eBay's Buy-It-Now Feature. Journal of Economics (Zeitschrift fur Nationalokonomie) 81(1), 25–52 (2004)
12. Onur, I., Tomak, K.: Buy-It-Now or snipe on eBay? In: Proceedings of the Twenty-Fourth International Conference on Information Systems (ICIS 2003), pp. 841–845. IEEE Computer Society Press, Seattle (December 2003)
13. Parsons, S., Marcinkiewicz, M., Niu, J., Phelps, S.: Everything You Wanted to Know about Double-auctions, but were Afraid to (Bid or) Ask, Working paper, Department of Computer and Information Sciences, Brooklyn College, City University of New York, p. 49 (August 18, 2006)
14. Plott, C.: Equilibrium, Equilibration, Information and Multiple Markets: From Basic Science to Institutional Design. Paper presented at the Nobel Symposium, Behavioral and Experimental Economics, Stockholm (December 4-6, 2001)
15. Roth, A., Ockenfels, A.: Last-minute Bidding and the Rules for Ending Second-price Auctions: Evidence from eBay and Amazon Auctions on the Internet. American Economic Review 92(4), 1093–1103 (2002)
16. Schwartz, R.A., Francioni, R.: Equity Markets in Actions: The Fundamentals of Liquidity, Market Structure and Trading. John Wiley & Sons Inc., Hoboken (2004)

17. Smith, V.L.: An Experimental Study of Competitive Market Behavior. The Journal of Political Economy 20(2), 111–137 (1962)
18. Smith, V.L.: Experimental Economics: Induced Value Theory. American Economic Review 66(2), 274–279 (1976); Papers and Proceedings of the Eighty-eighth Annual Meeting of the American Economic Association
19. Smith, V.L.: Constructivist and Ecological Rationality in Economics. American Economic Review 93(3), 465–508 (2003)
20. Vragov, R.: Why is eBay the King of Internet Auctions? An Institutional Analysis Perspective, e-Service Journal, Summer 3(3), 5–28 (2003)
21. Vragov, R., Shang, D., Lang, K.: Should Online Auctions Employ Dynamic Buyout Pricing Models? In: Proceedings of 38th Hawaii International Conference on Systems Sciences, Kona, Hawaii, pp. 381–391 (January 2008)
22. Vragov, R.: Operational Efficiency of Decentralized Internet Auction Mechanisms. In: E-Commerce Research and Application (Available online April 23, 2009) (in press), doi:10.1016/j.elerap.2009.04.008
23. Wang, Sh., Jank, W., Shmueli, G., Smith, P.: Modeling Price Dynamics in eBay Auctions Using Principal Differential Analysis, Robert H. Smith School Research Paper, No. RHS-06-052 (December 8, 2006)
24. Wenyan, H., Bolivar, A.: On-line Auction Efficiency: A Survey of eBay Auctions. In: Proceedings of WWW 2008 Conference, Beijing, China, April 21-26, pp. 925–934 (2008)
25. Whinston, A., Gopal, R., Tung, Y.: Efficiency Considerations in Online Auction Markets. Journal of Organizational Computing and Electronic Commerce 17(1), 311–328 (2007)
26. Yoo, B., Ho, K., Tam, K.: The Impact of Information in Electronic Auctions: An Analysis of Buy-it-now Auctions. In: Proceedings of 2006 Hawaii International Conference on Systems Sciences, Kona, Hawaii, pp. 167–174 (January 2006)
27. Zhang, H., Yin, F., Hsu, V.: The Impact of the Buy-It-Now Option on Online Auctions: An Empirical Investigation. In: Proceedings of the 6th International Workshop on E-Business (Web 2007), Montreal, Canada (December 9, 2007)

Electronic Commerce On-Site Search Services: A State of the Art Review

Nan Li[1], Peter Hitchcock[1], James Blustein[1], and Michael Bliemel[2]

[1] Faculty of Computer Science, Dalhousie University,
6050 University Avenue, Halifax Nova Scotia, B3H 1W5, Canada
[2] Faculty of Management, Dalhousie University,
6100 University Avenue, Halifax Nova Scotia, B3H 3J5, Canada
nan_ls@hotmail.com, {hitchcp,Jamie}@cs.dal.ca, m.bliemel@dal.ca

Abstract. Many Electronic Commerce websites have vast product catalogues, which require visitors to use an on-site search function to find and consequently purchase the product they desire. This paper illustrates the importance of successful on-site searches, the main Key Performance Indicators (KPI) for on-site searches, and introduces several popular on-site search algorithms and techniques.

Keywords: On-Site Search, Key Performance Indicators, E-Commerce.

1 Introduction

Over the last decade search engines continue to improve as they grow in popularity. With the rise of powerful search engines like Google, Yahoo! and Bing, why would we still need search services within a website? Why not let the search engines do all the search-related work? Here are the reasons:

A webpage may not be visible in the search result listings. Visitors tend to have little patience. People typically provide two words per search [1] and they do not often look past the first ten results returned by the search engine. Research shows that if a visitor cannot find what they are looking for within three clicks, the chance of the visitor leaving becomes much higher [2]. For a website owner, it does not make sense to let visitors leave the website and visit another link from the search engine's list of results if the item is available from your website. If allowed to leave, the chance that the visitor will return is very low. There are at least 50.6 billion web pages [3] but search engines usually display 10 search results a time. The majority of web pages are therefore invisible when search engines are the primary method of searching.

It is well known that search engines do not crawl web pages on a daily basis, so there are many pages that may have changed since they were last indexed. If search engines are the only method that visitors can use to browse a webpage, they can be mislead by out-of-date or incomplete information.

People are becoming accustomed to searching by inputting a search keyword rather than searching by category. Even if one website has its inventory in well organized categories, visitors may still want to search based on keywords that are in their minds,

R. Sharman, T.S. Raghu, and H.R. Rao (Eds.): WEB 2009, LNBIP 52, pp. 226–234, 2010.

instead of narrowing down their search category by category. Providing both a category and text search box on an e-commerce website has become a basic feature.

Almost all professional e-commerce websites now use a text search box and the inclusion of such a text search box, useful or not, is now the norm. By providing a search box search service, it becomes much easier to log what visitors are searching for on the website. By studying those search keywords, we can gain insight into what visitors are expecting from the website. Based on this, webpage content can be adjusted to better fit the visitors' expectations.

2 Background

Every e-commerce website has one common goal, which is to sell products or services to its visitors. No matter what the product or service is that is being sold, all visitors experience the same searching process as illustrated below in Figure 1, which is subsequently explained in detail.

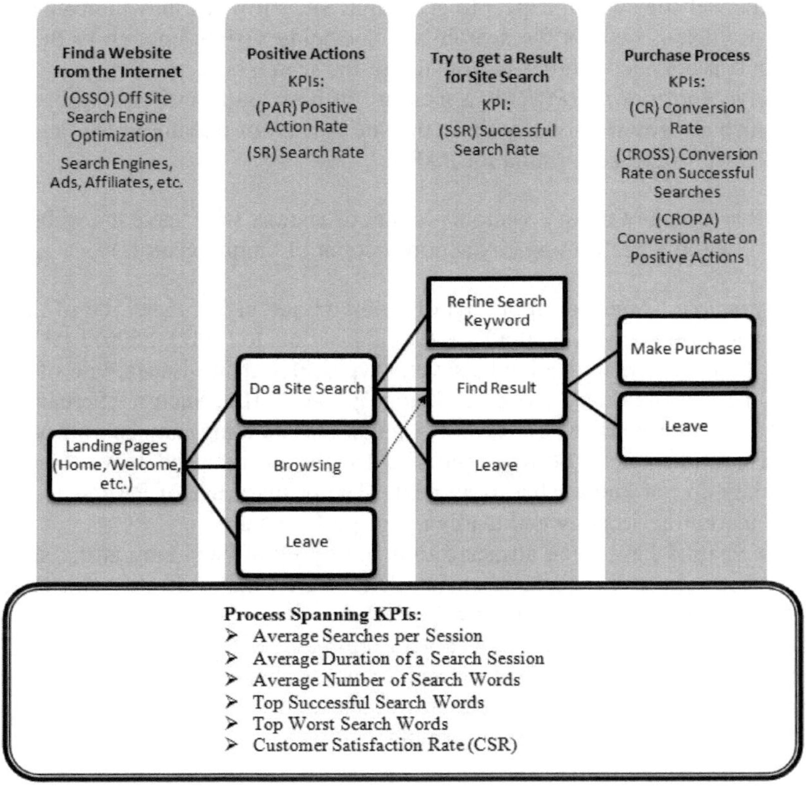

Fig. 1. E-Commerce Website Usage and KPIs from a Visitor's Point of View

The overall process is composed of two major parts: *off-site search optimization* (*OSSO*) and on-site search. For the site owner, the purpose of OSSO is to bring visitors to the website. On-site searches are intended to convert those visitors into customers. This paper concentrates on exploring on-site search approaches and performance measurement metrics.

2.1 Measuring Performance

Key Performance Indicators (*KPI*) are a set of measures or metrics used to define and evaluate certain aspects of e-commerce websites. There are several KPI to help gauge on-site search services. Some KPI are used to analyze how the current on-site search strategies are working, while others are used to design useful on-site search solutions.

Search Rate (*SR*) is the percentage of all the visitors who did at least a search by inputting a search keyword. The formula for SR is:

$$\text{SR} = \text{Count of unique visitors who performed at least one search} \, / \, \text{Count of unique visitors}\,. \tag{1}$$

For the websites which expect to get a high SR, a low SR may indicate several web design problems, such as the search box not being visible enough to the visitors or page content not encouraging visitors to use the search box.

Positive Action Rate (*PAR*) is a measure of how many visitors perform a positive action such as browsing or searching the site instead of leaving immediately after entering the website. The formula for PAR is:

$$\text{PAR} = (\text{count of unique visitors} - \text{count of visitors who leave the website without performing any action}) \, / \, \text{count of unique visitors})\,. \tag{2}$$

For example, if there were a total of 1,000 unique visitors and 500 of them left the site without doing anything, the PAR would be equal to (1000 – 500) / 1000 = 50%.

Low PAR can be indicative of several types of website issues; one of which may be that the website draws too much inappropriate traffic. Such traffic can be directly caused by a poor marketing strategy. Another shortcoming may be poor website content. The content may be too confusing for the visitors and leave them in a state where they do not know what to do next. The primary use of PAR is to analyze the off-site marketing strategy and landing page performance.

Once visitors have been attracted to a site by OSSO and stay at the site, the next step towards success is to have an intra-site search that will aid them to efficiently find products or services that they will purchase.

Successful Search Rate (*SSR*) is a very important KPI for on-site search. There are a couple of different definitions for SSR. Some website-owners calculate it based on unique visitors who performed searches. It shows the rate of how many visitors actually get a search result page. That formula is:

$$\text{SSR} = \text{Count of unique visitors who get at least one search result} \, / \, \text{Count of unique visitors}\,. \tag{3}$$

For example, assume that there are total of 1,000 unique visitors and 800 of the 1000 did 1,200 searches. Now assume that only 700 of them have ever seen the search result page. The SSR = 700/1000 = 70%.

Another definition of SSR is the rate for all of the search sessions that receive a search result page. That formula is:

$$\text{SSR} = \text{Count of search sessions that get a search result} / \text{Count of search sessions}\,. \tag{4}$$

As an example, if there are 1,000 unique visitors that make 1,500 searches and 1,125 of the search sessions return a search result, then the SSR is 1125/1500 = 75%.

To simplify the problem and focus on search only, we calculate the SSR according to the second formula. Therefore, we calculate SSR based on search sessions rather than visitors. SSR is the health meter of the current searching strategies. It directly affects the customer satisfaction rate and the very important KPI final conversion rate. Mondosoft [4] reported, "Among the 400 sites in our study, an average of 22% of all searches returned no results."

2.2 Purchase Related KPIs

There are some other website KPI that may also reflect how the on-site search solution is faring, or may detail the effect of the solution on on-site search performance.

Conversion Rate (*CR*) is the percentage of the all the visitors who actually buy something. For example, if the total number of unique visitors is 1,000 and 40 of them finally make a purchase, then the final CR = 40/1000 = 4%. Getting a high CR is the goal for all e-commerce websites. One of the motivations to increase SSR is to produce a higher CR. Aside from SSR, several other factors can affect a visitor's purchase decision. Examples of these alternative factors include price, shipping charges, and availability. A high conversion rate indicates a good SSR, but a poor conversion rate does not necessarily reflect a low SSR.

Conversion Rate on Successful Searches (*CROSS*) is the KPI that shows how many of the visitors who get at least one search result actually makes a purchase. If the total number of unique visitors is 1,000 and 400 of them gets at least one search result then forty of them actually purchase goods. The CROSS = 40 / 400 = 10%. This KPI focuses on the visitors who performed at least one successful search. A low CROSS indicates that there may be some pricing, shipping or availability issues that are stopping the visitors from buying the product after finding it through the search function.

Conversion Rate on Positive Actions (*CROPA*) shows how many visitors who performed a positive action actually buy something. If the total number of unique visitors is 1,000 and 500 of them performed a positive action and forty of them actually buy something, then CROPA = 40 / 500 = 8%. Some site owners prefer this KPI since it focuses attention on the performance of on-site features only by filtering out inappropriate traffic.

2.3 Spanning the Entire Process

Average Searches Per Session (*ASPS*) refers to the number of searches a typical visitor will usually do on a website. This KPI relates to visitor search behavior. Based on the Mondosoft website search survey [4], the average searches per session is between two and four. That research indicates that visitors are likely to refine their search keywords four times during a search process, at the most. If the visitor still cannot find a positive search result within the maximum four searches, the chance that the visitor will leave the website is high.

All website owners must study this KPI and learn the patience limits of visitors in order to survive. This KPI can also be a reference when filtering out suspected unwanted visitors. If one visitor searches too many unusual terms or too many times, it may be an indication that the visitor may be software and not really a potential customer.

Average Duration of a Search Session measures how much time users spend on each search, on average. A search session represents the entire process of a visitor trying to find a product by searching using a keyword. A visitor may have many search sessions. This KPI shows the time between search sessions. By studying this KPI, we can get an idea if the content on the search result page is appropriate. For example, if most of the search result pages provide many search results, you may expect people to finish the reading the entire list within 2–3 minutes. However, if the KPI shows that duration of the search is only 1 minute, then it either means that the visitor did not find what they were looking or they simply gave up reading. The challenge is how to get the right number for this KPI. One must consider that visitors may do something not related to search between search sessions, such as loading another static information page between searches on the same site or grabbing a cup of coffee.

Average Number of Search Words answers the question "Are most of the visitors searching using multiple words or single words?" This KPI is very important in determining the right search strategies. Searches that use multiple words strongly suggest a search approach that understands natural language.

Top Successful Search Words is the certain number of search keywords that visitors used most frequently to search in the website to get a search result. This measure indicates what most of the visitors are expecting from the website. Those search words may present some products or certain information. With the help of this KPI, a website owner will know what products or information should be promoted throughout the website. This KPI also indicates whether the searching strategy applied to this kind of search is working properly.

Top Worst Search Words are the most commonly used search terms that do not match anything in the index. The inability to get results from a search results in a poor situation for both the visitor and the website. However, the top "worst" search words can provide very important and valuable information. If a search keyword constantly returns no results but different visitors keep using it in their searches, it may indicate several things:

- The keyword may refer to a product that visitors are expecting to be on this website and considerations regarding adding the item to the website's inventory should be made.
- Visitors may be searching for an item that is in the inventory but the visitors are not using the correct term that refers to the item. It shows a need for a change to the site's searching strategy as changing a visitor's search habits is an unreasonable solution.

Customer Satisfaction Rate (*CSR*) indicates if customers are satisfied with the website and how much they appreciate the services that are provided by the website. CSR is difficult to measure. Some websites provide a survey, asking customers if they were satisfied with the services offered and if not, what factors caused the dissatisfaction. By analyzing the survey data, website owners can get some measure of the CSR. However, for those who do not have, or have but do not analyze, this kind of survey, it may be difficult to know customer satisfaction levels. Some other KPI can help in this regard. SSR in particular has a strong affect on CSR. A low SSR leads to low CSR —no one appreciates a poor search service.

3 On Site Search Approaches

In this part, we introduce major text search approaches. Website owners should pick the right searching strategy based on the websites' searching requirements and data characteristics. For most websites, one searching strategy will not fulfill all of the searching requirements. Implementing and applying two or even more searching strategies on one website may be needed.

Exact Search is the strategy that returns exact matches for the searched keyword only. In SQL, the syntax for exact search is select * from table where column = 'keyword'. This gives visitors the most accurate results. There is no additional technique challenge in this kind of search except improving searching speed. Creating proper indexes for the data will improve searching speed. Exact search is the best solution when visitors know precisely what they are searching for, and under what name it is indexed. Unfortunately, the system cannot find exact matches to visitors' search text most of the time and will return no search results if no other search strategies are used to follow up.

Partial Search is also known as wildcard or pattern search. Based on the wildcard's position, it can return different results. In SQL, the syntax for partial searches can be one of the following:

```
select * from table where column like 'keyword%'
select * from table where column like '%keyword'
select * from table where column like '%keyword%'
```

This type of search returns the results that contain the search keyword if the keyword shows up in any part of the searched data.

The wildcard can be a single character, such as "?". If searching for "n?t" the results will include words such as "not" and "net". The wildcard can be multiple characters, using "*". For example, a search for "scien*", the results can include "science" and "scientific" [5]. A leading wildcard in the search terms may cost more time than a term that has a wildcard in the end. The reason is that the searcher cannot ignore any section for the leading wildcard search, and it must go over the entire index until it finds the entries for the term. On the other hand, if we know what the results start with, we can jump to matching sections directly. Proper indexing can increase partial search speed as well.

Both of these SQL-based approaches require care to implement. The most straightforward approaches leave gaping security holes [6]. Other approaches, which are less risky and more forgiving of users' mistakes, depend on comparing relaxed versions of the user's search terms against a similarly relaxed version of the database index.

Phonetic Search is defined as strategic indexing and searching through words based on their pronunciation. Most of the phonetic algorithms are restricted to words in English. If those algorithms are applied to a non-English language, the results will surely be a mess [7, 8]. The following are some techniques for phonetic search.

The most common phonetic search algorithms are Soundex [8] (which was patented over 70 years ago) and some of its variants: Metaphone [9], Double Metaphone [10], Phonix [11], and Editex [8]. In brief, they all work by creating indexes in which codes represent letters and combinations of letters (such as "ph"). In this way, many words with similar pronunciations are identical in the index. The entries in the index point to the actual words.

Grammatical Searches are algorithms that try to match two strings using their grammatical characteristics. Like phonetic searching, they are also specific to a single natural language, e.g. English. Different languages require a different design algorithm to fulfill this search strategy. To implement grammatical search algorithms, it may be necessary to work out a library for mapping purposes. Stemming and synonym searches are two of the major grammatical search strategies.

Stemming Search is a strategy that uses the etymological root of the search keyword instead of the search keyword itself to search through the data and return matches that contain the same root. The stemming search matches all different types of a words including its verb, noun and adjective. For example if the keyword is "mice", it will match both "mouse" and "mice". If the keyword is "running", it matches "run", "running", "ran" and "runs". It was first published by Lovins [12]. Since then, several types of algorithms appeared. Among them is an algorithm written by Porter [13] which was widely used. His "Surfix Stripping" algorithm set up a rule that was formed through several steps.

All stemming algorithms are attempts to reach a balance between two types of error: overstemming and understemming. Overstemming means stem two words to the same root that should not. On the other hand, understemming means stem to different roots for two words that should have the same root [14].

Synonym-based search is more complex than stemming but can yield better results. Sometimes synonyms search and stemming search are quite confusing. For example, if the search keyword is "cars", the word "car" will also be in the search result for both algorithms. However, "automobile" will be in the result for synonyms search but not stemming search. Another example is a search of "intelligent". A synonym search might return matches that include the words "smart" and "clever". To implement synonyms search, a set of rules is not enough. We may need another dictionary for those matches that cannot be covered.

Fuzzy Search can be defined to include all of the string similarity matching algorithms that include phonetic and grammatical matching. We however, limit the term to algorithms that focus on correcting the misspelling (typo) problems in the search keyword only. This focus should be a strategy applied only after the failures of phonetic, stemming and synonyms searching or where those three strategies are not applicable. Levenshtein string distance [15] is one of the most well-known fuzzy search algorithms. It is also referred to as edit distance. It calculates the number of deletions, insertions or substitutions to translate a string (source string) to another string (target string). This calculated number is called the distance between these two strings. If the distance is 0, means the two strings are identical. The larger the number is, the more difference there is between the two strings. This algorithm can be used to return all of the strings that are close to the search keyword. However, since it is based on the string distance only, the majority of the time, it may only return words that are totally unrelated. That is why there are many hybrid solutions that implement string distance and other ranking algorithms to get more accurate results. Editex, referred to above in the section on phonetic algorithms, is one of them.

All of the algorithms described here in section 6 can be implemented by all of the programming languages, such as Java, C++, VB, or SQL server. They are all designed to solve the issue of accuracy in the returned search results to lead to a higher successful search rate (SSR). This in turn can lead to increased customer satisfaction rates with the site (CSR) as well as higher conversion rate on successful searches (CROSS).

4 Recommendations

Many electronic commerce websites continue to frustrate potential customers by providing a search box which often does not provide usable results. These poor results are the responses to queries that are not exact matches to the names of products contained within their databases. Most visitors are users that have become accustomed to finding millions of results with search engines, and often do not realize that on-site search services are far less sophisticated than those of commercial search engines. It is imperative for electronic commerce website operators to improve their visitors' experience with on-site search services if they wish to remain competitive.

In this paper we showed what key performance metrics can be used to assess how well on-site search services are functioning. As product catalogues and customer expectations continue to evolve, it is important to measure and monitor how well on-site search services are performing. We recommend that website operators consider using some or many of the search approaches outlined in this paper to reduce the number of failed searches that visitors are experiencing.

Acknowledgements. The authors wish to thank the anonymous reviewers for their valuable feedback that served to make this a better article, as well the first author's employer who wished to remain anonymous. Publication of this research was also supported through a research grant from the Social Science and Humanities Research Council of Canada (SSHRC).

References

1. Pu, H.-T., Chuang, S.-L., Yang, C.: Subject categorization of query terms for exploring Web users' search interests. J. Am. Soc. Inf. Sci. Technol. 53(8), 617–630 (2002)
2. Hobo. The 3 Click Rule of website design, http://www.hobo-web.co.uk/tips/31.htm

3. Netcraft, Web Server Survey (January 2009), http://news.netcraft.com/archives/2009/01/16/january_2009_web_server_survey.html
4. Mondosoft. Web Site Usability Metrics; Search Behavior and Search Trends (May 2004), http://www.mondosearch.com/upload/pdf/whitepaper/wp-searchbehavior.pdf
5. Microsoft. Wildcard Characters. MSDN Visual Studio Developer Center, http://msdn.microsoft.com/en-us/library/069b0htd(VS.71).aspx
6. Schwartz, R.: Processing Web Forms Carefully. Linux Magazine 4(9), 56–59 (2002)
7. Repici, D.J.: Understanding Classic SoundEx Algorithms (2007), http://www.creativyst.com/Doc/Articles/SoundEx1/SoundEx1.htm
8. Zobel, J., Dart, P.: Phonetic string matching: lessons from information retrieval. In: Proceedings of the 19th Annual International ACM SIGIR Conference on Research and Development in Information Retrieval, ACM, Zurich (1996)
9. Nelson, A.: Implement Phonetic ("Sounds-like") Name Searches with Double Metaphone Part VI: Other Methods & Additional Resources (2007), http://www.codeproject.com/KB/string/dmetaphone6.aspx
10. Atkinson, K.: Lawrence Philips' Metaphone Algorithm (2001), http://aspell.net/metaphone/
11. Zobel, J., Dart, P.: Finding approximate matches in large lexicons. Softw. Pract. Exper. 25(3), 331–345 (1995)
12. Lovins, J.B.: Development of a Stemming Algorithm. Mechanical Translation and Computational Linguistics 11(1&2), 22–31 (1968)
13. Porter, M.F.: An algorithm for suffix stripping, in Readings in information retrieval, pp. 313–316. Morgan Kaufmann Publishers Inc., San Francisco (1997)
14. Paice, C.D.: Method for evaluation of stemming algorithms based on error counting. Journal of the American Society for Information Science 47(8), 632–649 (1996)
15. Gilleland, M.: Levenshtein Distance. In: Three Flavors, http://www.merriampark.com/ld.htm

A Framework for CRM E-Services: From Customer Value Perspective

Wei-Lun Chang and Yu-Xin Wu

Department of Business Administration, Tamkang University,
NO 151, Ying-chuan Road, Tamsui, Taipei County, Taiwan
wlchang@mail.tku.edu.tw, nick2581@yahoo.com.tw

Abstract. The global competition for enterprises has been the significant issue for recent years. However, the customer needs are difficult to satisfy due to specialized characteristic of existing customers. A good CRM strategy may assist firms to earn advanced profits, increase customer perceived value, and acquire new customers. This research aims to provide a holistic framework based on two dimensions. The first dimension is the level of customer needs which is related to customer perceived value. The second value is the process of CRM; for instance, attracting, interacting, and retaining customers. This paper intends to: (1) identify the level of needs based on perceived value, (2) recognize the possible step of CRM processes, and (3) recommend an appropriate CRM e-service to a customer.

Keywords: E-Service; Customer Value; Internet-Enabled CRM.

1 Introduction

The global competition for enterprises has been the significant issue for the past years. However, the customer needs are difficult to satisfy due to specialized characteristic of existing customers. Companies need to manage the relationships with customers more efficient than competitors. For example, firms can get closer to their customers by interactive communication and needs/habits identification and enhance the value of customer. The profitability of customers can also be increased through sustainable attracting, interacting, and retaining customers. Consequently, the key for enterprises is offer superior customer relationship management strategies.

Customer relationship management (CRM) is a significant issue for today's companies. In particular, a good CRM strategy may assist firms to earn advanced profits, increase customer perceived value, and acquire new customers. The popularity of information technology and Internet has changed the concept to deliver services over the Internet. Certain enterprises provide the opportunity to deliver services over the Internet, which is considered as a way to decrease service cost, tighten with customers, and furnish mass communication.

In this study, CRM is transformed from traditional CRM (face-to-face) to Internet-Enabled CRM (over the Internet). This paper defines Internet-Enabled CRM as conducting CRM by utilizing devices which can deliver e-services through the Internet.

R. Sharman, T.S. Raghu, and H.R. Rao (Eds.): WEB 2009, LNBIP 52, pp. 235–242, 2010.

The extent of Internet-Enabled CRM includes electronic CRM (E-CRM), mobile CRM (M-CRM), and ubiquitous CRM (U-CRM). The existing CRM framework is based mostly on the company's perspective; for example, it considers how to acquire customers, retain customers, and create profits from customers. Hence, a holistic framework for both sides is still lacking, especially for e-service industry.

Furthermore, Internet is also the major problem for e-CRM which cannot provide face-to-face contact and difficult to grasp customer needs. Hence, it is important to obtain customer needs accurately and interact with customers efficiently to put effort on valuable customers. This research aims to provide a holistic framework based on two dimensions. The first dimension is the level of customer needs which is related to customer perceived value. The second value is the process of CRM; for instance, attracting, interacting, and retaining customers. We believe each customer has different perceived value for a same service. That is, this paper intends to: (1) identify the level of needs based on perceived value, (2) recognize the possible step of CRM processes, and (3) recommend an appropriate CRM e-service to a customer.

The rest of this paper is organized as follows. Section 2 surveys the extant literature, such as customer perceived value and e-service. Section 3 devises a conceptual framework for customer value management. Section 4 provides the implications of the proposed framework, and section 5 provides a conclusion.

2 Background

2.1 Definition of Perceived Value

The definition of perceived value is proposed by Zeithaml [11], which indicates customer perceived value is the consumer's overall assessment of the utility of a product based on what is received and what is given. Kolter [5] specifies customer delivered value is the difference between total customer value and total customer cost. That is, the benefit of a specific product or service for a customer. The total value includes product value, service value, and personnel value and the total cost enfolds monetary cost, time cost, and spirit cost. Holbrook [1] defines customer value is interactive, experienced, relative, and favorable. This study considers customer value is the difference between obtaining and devoting and various from people.

However, why value is important? Companies attempt to create profit from their customers who evaluate the firms that can provide products or services to satisfy their value [5]. Consumers always consider value as the most important factor when they purchase the products or services. The value stands for what the customers obtain from the transaction. Yan [10] indicates customer value reflects consumer behavior and affects the order of needs. Kim et al. [4] specifies that needs emerge before attitude and purchase and can create value, trigger behavior, and satisfy required level of needs. Hence, the concept of customer value and customer needs is relative (see Fig. 1). Customer value is the obtained benefit from the perception of products or services. Customer need is the motivation to achieve goals that belongs to a type of spontaneous behavior. Hence, this research will utilize the concept of value to build the holistic framework in terms of customer perspective.

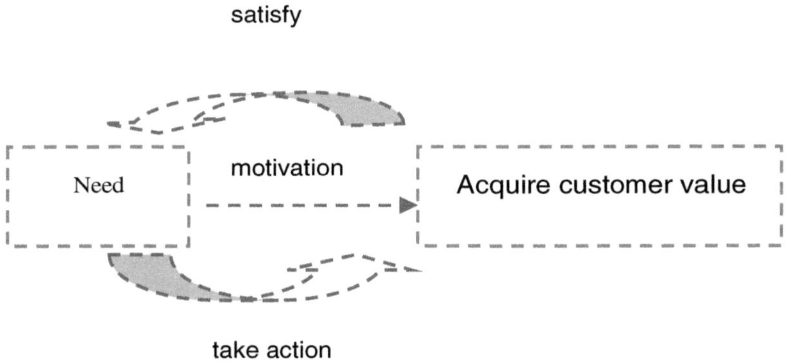

Fig. 1. Relationship between customer value and customer needs

2.2 CRM E-Service

Järvinen and Lehtinen [2] define e-service as a benefit providing object of transaction that can be characterized as an intangible process that is at least partially produced, marketed and consumed in a simultaneous interaction through electronic networks. The implement of e-business not only enhances the efficiency of business but creates markets and profit [7]. Meanwhile, e-services generate new service experience and customer value, such as functional value (time saving, convenience), emotional value (interaction), social value, and network value (security and privacy) [3][6].

In this study, we attempt to classify existing CRM e-services into four major components: attractive e-service, interacting e-service, analytic e-service, and retaining e-service. Attractive e-service provides e-services which employ marketing methods. For example, blog marketing, experience marketing, and 1-to-1 marketing are extremely suitable for e-services. The second component is interacting e-service, which allows firms and customers interact over the Internet. In this category, e-service providers can furnish post-purchase survey e-services, online responding e-services, and collected FAQ e-services. Post-purchase survey e-services allow firms to get a better understanding of their customers after purchase, and online responding e-service enables customers to obtain real-time answers when they have a problem.

The third component is analytic e-service, which is used to analyze customers through two main e-services: statistic analysis and data mining e-services. Statistic analysis employs conventional statistical approaches, like clustering and linear regression, while data mining employs artificial intelligence approaches, like neural networks and genetic algorithms, to analyze customers. Finally, retaining e-service includes customer segmentation e-service and performance measurement e-service. In this category, the aim is to help firms retain their customers. For example, customer segmentation e-service can assist firms to segment their customers, identify key value, and provide retaining strategies. Hence, this study will utilize the classification as the basis to build the holistic framework in terms of enterprise perspective.

3 A Conceptual Framework

3.1 A Value Cube for Internet-Enabled CRM

In the era of wireless technology, three dimensions of value are identified for Internet-enabled CRM: (1) business value, (2) customer perceived value, and (3) social value (see Fig. 2). Business value is generated from companies and is always represented by monetary value (e.g., profits). Firms can easily observe the changes in profit (customer profitability) for a given time period and can modify their CRM strategies accordingly. Customer retention another indicator with which to measure profits. According to the 80/20 rule, 20 percent of customers will generate 80% of a company's profits, so it is important to retain those customers. Internet-enabled CRM provides Internet-based e-services that customers can access anytime and anywhere, and companies can utilize new technologies (e.g., wireless and mobile devices) to help earn profits based on certain e-services, so Internet-enabled CRM is believed to attain high business value.

Customer perceived value is generated by customers and reflected in their willingness to pay. The concept of willingness-to-pay represents how much customers intend to pay for furnished e-services, and different CRM strategies may result in different behaviors of customers. For example, customers will not pay for the e-services which are inappropriate for them, even if they are delivered. Internet-enabled CRM provides opportunities for customers to acquire the most appropriate e-services when they face problems, and the technology helps companies identify customers' information, such as location, personalized preferences, and behaviors. Thus, Internet-enabled CRM can help attain high customer perceived value.

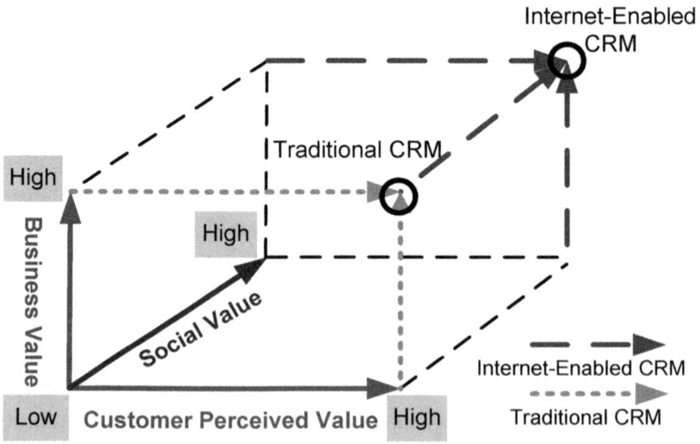

Fig. 2. A Value Cube for Internet-Enabled CRM

Social value is generated by collective intelligence—the wisdom of crowds—over the Internet. According to certain theories (e.g., Delphi method, brainstorming), group decision-making is superior to individual decision-making. Internet-enabled CRM allows peers to assist each other in solving problems based on wireless technologies (e.g., agent-based approach). Traditional CRM merely allows firms to decide what services to deliver—a one-way delivery concept—but Internet-enabled CRM allows peers from the social network to collaborate to decide what e-services will be furnished right away. Thus, Internet-enabled CRM is believed to attain high social value.

In short, Internet-enabled CRM facilitates high business value, customer perceived value, and social value in our proposed value cube. Traditional CRM may attain high business value and customer perceived value, but it lacks a social network effect in the e-service delivery process. We believe Internet-enabled CRM is superior to traditional CRM in terms of collaboration for Internet-enabled services. Hence, Internet-enabled CRM is expected to extend social value dimension from low to high and to provide complete solutions for managing customers well.

3.2 A Value-Based Model for Internet-Enabled CRM

This research uses the dimensions of customer value and CRM process of e-services to propose a customer value creation model (CVCM), which is also a value-based model for Internet-enabled CRM. Wooddruff [9] separates customer value into level of attribute, end, and goal from information processing perspective. Level of attribute describes the products or services, level of end indicates the interaction of users and products/services, and level of goal specifies the goal of individual or organization. Sheth *et al.* [8] indicate the determinants of customer decision for consuming value which are functional value, social value, emotional value, cognitive value, and conditional value. The existing literature specifies the significance for separating customer value into several levels. The lowest level of customer value is concrete and the highest of customer value is abstract. All levels of customer value are interconnected and the higher level of customer value needs to be satisfied from lower level of customer value. In this research, we synthesize the existing concepts to classify customer value into self-actualized value, social and emotional value, added value, and functional value.

In Fig. 3, we utilize customer value and CRM e-service process as two major dimensions to construct a customer value creation model. The lowest two levels of customer value are functional and added value which enfold the concept of CRM 1.0. In the past, CRM 1.0 allows merely closed or one-way communication which indicates only firms can decide when to communicate with customers or not. In these two levels, customers desire to accept useful e-services with basic functions and certain extended e-services to obtain added value. For example, customers need Google to help them search some information and guide them to the related websites. These two levels of customer value are based on basic and expectant value. Companies need to provide e-services that the customers perceive usefulness and completeness to fulfill their needs.

The third level is social and emotional value, which is enhanced to CRM 2.0 concept. CRM 2.0 allows value co-creation and is a type of two-way interaction. In this level, companies provide e-services that fulfill customers' desired value and perceived belongingness from customers. The effect of word-of-mouth can be applied in this level. The most important to firms is the satisfaction of social and emotional value that can retain and create more customers. The highest level is self-actualized value

Concept		Pre-Sale	Transaction		Post-Sale
Process for Creating Customer Value		**Acquire**	**Use**	**Feedback**	**Retain**
Process for Creating Business Value		**Marketing**	**Sale**	**Post-Service**	**Revise**
		CRM E-Service Process			
Level of Customer Value		Attract	Interact		Retain
Surprise from customers (CRM 3.0 concept: Self-problem solving and self -control)	Self-actualized value (Unexpected Value)	*Products and services provide self-actualized value.*	*Customer-centric radiation* B, C (arrows radiating from C)		*Customer domination*
Satisfaction from customers (CRM 2.0 concept: Value co-creation from social network)	Social and emotional value (Desired Value)	*Products and services provide belongingness.*	*Two-way interaction* B ↔ C		*Social and emotional satisfaction*
Comprehensiveness from customers (CRM 1.0 concept: E-service standard)	Added value (Expectant Value)	*Products and services are comprehensive.*	*One-way communication* B → C		*Completeness*
Usefulness from customers (CRM 1.0 concept: Basic functions of e-services)	Functional value (Basic Value)	*Products and services provide functional value.*	*Closed* [B] C		*Perceived usefulness*

Fig. 3. Customer value creation model

which is also the expected value to customers. In this level, customers expect surprises from companies and the concept is promoted to CRM 3.0. CRM 3.0 allows customers to solve problems on their own and furnish suggestions and comments for improving e-services sustainably. The customers play a vital role to provide much valuable information to enterprises, which is also the concept of customer-centric radiation. In this level, customers dominate the process of CRM and help the companies to retain most of their customers and create profits.

4 Implications

4.1 Customer-Centric Management

This paper provides a new perspective for CRM in terms of motivation and value. Different customer background may result in various levels of needs and perceived value. Companies need to differentiate marketing methods according to different targets. Our proposed framework provides the opportunity to identify customer needs and furnish a combination of CRM e-services in time. In addition, we assist firms to identify psychological perception from customer value. Enterprises can earn more profits from the concept of customer-centric management.

4.2 Collective Wisdom Empowerment

The proposed framework allows customers to collaborate in order to release the power of collective wisdom. Collective intelligence (wisdom) refers to the concept that people can contribute together in order to attain good performance of Internet-Enabled CRM. Our framework can assist companies to identify the level of needs for customers and predict what CRM e-service(s) can be delivered for the next step.

4.3 Real-Time E-Service Composition

Real-time e-service composition is also a significant issue for Internet-Enabled CRM. E-service providers should be aware of what customers really want at any time, based on their needs. Even when e-service providers acquire customer needs, they still have to compose the required e-services and deliver them to the customer quickly. Certain e-service providers can discover required e-services from the framework more efficiently and dynamically bundle them as a package. Our framework advances the e-service delivery process and implements the concept of service-oriented management.

5 Conclusion

CRM is an essential issue for companies in recent years. The emergence of e-services has been changed the essence of traditional CRM services. CRM e-services will dominate future CRM processes. This study proposes a value cube for Internet-enabled CRM in terms of business value, social value, and customer perceived value. The value cube also illustrates the revolution of CRM. In addition, this research investigates the significance of customer value to provide a different perspective for CRM process. Thus, we propose a value-based model for Internet-enabled CRM e-services. This paper extends the concept of customer value from Maslow needs hierarchy based on existing literature. In particular, we separate customer value into four levels: self-actualized value (highest), social and emotional value, added value, and functional value (lowest). The fulfillment of customer value may be caused by different combination of CRM e-services. Hence, we aim to provide a holistic framework for future CRM e-service providers with customer and business perspectives.

Moreover, there are still some limitations for this research. For example, the proposed value cube and value-based model need to be verified in details. Real-world cases or simulation of collected data can examine the feasibility and validity. Although the proposed frameworks are novel and preliminary, the value is existed for further investigated. The other limitation is the separation of level of customer value. We extend the concept from Maslow needs hierarchy to construct our framework. However, some other concepts that can separate the level of customer value are existed. The different separation of levels can be applied to compare the difference between our model and others. In sum, we believe our proposed model/framework is crucial and potential for future CRM studies. Additionally, the contribution will be significant if the real-world cases are applied in details.

References

1. Holbrook, M.B.: Consumer Value: a framework for analysis and research. Routledge, London (1999)
2. Järvinen, R., Lehtinen, U.: Services, e-Services and e-Service Innovations Combination of Theoretical and Practical Knowledge. In: Marko, S., Mika, H., Anne-Mari, J., Johanna, K., Mikko, R., Tarja, T. (eds.) FeBR 2004 Frontiers of e-Business Research 2004 e-Business Research Center, Tampereen yliopiston laitosten julkaisut, pp. 78–89 (2004)
3. Keeney, R.L.: The Value of Internet Commerce to the Customer. Management Science 45(4), 533–542 (1999)
4. Kim, J.-O., Forsythe, S., Gu, Q., Moon, S.J.: Cross-cultural consumer values, needs and purchase behaviour. Journal of Consumer Marketing 19(6), 481–502 (2002)
5. Kotler, P.: Marketing Management-Analysis, Planning, Implementation and Control, 9th edn. Prentice-Hall Inc., New Jersey (1997)
6. Korgaonkar, P.K., Wolin, L.D.: A multivariate analysis of web usage. Journal of Advertising Research 39, 53–68 (1999)
7. Rust, R.T., Kannan, P.K.: e-Service: New Direction in Theory and Practice. M.E. Sharpe, Armonk (2002)
8. Sheth, J.N., Newman, B.I., Gross, B.L.: Why We Buy What We Buy: A Theory of Consumption Values. Journal of Business Research 22, 159–170 (1991)
9. Woodruff, R.B.: Customer Value: The Next Source for Competitive Advantage. Journal of the Academy of Marketing Science 25(2), 139–153 (1997)
10. Yan, O.H.M.: Consumer Behavior in China: Customer Satisfaction and Cultural Value. Routledge, New York (1994)
11. Zeithaml, V.A.: Consumer Perceptions of Price, Quality, and Value: A Means-EndModel and Synthesis of Evidence. Journal of Marketing 52, 2–22 (1988)

An Integrated Approach to Managing IT Portfolio

Yu-Ju Tu and Michael J. Shaw

University of Illinois at Urbana-Champaign,
61820 Champaign, IL, U.S.A

Abstract. As IT portfolio management (ITPM) has been increasingly regarded as solution to governing IT investment, enterprises are faced with the challenge to develop and manage IT portfolio. We argue that IT portfolio needs to additionally consider managerial flexibilities and interdependencies in terms of a balanced portfolio return and risk. Moreover, we propose an IT portfolio model that is capable of considering option and synergy to make decision. Finally, we demonstrate an example to show the use our proposed model.

Keywords: IT portfolio, synergy, managerial flexibility, options, interdependency.

1 Introduction

Increasingly, IT portfolio management (ITPM) has garnered significant attentions among enterprises. It is generally said that IT portfolio management is able to provide a portfolio-based approach to help manage various IT asset or project. Since McFarlan[20], the basic concept of IT portfolio has existed for almost 30 years. So far, however, the IT portfolio researches are still very limited in the Information Systems literature.

To a certain degree, IT portfolio management is seen as an extension of IT valuation and prioritization. In this regard, discounted-cash-flow based models and real-options based models are main financial modeling approaches. In contrast with discounted-cash-flow based models, real-options based models in recent years have developed a stream of research in information systems (IS) literature [3][4][5][8][9][26]. Nevertheless, real-options based models have their own limitations. For example, because of their complicated theoretical assumptions, some enterprises tend to see such models as the black-box model for managing IT investment. It is also one of reasons why the real-options based models are still precluded from being widely used and discounted-cash-flow based models are still dominant.

Actually, IT portfolio management should cover not only simply IT valuation and prioritization, but also portfolio analysis. Nonetheless, usually the IT portfolio-level analysis used to be overlooked, because the analogy between an IT portfolio and stock portfolio is not easily perceived. For instance, a stock portfolio can be composed of numerous different stocks from the public market, but an IT project portfolio can only be composed of IT projects proposed. Besides, each IT project is usually singular in an IT project portfolio, but same stock can be multiple in the stock portfolio. On the other hand, the value of a stock portfolio could not be influenced by any

R. Sharman, T.S. Raghu, and H.R. Rao (Eds.): WEB 2009, LNBIP 52, pp. 243–253, 2010.

managerial flexibility, whereas the value of an IT project portfolio could. For instance, a senior IT manager could let some IT projects postpone for a while, or make them share some function with other IT projects in order to save certain cost. In other words, the value of the resultant IT project portfolio could change by IT manager's certain managerial action. Specifically, from our observation, managing IT project portfolio can exploit considerable possibilities of managerial flexibilities and interdependencies. With technology advancing, IT projects are often capable of benefiting from time because of Moore's law. For instance, because of the digital data and modular design, IT projects are relatively easy to share component with each other; because of the compatible managerial principles, IT projects are relatively feasible to be coordinated to support each other. Put simply, these nuances make managing IT portfolio very different from managing a traditional stock portfolio.

Accordingly, how to make the bridge between financial modeling approach and IT project context is one of main challenges in IT portfolio management. Although such researches in the Information Systems literature are stark, similar researches can be found in related research area. In the context of computer programming, Kersten and Verhoef employed the discounted-cash-flow based model and Markowitz's portfolio theory to optimize the IT product portfolio [10]. In the context of R&D management, Ong and Wu propose a descriptive IT investments portfolio framework incorporating real-options thinking [26]. In the context of operations research, Liesio et al. propose a project portfolio model which takes into account the project interdependency [13]. Clearly, however, more investigations are needed to explore the IT portfolio management in the Information Systems area.

In this paper we are to facilitate IT project portfolio management in a quantitative manner. Particularly, by providing a model for developing a balanced IT project portfolio, we are to improve the communication of IT investment decision. Also, we will demonstrate an example to illustrate the use of our proposed model. In this example, we will show how IT project deferral option and cost synergy could have impacts on IT project portfolio compositions. Finally, we will discuss this paper's managerial implications, research contribution, and future direction.

2 Related Literature

On the basis of real-options model, Luehrman proposes a two-parameters model to help deal with selecting projects embedded with a deferral option [15][16]. He creates an option space to help make strategy for projects under uncertainty. Basically, his model depends on the two logics. First, if we wait longer to make the decision for a project, we will have more uncertainties on its value. In other words, the project risk will increase. Second, if we wait some time to make decision for a project, the project's cost also needs to be discounted, since we should consider the interest that the money of the cost might accrue when we are waiting.

Luehrman's model fits in with measuring IT project, since most of IT project are deferrable and therefore deferral options of IT investment are well regarded and investigated in the IT related literature [1][3][4][11][20]. Besides, Luehrman's model is compatible with discounted-current-flow based data, so that it is more likely to be accepted by decision makers in the enterprise. As Kleinmuntz states, for the resource allocation decision, a complex model will be in danger to be treated as a mysterious black box by decision makers, who will be reluctant to rely on it [12]. Since Luhrman's model has several merits and concise to use, we adopt similar measurements to evaluate the IT project.

Modern portfolio theory [18] has been successfully applied in several disciplines. In a way, this model is not only dominant in finance discipline, but also suitable for being applied in other disciplines [21]. Basically, Markowitz reasons that asset return, asset standalone risks, and correlated risks are three main constructs for determining portfolio efficiency. Further, he proposes to use expected value of the asset, the standard deviation of the asset, the correlation between assets, and mean-variance criteria (MV) to select the portfolio. Namely, it is stated that a portfolio can dominates the other portfolio, if it is of higher return, give the same risk for both portfolios. In the same vein, a portfolio can dominate the other portfolio, if it is of lower risk, given the same return for both portfolios. Accordingly, the famous efficient frontier curve can be derived and those dominant portfolios are also called efficienct portfolios. In many perspectives, certain adjustment of Markowitz's model is still needed to fit in with the various portfolio contexts. However, the basic logics can still be analogous and thus Modern portfolio theory can be so influential.

Synergy is generally believed to bring the advantage to the project portfolio. Further, interdependency is often associated with synergy, which is a synergistic effect to bring in the additional advantages for interdependent projects. For example, in the Engineering Management, Stummer and Heidenberger model the project interdependency in order to reflect the effect of synergism in R&D project portfolio [27]. In their example, this synergism not only can increase the value but also can save the cost in the portfolio. Similarly, in the Operations Research, Liesio et al. account for the project interdependency in order to reflect the effect of synergy, or cannibalization, in the project portfolio. In their definition, synergy means when overall value and, or the cost, of a set of projects differs from the sum of the individual projects' overall values and costs. In the Information Systems, Tanriverdi and Venkatraman define two types of synergy: super-additive value synergy and sub-additive cost synergy [22]. Super-additive value synergy refers to the phenomenon—Value (a, b) > Value (a) + Value (b). Sub-additive cost synergy refers to the phenomenon—Cost (a, b) < Cost (a) + Cost (b). Moreover, Tanriverdi argues that IT relatedness would induce sub-additive cost synergy and IT complementarity would lead to super-additive value synergy in the multi-business firm [24]. Overall, in the project level, synergy could mean positive effect in the project portfolio and usually results from the interdependency between the projects; in the firm level, IT synergy is related to IT resource relatedness and complementarity.

3 Proposed Solution

In order to foster a general understanding of our propose model, we firstly propose a method for analyzing IT project portfolio (figure 1). With it, we argue that we can have analysis layers to go through to evaluate an IT project portfolio: IT project common analysis, IT project managerial flexibility analysis, IT project interdependency analysis, IT portfolio analysis, and IT portfolio selection. In the first layer of IT project common analysis, IT project is estimated by the similar way we evaluate other non-IT project. For example, we need to analyze and project IT project value and cost. The derived analysis outputs, such as the IT project's net present value (NPV), can usually be found in the IT project proposal, IT project business case, and etc. In the next layer of IT project managerial flexibility analysis, we can consider how to exploit IT project options, such as the deferral option. In the layer of IT project interdependency analysis, synergy is our focus. For instance, we could think whether certain IT projects can work together to save the cost (i.e., sub-additive cost synergy). In the layer of IT portfolio analysis, we need to find a way to evaluate our IT projects in an aggregate view. For example, we might want to generate all possible IT project portfolio combinations and their respective returns and volatilities for making decision. Finally, in the layer of IT portfolio selection, we need to develop our selection criteria. Usually, the trade-off is unavoidable in this layer, such as a trade-off between the IT project portfolio return and risk. In our understanding, so far very few enterprises have touched on the last two layers, so that we propose this method for enterprise reference.

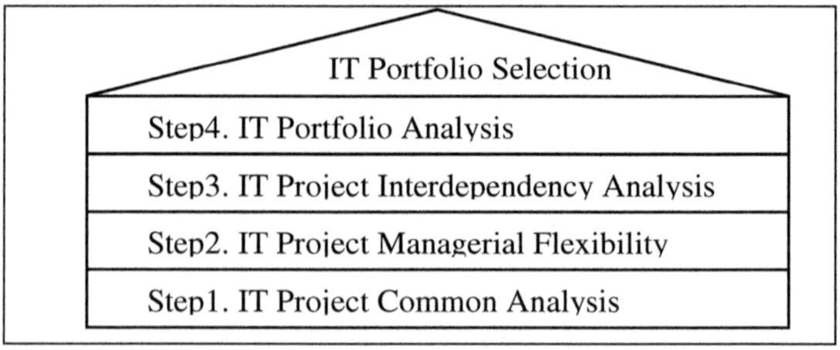

Fig. 1. Proposed Method for Analyzing IT Portfolio

3.1 Step 1: IT Project Common Analysis

Deriving IT project value and cost is the focus here. Most enterprises already have their financial practices to evaluate IT project value and cost, such as IT project's net present value (NPV). Thus, our proposed model assumes the IT project value and cost are already available for use.

3.2 Step 2: IT Project Managerial Flexibility Analysis

Analogous to Luehrman's model[15][16], our proposed model employs IT project return and IT project risk to further IT project common analysis into IT project managerial flexibility analysis. The deferral option of an IT project is our target to be considered in our proposed model. In other words, once an IT project is deferred, our model would consider the extra interest earning from the unused cost in the deferral time, as well as the accompanied risk. Basically, the return means a ratio of IT project value to its cost. The risk refers to the degree to which the IT project value would fluctuate in the deferral time. They are defined as follows.

$$Value\text{–}to\text{–}\cos t = S\frac{X}{(1+r)^t} \tag{1}$$

$$Volatility = \sigma\sqrt{t} \tag{2}$$

In the formula 1, we have S: IT project present value, X: IT project cost, r: risk-free interest rate, t: the time we can wait for making decision of the IT project, and actually traditional NPV = S – X. And in the formula 2, we haveσ: the standard deviation of IT project value in the deferral time, and t: the deferral time

3.3 Step 3: IT Project Interdependency Analysis

In our proposed model, we depend on IT project interdependency to approximate the value of IT project synergy. Moreover, we assume that we can estimate this interdependency by analyzing the degree to which IT projects are related. For example, whether IT projects are related to sharing similar tangible resources or utilizing the similar know-how, and whether they can be pooled for increase negotiation power for purchase. Since the research investigating the IT project interdependency and synergy is very sparse, we make our assumption mainly grounded on the finings of the sub-additive cost synergy and IT resource relatedness. According to Tanriverdi [24], the sub-additive cost synergy can be measured by four dimensions of IT resources relatedness. These dimensions are (1) shared tangible resources, (2) coordinated strategies, (3) pooled negotiating power, and (4) shared know-how. Besides, the conventional observation is also in support of our assumption. For instance, when thinking about reducing the total development cost of overall IT projects, the senior IT manager usually would consider whether there are some modules, functions, applications, software, and hardware which can be shared in these IT projects (i.e., shared tangible resource and shared know-how), or whether we can increase our bargain power by aggregating these IT projects' purchases (i.e., pooled negotiating power). Therefore, we reason analyzing IT project cost interdependency is a possible way for us to approximate the value of IT project cost synergy.

Accordingly, we assume that the cost-saving synergy (Syn_{ij}) is a function of the degree (%) to which two IT project are interdependent (Itd_{ij}). For instance, if the interdependency between IT project i and j is 0%, it is implied that both projects are independent and thus could hardily have any cost-saving synergy. On the contrary, if the degree of interdependency is 100%, there is likely a cost synergy for IT project i and j. Further, assuming today we can derive a function as $Syn_{ij} = 0.5(Itd_{ij})$ by either the expert judgment or by an educated guess, if we estimate two IT projects can have 10% interdependency on sharing certain cost component, we could project that there will probably be a cost synergy worth 5% of total cost of IT project i and j. In short, we assume the cost synergy magnitude of IT project i and j (Syn_{ij}) depends on the function of their interdependency (f (Itd_{ij}))

$$Syn_{ij} = f\left(Itd_{ij}\right) \tag{3}$$

In the formula 3, we have Syn_{ij} : synergy of IT project i and IT project j, and Itd_{ij} : interdependency between IT project i and project j.

3.4 Step 4: IT Portfolio Analysis

On the basis of Markowitz portolio model, we develop our model to measure the return and riks of an IT project portfolio. The cost synergy is also taken into account in this model. In a sense, a stock portfolio return is analogous to our IT project portfolio $return_p$. So, it is derived as follows.

$$return_p = \sum_{i=1}^{n} w_i \left(S_i \frac{(1+r)^{ti}}{X_i - \sum_{j=i+1}^{n} Syn_{ij}} \right) \tag{4}$$

In the formula 4, we have w_i : the weight of IT project i in the portfolio, Syn_{ij} : the synergy of IT project i and IT project j in the portfolio, X_i : the cost of IT project i in the portfolio, S_i : the value of IT project i in the portfolio, r : the risk-free interest rate, and ti : the deferral time for IT project i.

The stock portfolio risk is analogous to our IT project portfolio $risk_p$, and it is derived as follows.

$$risk_p = \sqrt{\left(\sum_{i=1}^{n} (w_i \sigma_i)^2 + \sum_{i=1}^{n} \sum_{\substack{j=1 \\ j \neq i}}^{n} w_i w_j \rho_{ij}\ \sigma_i\ \sigma_j \right)} \tag{5}$$

In the formula 5, we have w_i : the weight of IT project i in the portfolio, w_j : the weight of IT project j in the portfolio, ρ_{ij} : the correlation between IT project i and j, σ_j : the standard deviation of IT project *j*, and σ_i : the standard deviation of IT project *i*.

3.5 IT Portfolio Selection

We follow Markowitz's mean-variance criterion to select IT project portfolio. This criterion is well-regarded in financial portfolio analysis and also found effective in other non-financial areas. Its basic logic is that, given the same risk, a portfolio A with a higher return will be dominant than a portfolio B with a lower return, and vice versa. Moreover, this mean-variance criterion can lead to a so-called efficient frontier where the portfolio risk is minimized and return is maximized. Following the same logic, we adopt this mean-variance criterion to determine whether an IT project portfolio A is more efficient than an IT project portfolio B. In our model, the efficient IT portfolio frontier will be defined as the following rule.

$$\text{\textit{IT project portfolio A is more efficient than IT project portfolio B, if}} \quad return_A > return_B \text{ and } risk_A \leq risk_B \tag{6}$$

4 An Illustrative Example

In this section, we illustrate a simplified example to further the understanding of our proposed model. Hypothetically, we have only three IT projects A, B, and C to select (Table 2). Thus, initially there will be only three IT project choices a, b, c to make decision in order to develop the IT project portfolio. In addition, we assume we can also decide to defer these decisions to the next year. Thus, we can add choice a1, b1 and c1 to represent choices when the original projects are deferred for one year to make decision. For example, we can decide to invest IT project A, B, and C at the current time (i.e., choices a, b, and c), or defer to decide them until the next year (i.e. choices a1, b1, and c1). Noticeably, since a and a1, b and b1, and c and c1 are physically the same project, they are precluded from being selected concurrently. Consequently, with the 6 choices (i.e., a, b, c, a1, b1, and c1), we will have many different portfolio compositions to determine whether they are efficient IT portfolios.

Table 1. IT project profiles

Heading level	IT project A	IT project B	IT project C
IT project present value (S)	\$102	\$99	\$97
IT project cost (X)	\$100	\$100	\$100
The deferral time (t) (per year)	1	1	1
Standard deviation (per year) (σ)	0.3	0.2	0.1
Risk-free interest rate(r_f)	0.06	0.06	0.06

Moreover, we design 3 scenarios to verify the importance of taking the options and synergy in into the consideration of an IT project portfolio. In the first scenario, the base case, we consider neither options nor synergy. And we depend on the traditional net-present-value to determine the efficient IT project portfolio. In other words, in this way what we do will be similar to prioritizing IT project based on its net-present-value only. In the second scenario, the case 1, we add options consideration. In the last case, case 2, we consider both options and synergy. To this end, we assume the IT project B and IT project C have the 10% interdependency on sharing certain cost component. In addition, we assume the correlation between two IT projects will also be half of the IT projects' interdependency. Similarly, we assume the amount of we can save from both IT projects' total cost (synergy) will be half of the IT projects' interdependency. Namely, in this case the correlation between IT project B and C will be set as 0.05, and 5% of their total cost will be saved as cost synergy benefit.

Consequently, for each scenario we can derive the efficient portfolios from its overall IT project portfolio combinations. In the figure 2, we can see there are 3 groups of efficient portfolios, each of which will be presented with the same color, the same shape, and the same first digit. For example, the green-diamond-0a means that, in the base case, a portfolio composed of the choice a is derived as efficient, the blue-triangle-1a means that, in the case 1, a portfolio composed of the choice a is derived as efficient, and the red-square-2bc means that, in the case 2, a portfolio composed of the choice b and c is derived as efficient.

As for the base case, the most efficient portfolio is only the portfolio (a), i.e., doing the IT project A now. This result is actually not surprised, since only IT project A is of a positive net-present-value (i.e., 2$). According to the mean-variance criteria, other portfolio combinations could generate only the worse return, given the same risk in each IT project choice (i.e., a, b, and c) in the base case. In the case 1 where we begin to consider the IT project deferral option, we will have 7 efficient portfolios (i.e., a1, a1b1, a1c1, b1c1, ab1, ac1, and a). Among these efficient portfolios, the portfolio (a1), i.e., doing the IT project A 1-year later, will be of the highest return as well as highest risk. And the portfolio (a), i.e., doing the IT project A now, will be of the lowest return as well as highest risk. Clearly, the results together reflect the trade-off between the portfolio return and risk. That is, the deferral option could bring in not only additional advantage but also additional risk. This is also why the portfolio (a) is the efficient portfolio either in the base case or case 1. It is the efficient portfolio with lowest risk, given the no-synergy situation. In the case 2 of example where we consider both IT project deferral option and cost synergy, the situation change and we will have 3 efficient portfolios (i.e., bc, a1bc, b1c1). Currently, the efficient portfolio

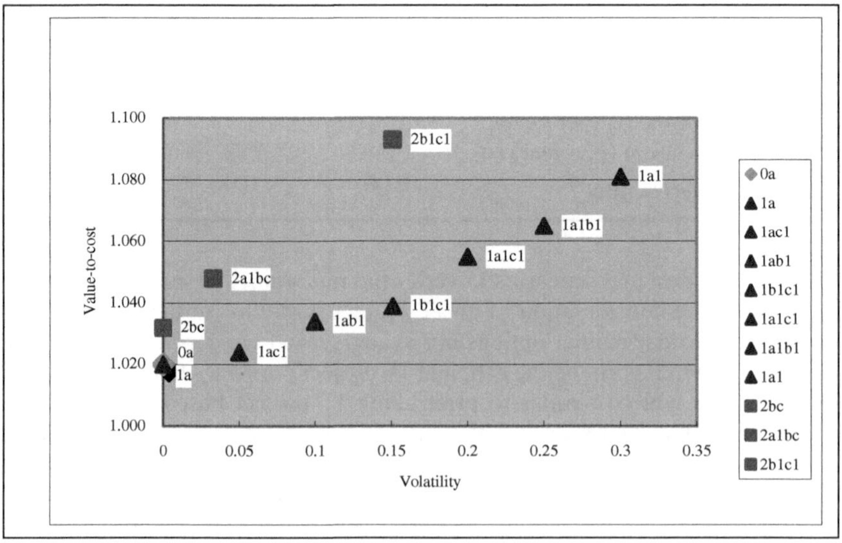

Fig. 2. Efficient portfolio frontier of illustrative example scenarios

with lowest return and risk is the portfolio (bc), i.e., doing the IT project B and C now, the in-between efficient portfolio is the portfolio (a1bc), i.e., doing IT project B and C now and doing IT project 1-year later, and the efficient portfolio with highest risk as well as highest return is the portfolio (b1c1), i.e., doing the IT project B and C 1-year later. Noticeably, the interdependency between IT project B and C have the impact on the efficient portfolio composition, since each of three efficient portfolios comprise choices originated from both IT project B and C (i.e., bc and b1c1). If we contrast the efficient portfolios in the three cases, we will find the efficient portfolio in base case happens to be one of the efficient portfolios in case 1. And the efficient portfolios in case 2 of example are better than those in the base 1 and base case.

5 Discussion and Conclusion

Thus far, we can see if we consider IT project managerial flexibility and interdependency, more and better portfolio choices might emerge. In our case 2 of example, the derived efficient IT project portfolios are obviously better than those in the base 1 and base case. Specifically, in our case 2, if an enterprise is conservative (i.e., risk-averser), it is likely that portfolio (bc) is favored because it has lowest risk. Conversely, if the enterprise is comfortable with high risk (e.g., risk-seeker), the portfolio (a1bc) becomes a good choice because it has the largest the return as well as risk. In between, the portfolio (b1c1) could be good portfolio choice because its risk is neither lowest nor highest. Even if there is no IT project interdependency to exploit, there still could be better choices if we have some IT managerial flexibility to utilize. In our case 1 of example, portfolio (a1), portfolio (a1b1), portfolio (a1c1), portfolio (b1c1), portfolio (ab1), and portfolio (ac1) are all efficient, as long as we are willing to bear certain risk in our IT project portfolio.

Another important point reflected in this paper is that we need to pay attention to the balance between the return and risk in the IT project portfolio. If we fully rely on real-options based models to select IT projects, we could unconsciously constitute an IT project portfolio with very high risk. Besides, there is also a possibility of a synergy risk, although it is beyond the scope of this paper. In our example, the portfolio (a1) is better than portfolio (a) because it is with a higher return, whereas portfolio (a) can be better than portfolio (a1) because it is with a lower risk. Therefore, although we have shown that additional return could be brought by considering managerial flexibility and interdependency, we want to underlie that we also have to consider the additional risk. It is very risky to make IT project portfolio without a balance consideration.

Additionally other than options, the IT interdependency and synergy are crucial to the IT project portfolio decision. Although such investigations in the literature are still stark, we argue the IT project interdependency is a helpful index to approximate the synergy effect. For example, if we find that several independent IT projects actually more or less need to get some hardware from the same vendor, it would be sensible if we estimate their cost synergy by evaluating the degree to which their hardware cost are interdependent.

Moreover, considering IT interdependency and synergy could really make difference in the IT portfolio decision making. Only considering discounted-based-models and real-options-models are sometimes not sufficient. For example, initially we could just decide to defer an IT project because of its low net-present-value (NPV) but high future risk, ex: a costly and advanced IT platform project. However, after considering this IT platform's possible interdependencies with other IT application projects, we could decide not to defer it due to the cost synergy. Actually, it is also very likely to have the value synergy in the IT portfolio, although we have not addressed it in this paper. Therefore, the consideration of interdependency and synergy really matter in the IT project portfolio.

On the other hand, this paper provides a useful implication for further investigation of the relationship between synergies and options. In our case 2 of example, we can find one of efficient portfolios is portfolio (b1c1). Actually, it is not a surprised result because we assume IT project B and C have the interdependency. And resultant synergy could also be exploited even if the two projects are deferred for 1 year later, i.e., the choice b1 and c1, as long as the two projects were not dropped off. In this regard, we make a conjecture that there an interesting relationship between synergy and option, a right, instead of the obligation, to utilize the IT project interdependency. Moreover, if we combine it with the deferral option, this relationship could be treated as the enterprise discretion to exploit the IT project interdependency now or later. For example, when two similar IT projects are proposed by two different units, enterprise usually would think of whether to integrate, or merge them to the unified one. However, the timing of doing so could very depend. It could be in their development processes, or we can wait until they have both been successfully developed.

Overall, this paper makes contributions. First, we demonstrate how to manage IT portfolio in a quantitative manner. Besides, our proposed approach is fully compatible with financial data and can easily be understood by other non-IT departments, executive levels, or even other enterprise shareholders. Additionally, in the information systems literature, most related papers investigating IT portfolio management are still focused on the discounted-based-model and real-options based model. In this paper, we point out we need to consider managerial flexibility influence, interdependency influence, and their mutual influences in the IT portfolio decision, bring out an promising research area in terms of a more integrated IT portfolio management.

References

1. Amram, M., Kulatilaka, N.: Disciplined Decisions: Aligning Strategy with the Financial Markets. Harvard Business Review (77), 95–104 (January-February 1999)
2. Benaroch, M.: Managing Information Technology Investment Risk: A Real Options Perspective. Journal of Management Information Systems 19(2), 43–84 (2002)
3. Benaroch, M., Kauffman, R.J.: Justifying electronic banking network expansion using real options analysis. MIS Quarterly 24(2), 197–226 (1999)
4. Benaroch, M., Lichtenstein, Y., Robison, K.: Real Options in Information Technology Risk Management: An Empirical Validation of Risk-Option Relationships. MIS Quarterly 30(4), 827–864 (2006)
5. Cho, W., Shaw, M.J.: Does IT Synergy Matter in IT Portfolio Selection? In: Proceedings of ICIS (2009)
6. Dixit, A., Pindyck, R.: Investment under Uncertainty. Princeton University Press, Princeton (1994)

7. Fichman, R.G.: Real options and IT platform adoption: Implications for theory and practice. Information Systems Research 15(2), 132–154 (2004)
8. Fichman, R.G., Keil, M., Tiwana, A.: Beyond valuation: Real Options thinking in IT project management. California Management Review 47(2), 74–96 (2005)
9. Jeffery, M., Leliveld, L.: Best Practices in IT portfolio Management. Sloan Management Review 45(3), 41–49 (2004)
10. Kersten, B., Verhoef, C.: IT portfolio management: A banker's perspective on IT. Cutter IT Journal 16(4), 27–33 (2004)
11. Kim, Y.J., Sanders, L.G.: Strategic Actions in Information Technology Investment Based on Real Option Theory. Decision Support Systems 33(1), 1–11 (2002)
12. Kleinmuntz, D.N.: Resource Allocation Decisions. In: Edwards, W., Miles, R.F., von Winterfeldt, D. (eds.) Advances in Decision Analysis (2007)
13. Liesio, J., Mild, P., Salo, A.: Robust portfolio modeling with incomplete cost information and project interdependencies. European Journal of Operational Research 190(3), 679–695 (2008)
14. Lin, B., Chen, J.: Corporate technology portfolios and R&D performance measures: A Study of Technology Intensive Firms. R&D Management 35(2), 153–166 (2005)
15. Luehrman, T.: Investment Opportunities as Real Options: Getting Started on the Numbers. Harvard Business Review, 51–67 (1998)
16. Luehrman, T.: Strategy as a Portfolio of Real Options. Harvard Business Review, 89–99 (1998)
17. Maizlish, B., Handler, R.: IT Portfolio Management. John Wiley & Sons, Chichester (2005)
18. Markowitz, H.M.: Portfolio selection. Journal of Finance 7(1), 77–91 (1952)
19. McFarlan, F.W.: Portfolio approach to information systems. Harvard Business Review 59(5), 142–150 (1981)
20. Schwartz, E.S., Zozaya-Gorostiza, C.: Investment under Uncertainty in Information Technology: Acquisition and Development Projects. Management Science 49(1), 57–70 (2003)
21. Sharpe, W.F.: The Sharpe Ratio. Journal of Portfolio Management 21(1), 49–58 (1994)
22. Tanriverdi, H.: Information Technology Relatedness, Knowledge Management Capability, and Performance of Multi-business Firms. MIS Quarterly 29(2), 311–334 (2005)
23. Tanriverdi, H., Venkatraman, N.: Knowledge Relatedness and Performance of Multibusiness Firms. Strategic Management Journal (26), 97–119 (2005)
24. Tanriverdi, H.: Performance Effects of Information Technology Synergies in Multibusiness Firms. MIS Quarterly 30(91), 97–108 (2006)
25. Taudes, A., Feurstein, M., Mild, A.: Option Analysis of Software Platform Decisions: A Case Study. MIS Quarterly 24(2), 227–243 (2000)
26. Wu, L.C., Ong, C.S.: Management of information technology investment: A framework based on a Real Options and Mean–Variance theory perspective. Technovation 28(3), 122–134 (2008)
27. Stummer, C., Heidenberger, K.: Interactive R&D portfolio analysis with project interdependencies and time profiles of multiple objectives. IEEE transactions on Engineering Management 50(2), 175–183 (2003)

The Effect of Positive Quadrant Dependence between Projects on Portfolio Value

John C. Burke and Michael J. Shaw

University of Illinois at Urbana-Champaign, University of Illinois at Urbana-Champaign
{jcburke1,mjshaw}@uiuc.edu

Abstract. Increasingly CIO's are interested in managing their IT Project Portfolios centrally. This may be done for a variety of reasons, e.g. to manage costs, reduce duplication of effort, reduce the number of silos in the organization, better understand what the firm is doing, or to align their IT investments with their firm's strategy. In particular, during this time of an economic downturn managers want to use their resources efficiently in response to tightening IT budgets. An important question then becomes how to value these projects. Real Option Analysis (ROA) has become one of the common tools used for valuing projects. However, the assumption of independence between projects often made by researchers may undervalue growth options under a wide variety of assumptions when these projects are positive quadrant dependent (PQD), a form of positive correlation.

Keywords: Portfolio Management, Copula, Project Management.

1 Introduction

Increasingly CIO's and IT managers are centralizing their IT Project Portfolios for a variety of reasons, e.g. to manage costs, reduce duplication of effort, reduce the number of silos in the organization, better understand what the firm is doing, or to align their IT investments with their firm's strategy etc. An important question is how should IT projects be valued? The difficulty of this problem is due to the nature of IT project portfolios. Unlike financial portfolios, which can often be valued through a public marketplace, IT projects are generally specific to a firm. While financial portfolios are commonly diversified (Markowitz, 1952), IT project portfolios are often very homogeneous. That is, firms invest in specific technologies and vendors that hopefully support their firm's overall goals and strategies. In a way, IT portfolios can be viewed as open complex systems with many interactions (Bak, 1996). The importance of this is that such systems often exhibit:

- Non-linear relationships
- Non-normal distributions
- Many interdependencies

All three of the above characteristics make valuing an IT portfolio difficult using the traditional techniques found in MIS research, which has until recently been dominated

R. Sharman, T.S. Raghu, and H.R. Rao (Eds.): WEB 2009, LNBIP 52, pp. 254–268, 2010.

by assumptions of independence, normal distributions and linear relationships. In this paper, these issues are dealt with using a modeling technique involving mathematical copulas.

The interdependencies between projects are often significant. This can be logically understood by the simple observation that many projects use the same technologies, have the same managers, share the same employees, are in the same group or division and are run under the same budget, i.e. Economies of Scope or Scale (Panzar and Willig, 1981). It is also often observed that the success or failure of projects often move together, i.e. two projects that are related are both successful or both unsuccessful. This may be because one project depends on the other, or simply because they share many of the same inputs, which makes the projects' success correlated with one another. Therefore, when valuing projects, they should be considered in the context of the other projects in the portfolio, not independently (Markowitz, 1952).

The main question of this paper is what is the affect of these interdependencies on the valuation of IT projects? The short answer is that when projects are correlated and built in series, traditional techniques that assume independence will tend to undervalue them. This paper can be best understood in the general framework of research done by Fichman (2004) and Bardharn, Bagchi, and Sougstad (2004). The rest of this paper continues as follows, first a brief literature review is given. Second, bivariate distributions and the theory of mathematical copulas are reviewed, followed by analysis of a simple theoretical portfolio with positive quadrant dependence between projects and a discussion of the findings. Finally, we conclude with ideas for future research.

2 Literature Review

2.1 Valuation of Technology Projects

Since Markowitz introduced modern portfolio theory in 1952, it has been generally recognized that investments should be managed as a portfolio rather than as independent investments. Each new project should be evaluated based on how it affects the firm as a whole, rather than as an independent asset. Ultimately, the overall goal of an organization is to balance the overall risk vs. return of an entire portfolio of projects, rather than just managing the risk vs. return of an individual project. Conceptually this can be related to the an individual's personal investments where a person may invest in a range of assets depending on their risk tolerance, e.g. some very low risk-low yield government bonds, some medium risk-medium yield blue chip stocks and some high risk-high yield investments. This mix of investments is made to minimize risk and maximize return in a business environment that is recognized as being inherently uncertain.

However many traditional financial techniques, such as NPV or ROI, assume static business environments, which is often not a valid assumption for IT. Costs, benefits, and risks for IT projects are often highly uncertain or stochastic in nature. Real Option Analysis (ROA) offers greater flexibility in capturing the value inherent in these processes. When complicated investment scenarios arise, ROA can be combined with Monte Carlo techniques to calculate portfolio value. Modeling portfolios in this way has the advantage that the distributions used in these models and their characteristics, such as mean, median, mode, standard deviation etc., can be easily and transparently tracked over time.

In order to model an IT project effectively for ROA, at a minimum the joint distribution of costs and benefits have to be modeled. However, even relatively simple joint distributions are difficult to conceptualize if the number of variables involved is beyond two. A useful tool which greatly adds to the transparency of joint distributions is mathematical copulas. Copulas allow for multivariate joint distributions to be separated into their marginal and joint components, enabling executives to monitor a project's overall costs separately from its overall benefits or from their joint relationship.

2.2 IT Project Valuation Using Real Option Analysis

Over the last ten years several different research streams on Real Option Analysis (ROA) have developed in the mainstream MIS literature. One early stream of research focused on the utility of using ROA for valuing IT projects that are fundamentally risky. These high risk investments are usually undervalued using traditional valuation tools, such as NPV, because they assume managers have little flexibility to kill poorly performing projects or expand superior projects (Benaroch and Kaufman, 1999, 2000; Taudes, Feurstein, and Mild, 2000).

A second important stream of literature focuses on the importance of actively imbedding Real Options into initial IT project design. For example, expressly putting escape clauses into contracts so that failing projects can be abandoned without financial loss will protect the option to abandon assumed in many project valuations. Likewise, many infrastructure projects assume that there will be follow on projects that will enhance their overall value to the firm (Benaroch 2001, 2002; Bardharn, Bagchi, and Sougstad, 2004; Benaroch, Lichtenstein, and Robinson, 2006).

The above two streams of research have focused mainly on the traditional Black-Scholes and Binomial Option Models. However, other researchers have begun to question the appropriateness of the assumptions embedded in those models and have suggested that there may be significant interactions, dependencies, and synergies between IT projects (Fichman, 2004). Bardharn et al. (2004) used the Margrabe option model to capture the correlation between costs and revenues, and incorporated a way to capture some inter-project dependencies through nesting options. A limitation of their method was that it allowed for a few discrete possibilities rather than a range of possible revenue outcomes for interacting projects. This paper seeks to build on their technique by showing how to incorporate a continuous range of possibilities into revenue projections and also to show the affect PQD between projects has on IT project valuations.

One relatively simple and flexible technique for handling situations that involve complex interactions is using Monte Carlo simulation. Monte Carlo methods can simulate many different types of dependence structures and quickly allow managers to investigate different business scenarios. The results of the simulations can then be used to determine individual project and portfolio valuations (Rogers, 2002).

2.3 Typology of Basic Real Options

There have been many types of real options identified within the literature, however the most common options discussed are either to defer or abandon a project vs. the option to expand or build upon a project. Within R&D and high tech industries the option to explore different uncertain technologies using pilot programs and prototypes is also common. Other important options in high tech are the options to lease equipment or outsource work and in the case of this paper the option to stage a series of projects called Growth options (Table 1) (Mun, 2002; Trigeorgis, 1996; Dixit and Pindyck, 1995).

Table 1. Common Types of Options

Option	Description
Defer	The option to delay investment until more information can be learned about the project, such as costs, prices, demand etc.
Stage	The option to build a project in stages, where investment can be delayed or even killed if the environment changes.
Explore	The option to use a pilot program to better learn about a project before initiating it on a full-scale basis.
Scale	The option to increase or decrease the scale of a project depending upon its success.
Abandon	The option to kill a project if it goes badly.
Outsource	The option to subcontract a project or part of a project to shift some downside risks to a third party.
Lease	The option to lease some resources to shift some downside risks to a third party.
Growth	A set of projects where the value of earlier projects depends largely on investments in additional projects, i.e. an infrastructure investment that assumes follow-on investments will be made using that infrastructure.
Compound	A combination of the above options in one project.

2.4 Copulas and Real Options

Copulas are a relatively new topic in business research journals, although their origin goes at least back to Sklar (1959), they remained largely regulated to mathematicians until the arrival of powerful desktop computers and statistical packages such as SAS, R, MatLab etc. It was not until Nelson's seminal works (2006, 1999) and works written for practitioners (Schmidt, 2006), that copulas became accessible to non-mathematicians. Since that time, copulas have been used in insurance, hydrology (Salvadori and De Michele, 2004; Gaume, 2006), the petroleum industry (Armstrong et. al, 2004; de Melo e Silva Accioly and Chiyoshi, 2004), decision analysis (Clemon and Reilly, 1999) and in many financial applications.

In this paper, we will show how to apply copula methods to the study of a simple IT project portfolio in order to enhance ROA techniques developed by Benaroch et al. (2000, 1999) and Bardhan et al. (2004). Considering that average IT spending can be 20% of a firm's operational costs, any technique which better values a firm's IT project portfolio can significantly improve a firm's bottom line (Kersten and Verhoef, 2004).

3 Review of Mathematical Copulas

3.1 Issues in Modeling IT Project Portfolios

As mentioned above, IT Project Portfolios have three characteristics that make their study difficult using traditional methods. First, they tend to follow non-normal

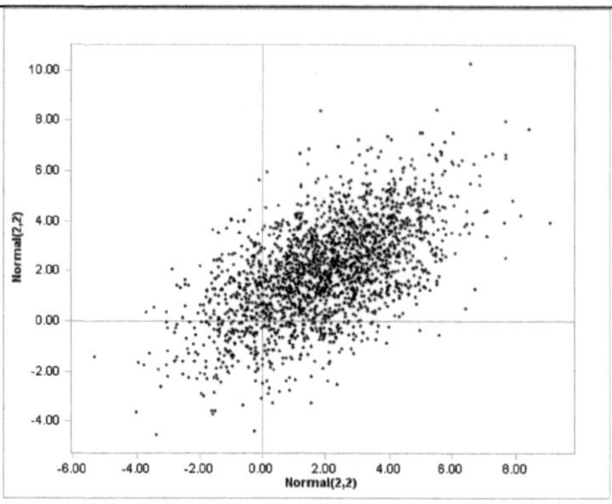

1. a. Bivariate Normal distribution, with 0.60 rank correlated marginals

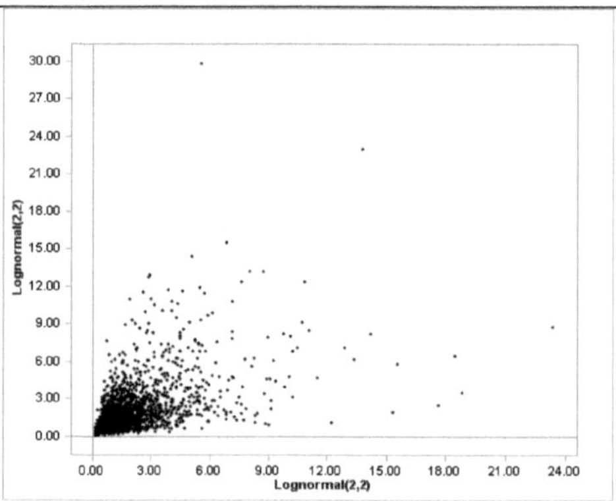

1. b. Bivariate Lognormal distribution, with 0.60 rank correlated marginals

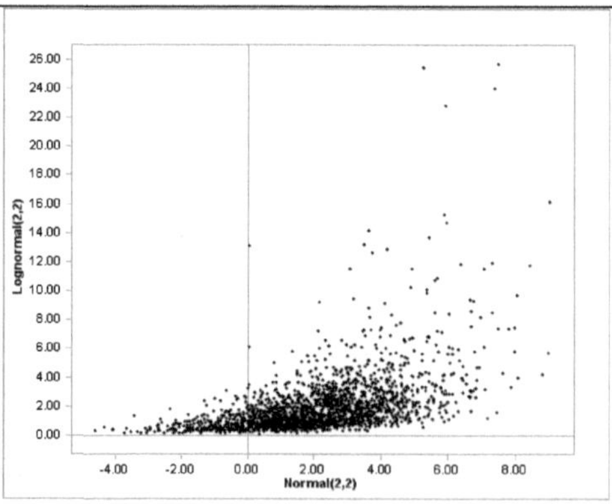

1. c. Bivariate Normal-Lognormal distribution, with 0.60 rank correlated marginals

Fig. 1. Different correlated bivariate distributions, a.) Normal-Normal b.) Lognormal-Lognormal c.) Normal-Lognormal. As can be seen these distributions are quite different and assuming a distribution is Normal or Gaussian can lead to large errors.

distributions. Second, they tend to have non-linear behavior. Third, unlike financial investments, IT projects within a company have many interdependencies. Linear correlation and linear regression are very powerful and useful tools. However, not all systems are normally distributed or linearly related. As can be seen in Figure 1, bivariate normal (or by extension multivariate normal) systems are quite different in shape from other bivariate or multivariate distributions. Therefore, assuming a process follows a normal or a linear distribution when it does not can lead to large errors, particularly in the tails of a process. For example, the growth of the Internet, cell phone usage, digital music and digital cameras are all non-normal, non-linear phenomena that occurred so rapidly that they caused whole industries to be thrown into turmoil.

Typically, non-normal data in IS research has been handled through transforming variables, such as by taking the Natural Log of certain variables. However, manipulating non-linear, non-normal data in order to model distributions using traditional linear techniques has two huge disadvantages. First, it is often difficult for managers or even researchers to explain the need to transform the data to others. Second, the user of the information is no longer dealing in the processes natural distribution. This is simply not an easy or natural process for most people especially if the number of random variables is greater than two. As will be seen, mathematical copulas allow the data to be investigated using its natural marginal distributions rather than by using an unfamiliar joint distribution.

3.2 Copula Definition and Sklar's Theory

The most important theory regarding copulas is Sklar's Theory which states:

"Let H be a joint distribution function with margins F and G. Then there exists a copula C such that for all x,y in R, H(x,y) = C(F(x), G(y)). If F and G are continuous, then C is unique; otherwise, C is uniquely determined on Range F x Range G."

where C is the copula function (Nelson, 2006, pg.21; Sklar, 1959) .

The importance of Sklar's theory is that it reduces the problem of finding a joint density function to simply (1) identifying the appropriate marginal density functions and (2) finding the appropriate Copula function. Both of these can be done using modern statistical packages such as SAS, SPSS, Matlab, R etc. all of which have libraries available for working with Copulas.

In essence what copulas do is split a bivariate joint distribution into two pieces, first the two marginal distributions which can then be investigated independently and second the copula which handles any correlation between them. The two marginal distributions are transformed, using the appropriate Cumulative Distribution Functions, and an appropriate mathematical copula, into a unit cube $[0, 1]^n$ in which both marginal distributions are uniform on the interval [0, 1]. Since these uniform marginal distributions can be transformed back into their original functions using the appropriate inverse functions (Figure 2), in theory the marginal distributions involved can be any well behaved distribution. That is, Normal-Normal, LogNormal-Normal, Weibull-Cauchy and many other combinations can be modeled quite easily.

For example, if the X-axis of Figure 1.a. represented a person's height and the Y-axis represented a person's weight the two would be expected to be positively correlated, in this case with a rank correlation of 0.60. Using traditional methods the joint distribution would be evaluated using statistical tables for a bivariate normal distribution. Alternatively, using copula methods, each marginal, (height and weight), would be separately transformed into a uniform distribution over [0-1] using the appropriate CDF function (Figure 2), and the 0.6 correlation would be handled by a separate copula function. The advantage of this is that the mean and standard deviation of the two marginal distributions and/or the correlation between them can be investigated individually. When the joint distribution is bivariate normal, a well behaved joint distribution, the advantages of using a copula may be minimal, but when the marginal distributions are more exotic, traditional statistical tables may not exist, e.g. for a Cauchy-LogNormal bivariate distribution. Copulas handle this situation easily, even in the multivariate case.

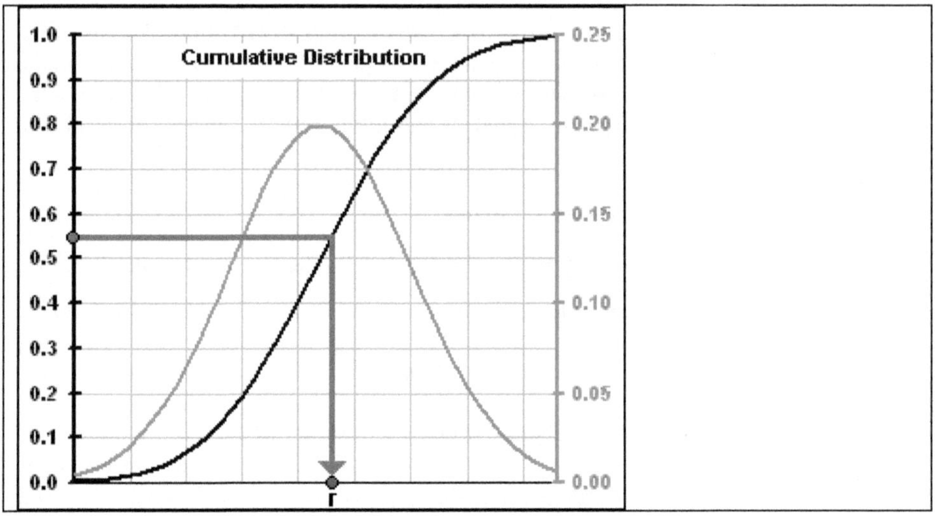

Fig. 2. Inverse Function and Cumulative Distribution Function used to transform a Normal Marginal Distribution into a Uniform Distribution and back, (Ponzo, 2008)

3.3 Archimedean Copulas

Since marginal distributions are relatively familiar to most researchers, the main difficulty for those new to copula methods will be identifying the appropriate copula function. For bivariate data there is a class of easily constructed functions known as Archimedean copulas which can fit the three basic types of tail dependence, 3.a. symmetric-tail dependence, where correlation is symmetric throughout the joint distribution, 3.b. lower-tail dependence, where lower values of X are more correlated with values of Y than higher values of X, and 3.c. upper-tail dependence, where higher values of X are more correlated with values of Y than lower values of X. Archimedean Copulas have the following properties (Nelson, 2006):

- For each pair x and y lying in [0,1], C(x,y), generates a number in [0,1].
- C(x,y) = 0 if either one of x or y is 0. (That is: C(0,y) = C(x,0) = 0 for x and y in [0,1].)
- C(x,1) = x and C(1,y) = y. (That is, for y = 1, C(x,1) = x increases from 0 to 1 as x increases from 0 to 1.)
- C(x,y) is increasing in both x and y.
- Satisfy the general equation $C(x,y) = \Phi\text{-}1(\Phi(x) + \Phi(y)); 0 < x, y < 1$

Three of the most commonly used Archimedean copulas are the Frank, Clayton, and Gumbel copulas, which have symmetric (Figure 3.a.), lower tail (Figure 3.b.), and upper tail (Figure 3.c.) dependence respectively. Nelson (2006, 1999) lists 22 different classes of copula that exhibit a variety of different dependence behavior which are further catalogued in Armstrong (2003). These three families are defined by the equations in Table 2.

Table 2. Three common copulas and their formulas; θ is a shape parameter, (Ponzo, 2008)

Name	Equation	Parameter	Dependence
Frank Copula	$C(u,v) = (-1/\theta) \ln [1 - (1-e^{-\theta u})(1 - e^{-\theta v})/(1-e^{\theta})]$	θ in (-∞ , ∞)	Symmetric Tails
Clayton Copula	$[u^{-\theta} + v^{-\theta} -1]^{-1/\theta}$	θ in [0 , ∞)	Lower Tail
Gumbel Copula	$\mathrm{Exp}[-((-\ln(u)^{\theta} + (-\ln(v)^{\theta})^{1/\theta}]$	θ in (1 , ∞)	Upper Tail

The three copulas in Figure 3, represent three common types of tail dependence. As an example, if the revenues of two projects are positively correlated the Frank copula might be used to represent the stochastic properties of their joint distribution. However, if the same two projects are more likely to be more tightly correlated when revenues are low, than when they are high, the Clayton copula might be used because it has lower tail dependence. Likewise, if two projects are more likely to be correlated when things go well then when things go poorly; the Gumbel copula might be used.

3.4 Generating Data with Copulas for Monte Carlo Analysis

Once the appropriate copula family is chosen, the copula equations can then be used in Monte Carlo simulation using the following procedure (Ponzo, 2008).

1. Assume a copula C(u,v), in this case the Clayton copula
   $C = [\, u^{-\theta} + v^{-\theta} - 1 \,]^{-1/\theta}$
2. Calculate the partial derivative $\partial C/\partial u$ and set $w = \partial C/\partial u$
   $w = u^{-1-\theta} [\, u^{-\theta} + v^{-\theta} - 1 \,]^{-1/\theta - 1}$
3. Solve $w = \partial C/\partial u$ for v in terms of u and w.
   $v = [\, w^{-\theta/(1+\theta)} u^{-\theta} - u^{-\theta} + 1 \,]^{-1/\theta}$
4. Randomly generate u and w as uniformly distributed random variables on [0,1]
5. Then the v value associated with the selected u-value is given in step 3, above.

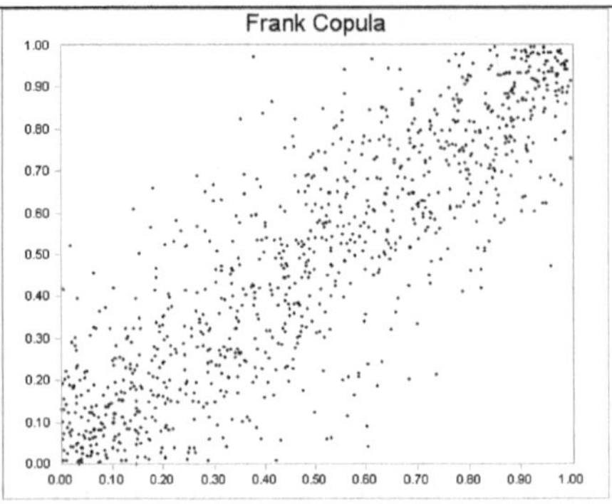

3. a. Frank Copula with no tail dependence

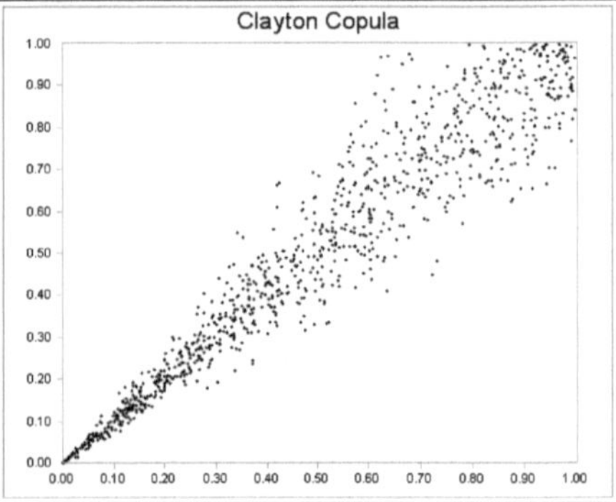

3. b. Clayton Copula with lower table dependence

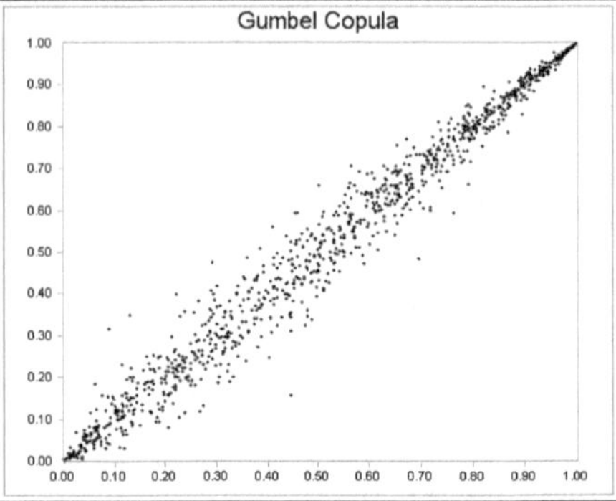

3. c. Gumbel Copula with upper tail dependence

Fig. 3. Different common copulas and their tail dependence

The result of this process is to create a copula with the desired tail dependence on the unit square, [0,1]. Typically the correlation of the copula is measured using Spearman's rho rank correlation or by Kendall's Tau. Different desired correlations can be created by changing the value of θ in the equations above.

Once the copula is constructed on the unit square [0,1], the X and Y values for any bivariate distribution can then be generated from u and v using the appropriate inverse functions of the marginal distributions. That is, if the marginal distributions are both Normal, then x and y can be found by using the function NORMINV() in Excel. If they are both Log-Normal then the LOGINV() function can be used. If X is Log-Normal and Y is Normal, then simply apply the appropriate inverse function to u and v. SAS, MatLab, SPSS, R etc. have extensive libraries of inverse functions so that almost any common marginal distribution can be found. Although beyond the scope of this paper, a similar procedure can be used to construct multivariate copula functions. Typically the process is automated in the commonly available statistical packages and data can be generated relatively easily.

4 Research Question and Methodology

For the purposes of this paper it is assumed there are two generic possibilities for interactions between IT projects in a firm. The first is that two projects that are built in parallel will interact, although they are not explicitly dependent on one another, such as a Wifi project and a database project. Although they may seem completely unrelated, they may still interact or be Positive Quadrant Dependent (PDQ) if for example the same project manager is responsible for both, if funds from one project are used to bolster the other, or if the same employees using the same company standards are used in both projects etc. Formally, projects are PQD, if the following inequality holds, $Pr(X > x, Y > y) \geq Pr(X > x) Pr(Y > y)$. PQD is a somewhat weaker version of linear correlation in that it means that the value of two projects increases or decreases together, but not necessarily linearly.

A second fundamental way projects can interact is if they are built in series, such as an Ecommerce Web site being built on top of a product database. In this case the database must be built first, and if successful, the Web site can be built on top of it as a growth option. If the database is particularly successful, it is somewhat reasonable to expect that the Web site will also do well. At the opposite extreme, if the database project goes very poorly and is canceled the Web site cannot be built at all.

In the first case, the Wifi project and the database should be considered two separate investments, although their interaction should be accounted for. In the second case, the value of the Ecommerce Website should be explicitly included in the valuation of the initial database project because the Website is actually a growth option off the first investment. The valuation of this type of situation has been expressed as a nested option (Bardhan, 2004). The adjustment made in this paper is the explicit addition of the value of interaction. This value of this interaction can in theory be negative as when two IT projects interfere with one another.

Case 1:
Value of Portfolio = Real Option Value of Project 1 + Real Option Value of Project 2 + interaction value

Case 2:
Value of Portfolio = Real Option Value of {Project 1 + Call Value[Project 2] + interaction value}

The research question of this paper is what is the value of a portfolio made of two projects, X and Y, where the value of two projects X and Y are PQD? The revenues of a simplified portfolio of two projects was simulated, the first case involving two projects that were built in parallel, the second case where the two projects were built in series. Further, the two projects were related through three types of copulas; Clayton, Frank, and Gumbel Copulas. Rank correlations approximating 0%, 20%, 40%, 60%, 80% and 98% were simulated for each case. Finally, three types of Marginal distributions were considered, Uniform, Normal and LogNormal.

10,000 trials were run in each case using Vose ModelRisk software to generate the Copula data. Random numbers were generated that simulated the proposed dependence structure between the revenues of the two projects. For example, two projects that were assumed to have no interactions and had no tail dependence were generated using a Frank copula 10,000 times and their revenues averaged. Next two projects that had a rank correlation of 20% were generated using a Frank copula 10,000 times and their revenues recorded and averaged. Next two projects that had a rank correlation of 40% were generated using a Frank copula 10,000 times and their revenues recorded and averaged etc. The process was repeated for a Clayton copula (lower tail dependence) and for a Gumbel Copula, (upper tail dependence).

To value the simulations, real option logic was used rather than a formal option model such as Black-Scholes. A project was considered a success if it reached the 0.4 quantile of its projected revenue. A project was considered a failure, and discontinued, if it was less than the 0.4 quantile of revenue; for reference, in the case of a normal distribution that corresponds to a z-score of about -0.25. For two projects in series, (that is a project that had a potential growth option available to it), if the first project failed and was canceled, the second project was also automatically cancelled, i.e. it had a revenue of 0. In the case of two projects in parallel, if the first project failed, the second project could still survive if it also was above the 0.4 quantile of its expected revenue.

5 Results and Analysis

The results were somewhat counter intuitive to what was expected and are shown in Table 3, 4, and 5. The base case in each table is the assumption of independence between two projects, or a rank correlation of 0. These projects are listed as 100%. Every other cell in the tables represents the average simulated revenue for various assumptions of tail dependence and PQD relative to the independent case. For example, when there is no tail dependence, (Table 3), rank correlation is close to 1, and the two projects have bivariate lognormally distributed revenues, revenues are 128% what they would be as compared to two projects that were independent.

As can be seen when projects are in series, higher dependency leads to higher revenues and thus higher profits. In the extreme case, revenues can be 30% or more higher for projects that are highly correlated, have a rank correlation near 1 and run in series. This compares favorably to projects that are completely independent, and have a rank correlation near 0. However, when the projects were run in parallel, higher rank correlations did not necessarily correspond to greater or lesser revenue figures for uniform or normally distributed projects. In fact, higher correlation appears to have little effect for parallel projects, except when the projects are lognormally distributed, in which case the highly skewed distributions led to some unstable results.

It is fairly easy to understand why higher PQD leads to greater profitability when projects run in series. If the first project is successful, higher correlation leads to success in the second project as well, in a domino effect, or "success breeds success". When projects run in parallel however, the picture is not so clear. It appears that when the distributions are symmetrical, higher correlations do not add much to overall profitability. This does make some sense, because failures are balanced out by successes. What is very interesting is that when revenues are highly skewed, such as is the case of the lognormal distribution there seems to be an effect on profitability. This is important because our empirical investigations of several Fortune 500 companies have all had projects that have lognormally distributed revenue patterns.

Table 3. Comparison of Profitability when projects are in series vs. in parallel with various assumptions of PQD and No Tail Dependence

Rank Correlation	**Uniform Distribution** **Frank Copula** **Projects in Series**	**Normal Distribution** **Frank Copula** **Projects in Series**	**LogNormal Distribution** **Frank Copula** **Projects in Series**	**Uniform Distribution** **Frank Copula** **Projects in Parallel**	**Normal Distribution** **Frank Copula** **Projects in Parallel**	**LogNormal Distribution** **Frank Copula** **Projects in Parallel**
0	100%	100%	100%	100%	100%	100%
0.2	104%	104%	105%	100%	100%	102%
0.4	109%	108%	108%	101%	100%	101%
0.6	115%	114%	120%	101%	101%	106%
0.8	117%	115%	119%	99%	98%	102%
0.98	122%	122%	128%	99%	99%	106%

Table 4. Comparison of Profitability when projects are in series vs. in parallel with various assumptions of PQD and Lower Tail Dependence

Rank Correlation	**Uniform Distribution** **Clayton Copula** **Projects in Series**	**Normal Distribution** **Clayton Copula** **Projects in Series**	**LogNormal Distribution** **Clayton Copula** **Projects in Series**	**Uniform Distribution** **Clayton Copula** **Projects in Parallel**	**Normal Distribution** **Clayton Copula** **Projects in Parallel**	**LogNormal Distribution** **Clayton Copula** **Projects in Parallel**
0	100%	100%	100%	100%	100%	100%
0.2	104%	104%	108%	100%	100%	103%
0.4	109%	109%	111%	100%	100%	101%
0.6	113%	112%	114%	100%	100%	99%
0.8	118%	117%	121%	100%	100%	101%
0.98	123%	123%	131%	100%	100%	104%

Table 5. Comparison of Profitability when projects are in series vs. in parallel with various assumptions of PQD and Upper Tail Dependence

Rank Correlation	**Uniform Distribution**	**Normal Distribution**	**LogNormal Distribution**	**Uniform Distribution**	**Normal Distribution**	**LogNormal Distribution**
	Gumbel Copula	**Gumbel Copula**	**Gumbel Copula**	**Gumbel Copula**	**Gumbel Copula**	**Gumbel Copula**
	Projects in Series	**Projects in Series**	**Projects in Series**	**Projects in Parallel**	**Projects in Parallel**	**Projects in Parallel**
0	100%	100%	100%	100%	100%	100%
0.2	102%	101%	89%	99%	99%	92%
0.4	107%	106%	101%	100%	100%	95%
0.6	112%	112%	102%	99%	100%	92%
0.8	114%	113%	107%	99%	99%	94%
0.98	119%	119%	115%	98%	98%	97%

6 Conclusions and Future Work

Real option analysis has been a major stream of research in IS for two decades. However, it has only been relatively recently that ROA has begun to investigate portfolios of projects in IT. This is unfortunate as popular IT management frameworks such as COBIT and VALIT recognize the limitations of traditional valuation techniques like NPV and ROI and suggest using ROA for evaluating IT investment programs. The necessity of using more advanced techniques of valuation stems from the homogeneity of IT project portfolios and the inherent interdependencies produced from sharing resources, technologies and personnel. The economies of scope and scale created lead to portfolios that exhibit non-normal and non-linear relationships.

This paper contributes to the existing literature by investigating the implications of running projects in parallel or in series. From the results given above, it is clear that when projects are run in series, higher correlations lead to greater success. This is significant because in the authors' dealings with Fortune 500 companies, we have found that projects often include growth options where a particular successful project leads to further investments in the same technology or vendor.

Another current trend we have seen is companies are trying to use similar technologies in parallel across company divisions, e.g. using Java across all departments. The justification used is that the economies of scope created by investing in such projects will save money. However, as can be seen above, projects that run in parallel do not gain much benefit from being positively correlated, indeed traditional portfolio analysis would suggest that overall portfolio risk would be lowered if the projects were not highly correlated. Thus, the benefit of using the same technologies in parallel projects is not immediately apparent, but the added risk could be significant, e.g. if Java later needs to be significantly upgraded all departments will be affected.

To sum up, the important insight from this work is that if projects are PQD, i.e. if the success of a base project is positively correlated with the success of a follow on project, traditional assumptions of independence between projects in Real Option Analysis valuation will tend to undervalue growth options. On the other hand, if projects are run in parallel, PQD will not necessarily create greater returns in a portfolio.

This was unexpected as firms that we are working with are generally trying to spread technologies across departments, horizontally not vertically within an organization.

In general, this work agrees with the work done by Bardharn (2004), but the contribution of this work is two-fold. First, it shows how copulas can be used to simulate PQD between projects, which was a suggestion of Bardhan et al., and it shows that failure to account for PQD is dangerous and will tend to undervalue projects that run in series, i.e. projects that have growth options and have little affect on projects that run in parallel.

Future work contemplated by our team involves investigating the source of value created by spreading technologies horizontally across firms. Mathematically, PQD seems to have little effect on projects that run in parallel, yet firms that we work with are actively pursuing this strategy. In the actual cases, this restructuring involves significant costs to reengineer the organizations by tearing down legacy technological silos, e.g. one division uses COBOL, another uses PL/1, a third uses Visual Basic etc., and they all will be replaced by Java. If the primary savings is from sharing information across the firm then adding Data services between silos may be cheaper and less risky than reengineering the silos.

References

Armstrong, M.: Copula Catalogue. Part 1: Bivariate Archimedean Copulas, `http://www.cerna.ensmp.fr` (downloaded April 13, 2008)

Armstrong, M., Galli, A., Bailey, W., Couët, B.: Incorporating Technical Uncertainty in Real Option Valuation of Oil Projects. Journal of Petroleum Science and Engineering (44), 67–82 (2004)

Bardhan, I., Bagchi, S., Sougstad, R.: Prioritizing a portfolio of information technology investment projects. Journal of Management Information Systems 21(2), 33–60 (2004)

Bak, P.: How Nature Works. Copernicus, New York (1997)

Benaroch, M.: Option-Based Management of Technology Investment Risk. IEEE Transactions on Engineering Management 48(4), 428–444 (2001)

Benaroch, M.: Managing Information Technology Investment Risk: A Real Options Perspective. Journal of Management Information Systems 19(2), 43–84 (2002)

Benaroch, M., Kauffman, R.J.: A Case for Using Real Options Pricing Analysis to Evaluate Information Technology Project Investments. Information Systems Research 10(1), 70–86 (1999)

Benaroch, M., Kauffman, R.J.: Justifying Electronic Banking Network Expansion Using Real Options Analysis. MIS quarterly 24(2), 197–225 (2000)

Benaroch, M., Lichtenstein, Y., Robinson, K.: Real options in information technology risk management: An empirical validation of risk-option. MIS Quarterly 30(4), 827–864 (2006)

Clemon, R.T., Reilly, T.: Correlations and Copulas for Decision and Risk Analysis. Management Science 45(2), 208–224 (1999)

Cyert, R.M., March, J.G.: A Behavioral Theory of the Firm. Prentice Hall Englewood Cliffs, New Jersey (1963)

de Melo e Silva Accioly, R., Chiyoshi, F.Y.: Modeling Dependence with Copulas: a Useful Tool for Field Development Decision Process. Journal of Petroleum Science and Engineering 44, 83–91 (2004)

Dixit, A.K., Pindyck, R.S.: Investment under Uncertainty. Princeton University Press, Princeton (1994)

Fichman, R.: Real Options and IT Platform Adoption: Implications for Theory and Practice. Information Systems Research 15(2), 132–154 (2004)
Gaume, E.: On the Asymptotic Behavior of Flood Peak Distributions. Hydrology and Earth System Sciences 10, 233–243 (2006)
Kersten, B., Verhoef, C.: IT Portfolio Management: A Banker's Perspective on IT. Cutter IT Journal 16(4), 34–40 (2003)
Markowitz, H.M.: Portfolio Selection. Journal of Finance 7(1), 77–91 (1952)
Mun, J.: Real Options Analysis. John Wiley & Sons, Hoboken (2002)
Nelson, R.B.: An Introduction to Copulas. Lecture Notes in Statistics. Springer, New York (1999)
Nelson, R.B.: An Introduction to Copulas, 2nd edn. Lecture Notes in Statistics. Springer, New York (2006)
Nelson, R., Winter, S.: An Evolutionary Theory of Economic Change. Harvard University Press, Cambridge (1981)
Panzar, J.C., Willig, R.D.: Economies of scope. American Economic Review 71, 268–272 (1981)
Ponzo, P.: Copulas, `http://www.gummy-stuff.org/copulas-2.htm` (retrieved May 3, 2008)
Salvadori, G., De Michele, C.: Frequency Analysis via Copulas: Theoretical Aspects and Applications to Hydrological Events. Water Resources Research 40, 1–17 (2004)
Schmidt, T.: Coping with Copulas. In: Rank, J. (ed.) Copulas - From Theory to Application in Finance, pp. 3–34. Risk Books, London (2007)
Sklar, A.: Fonctions de répartition à n dimensions et leurs marges. Publications de l'Institut de Statistique de L'Université de Paris 8, 229–231 (1959)
Trigeorgis, L.: Real Options: Managerial Flexibility and Strategy in Resource Allocation. MIT Press, Cambridge (1996)

Assessing the Effect of External Pressure in Inter-organizational IS Adoption – Case Electronic Invoicing

Esko Penttinen and Virpi Kristiina Tuunainen

Aalto University School of Economics, P.O. Box 21220, FI-00076 AALTO, Finland
{esko.penttinen,virpi.tuunainen}@aalto.fi

Abstract. We assess the effect of external pressure in IS adoption in the inter-organizational settings of electronic invoicing. Electronic invoicing has been hailed as one of the biggest savings generators for businesses in recent years. However, the adoption in different countries has been much slower than anticipated. Based on earlier literature on diffusion of innovations, adoption of inter-organizational information systems, and institutional theory, we build a research model to empirically estimate the relative importance of external pressure in the context of an IOS implementation. We test the research model empirically using a survey data of companies that have received a letter enforcing them to move to electronic invoicing. We find that organizational readiness, external pressure, and perceived benefits are the most important factors affecting the adoption of electronic invoicing systems in small and medium sized companies (SMEs). We also find evidence for the "bandwagon effect" as well as for the supplier pressure.

Keywords: Adoption of IS, external pressure, electronic invoicing, survey.

1 Introduction

In this study, our focus is on inter-organizational information systems, more precisely on electronic invoicing. Electronic invoicing is defined as the electronic transmission of invoice data in a structured and standardized format, allowing the automated processing of the invoice at the buyer site [1]. Its importance is highlighted by the attention it has received from the European Commission, naming it as one of most important sources of productivity growth in Europe [2].

In Europe, the two most commonly used forms of electronic invoicing are PDFs and EDI messaging. PDFs, however, do not allow for the invoice data to be automatically processed in the receivers' information systems as the data transmitted is not in structured format. EDI messaging, on the other hand, is mainly used in point-to-point systems, requiring usually somewhat heavy investments in information systems. In the Nordic countries, there are standards for exchanging invoice data electronically, in a structured format, through many-to-many networks. In Finland, these standards are TEAPPSXML and Finvoice standards, with which the invoice data is electronically transmitted in structured format between two trading partners.

R. Sharman, T.S. Raghu, and H.R. Rao (Eds.): WEB 2009, LNBIP 52, pp. 269–278, 2010.

Compared to paper-based invoicing or e-mail based PDF-invoicing, true electronic invoicing in structured format presents numerous benefits for both trading partners, including processing cost savings, time and material savings, and decreased number of errors in the invoicing process [3]. Despite the benefits, the transition to electronic invoicing has been slow [4]. As a result, some companies and government units have begun enforcing their suppliers to send their invoices in electronic format (see e.g. [5]). The objective in this study is to evaluate the effect of these enforcement initiatives in the adoption process of electronic invoicing. In other words, our main focus is on assessing the effect of external pressure in an IS diffusion. To do this, we build a research model based earlier research on diffusion of innovations and adoption of inter-organizational information systems, to empirically estimate the relative importance of external pressure in the context of electronic invoicing. Our objective is to enhance the current understanding of the external pressure component in IOS diffusion.

The extant literature offers many avenues for examining the factors affecting the rate of adoption of information systems [6], [7], [8], [9]. We took the existing studies on IS adoption as a starting point and gathered a set of factors that had been identified as important in IS adoption. Using principal component analysis to reduce the number of constructs, we found eight easily identifiable constructs: (1) perceived benefits, (2) complexity, (3) perceived competitor benefits, (4) supplier pressure, (5) bandwagon effect, (6) organizational readiness, and (7)-(8) two constructs measuring the external pressure from customers.

The results of the regression analysis suggest that perceived benefits, supplier pressure, bandwagon effect, external pressure from customers, and organizational readiness can be used to explain the adoption of electronic invoicing in small companies. Concerning the items related to the focus of our study, external pressure from customers, these items loaded on two separate constructs in the principal component analysis. The component which included the reception of the enforcement letters and the attitude towards these letters (positive vs. negative) was statistically significant in explaining the adoption of electronic invoicing.

The paper is organized as follows. We will next review the relevant literature on IS diffusion and adoption of inter-organizational IS. Then, we will present our research model and its operationalization to the context of electronic invoicing. Finally, we provide the results using the 96 responses we have gathered so far.

2 Literature Review

For the purposes of our study, we collected a set of factors from earlier research on IS adoption. We were especially interested in exploring the research addressing the external pressure component in IS adoption.

2.1 IS Adoption

The extant literature provides a plethora of factors affecting the rate of diffusion of technological innovations. The diffusion of innovations (DoI) theory [10] addresses how, why, and at what rate new ideas and technology spread through organizations. The theory suggests a number of variables that determine the rate of adoption of an innovation. First, it identifies five factors or innovation characteristics impacting the adoption rate of innovations: relative advantage, compatibility, complexity, trialability, and observability. Second, it distinguishes between optional, collective, and authority innovation decision types. It also distinguishes between different channels through which the innovation is communicated, and presents the nature of the social system as a factor affecting the rate of adoption. Finally, it acknowledges the extent of change agents' promotion efforts. [10]

The diffusion of innovations theory has been used in numerous studies in the field of information systems. Most importantly, Moore and Benbasat expanded the five factors impacting the adoption of innovations, generating eight factors (voluntariness, relative advantage, compatibility, image, ease of use, result demonstrability, visibility, and trialability) that impact the adoption of IT [11]. Furthermore, they presented scales to operationalize these factors and validated them in their empirical study. Since the early applications of DoI to IS research the theory has been applied and adapted in numerous ways. Research has, however, consistently found that technical compatibility, technical complexity, and relative advantage (perceived need) are important antecedents to the adoption of innovations (see e.g. [12], [13]).

2.2 Institutional Factors

Utilizing the institutional theory, DiMaggio & Powel discuss the three mechanisms of institutional isomorphic change - coercive, mimetic, and normative - as sources of organizational change [14]. Coercive pressures result from both formal and informal pressures exerted on organizations by other organizations upon which they are dependent and by cultural expectations in the society within which organizations function. Such pressures may be felt as use of force, as persuasion, or as invitations to join in collusion. Mimetic pressure stems from uncertainty. When organizational technologies are poorly understood, or when the goals of the organization are ambiguous, or when the environment creates symbolic uncertainty, organizations may model themselves on other organizations, in other words, imitate existing organizational models. Therefore, the process of imitation can be seen as a response to uncertainty. When an organization faces a problem with ambiguous causes or unclear solutions, it is tempted to imitate similar organizations in their field that it perceives to be more legitimate or successful. Normative pressures stem primarily from professionalization. According to DiMaggio and Powell, there are two main aspects of professionalization that act as the sources of normative isomorphism. First, universities and professional training institutions are important centers for the development of organizational norms among managers and staff. Second, professional and trade associations are another vehicle for the definition and promulgation of normative rules about organizational and professional behavior. [14]

Teo et al. used the institutional isomorphism framework to empirically test the contribution of these three factors to the adoption of inter-organizational linkages (IOL) [9]. Consistent with the institutional-based theories, they found that all three institutional influences – mimetic pressures, coercive pressures, and normative pressures – can be dearly distinguished conceptually and empirically in terms of their influence on organizational predisposition toward an IT-based IOL [9]. Furthermore, when institutional forces are examined as a whole, and their influence is evaluated within a larger set of factors that include organizational readiness to adopt financial EDI (FEDI) and attitudes toward adopting FEDI, institutional factors still exhibit a significant and high influence on intentions to adopt. Overall, there is strong empirical support for institutional-based variables as predictors of adoption intentions for inter-organizational linkages.

2.3 External Pressure in IOS Adoption

Earlier research has identified two main sources of external pressure to adopt information systems: competitive pressure, and even more importantly, imposition by trading partners. The impacts of these factors have been exemplified, for instance, in automotive industry, where car manufacturers have required their suppliers and subcontractors to use EDI in their transactions with them [6], [15]. Imposition from trading partners is expected to be one of the most critical factors for EDI adoption by small firms; as the typically weaker partners in inter-organizational relationships, small businesses are extremely susceptible to coercion by their larger partners [8]. Such impositions are especially prevalent in the case of EDI because of its network nature [6].

The pressure exercised by trading partners is a function of two factors: the potential power of the imposing partner and its chosen influence strategy [16], [6]. Provan discusses potential and enacted power in organizational relationships [16]. A powerful partner may pursue three different strategies to induce a small partner to adopt EDI: (1) recommendations, (2) promises, and (3) threats [6]. Threats have been invoked, for instance, by large automobile manufacturers and department store chains [17].

Mehrtens et al. developed a model of Internet adoption by SMEs [7]. Their model included perceived benefits, organizational readiness (technical and financial), and external pressures by trading partners. The findings of their multiple case study indicate that all three factors had an impact on the decision making process to adopt Internet in small and medium sized enterprises [7].

2.4 Research Model and Operationalization of Constructs

Based on the above discussion, our model for assessing the importance of external pressure in the diffusion of electronic invoicing includes four sets of factors: institutional factors (coercive, mimetic and normative), perceived benefits, complexity, and organizational readiness (financial and technical).

In operationalizing the research model, we measured the dependent variable, the intention to adopt electronic invoicing by asking the respondent to evaluate the following statement on a LIKERT scale from 1 to 7: "During the next six months, we plan to regularly use electronic invoicing in our organization". For our independent variables, we utilized the constructs from earlier studies (mainly from [7], [9]).

To study the effect of external pressure, in addition to the constructs provided by [9], we included questions about the enforcement letter sent to the suppliers indicating that they should send their invoices in electronic format in order to continue the business relationship. The question "My organization has received requests to adopt e-invoicing" was a 0/1 variable, whereas the questions "We perceived the requests positively", "We perceived the requests as a means to deepen the relationship with the customer", and "We perceived the requests as a burden that increases our costs of invoicing" were measured on a LIKERT scale 1-7.

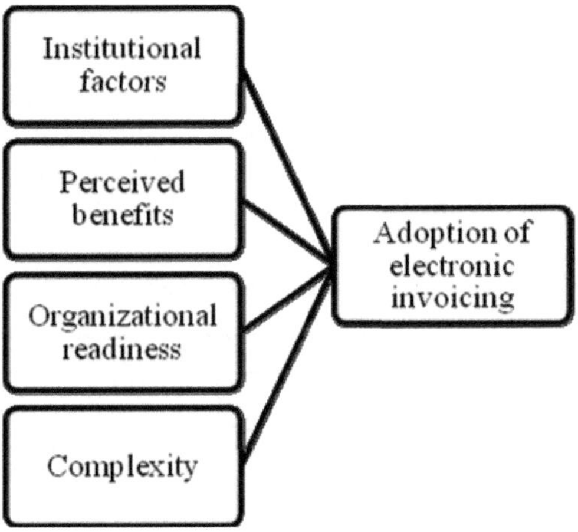

Fig. 1. Research Model

3 Empirical Study

3.1 Key Variables and Sample

Following our research model depicted in the section above, we created a questionnaire to be used in the survey. The questionnaire included background questions (industry, size of the organization, country, etc.) and questions related to the penetration of electronic invoicing and the intention to adopt electronic invoicing in the near future. In addition, we asked 33 questions related to the independent constructs in our research model. These items can be found in Appendix 1. The questionnaire was tested by piloting it with a group of academics and practitioners.

Our empirical study consisted of four groups of survey data collection. First, invitation to participate in the electronic survey was sent to companies that had received a letter by a large Finnish company, sent to their suppliers requesting them to supply the invoices in electronic format. Second, the invitation was sent to organizations that had received a similar letter sent by a government unit to their suppliers. Third, the invitation was sent to a list of respondents provided by an electronic invoice operator to study the effect of third-party persuasion. Fourth, the survey questionnaire was sent to a group of organizations that had not received, to our knowledge, a letter enforcing them to move to the use of electronic invoicing. The questionnaire used in these surveys was not changed between the rounds of data gathering. The data collection for each of these rounds was conducted in August – September 2009. We received 105 responses to the survey, of which 96 had all questions answered.

3.2 Principal Component Analysis

First, we conducted a principal component analysis (varimax rotation) to the set of 33 independent variables to reduce the number of variables to be used in the regression analysis. We decided to use eight variables using the threshold of Eigenvalues above 1. The rotated factor pattern can be found in Appendix 1 and the Eigenvalues of the correlation matrix in the following table (Table 1). All of the eight components can be clearly distinguished. We named the constructs as (PC1) perceived benefits, (PC2) complexity, (PC3) perceived competitor benefits, (PC4) supplier pressure, (PC6) bandwagon effect, (PC8) organizational readiness, and two constructs measuring the external pressure from customers (PC5 and PC7).

Table 1. Principal Component Analysis Eigenvalues

Component	Eigenvalue	Difference	Proportion	Cumulative
PC1 (perceived benefits)	8.69205080	3.85517836	0.2634	0.2634
PC2 (complexity)	4.83687244	1.45476555	0.1466	0.4100
PC3 (perceived competitor benefits)	3.38210689	1.30537037	0.1025	0.5125
PC4 (supplier pressure)	2.07673652	0.20504346	0.0629	0.5754
PC5 (ext. pressure from customers 1)	1.87169305	0.39212708	0.0567	0.6321
PC6 (bandwagon effect)	1.47956597	0.20143047	0.0448	0.6769
PC7 (ext. pressure from customers 2)	1.27813550	0.15094716	0.0387	0.7157
PC8(organizational readiness)	1.12718834	0.11481809	0.0342	0.7498

Next, we used these eight principal components to explain the dependent variable in the model. We will next proceed to discussing the results of the regression analysis.

3.3 Regression Analysis

We used linear regression to analyze the data. By examining the residuals of the regression analysis, we decided to test the model separately for large and small companies. We used the turnover of the company as an indicator of size; large companies in our sample had turnovers of more than 50 million Euros. There were 72 responses in the data set from small companies with less than 50 million Euros turnover.

By using the eight constructs to explain the intention to regularly use electronic invoicing, we were able to explain more than 50% of the variance in the dependent variable (R2 = 0.5628, adjusted R2 = 0.5072).

The results of the regression analysis for small companies suggest that (PC1) perceived benefits, (PC4) supplier pressure, (PC6) bandwagon effect, (PC7) external

Table 2. Results of the Linear Regression (small, n = 72)

Variable	DF	Estimate	Error	t value
Intercept	1	4.95748	0.17859	27.76
PC1 (perceived benefits)	1	0.58675	0.19661	2.98
PC2 (complexity)	1	-0.22735	0.18574	-1.22
PC3 (perceived competitor benefits)	1	0.34295	0.18972	1.81
PC4 (supplier pressure)	1	0.59160	0.19315	3.06
PC5 (ext. pressure from customers 1)	1	0.13111	0.18258	0.72
PC6 (bandwagon effect)	1	0.39507	0.16767	2.36
PC7 (ext. pressure from customers 2)	1	0.81933	0.19140	4.28
PC8 (organizational readiness)	1	1.02626	0.17126	5.99

pressure from customers, and (PC8) organizational readiness affect the intention to regularly use electronic invoicing.

Unfortunately, the survey data set only has 24 observations for large companies, therefore not allowing the regression analysis to be done on the companies with turnover of more than 50 million Euros.

4 Summary and Conclusions

In this study, we set out to explore the effect of external pressure in IOS adoption, particularly in the context of electronic invoicing. Based on earlier research, we developed a research model and operationalized it into a survey questionnaire. The questionnaire included background questions, one question measuring the intention to adopt electronic invoicing, and 33 items to measure the independent constructs.

We sent the survey out to the recipients of an enforcement letter indicating that the supplier should send their invoices in electronic format in order to continue the business relationship, and received altogether 105 responses, of which 96 were usable.

Using principal component analysis, we were able to reduce the number of variables to eight easily identifiable constructs. The variables related to the external pressure from customers loaded on two separate components. One of the two components included items used in earlier research [9] to measure the extent of external pressure from customers. Another component included the question of whether the company had received an enforcement letter from their customers (either from customer companies or from public organization). In the next phase of the study, we used these eight principal components in the regression analysis to explain the adoption of electronic invoicing.

Using our survey data, we were able to identify factors that affect the adoption of electronic invoicing by small and medium sized companies (with turnover of less than 50 million Euros). The results show that perceived benefits, supplier pressure, bandwagon effect, organizational readiness, and external pressure from customers affect the adoption of electronic invoicing practices.

The small number of responses is the main limitation of our study. We decided to examine separately the factors affecting the adoption of electronic invoicing in small companies and in large companies. In this paper, we report the findings addressing the small companies with less than 50 million Euros turnover. We plan to gather more data especially from large organizations, and our objective is to compare the factors in the case of small versus. large companies. We assume that the external pressure component and the organizational readiness component are less significant in the case of large companies' IS adoption. We predict the perceived benefits to be the most important factor for large companies. This will be addressed in our future research.

Acknowledgments. We thank the organizations involved in the study for providing contact lists for the empirical study. We thank the Business Technology department research seminar participants at the Helsinki School of Economics for the feedback on an earlier version of the paper.

References

1. Penttinen, E. (ed.): Electronic Invoicing Initiatives in Finland and in the European Union – Taking the Steps towards the Real-Time Economy (2008); Dorota, K., Harald, B., Hyytiäinen, M., Kuivalahti, T., Penttinen, E., Poteri, J., Turunen, T. (contributors): Helsinki School of Economics Series B-95
2. EEI : European Electronic Invoicing (2007), http://www.epractice.eu/files/media/media1364.pdf (accessed 31.8.2009)
3. Lempinen, H., Penttinen, E.: Assessing the business value of electronic order-to-payment cycle. In: The Proceedings of the European Conference in Information Systems (ECIS), Verona, Italy, June 8-10 (2009)
4. Penttinen, E., Hyytiäinen, M.: The Adoption of Electronic Invoicing in Finnish Private and Public Organizations. In: The Proceedings of the European Conference in Information Systems (ECIS), Dublin, Ireland, June 8-11 (2008)
5. Brun, M.: Electronic Invoicing to the Public Sector in Denmark (2007), http://www.epractice.eu/cases/EID (accessed 29.11.2007)
6. Iacovou, C.L., Benbasat, I., Dexter, A.S.: Electronic Data Interchange and Small Organizations: Adoption and Impact of Technology. MIS Quarterly (December 1995)
7. Mehrtens, J., Cragg, P., Mills, A.: A model of Internet adoption by SMEs. Information and Management 39, 165–176 (2001)
8. Saunders, C., Hart, P.: Electronic Data Interchange Across Organizational Boundaries: Building a Theory of Motivation and Implementation. In: Paper Presented at The Administrative Sciences Association of Canada Twenty First Annual Conference, Lake Louise, Alberta, Canada (May 1993)
9. Teo, H.H., Wei, K.K., Benbasat, I.: Predicting intention to adopt interorganizational linkages, an institutional perspective. MIS Quarterly 27(1), 19–49 (2003)
10. Rogers, E.M.: Diffusion of Innovations, 4th edn. Free Press, New York (1995)
11. Moore, G.C., Benbasat, I.: Development of an instrument to measure the perceptions of adopting an information technology innovation. Information Systems Research 2(3), 192–222 (1991)
12. Bradford, M., Florin, J.: Examining the role of innovation diffusion factors on the implementation success of enterprise resource planning systems. International Journal of Accounting Information Systems 4(3), 205–225 (2003)
13. Crum, M.R., Premkumar, G., Ramamurthy, K.: An assessment of motor carrier adoption, use, and satisfaction with EDI. Transportation Journal 35(4), 44–57 (1996)
14. DiMaggio, P.J., Powell, W.W.: The Iron Cage Revisited: Institutional Isomorphism and Collective Rationality in Organizational Fields. American Sociological Review 48(2), 147–160 (1983)
15. Tuunainen, V.K.: Opportunities of Effective Integration of EDI for Small Businesses in the Automotive Industry. Information & Management 36(6), 361–375 (1998)
16. Provan, K.G.: Recognizing, Measuring, and Interpreting the Potential/Enacted Power Distinction in Organizational Research. Academy of Management Review 5(4), 549–559 (1980)
17. Brent, P.: Store Chains Put The Squeeze on Suppliers. The Financial Post 26, 13 (1994)

Appendix: Rotated Factor Pattern (Principal Component Analysis, Varimax Rotation)

	F1	F2	F3	F4	F5	F6	F7	F8
My organization has received requests to adopt e-invoicing	0.08	-0.01	0.03	0.17	0.01	-0.13	**0.73**	-0.08
We perceived the requests positively	0.34	-0.02	0.07	0.15	0.07	0.10	**0.74**	0.22
We perceived the requests as a means to deepen the relationship with the customer	0.22	0.09	0.17	-0.03	0.15	0.08	**0.74**	0.05
We perceived the requests as a burden that increases our costs of invoicing	-0.07	**0.52**	-0.05	0.11	0.19	0.10	0.14	-0.42
The extent of electronic invoicing adoption by competitors	0.06	-0.04	-0.23	0.01	0.23	**0.71**	0.06	0.09
The extent of electronic invoicing adoption by suppliers	0.15	0.01	-0.01	0.15	0.05	**0.82**	0.01	-0.18
The extent of electronic invoicing adoption by customers	0.25	0.01	0.15	0.16	-0.14	**0.80**	-0.07	0.16
Competitors have benefitted from e-invoicing in terms of time and monetary savings	0.09	-0.06	**0.91**	0.23	0.10	-0.04	0.06	0.07
Competitors are perceived favorably by others in the same industry	0.07	0.01	**0.91**	0.21	0.08	0.00	0.19	-0.07
Competitors are perceived favorably by suppliers	0.10	-0.09	**0.89**	0.16	0.18	-0.01	-0.01	-0.08
Competitors are perceived favorably by customers	0.06	-0.03	**0.91**	0.19	0.24	-0.06	0.06	0.02
Concerning the suppliers that have adopted e-invoicing, my firm's well-being depends on their resources	0.15	-0.03	0.38	**0.71**	0.11	0.07	0.10	0.11
Concerning the suppliers that have adopted e-invoicing, my firm cannot easily switch away from them	0.12	0.10	0.18	**0.85**	0.05	0.18	0.05	0.02
Concerning the suppliers that have adopted e-invoicing, my firm must maintain good relationships with them	0.27	0.08	0.30	**0.67**	0.06	0.05	-0.06	0.11
Concerning the suppliers that have adopted e-invoicing, they are the core suppliers in a concentrated industry	0.07	0.06	0.14	**0.79**	0.17	0.06	0.22	0.08

Concerning the customers that have adopted e-invoicing, my firm's well-being depends on their purchases	0.18	0.11	0.23	0.22	**0.80**	0.13	0.05	0.08
Concerning the customers that have adopted e-invoicing, my firm must maintain good relationships with them	0.29	0.12	0.14	0.13	**0.78**	-0.05	0.12	0.06
Concerning the customers that have adopted e-invoicing, they are the largest customers in the industry	0.19	0.15	0.28	0.07	**0.79**	0.09	0.06	0.09
E-invoicing is difficult to understand from a business perspective	-0.11	**0.74**	-0.09	0.34	0.00	-0.17	-0.12	-0.03
E-invoicing is difficult to understand from a technical perspective	-0.15	**0.76**	0.00	0.04	0.01	-0.03	0.09	0.09
Using e-invoicing is difficult	-0.06	**0.78**	-0.05	-0.06	-0.06	-0.23	0.09	0.19
Maintaining audit trail is difficult with e-invoicing	-0.07	**0.87**	-0.05	-0.05	0.00	0.15	0.00	-0.06
Tracing errors is difficult with e-invoicing	-0.09	**0.77**	0.00	-0.12	0.24	0.12	-0.01	-0.09
Understanding the whole process of cash disbursement and collection is difficult with e-invoicing	-0.09	**0.88**	0.04	0.08	0.09	0.02	-0.09	-0.13
We have the necessary monetary resources to implement e-invoicing	0.32	-0.09	-0.06	0.07	0.15	0.04	0.17	**0.80**
We have the necessary technical resources to implement e-invoicing	0.24	0.02	-0.01	0.26	0.12	0.03	0.01	**0.81**
E-invoicing generates cost savings	**0.85**	-0.14	0.05	0.10	-0.03	0.01	0.08	0.19
E-invoicing generates material savings	**0.85**	-0.04	0.06	0.08	0.16	0.13	0.01	0.09
E-invoicing generates time savings	**0.81**	-0.20	-0.03	0.12	-0.03	0.15	0.08	0.05
E-invoicing reduces the number of errors	**0.54**	-0.11	0.05	0.46	0.15	0.04	0.22	0.08
E-invoicing improves the image of my organization	**0.80**	-0.05	0.12	0.22	0.23	0.08	0.18	0.08
E-invoicing our customer retention	**0.76**	-0.14	0.08	0.12	0.26	0.09	0.22	0.13
E-invoicing our customer satisfaction	**0.64**	-0.08	0.27	-0.06	0.31	0.13	0.21	0.15

PC1: Perceived benefits, PC2: Complexity, PC3: Perceived competitor benefits, PC4: Supplier pressure, PC5: External pressure component1, PC6: Bandwagon effect, PC7, External pressure component2, PC8: Organizational readiness.

Open Source versus Proprietary Software: A Case of Fully Covered Market

Yipeng Liu[1] and Hsing K. Cheng[2]

[1] 320 Brennan Hall, Kania School of Management, University of Scranton
Scranton, PA, 18510, U. S. A.
[2] 361C Stuzin Hall, Warrington College of Business, University of Florida
Gainesville, FL, 32611, U. S. A.
yipeng.liu@scranton.edu, hkcheng@ufl.edu

Abstract. This paper analyzes the impact of network externalities on the competition between open source software (OSS) and proprietary software (PS) in a fully covered market. The installed base and the profit of proprietary software are found increasing at the expense of decreasing user base for OSS. Furthermore, we find that a threshold corresponding to the quality ratio between OSS and proprietary software can be derived such that if the network effect intensity of the OSS is greater than that of the proprietary software multiplied by this threshold value, then OSS benefits from the presence of network externality; Finally, we find that making software products compatible with competing rival is not desirable by proprietary software vendors but favored by OSS venders.

Keywords: Open source software, network externalities, competition, compatibility.

1 Introduction

As opposed to commercial proprietary software (PS), open source software (OSS) refer to those programs "whose licenses give users the freedom to run the program for any purpose, to study and modify the program, and to redistribute copies of either the original or the modified program without having to pay royalties to previous developers" [16]. Apache, OpenOffice, mySQL and Linux are some notable examples of OSS that have achieved remarkable success against their closed source or proprietary alternatives as is evident in their large user base.

Increasing number of OSS products have become available in the market, ranging from major operating systems, database systems, to thousands of specialized scientific applications. The increasing adoption of OSS at the same time poses a challenge for proprietary software vendors. For decades, commercial software makers charge consumers licensing fees of their programs for a steady flood of ever-cheaper computers. But now, the suppliers face a growing threat from "the open source", which gives customers a free or low-cost alternative to commercial products. "It's very hard to compete with free," says John Chen, chief executive of Sybase Inc., the No. 4 largest database provider. "It lowers the price point."

R. Sharman, T.S. Raghu, and H.R. Rao (Eds.): WEB 2009, LNBIP 52, pp. 279–288, 2010.

Several factors contribute to the lower total ownership cost of using OSS. For instance, "OSS costs less to initially acquire, upgrade and maintain, and runs more efficiently on older hardware, among others" [16]. Cyber source found that using OSS saves 24 to 34 percent of the total ownership cost over a three-year time span compared with using Microsoft's proprietary approach for a typical organization of 250 computer-using employees (www.cybersource.com).

2 Literature Review

The successes of OSS have led to an increasing interest in understanding this form of software about its development and its impact on the software industry. Pioneering research on OSS to date focuses mainly on why developers participate in OSS projects (e.g., [7, 8, 11, 12]), the incentives of firms to adopt open source initiatives (e.g., [13]), and the success factors of OSS projects (e.g., [3, 4, 6, 15]). As OSS proves to be a viable technology solution for businesses, another stream of OSS research turns attention to the competition dynamics between OSS and proprietary software. This stream of research includes analysis – both empirical and theoretical – of the public and free nature of OSS products and their impact on the marketplace for software products. However, the majority of these studies either focus primarily on the result of competition between particular operating systems (e.g., [2]) or consider open source to be privately provided public goods and concentrate on software vendor's choice between producing open source or proprietary software (e.g., [1, 9]). Furthermore there are few studies that analyze the extent of this competition under the presence of network externalities.

Our paper aims at a similar topic but differs from the past literature in two major aspects. First, our work focuses on the impact of network externalities on the competition rather than the result of competition between open source and proprietary software. We model the heterogeneous consumers' preferences for products to depend on two major factors – the software quality and the network size, and we allow the extent of network effect to be different between OSS and proprietary software. Second, we investigate the strategic choices and incentives for compatibility between OSS and proprietary software venders – a topic majorly overlooked in previous studies on open source software.

Table 1. Four different cases of analyses

	OSS and Proprietary Software are compatible	OSS and Proprietary Software are incompatible
Both OSS and Proprietary Software exhibit same network effect (γ)	Case 1	Case 3
OSS and Proprietary Software exhibit different network effect (γ_o & γ_p)	Case 2	Case 4

We use a purely analytical approach to study the competition between open source and proprietary software with focus on the following research questions: Does the positive network effect always yield positive impact? How would the choice of compatibility affect network externality's impact? Furthermore, which software vendor (PS or OSS) has the most incentive to make its product compatible? We address these research questions by separating our analysis into four different cases (see Table 1) depending on whether the rivalry software are compatible with each other and whether they share the same network effect intensity.

3 The Model

Assume that the total number of potential customers who will adopt either open source software (OSS) or proprietary software is N, which is normalized to 1 without loss of generality. Let θ represent a customer's preference for software quality and θ is uniformly distributed between 0 and 1. In the absence of network externalities, a customer derives:

$$u = \theta \cdot s - p$$

utility of adopting the software of quality s charging price p.

Let γ model the intensity of the network externalities effect. When Q is the installed base of the software (i.e., the total number of users adopting the software), network externalities effect increases each consumer's preference θ by γQ in accordance with the increase in willingness to pay when an additional user joins the network. When purchasing a software product of quality s in a network of size Q at price p, consumer θ obtains net utility:

$$u = (\theta + \gamma Q) s - p$$

under the influence of network externalities. In [5], $\theta \cdot s$ is the product's "network-independent" or standalone value, which depends on both consumer's preference and product quality. The "network-generated" value is $\gamma Q s$ and exhibits complementary effects between network size and quality. Therefore in the same network, a high quality product has both higher standalone and network values than a lower quality one. In [10], and most other research on network externalities, product are homogeneous and consumers differ in their total willingness to pay. The network-generated benefit therefore only depends on the network size.

Let s_o and s_p describe respectively the quality of open source software and proprietary software. Generally, software quality can be measured in several dimensions, such as performance, ease of use, customer support, reliability and security, etc. For the sake of generality, our study is not restricted to any particular dimension. Rather, we define software quality as the characteristics of software other than the price. For practical purpose, we assume $s_p > s_o$, since all customers will adopt OSS if the quality of the free OSS exceeds that of the commercial counterpart. In reality, we indeed observe certain quality advantages enjoyed by the proprietary software, such as more user-friendly interface, more reliable and professional customer support, continuous product upgrade and so forth. Let Q_o and Q_p denote the installed user base of open source software and proprietary software respectively.

4 Competition between OSS and Proprietary Software

We first present the case where there is no network externalities effect in Section 4.1 as a benchmark, followed by analyses of competition between OSS and proprietary software in the presence of network externalities under different scenarios. Several key propositions are derived to examine the impact of network externalities on the competition.

4.1 Benchmark Case – No Network Externalities

In the benchmark model (see Figure 1), we assume that the market is fully covered, i.e., all consumers choose to use one of the two software products. This is always true when the benefit of the product is sufficiently large. In addition, we assume that the open source software is freely available hence there is no price component in the net utility. Without network effect, a consumer of type θ derives net utility

$$u_o = \theta \cdot s_o$$

by using the open source software and the net utility of buying the proprietary software is

$$u_p = \theta \cdot s_p - p.$$

Suppose consumer $\theta_b \in [0,1]$ is indifferent between the open source and proprietary software products, then one has

$$\theta_b s_p - p = \theta_b s_o .$$

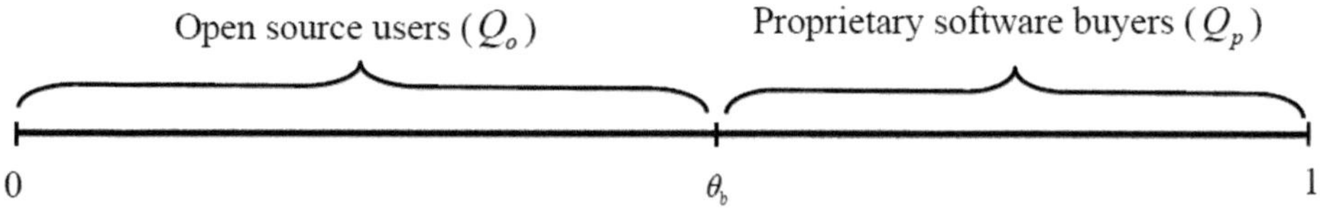

Fig. 1. Demand of Open Source and Proprietary Software

Thus, $\theta_b = p/(s_p - s_o)$ and the resulting installed bases for OSS and proprietary software are θ_b and $1-\theta_b$ respectively. In contrast with conventional Hotelling model, only one party—the proprietary software producer aims at maximizing profit and the open source software vender is passive. Due to the negligible marginal cost of production, proprietary software firm solves the following profit maximization problem:

$$\max_{p} p(1-\theta_b)$$
$$s.t.\ \ 0 \le p \le s_p - s_o \ .$$

Accordingly, the optimal price of the proprietary software in the benchmark case is,

$$p_b^* = \left(s_p - s_o\right)/2\ ,$$

and the demands of proprietary and open source software and the profit of the proprietary software vender are given by

$$Q_{bp}^* = Q_{bo}^* = \frac{1}{2}$$
$$\pi_b^* = \left(s_p - s_o\right)/4$$

where the subscript b denotes the benchmark case of no network externalities, p for proprietary software, and o for OSS. Even though proprietary software is of higher quality, since OSS is free, the benchmark-level demands (e.g. installed user base) of proprietary and open source software are the same.

4.2 The Impact of Network Externality

We first present how consumers' utility functions of the open source and proprietary software change according to different network effect intensities and compatibility strategies. Next, we summarize the impact of network externalities by comparing the demands of OSS and proprietary software with the benchmark demands reported in Section 4.1.

4.3 Case 1: OSS and Proprietary Software Are Compatible and Exhibit Same Network Externality Effect

When the rivalry products are compatible with each other, the network size for either software product is equivalent to the sum of the two networks (i.e. $Q = Q_o + Q_p = 1$, since the market is fully covered). In addition, both OSS and proprietary software exhibit the same network effect intensity in Case 1 (i.e., $\gamma_o = \gamma_p = \gamma$). Therefore, in the presence of direct network effect, the net utility for OSS and proprietary software consumers are given by:

$$u_o = \left(\theta + \gamma Q\right) s_o \text{ and } u_p = \left(\theta + \gamma Q\right) s_p - p\text{, where } Q = 1\,.$$

Marginal consumer θ_o who is indifferent between open and proprietary software is characterized by

$$(\theta_o + \gamma Q) s_o = (\theta_o + \gamma Q) s_p - p \ .$$

The demands of open source and the proprietary software are therefore defined as:

$$Q_o = \theta_o \text{ and } Q_p = 1 - \theta_o \ .$$

Simple algebra indicates that:

$$\theta_o = \left(\left(s_o - s_p \right) \gamma + p \right) / \left(s_p - s_o \right) \ .$$

Accordingly, the number of proprietary software buyers is:

$$Q_p = \left(\left(s_p - s_o \right) (1 + \gamma) - p \right) / \left(s_p - s_o \right) \ .$$

In order to guarantee non-negative demand for both OSS and proprietary software, the following condition must hold

$$\gamma \left(s_p - s_o \right) \le p \le (1 + \gamma) \left(s_p - s_o \right) \ .$$

Proprietary software vender maximizes its revenue by setting the price optimally. The decision problem of the proprietary software vender is therefore formulated as:

$$\begin{aligned} &\max_p pQ_p = p \cdot \frac{\left(s_p - s_o \right)(1+\gamma) - p}{s_p - s_o} \\ &\text{s.t. } \gamma \left(s_p - s_o \right) \le p \le (1+\gamma)\left(s_p - s_o \right) \end{aligned} \ .$$

Kuhn-Tucker conditions lead to:

$$p^* = \frac{\left(s_p - s_o \right)(1+\gamma)}{2}, \ Q_o^* = \frac{1-\gamma}{2}, \ Q_p^* = \frac{1+\gamma}{2}, \text{ and } \pi_p^* = \frac{\left(s_p - s_o \right)(1+\gamma)^2}{4} .$$

By comparing these optimal results to the benchmark level demands and profit, we have the following proposition.

Proposition 1. *In Case 1, the installed base of proprietary software increases, the installed base of open source software decreases, both the optimal price and the optimal profit of proprietary software increase in the presence of network externalities.*

4.4 When the Network Effect Intensity Is Different

Unlike past literature, our model allows the possibility that the OSS has higher network effect intensity than the proprietary software. To address this issue (i.e., Cases 2 and 4 in Table 1), we use different parameters γ_o and γ_p ($\gamma_o > \gamma_p$) to capture the different network effect intensities for OSS and proprietary software respectively.

4.5 When Software Products Are Not Compatible

Users in OSS network will not be able to benefit from the contribution of the users in the proprietary software network and vice versa. As a result, the network size, from which the network value is generated, shrinks for both software products. To address this issue (Cases 3 and 4 in Table 1), we use Q_o and Q_p to denote the installed base of OSS and proprietary software respectively. Full market coverage leads to $Q_o + Q_p = 1$. Following the same approach in Case 1, Table 2 reports the optimal outcomes of the open source and proprietary software under different scenarios. A series of key propositions are thus derived from Table 2.

Table 2. Fully covered market: optimal outcomes

	Case 1	Case 2	Case 3	Case 4
u_o	$(\theta+\gamma Q)s_o$	$(\theta+\gamma_0 Q)s_o$	$(\theta+\gamma Q_o)s_o$	$(\theta+\gamma_o Q_o)s_o$
u_p	$(\theta+\gamma Q)s_p-p$	$(\theta+\gamma_p Q)s_p-p$	$(\theta+\gamma Q_p)s_p-p$	$(\theta+\gamma_p Q_p)s_p-p$
p^*	$\frac{(s_p-s_o)(1+\gamma)}{2}$	$\frac{s_p(1+\gamma_p)-s_o(1+\gamma_o)}{2}$	$\frac{s_p-s_o(1+\gamma)}{2}$	$\frac{s_p-s_o(1+\gamma_o)}{2}$
Q_o^*	$\frac{(1-\gamma)}{2}$	$\frac{s_p-s_o+s_o\gamma_o-s_p\gamma_p}{2(s_p-s_o)}$	$\frac{s_p-s_o-s_o\gamma-2s_p\gamma}{2(s_p(1-\gamma)-s_o(1+\gamma))}$	$\frac{s_p-s_o-s_o\gamma_o-2s_p\gamma_p}{2(s_p(1-\gamma_p)-s_o(1+\gamma_o))}$
Q_p^*	$\frac{(1+\gamma)}{2}$	$\frac{s_p-s_o+s_p\gamma_p-s_o\gamma_o}{2(s_p-s_o)}$	$\frac{s_p-s_o-s_o\gamma}{2(s_p(1-\gamma)-s_o(1+\gamma))}$	$\frac{s_p-s_o-s_o\gamma_o}{2(s_p(1-\gamma_p)-s_o(1+\gamma_o))}$
π^*	$\frac{(s_p-s_o)(1+\gamma)^2}{4}$	$\frac{(s_o(1+\gamma_o)-s_p(1+\gamma_p))^2}{4(s_p-s_o)}$	$\frac{(s_o-s_p+s_o\gamma)^2}{4(s_p(1-\gamma)-s_o(1+\gamma))}$	$\frac{(s_o-s_p+s_o\gamma_o)^2}{4(s_p(1-\gamma_p)-s_o(1+\gamma_o))}$
Valid γ range	$0\le\gamma\le1$	$0\le\frac{1+\gamma_o}{1+\gamma_p}\le\frac{s_p}{s_o}$	$0\le\gamma\le\frac{s_p-s_o}{2s_p+s_o}$	$0\le\frac{1+\gamma_o}{1-\gamma_p}\le\frac{s_p}{s_o}$

4.6 The Effect of Network Externalities – Positive or Negative

By comparing the optimal outcomes of OSS and PS under Cases 3 and 4 with the benchmark results, we find that network externalities have positive impact on the demand and profit of proprietary software, but negative impact on the demand of open source software.

Proposition 2. *When OSS is incompatible with its proprietary software counterpart (Case 3 and 4), the installed base of open source software decrease, the installed base of proprietary software increases, the optimal price of proprietary software drops,* *but the optimal profit of proprietary software improves in the presence of network externalities.*

Comparing the optimal outcomes of Case 2 with benchmark results, however, shows mixed results. We find that if the ratio of network effect intensities between OSS and proprietary software (i.e. γ_o / γ_p) falls short of the inverse quality ratio between the two (i.e. s_p / s_o), then proprietary software benefits from the presence of network externalities; otherwise, OSS is favored by more users in the presence of network externalities. Our findings can be summarized by the proposition below.

Proposition 3. *Define the threshold value* $T_1 = \frac{s_p}{s_o}$. *In case 2, When* $\gamma_o < T_1\gamma_p$ *, the installed base, the optimal price and the overall profit for proprietary software all increase and the installed base of OSS decreases in the presence of network externalities. The results are reversed when* $\gamma_o > T_1\gamma_p$.

4.7 What Is the Best Strategy – Compatible or Incompatible?

For either OSS or proprietary software vender, making its product compatible to its competitor allows the user of that product benefit from the network of its opponent, which therefore adds to the value of the product and increases consumer's willingness to pay and their net utility of adopting the software. However, in a fully covered market, the increase of one party's user leads to the decrease of the other party's user and the best response for the competitor in such a situation is to make its product compatible too. Therefore in equilibrium we will see software products are either incompatible with each other or fully compatible with each other. One-way compatibility (one product compatible with the other, but not the other way around) is therefore ignored in our analysis. Furthermore, we are more interested in the question about which party has the most incentive to make its product compatible. The answer to this question can be found by a head to head comparison (e.g. Case 3 vs. Case 1, Case 4 vs. Case 2) between the payoffs (e.g. market shares and profits) for both OSS and proprietary software venders when the software is made from incompatible to compatible with its rival product.

Proposition 4. *Whether OSS and proprietary software exhibit the same network effect intensity or not, OSS vender always has the most incentive to make its product compatible with its proprietary counterpart, as manifested by the expanded market share after the change. Proprietary software vender, on the other hand, is not willing to make its product compatible with the OSS as doing so will decreases its market share and profit.*

5 Conclusion

We investigate the impact of network externalities on the competition between open source and proprietary software. We analyze four different scenarios depending on whether OSS and proprietary software are compatible with each other and whether they exhibit the same network effect intensities. When the market is fully covered, network effect benefits the proprietary software more than OSS in all cases except Case 2. Compared with the benchmark case of no network externalities, the installed base and the profit of proprietary software both increase at the expense of OSS losing user base in the presence of network externalities. In Case 2, we find that a threshold corresponding to the quality ratio between OSS and proprietary software can be derived such that if the network effect intensity of the OSS is greater than that of the proprietary software multiplied by this threshold value, then OSS benefits from the presence of network externality; otherwise, proprietary software benefits from the presence of network effect. Finally, we find that making software products compatible with competing rival is not desirable by proprietary software vendors but highly favored by OSS venders. Hence, in order to maintain its dominant position in market shares, the proprietary software vendor should make it hard for the OSS software to be compatible with its product.

References

1. Bessen, J.: What good is free software?. In: Hahn, R. (ed.) Government Policy Towards Open Source Software. AEI Brookings Joint Center for Regulatory Studies, Washington (2002)
2. Casadesus-Masanell, R., Ghemawat, P.: Dynamic mixed duopoly: a model motivated by Linux vs. Windows. Management Science 52(7), 1072–1084 (2006)
3. Chengalur-Smith, S., Sidorova, A.: Survival of open-source projects: a popular ecology perspective. In: Proceedings of the International Conference on Information Systems, pp. 782–787 (2003)
4. Crowston, K., Annabi, H., Howison, J.: Defining open source software project success. In: Proceedings of the International Conference on Information Systems, pp. 329–340 (2003)
5. Farrell, J., Saloner, G.: Installed base and compatibility: innovation, product preannouncements, and predation. American Economic Review 76(5), 940–955 (1986)
6. Fitzgerald, B., Kenny, T.: Open source software in the trenches: lessons from a large-scale OSS implementation. In: Proceedings of the International Conference on Information Systems, pp. 316–326 (2003)
7. Hann, I.-H., Roberts, J., Slaughter, S.A., Fielding, R.: Economic incentives for participate in open source software projects. In: Proceedings of the International Conference on Information Systems, pp. 365–372 (2002)
8. Hann, I.-H., Roberts, J., Slaughter, S.A.: Why developers participate in open source software projects: an empirical investigation. In: Proceedings of the International Conference on Information Systems, pp. 821–830 (2004)
9. Johnson, J.P.: Economics of open source software. Journal of Economics and Management Strategy 11, 627–662 (2002)
10. Katz, M., Shapiro, C.: Network externalities, competition and compatibility. American Economic Review 75, 420–440 (1985)
11. Lerner, J., Tirole, J.: The open source movement: key research questions. European Economic Review 45, 819–826 (2001)
12. Lerner, J., Tirole, J.: Some simple economics of open source. Journal of Industrial Economics 50, 197–234 (2002)

13. Mustonen, M.: Copyleft – the economics of Linux and other open source software. Information Economic Policy 15, 99–121 (2003)
14. Rosenberg, D.K.: Open source: The unauthorized white papers. IDG Book Worldwide, Inc. (2000)
15. Sagers, G.W.: The Influence of network governance factors on success in open source software development projects. In: Proceedings of the International Conference on Information Systems, pp. 427–438 (2004)
16. Wheeler, D.A.: Why open source software/free software (OSS/FS)? Look at the number! (2003), `http://www.dwheeler.com/oss_fs_why.html`

When Is RFID Perceived as a Radical Technology?

Aditya Sharma, Dominic Thomas, and Benn Konsynski

Abstract. RFID Technology has been in existence since the 1940's when it was used to differentiate between friendly and enemy aircraft in World War II. Its application in the business world is however relatively new. RFID has the potential to revolutionize supply chains and take product tracking to a new level. However, its adoption has been slow not only because of the higher cost of tags compared to barcodes but also because many companies have not been able to figure out how to effectively use it. In this study we focus on one of the key issues companies face when they try to evaluate RFID i.e. its radical and disruptive nature. Using data from semi-structured interviews we build a case for why organizations may perceive RFID as a disruptive and radical technology. Perceived radicalness of a technology is presented as a second order formative with five critical dimensions. Testable hypotheses are proposed for each dimension and its contribution towards the "radicalness of RFID".

Keywords: Radical Technologies, Perceived Radicalness, Adoption, RFID, Emerging Technologies.

1 Background and Introduction

"RFID will have a pervasive impact on every aspect of civilization, much the same way the printing press, the industrial revolution and the Internet and personal computers have transformed society.... RFID is a big deal. Its impact will be pervasive, personal and profound. It will be the biggest deal since Edison gave us the light bulb."

-Rick Duris, Frontline Solutions Magazine, December 2003

The "digital wallet," "the personal data warehouse," "unison," "ubiquity," and "universal:" these terms characterize current discussions of cutting-edge information technologies. Information technologies (ITs) pervade modern daily life and continue to move into previously analog spaces, such as our money management (smart phones with digital cash chips built in), basic information in our lives (PDAs, smart phones, etc.), and any communications we conduct (email, SMS, cellular communications, MySpace and blogs, etc.). Radio Frequency Identification (RFID) technology provides the necessary cornerstone for identifying almost any item uniquely and digitally from a distance enabling new efforts with "blink" debit and credit cards, mass transit ticket systems, and a variety of industrial applications beyond the well-known application of replacing bar codes (i.e. Walmart's initial RFID efforts). Many of RFID applications in business promise to extend far beyond simple logistics. They can include smart sensor units that track and report their status and self-reporting receipts and warranties built into items and controlled by their owners. A breakthrough

R. Sharman, T.S. Raghu, and H.R. Rao (Eds.): WEB 2009, LNBIP 52, pp. 289–297, 2010.

application of this fundamental change in identification technology (from prior analog or barcode systems) could disrupt the way businesses compete. RFID hence may be perceived as a radical technology offering great opportunity. Businesses know that there is great risk to attempting to apply such a radical technology. It will cost a lot and it will require substantial business process change to leverage its true potential. At the same time, businesses are also aware that great risk is present in failing to address RFID: it could displace the rules of business which lead to their current profitability.

The developer and the adopter of a new technology innovation represent two sides of the same coin. While one side helps create new and better technologies the other helps determine its impact and eventual success. Most characterizations of an emerging technology innovation such as radical, breakthrough, revolutionary and discontinuous are from the *creator/developer perspective* where these labels are used interchangeably to suggest technologies that are new and distinct and that provide significantly large rewards. The innovations are also characterized as disruptive because they have the potential to alter competitive position of innovating firms [16]. This research began with a broad, qualitative inquiry into the current efforts in business to apply RFID. A substantial literature review showed that research has yet to address the issue of RFID's radicalness and its implications from the adopter's perspective. Thus, we conducted intensive 1-2 hour interviews with 12 senior managers in 10 large or medium organizations (6 Fortune 500, 1 Major IT consulting firm) to better understand what are the special risks and opportunities present in a radical platform IT innovation such as RFID and how organizations deal with them. We report the findings of this research here. We show how research must clarify the meaning of radicalness as it applies to adoption of new IT in order to make it useful for academic and practice purposes.

It is often assumed that term radicalness of an innovation is clearly understood and means the same for all researchers and managers. This however is far from truth. Different people characterize the same innovation as radical for very different underlying reasons. This lack of definitional clarity belies understanding the inherent attributes of radicalness for effectively understanding radical technologies and innovations. Researchers often face ambiguity in understanding and explaining the effects of radicalness on adoption and implementation decisions and outcome due to this lack of clarity.

We address this literature gap and argue that the radicalness of a technology innovation is inherently related to technology adoption. To be understood more completely the IS research community needs to conceptualize radicalness as a multi-dimensional construct including user perceptions and their application context along with the inherent technology attributes. The conceptualization of radicalness in technology adoption we present herein extends work by Sood and Tellis [17]; Chandy and Tellis [2]; Henderson and Clark [10] on innovation attributes by incorporating technology-organization-context focused dimensions which, we argue, will enable radicalness to better explain when and why a technology will experience adoption resistance or success.

We begin by discussing the role of technology radicalness in new technology adoption and making a case for its relevance in adoption studies. We follow with a discussion on prior conceptualizations of technology radicalness in the innovation literature. We define perceived radicalness of a technology as a second order formative construct and present its five critical dimensions while discussing their contribution towards RFID's radicalness. Testable hypotheses are proposed for each dimension and its effect on perceptions of RFID's radicalness. We support our conceptualization through the data collected from semi-structured interviews in an emerging technology adoption context and more specifically in our current empirical study of the adoption of Radio-Frequency Identification (RFID) technology.

2 Literature Review

As technology relates to innovations, configurations of business process can be implied by and built into the structure of technologies, directing specific usage behaviors that, if faithfully followed, will yield the intended benefits of the technology [4]. Radical technologies are very different from incremental technologies. They are likely to require specific usage behaviors that vary greatly from the existing behaviors within the affected organizational business processes for their implementation. As a result, radical technologies are less frequently adopted than incremental innovations [3], appear more complex to adopters and generate uncertainty about the resources required to use them effectively [8]. It has been suggested that perceptions of a technology's radicalness may influence its adoption and need to be better understood [1].

To address differences in adoption patterns, we focus on radical technology-enabled business process innovations, as this is an area where consultants and practitioners focus their efforts to improve business. These innovations require a higher perspective than that of the individual user. At a minimum, we must look at multiple users to isolate steps and sequences in adoption. Business process innovations involve group level convergence of technology, people, and process producing some non-incremental change in the status quo – a "radical" innovation. It follows that any conceptualization of radicalness to understand business innovation will need to address at least a group or in some cases a business unit or an organization.

2.1 Radicalness in RFID

RFID is an infrastructure technology [11] associated with platform innovation [17]. As such it requires substantial initial investment and future follow on investments with significant changes in the routines and practices of organizations to realize benefits. This degree of change coupled with the newness of RFID to commercial endeavors indicates that decision-makers would likely perceive it as highly radical. RFID technology has a potential to become a disruptive technology [13] with a profound impact on business and society. RFID adoption in a firm poses the issue of modifying and altering the business processes to leverage the benefits from it, and it has yet to be widely applied in practice, indicating substantial newness. In this sense, adoption of RFID may be characterized as risky and disruptive as it brings about changes in structure and functioning of organizations. To realize supply chain benefits from RFID adoption, synergies need to be built propagated through multiple organizations, as is happening with Wal-Mart and its suppliers. Such inter-organizational systems changes are complex and involved heightened uncertainty and potential for gain [12]. Though some technologies exhibit one or two of the characteristics of radicalness, few exhibit them all. RFID presents a context ideal for studying radicalness because it involves high expense and risk as well as great potential for gain.

2.2 Prior Conceptualizations of Innovation Radicalness

Most of the prior literature views innovations dichotomously (i.e. product or process, administrative or technological and incremental or radical) [9]. An innovation is defined as radical if it is both new and introduces a magnitude of change [6]. Radical innovations are characterized as competence destroying [18] often making existing skills and knowledge redundant. Dewar and Dutton [5] recognize radical innovations with high degree of new knowledge embedded in them. These categorizations while useful are incomplete as they leave out perceptions of radicalness within an application context. The fact that existing technologies may display a characteristic of radicalness directly contradicts the notion that radicalness must be new-to-the-world or inherent in a technology. Indeed, taken as a whole, existing literature argues that radicalness is in the eye of the beholder but that beholder may be a group or organization when it comes to understanding radicalness of platform technologies such as RFID. A conceptualization of technology radicalness that includes perceptions of its radicalness within its application context has yet to be well formulated.

3 Conceptualization and Hypotheses: Perceived Radicalness a Multidimensional Construct

A five item scale for perceived radicalness was proposed [7] that tried to capture the radicalness inherent in a technology innovation. The scale was later extended and used [15]. However, we believe that radicalness as a concept needs to be looked at from the adopter's perspective where attributes inherent to the technology interact with its application context. Henderson and Clark [10] provide three factors that capture radicalness in terms of the changes in a product innovation. We extend their conceptualization into a technology adoption context by including the new knowledge and changes an innovation mandates for successful adoption. Hence we propose a multi dimensional construct of "Perceived Radicalness". Consistent with this prior work we have defined the perceived radicalness to include the following five dimensions: 1) embedded knowledge in the technology or product knowledge; 2) knowledge and prior experience in the application of technology or business application knowledge; 3) changes in fundamental concepts of the business activities to which it is applied or business concept change; 4) changes in the resources needed for the business activities to which it is applied or business component change and 5) changes in the business processes of the business activities to which it is applied or business linkage change.

The following sub-section delineates each dimension along with its role in RFID being perceived as radical:

1) Product knowledge: Encompasses the knowledge about a specific technology, particularly its features and capabilities, resources required to operate it and its limitations. In the RFID context, the knowledge about RFID (How does it work? What are its limitations?) would constitute the knowledge about the technology or product knowledge. Organizations that are unaware of RFID's unique features and capabilities are likely to perceive it as radical due to high knowledge barriers. Hence,

H1: Lower level of product knowledge will contribute towards higher perception of radicalness of RFID

2) Business application knowledge: Encompasses knowledge about the settings and contexts in which a technology could be applied in a given business. The knowledge about how RFID could be utilized in a current business setting (for example inventory tracking, theft prevention etc) to leverage benefits would constitute business application knowledge. This knowledge can be thought of as an intersection of technology with business and may be very context specific. Greater application knowledge will allow businesses to visualize and use RFID in unique and unexpected ways contributing towards its radicalness.

H2: Higher level of business application knowledge will contribute towards higher perception of radicalness of RFID

3) Business Concept Change: Encompasses changes in underlying ideas of what a business does and can do including how it makes money and what its products or services are. RFID tag and reader enable the unique item-level identification, non-line of sight, real time and parallel processing of identification data. All of these scientific concepts are embedded in the technology. However, the use of RFID in business activities such as asset management would lead to a change in the concepts of how that activity is and can be conducted. Fundamental and conceptual changes in the way the business is conducted will contribute towards RFID's radicalness.

H3: Higher level of changes at the conceptual level of the business activity will contribute towards higher perception of radicalness of RFID

4) Business Component Change: Encompasses changes in assets and resources that are available to a firm including employee skills, IT, systems and equipment for doing its business. In the context of RFID use, the readers and tags, other hardware, software, systems and sub-systems and people would be components associated with the RFID innovation required to execute a business activity. Any improvements, replacements, additions or removals of existing components would mean a change in components for the business activities. The level of change in components will be high when RFID technology is to be used to accomplish business tasks that were manually performed in the past, because the innovation adoption may involve all of the above-mentioned changes. Greater need for change in resources will cause greater disruption in the current activities of the business contributing towards RFID's radicalness.

H4: Higher level of changes at the component level of the business activity will contribute towards higher perception of radicalness of RFID

5) Business Linkage Change: Encompasses changes in the processes including tasks and routines by which a firm links its business components to execute its business model. In context of RFID, linkage change applies to how the tags, readers, other hardware, software, middle-ware, other systems and people are inter-connected to accomplish the business activity. Any change in the way components are connected through tasks and processes for

accomplishing a business activity would mean a change in linkages. Greater linkage change will contribute towards RFID's radicalness.

H5: Higher level of changes at the linkage level of the business activity will contribute towards higher perception of radicalness of RFID

4 Data and Methodology

We wished to explore the meaning of radicalness of an innovation for the adopting organizations, why organizations perceive some innovations as more radical than others, and how radicalness may impact their decision to adopt and integrate a technology-based innovation. Prior literature showed inconsistent definitions and incoherence across fields in understanding radicalness in innovation adoption. In such a case, interpretive research focusing on exploring the unknown phenomenon best serves to initiate a valid and accurate line of inquiry [19], [14] precisely our underlying research goal. To accomplish the above-mentioned goals and to develop a better understanding of the adoption process, we conducted in-depth, semi-structured interviews using a convenience sample. The interviewees were executives and RFID program managers and supply chain managers across 10 organizations (12 interviews) involved in RFID initiatives at some level. We sampled from three perspectives in order to triangulate and, thereby, strengthen our understanding of radicalness of RFID adoptions. These perspectives were the adopter perspective (7 firms and 8 interviews in three industries: manufacturing, retailing, and logistics), the implementer perspective (1 top IT consulting firms and 2 interviews), and the vendor perspective (2 firms and 2 interviews).

The interviews were conducted over a period of three months (May-July, 2005) and were either face to face or over the phone, lasting between one and two hours. The questions for the interviews were a mix of open-ended questions and closed questions to allow both the flexibility of exploring new contexts but also to help maintain focus on some of the previously identified relevant themes. At the time of the interviews, we were not exploring radicalness as perceived or context dependent. These themes emerged from the data and were later developed conceptually, because of what we found from practice.

The interviews were recorded and later transcribed. The authors coded the interview data in an effort to extract key ideas underlying the concept of innovation radicalness for managers evaluating emerging technologies such as RFID. This coding process involved the first author identifying patterns and underlying themes that emerged from quotations in the raw text, excerpting them and bringing them to the other two authors for joint discussion and refinement over a period of 7 months and more than 20 hours of discussion.

5 Discussion

We became aware that all three perspectives were unified in seeing RFID adoption radicalness as a continuous, context-dependent phenomenon with multiple dimensions. Prior conceptualization of radicalness as dyadic or non-perceptual does not fit these data from practice. The context dependency fits well if we expect radicalness would be perceptual for innovation adoptions.

Some of the key quotes of managers that were interviewed are presented in Table 1 (Appendix) as a representative sample that supports our multi-dimensional conceptualization of radicalness as perceived and depending upon prior experience and application context. Table 1 also shows the major patterns and underlying themes found as a result of the coding and analysis process.

Repeated mentions of "need for learning" and "need for high level of changes in business processes and infrastructure that could prove disruptive" by the interviewees suggest support for multiple dimensions of product knowledge, business application knowledge, change in business linkages and business components. Another important theme that emerged from the interviews was about paradigm shift in the way a particular business activity is conducted. This idea is also reflected in our proposed dimension of change in business activity concepts.

6 Implications for Practice and Theory

This study addresses an important question i.e., why RFID might be perceived as radical by its adopters? In doing so it also discusses what radicalness means and how perceptions of radicalness may influence adoption decisions.

The conceptualization of radicalness as a multi-dimensional construct has implications for both theory and practice. For the practitioners our conceptualization addresses the issue of "lack of definitional clarity" and enables managers to understand the inherent attributes of innovation radicalness. This will allow managers to effectively develop or respond to radical innovations. From the theoretical and academic perspective, our conceptualization opens the "black box" of radicalness by proposing a multi-dimensional construct. This will enable researchers to reconcile seemingly disparate results and aggregate their understanding of role of radicalness in innovation adoption.

7 Conclusion

Overall the data from interviews supports our conceptualization of radicalness as a perceptual and formative multidimensional construct with the five proposed dimensions. We expect to test our proposed hypotheses as an extension of our current work. We believe that our conceptualization of radicalness will further the understanding of the role of "Perceived Radicalness" construct on RFID adoption and implementation decisions.

References

1. Ciganek, A., Zahedi, F.M.: Radical! The Influence of Perceived Radicalness on Technology Acceptance. In: Proceedings of the Tenth Americas Conference on Information Systems, New York, NY (August 2004)
2. Chandy, R.K., Tellis, G.J.: The Incumbents Curse? Incumbency, Size, and Radical Product Innovation. Journal of Marketing 64, 1–17 (2000)

3. Damanpour, F.: Organizational Complexity and Innovation: Developing and Testing Multiple Contingency Models. Management Science 42(5), 693–716 (1996)
4. DeSanctis, G., Poole, M.S.: Capturing the complexity in advanced technology use: Adaptive structuration theory. Organization Science 5, 121–147 (1994)
5. Dewar, R.D., Dutton, J.E.: The adoption of radical and incremental innovations: an empirical analysis. Management Science 32(11), 1422–1433 (1986)
6. Ettlie, J.E., Bridges, W.P., O'Keefe, R.D.: Organization Strategy and Structural Differences for Radical Versus Incremental Innovation. Management Science 30(6), 682–695 (1984)
7. Gatignon, H., Tushman, M.L., Smith, W., Anderson, P.: A Structural Approach to assessing Innovation. Management Science 48(9) (September 2002)
8. Gopalakrishnan, S., Damanpour, F.: Patterns of Generation and Adoption of Innovations in Organizations: Contingency Models of Innovation Attributes. Journal of Engineering and Technology Management 11, 95–116 (1994)
9. Hage, J.: Theories of Organizations. John Wiley and Sons, New York (1980)
10. Henderson, Clark: Architectural Innovations, The reconfiguration of existing product technologies and failure of the firms. Administrative Science quarterly 35 (1990)
11. Kauffman, R.J., Riggins, F.J., Curtin, J.: Working paper. University of Minnesota, Minneapolis (2004/2005)
12. Karimi, J., Konsynski, B.R.: Globalization and information management strategies. Journal of Management Information Systems 7, 7–26 (1991)
13. Krotov, V., Junglas, I.: RFID as a disruptive innovation. Journal of Theoretical and Applied Electronic Commerce Research 3(2), 44–59 (2008)
14. Lee, A.S.: Integrating positivist and interpretive approaches to organizational research. Organization Science 2, 342–365 (1991)
15. Lyytinen, K., Rose, G.M.: The Disruptive Nature of Information Technology Innovations: the Case of Internet Computing in Systems Development Organizations. MIS Quarterly 27(4), 557–595 (2003)
16. O'Connor, G.C., McDermott, C.M.: The Human Side of Radical Innovation. Journal of Engineering Technology Management 21, 11–30 (2004)
17. Sood, A., Tellis, G.J.: Technological Evolution and Radical Innovation. Journal of Marketing (69), 152–168 (July 2005)
18. Tushman, Anderson: Technological Discontinuities and Organizational Environments. Administrative Science Quarterly (31) (1986)
19. Yin, R.K.: The Information Systems Research Challenge: Qualitative Research Methods. In: Cash Jr., J.I., Lawrence, P. (eds.), vol. 1, pp. 1–6. Harvard Business School, Boston (1989)

Appendix

Table 1. Key Quotes from Managers

#	Key Quotes	Organization	Underlying Themes
1	We find benefits but RFID is not on our priority list and we don't think we are ready as we *don't have the infrastructure and expertise to process huge amount of data* that would be generated by it and make sense out of it. Lack of standards and cost of tags and readers is prohibitive. Also RFID will be *a major change for our company in over hauling our business processes.*	A	Business Application Knowledge, Business Component Change, Business Linkage change
2	For RFID we could easily identify which tag would work and what device would work for our products, that didn't take very long, less than six months but now we are facing a *major issue as far as its application. How much changes you have to do to all the existing ERP systems and front end business applications required in its application, we are not clear as there may be a lot.*	G	Business Application Knowledge
3	Smaller organizations see RFID as an opportunity to make two leaps at once and hence displace some of the existing organizations. Also I believe that it is *more perceptual and determined by the business context* in which it is applied. For us, in terms of retail checkout at this point it is not a major change, as it does not fundamentally change the business process. But going into the future, when there is item level tagging, and automated checkouts. It may be a paradigm shift because it *Eliminates the basis of our business. We may have to kiss our scanning and retail business goodbye.*	J	Business Concept Change, Business Component, Business Linkage Change
4	RFID would require *altering our existing optical scanners infrastructure and processes currently* in place. A lot of *learning, major changes in infrastructure may be required.* This would be *disruptive* for the organization.	C	Product Knowledge, Business Application Knowledge, Business Component Change, Business Linkage Change

My How You've Grown! eProcurement in the Post-Dot-Bomb Era

Tim McLaren, Catherine Middleton, and Xueying (Ci Ci) Fang

Ted Rogers School of IT Management, Ryerson University
350 Victoria Street, Toronto, Ontario, Canada M5B 2K3

Abstract. This study contrasts the results of a survey on eProcurement adoption rates, success factors, and challenges conducted in 2009, with findings from prior studies. The findings suggest that many of the barriers to success identified in earlier studies (such as lack of management buy-in) have largely been overcome, yet the technical challenges of integrating information systems and processes remain. Furthermore, while only 24% of respondents indicated they were satisfied with their organizations' current eProcurement implementation, 72% of respondents felt that their organization would benefit from more usage of eProcurement. This disparity is explored using principal components analysis of the factors associated with the usage, benefits, and challenges of eProcurement. The paper concludes with a discussion of how implementation success factors may continue to evolve as the technology and business practices mature.

Keywords: eProcurement, technology adoption, success factors, hype cycle, B2B ecommerce.

1 Introduction

This study investigates current experiences, benefits, and challenges of electronic procurement (eProcurement) in Canada. Many recent peer-reviewed studies suggest eProcurement adoption is still very limited [1,2]. In contrast, this survey of 334 purchasing management professionals in Canada found over 75% of the organizations have used eProcurement technologies for at least one year and over half have used eProcurement for at least three years.

The term eProcurement refers to using computer-based systems to facilitate the purchasing of goods or services. Six forms of eProcurement have been classified, including e-ordering/e-Maintenance Repair Operate (MRO), web-based enterprise resource planning (ERP), e-sourcing, e-tendering, e-reverse auctioning/e-auctioning and e-informing [3]. For the purposes of this study, eProcurement is defined as the use of computer-based information systems linked via the Internet or other data networks to facilitate the purchasing of goods or services.

eProcurement has matured significantly since its initial "hype" over a decade ago. Desperate to claw their way out of an economic downturn, firms jumped at early claims of eProcurement as a source of economic efficiency in virtually every aspect of

R. Sharman, T.S. Raghu, and H.R. Rao (Eds.): WEB 2009, LNBIP 52, pp. 298–309, 2010.

supply chain management [4]. Researchers and analysts promised that eProcurement technologies would, among other things, reduce administrative costs, increase cost efficiency, shorten order fulfillment time, and increase collaborations between business partners. Subsequent market observations were disappointing: existing adoption processes were slower and more complex and technologies were less developed than expected. Companies realized that they did not have a full understanding of the inter-organization collaboration and network effects underlying this new model [5]. In additional, many organizations acknowledged the potential benefits of eProcurement yet did not commit to its implementation. For one reason or another, the purchasing community appeared to be sitting on its hands [6]. Both these factors caused the incredible expected growth of eProcurement implementation to be revised downwards [5].

This progression of eProcurement technologies closely correspond to the shifts from the technology trigger, to the peak of inflated expectations, to the trough of disillusionment of the "hype cycle" concept popularized by Gartner Inc. [7]. As shown in Fig. 1, Gartner's hype cycle characterizes the typical evolution of an emerging technology from over-enthusiasm through a period of disillusionment to an eventual understanding of the technology's role in a market or domain. Now, years later, the eProcurement model is likely progressing on the slope of enlightenment, where the focus is on experimentation and real-world application.

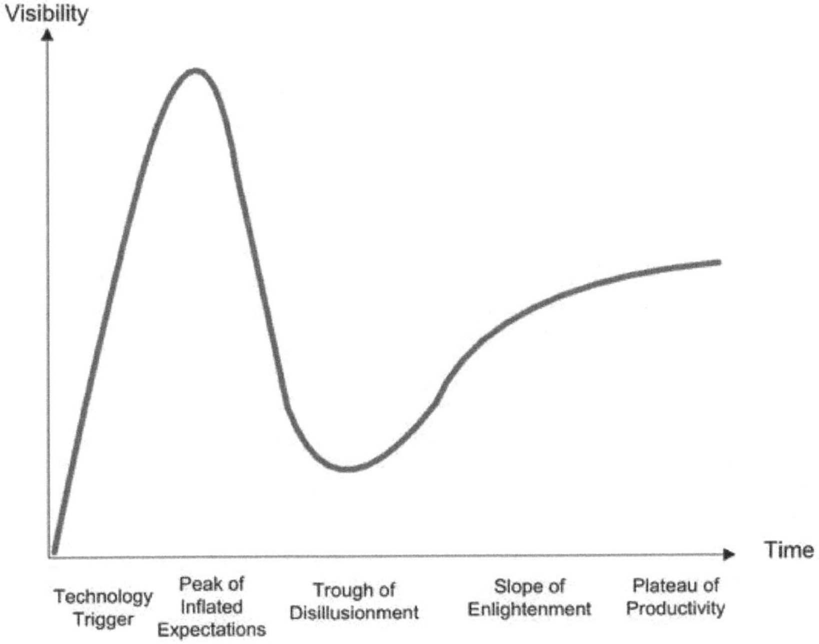

Fig. 1. Gartner's Hype Cycle Concept (adapted from Linden and Fenn 2003

While the impact of eProcurement technologies was previously overestimated in the short term, it is important to not underestimate its influence in the long term [8]. The goal of this paper is to provide a more recent analysis of (1) the current state of implementation and usage of eProcurement and (2) the benefits and challenges currently facing organizations in eProcurement implementation and usage.

2 Prior Literature

The mechanisms and processes for organizational purchasing have remained static for decades in many companies. Some businesses still employ a mostly paper-based method that is both error-prone and inefficient [4] . However, despite its obvious advantages, eProcurement cannot be instantly and seamlessly applied into an existing workplace with existing procedures, policies, and practices. The implementation of a new technology requires costly, complex, and time-consuming changes, updates, replacements, and adaptations throughout the infrastructure. Changing to eProcurement technologies requires a complete renovation of company systems and strategies, from which not all organizations are readily willing to resign [9]. In short, eProcurement is a process, not an easily learned, inconsequential tool to speed up online negotiation [10].

There are five main drivers that influence the success of eProcurement adoption—organizational, readiness, supply, strategic, and policy factors [11]. First, the main organizational factors are size and type of operation: eProcurement is usually more advantageous in bigger organizations and in more repetitive systems [11]. Second, employees and users' level of resistance to new systems is vital, as lack of readiness has been attributed mainly to human readiness [12]. Third, full integration throughout the supply chain ensures maximum benefit from eProcurement implementation [13]. Fourth, organizations should be strategic in their eProcurement adoption by creating and following a specific eProcurement strategic and aligning this in broader context to organizational strategy [14]. Lastly, research shows that public procurement organizations can use government spending as an instrument of industrial or social policy, helping to support regional developments and promoting industrial efficiency [15]. These five types of factors affect the degree of overall success, and experiences of benefits and challenges of the eProcurement implementation.

Adoption of a losing technology is costly not only in the money invested but also in terms of time to implement the technology. The majority of organizations have been taking the "wait and see" approach: they have been either aware of the developments but have not committed resources or have been investing selectively until the best eProcurement model can be identified [16]. As well, companies have mostly experimented with eProcurement technologies only in peripheral business processes [17].

In 2001, eProcurement was cited as an enabler for many best practices, automating transaction processing and thus freeing employees to do more value-added work. As well, the emergence of eProcurement developed new tools, such as reverse auctions and global sourcing. Reverse auctioning, for example, enables multiple users to bid and sell to individual buyers; this greatly increases the competition and improves the purchasing price of for buyers [4].

Early on, three key areas were identified as potential causes of eProcurement implementation failure: difficult software solutions, lack of integration/standardization, and buyer/seller/user resistance [4]. Instead of embracing the new technologies, employees adopted a "wait and see" approach in adopting eProcurement [18]. Managers worried about not getting the desired returns for the investment and over the security and confidentiality of data exchange in a virtual environment while workers were weary of being replaced by either automated machines or others more suited for the position after the changes [19]. The remainder of this paper introduces new findings to examine how usage, benefits, and challenges of eProcurement has changed now that the technologies and practices have matured further.

3 Methodology

In March 2009, the 2484 members of the Purchasing Management Association of Canada (PMAC) that had achieved the C.P.P. credential were invited to fill out questionnaires in English or French. In total, 334 members took part in the survey. The items for the survey were drawn from prior eProcurement studies [1,20,21] and pilot tested with two researchers and two managers to ensure the questions had strong face validity. The eProcurement usage, benefits, and challenges items used a five-point Likert-type scale from strongly disagree to strongly agree.

Respondents were from a diverse variety of industries, including manufacturing (22%), resources (17%), government/not-for-profit (17%), and utilities/transport (11%) which reflects the Canadian economy in general. the size of organizations in terms of annual sales was evenly distributed between $1M to $100M (19%), $100M to $1B (27%), greater than $1B (22%) and not applicable (28%).

Most respondents (55%) held titles of manager/director, while 16% were buyers, and 14% were analysts. On average, repondents had seven years of eProcurement experience at their present organizations and fourteen years at other organizations. Two-thirds (67%) of the respondents felt knowledgable about their organization's current plans for eProcurement; over half (56%) felt knowledgable about their organization's future plans for eProcurement. The majority of organizations (53%) have used eProcurement for more than three years , while 22% have used eProcurement for more than five years.

4 Results

Findings from the survey included data on how eProcurement is currently being used, what are the perceived benefits to the organization, and what are the perceived challenges. A principal components analysis was used to obtain estimates of the factors that account for the largest variance in the sample and uncover the underlying constructs for each set of items (Stevens, 1986). Factors with eigenvalues greater than one were retained. Varimax rotation with Kaiser normalization was used to transform the initial factors in to a more meaningful configuration. Items were assigned to factors if the loading was at least 0.40 and did not cross-load on more than one factor. Each of the three sets of data were found to be suitable for factor analysis using the criteria of Bartlett's test of sphericity ($P<0.000$) and the Kaiser-Meyer-Olkin (KMO) measure, which was greater than 0.70 for each of the data sets.

4.1 Usage of eProcurement

In earlier studies, eProcurement activities focused on purchasing nonproduction or indirect supplies [22]. The use of eProcurement in purchasing indirect supplies, defined as goods or services purchased for maintenance, repair, or operations, was mandatory in 28% of the organizations in this study. Conversely, the use of eProcurement in purchasing direct supplies, defined as components of the organization's product or service, was mandatory in only 19% of the organizations. Indirect goods is clearly the focus, perhaps due to the fact that indirect purchasing is generally a more secure and economical space for companies to try out eProcurement systems than direct purchasing [23].

There was some discrepancy between large and small businesses in mandatory eProcurement usage. Large businesses are defined as those with over 1000 employees in Canada and small businesses as those with under 1000 employees in Canada. The use of eProcurement in purchasing direct supplies was mandatory in 18% of the large businesses versus 21% of the small businesses. On the other hand, the use of eProcurement in purchasing indirect supplies was mandatory in 29% of the large businesses versus 26% of the small businesses. These results display a pattern of greater mandated eProcurement implementation in large businesses in terms of indirect supplies and greater mandated implementation in small businesses in terms of direct supplies.

Fig. 2 shows the extent to which respondents' organizations use eProcurement systems to support various procurement functions. The overall level of current usage, which encompasses widespread and minimal usage, was strong, with the greatest percentages of organizations currently using eProcurement for the purposes of purchasing from existing suppliers, purchasing from new suppliers, and placing orders through single supplier's website.

Of the organizations that are not yet utilizing eProcurement systems in each of the categories, almost half expected to be using eProcurement within one to three years. The most optimistic percentages of expected usage were in the purchasing from new suppliers, purchasing indirect supplies, and evaluating new suppliers categories, while the most pessimistic were in the making payments through a multi-supplier website, making payments through a single supplier website, and placing orders through a multi-supplier website categories. Once again, preference was displayed towards purchase- and single-supplier-oriented functions instead of payment- and multi-supplier-oriented functions.

Principal components analysis of the usage items indicated that three factors accounted for 77% of the variance in the items (see Table 1). These factors can be interpreted as three principal types of usage of eProcurement that are significant: *payments and reporting; evaluating suppliers;* and *ordering from suppliers.* The only exception to this grouping is the item "placing orders through a multi-supplier website" which loaded more strongly on the first factor rather than the third, which may be due to the relatively few respondents who currently used eProcurement for that activity. The identification of these three categories of usage is reduces the complexity of current conceptualizations of how eProcurement systems are used. Other items that did not

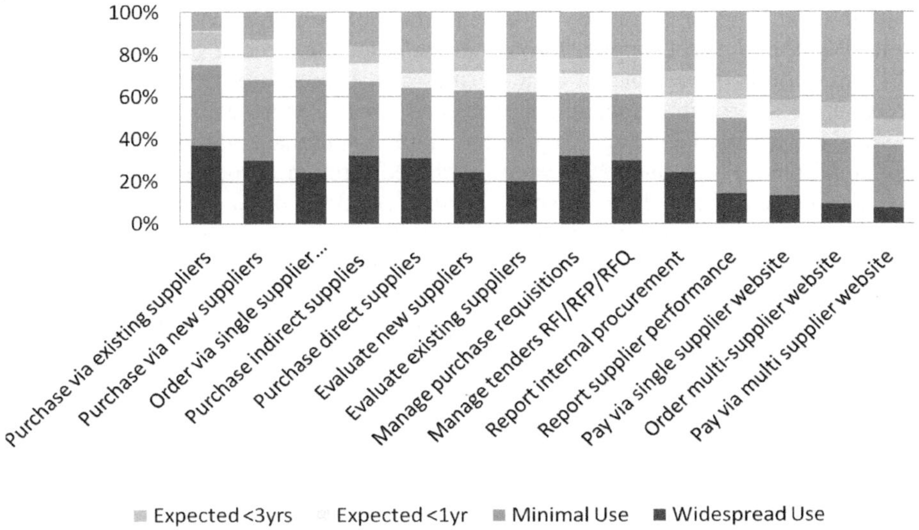

Fig. 2. Usage by Type of Activity

Table 1. Factor Loadings for Usage Items

Rotated Component Matrix[a]

	Component		
	1	2	3
making_payments_through_multisupplier	.887	.200	.161
making_payments_through_singlesupplier	.828	.094	.219
placing_orders_through_multisupplier	.813	.272	.221
reporting_on_internal_performance	.681	.354	.216
evaluate_new_suppliers	.259	.902	.133
evaluate_existing_suppliers	.244	.892	.201
purchasing_indirect_supplies	.092	.215	.873
placing_orders_through_singlesupplier	.330	-.046	.727
purchasing_direct_supplies	.253	.375	.706

Extraction Method: Principal Component Analysis.
Rotation Method: Varimax with Kaiser Normalization.

a. Rotation converged in 5 iterations.

load strongly on a factor (0.40) included "managing tenders", which suggests that most respondents did not identify that usage as being currently being significant.

Despite greater mandated eProcurement utilization in terms of direct supplies in small businesses, a greater share of total direct purchases is conducted through eProcurement in large businesses. The percentage of large businesses that purchased over 75% of total direct supplies through eProcurement exceeded small businesses by 10%. As well, the percentage of large businesses that purchased 50% to 74% of total direct supplies through eProcurement exceeded small businesses by 4%. Large businesses also purchased a greater share of total indirect purchases through eProcurement than small businesses: over 75% were purchased through eProcurement for 16% of large businesses versus 14% of small businesses. Both these results and previous research shows that larger businesses adapt and use eProcurement much more than small businesses [24]. eProcurement software requires larger investments than alternative e-procurement technologies, which explains why large corporations are the main adopters of this technology. More expensive e-procurement technologies, such as e-procurement software, may be better suited for organizations with large supply chains that expect larger savings from improving these processes, but not for smaller companies that do not have the scale to justify such a large investment. In contrast, these companies may benefit from cheaper e-procurement technologies [16]. Other reasons for small businesses' lagging patterns in eProcurement adoption include owners' attitudes, limited IT infrastructure, and limited knowledge and expertise with information systems [25].

4.2 Perceived Benefits and Challenges of eProcurement

As shown in Table 2, the greatest current benefits were attributed to spending less time on low-value tasks, finding new suppliers, and paying less for supplies. The benefits least mentioned were understanding suppliers' plans, involving suppliers in the organizations' plans, and reducing number of contracts. Agreed encompasses the strongly agreed and agreed categories. These results show that eProcurement has served to increase economic efficiency, but has not necessarily improved buyer-supplier relationships.

Table 2. Perceived Benefits of the Organization's eProcurement Systems

"eProcurement has helped my organization to..."	**Strongly disagree**	**Disagree**	**Neither agree nor disagree**	**Agree**	**Strongly agree**
Find new suppliers	6.9%	12.7%	15.8%	36.7%	18.5%
Reduce number of suppliers	6.6%	27.4%	27.4%	20.1%	8.5%
Reduce number of contracts	5.4%	28.6%	28.6%	20.5%	5.8%
Negotiate with suppliers	6.6%	19.3%	22.8%	32.8%	7.3%
Strengthen our supplier relationships	5.4%	15.1%	29.3%	30.9%	8.9%
Measure supplier performance	5.4%	18.5%	33.2%	21.2%	8.1%
Involve suppliers in our planning	6.2%	23.2%	29.0%	20.5%	3.1%
Understand our suppliers' plans	5.0%	28.2%	29.0%	16.6%	2.7%
Reduce off-contract buying	5.8%	19.3%	24.3%	30.5%	5.8%
Pay less for supplies	4.6%	14.3%	22.0%	40.5%	9.3%
Spend less time on low-value tasks	4.2%	8.9%	17.4%	43.2%	17.8%

As shown in Table 3, the greatest challenges in an organization's eProcurement implementation were difficulty integrating internal procurement systems, difficulty integrating organization's system with supplier's, and lack of standard data formats. As eProcurement is a relatively new development in the business application area, there is a lack of benchmark models especially in organizations that are still learning of these systems' functionalities and uses as applicable to their specific businesses [1]. In the short term, firms need to accommodate the trends in their key market segments. In the long term, a universal standard for eProcurement systems needs to be set across all industries [26]. For example, the key to the success of a single eProcurement network for the U.S. automotive industry, a goal pursued by GM, Ford, and Daimler Chrysler in their joint venture, is involving other leading automakers such as Japanese automotive manufactures [27,28]. In contrast, the least significant challenges were incurred in external supplier resistance (17% agreed), internal buyer resistance (19% agreed), and internal end-user resistance (22% agreed). Previously perceived to be a major obstacle, buyer/seller/user resistance and apprehension has been overcome with time and training. These results suggest that the major barriers to more effective eProcurement implementation are no longer due to user resistance or lack of management support but merely overcoming the current technological challenges.

Table 3. Perceived Challenges of the Organization's eProcurement Systems

"Implementing eProcurement in my organization has been challenging due to..."	**Strongly disagree**	**Disagree**	**Neither agree nor disagree**	**Agree**	**Strongly agree**
Lack of standard data formats	0.0%	12.0%	23.5%	39.0%	13.1%
Difficulty integrating internal procurement systems	0.8%	11.2%	15.1%	41.8%	20.7%
Difficulty integrating our systems with suppliers	0.4%	13.5%	19.9%	35.1%	18.3%
Difficulty maintaining our internal controls and policies	1.6%	22.3%	20.7%	29.1%	14.3%
Unexpected costs (catalog implementation, training, etc.)	0.4%	16.3%	30.7%	28.3%	9.6%
Immature eProcurement software	2.0%	16.7%	27.5%	30.3%	7.6%
Immature eProcurement service providers	2.4%	18.7%	33.1%	21.1%	8.0%
Internal buyer resistance	4.4%	32.3%	21.5%	23.1%	9.2%
Internal end-user resistance	3.6%	25.1%	21.9%	27.5%	11.6%
External supplier resistance	2.0%	27.9%	33.5%	19.5%	3.6%
Lack of internal management support	4.0%	18.3%	25.9%	25.5%	16.3%

Principal components analysis of the perceived benefits resulted in a two-factor solution (Table 4) that accounted for 70% of the variance. The first factor can be interpreted as *improved supplier relationship management*, while the second factor can be interpreted as *increased operational efficiency*.

Principal components analysis of the perceived challenges resulted in a three-factor solution (Table 5) that accounted for 76% of the variance. The first factor can be interpreted as the challenges with *integrating systems, processes, and controls*. The second factor can be interpreted as the challenge of using relatively *immature software*. The third factor relates to the challenge of overcoming *resistance from within the organization*. Interestingly, resistance from external suppliers and internal management did not load strongly on this factor, which suggests responses to these latter two items were inconsistent.

A final series of items focused on the respondents' satisfaction with the current eProcurement implementation in their organization. 41% of respondents agreed that the benefits outweigh the costs of eProcurement systems as opposed to the 13% who disagreed. However, only 24% of respondents indicated that they were satisfied with their organizations' current levels of eProcurement implementation. Despite this low level of current satisfaction, 72% felt that their organization would benefit from more usage.

Table 4. Factor Loadings for Benefits

Rotated Component Matrix[a]

	Component	
	1	2
understand_supplier_plans	.829	.287
finding_new_suppliers	.774	.118
involve_suppliers_in_planning	.754	.372
reduce_offcontract_buying	.102	.868
spend_less_time_on_lowvalue_tasks	.318	.760
pay_less_for_supplies	.382	.733

Extraction Method: Principal Component Analysis.
Rotation Method: Varimax with Kaiser Normalization.

a. Rotation converged in 3 iterations.

Table 5. Factor Loadings for Challenges

Rotated Component Matrix[a]

	Component		
	1	2	3
difficulty_maintaining_internal_controls	.793	.026	.191
difficulty_integrating_system_with_suppliers	.774	.185	-.002
difficulty_integrating_internal_systems	.766	.296	.058
immature_serviceproviders	.173	.892	.163
immature_software	.223	.889	.134
internal_buyer_resistenance	.150	.090	.884
internal_enduser_resistances	.037	.183	.879

Extraction Method: Principal Component Analysis.
Rotation Method: Varimax with Kaiser Normalization.

a. Rotation converged in 4 iterations.

5 Discussion and Conclusion

In contrast to prior reports which contend eProcurement adoption is not yet widespread [1,2], this survey of 334 purchasing management professionals in Canada found that, in 2009, over 75% of the organizations have used eProcurement technologies for at least one year and over half have used eProcurement for at least three years. eProcurement technologies were most frequently used for purchasing- and single-supplier activities and less so for payment- and multi-supplier activities. In comparing public- and private-sector organizations, the biggest difference in usage of eProcurement was in managing tenders, which was the second greatest area of eProcurement usage for the public sector but did make the top nine most common uses for the private sector.

5.1 Usage of eProcurement

The primary function of eProcurement has not changed significantly from 2003, when it was also to place and track orders [16]. The lowest percentages of current usage were in making payments through a multi-supplier website, placing orders through a multi-supplier website, and making payments through a single-supplier website. Current eProcurement usage was most widespread for purchase- and single-supplier activities and less prevalent in payment- and multi-supplier activities. Notably, order-processing of goods and services, especially in simple forms, has become a priority in terms of eProcurement functions for many companies [23].

One of the difficulties with researching enterprise systems is coming to terms with their complex functionality. However, principal components analysis of the survey responses on the current use of eProcurement in the organizations studied indicate they are primarily used for three principal functions: *payments and reporting; evaluating suppliers;* and *ordering from suppliers.*

5.2 Benefits and Challenges of eProcurement

Large and small businesses faced almost identical challenges in the implementation of eProcurement. The biggest distinction was in difficulty integrating systems with suppliers, which was a challenge for 14% more of the small business respondents than the large business respondents. Small businesses' lack of capital to participate in business-to-business procurement environments and the small transaction volumes associated with these firms' scale of business result in the incapacity to purchase and maintain the most up-to-date systems [1]. As well, small businesses' lack of marketplace influence often means that they have to provide and regularly update catalogue data in a variety of formats in order to accommodate each specific buyer [29]. Another notable discrepancy was in immature eProcurement software, which was an issue for 7% more of the large business respondents than the small business respondents. Small and medium enterprises are typically able to start using electronic developments earlier than large firms, as the bulk of their transactions are less complex and they can take advantage of new technologies for more advanced applications without bearing the full burden of the cost [30].

The most frequently cited benefits attributed to eProcurement systems were: spending less time on low-value tasks, finding new suppliers, and paying less for supplies. Surprisingly, the most frequently reported challenges reported did not include user or supplier resistance, but rather involved the technological difficulties in integrating information systems. As shown in the factor analysis, the many potential benefits of using eProcurement systems can be conceptualized using two underlying constructs: *improved supplier relationship management* and *improved operational efficiency.* Similarly, factor analysis revealed the many challenges with implementing eProcurement in an organization were related to three underlying challenges: *integrating systems, processes, and controls; immaturity of the software;* and *resistance from internal users.* Surprisingly, lack of support from management or external suppliers was not found to be consistently cited by the respondents, as has been found in earlier eProcurement studies (e.g., Angeles and Nath 2007, which reports on a survey conducted several years prior).

The respondents' overall ratings of satisfaction with eProcurement contained some interesting contrasts. As noted previously, the majority (41%) felt the benefits of eProcurement outweighed the costs for their organization. Only 24% of respondents were satisfied with their organizations' current eProcurement implementation and fully 72% felt that their organization would benefit from more usage of eProcurement. This broad consensus suggests an optimism among purchasing managers that the cost-benefit ratio for implementing eProcurement systems will continue to improve as the technologies and practices mature. In "hype cycle" terms, not only does eProcurement appear to have passed be well beyond the "peak of inflated expectations", but it appears to have passed the "trough of disillusionment" and is climbing into the "plateau of productivity". eProcurement appears to not be a managerial fad that has come and gone, but a maturing technology that is quietly becoming a critical component for many organizations.

The results of this study suggest that eProcurement usage is more widespread than previously reported. Despite the apparent complexity of eProcurement systems, a factor analysis of the results suggests the most consistent uses for eProcurement fall into just three categories: payments and reporting; evaluating suppliers; and ordering from suppliers. Similarly, the many potential benefits and challenges were found to load on five major factors. The most consistently reported benefits of eProcurement in an organization was improving supplier relationship management and improving operational efficiency. Similarly, the most consistently reported challenges were in integrating systems, processes, and controls; immaturity of the software; and resistance from internal users. This suggests that further efforts in researching and improving eProcurement technologies and practices should focus on each of the areas highlighted in these results.

References

[1] Angeles, R., Nath, R.: Business-to-Business e-Procurement: Success Factors and Challenges to Implementation. Supply Chain Management: An International Journal 12, 104–115 (2007)

[2] Pearcy, D.H., Giunipero, L.C.: Using e-Procurement Applications to Achieve Integration: What Role does Firm Size Play? Supply Chain Management: An International Journal 26, 34 (2008)

[3] de Boer, L., Harink, J., Heijboer, G.: A Conceptual Model for Assessing the Impact of Electronic Procurement. European Journal of Purchasing and Supply Management 8, 25–33 (2002)

[4] Attaran, M., Attaran, S.: Catch the Wave of e-Procurement. Industrial management-Chicago then Atlanta 11, 16–21 (2002)

[5] Antonio, D., Mahendra, G., Richard, P.: Moving Procurement Systems to the Internet: The Adoption and use of e-Procurement Technology Models. European Management Journal 21, 11–23 (2003)

[6] Walker, H., Harland, C.: E-Procurement in the United Nations: Influences, Issues and Impact. International Journal of Operations & Production Management 28, 831–857 (2008)

[7] Linden, A., Fenn, J.: Understanding Gartner's Hype Cycles, Technical Report R-20-1971 (2003)

[8] Hawking, P., Stein, A., Wyld, D.C., Foster, S.: E-Procurement: Is the Ugly Duckling Actually a Swan Down Under? Asia Pacific Journal of Marketing and Logistics 16, 3–26 (2004)

[9] Gaddis, S.E.: How to Design Online Surveys. Training & Development 52, 67 (1998)

[10] Bogucki Duncan, N.: Capturing Flexibility of Information Technology Infrastructure: A Study of Resource Characteristics and their Measure. J. Manage. Inf. Syst. 12, 37–57 (1995)

[11] Bergh, D.D., Fairbank, J.F.: Measuring and Testing Change in Strategic Management Research. Strategic Manage. J. 23, 359–366 (2002)

[12] Smith, N.C.: The Case Study: A Vital yet Misunderstood Method for Management. In: Mansfield, R. (ed.) Frontiers of Management, pp. 145–157. Routledge and Kegan Paul, London (1989)

[13] Creswell, J.W.: Research Design: Qualitative, Quantitative, and Mixed Methods Approaches. SAGE Publications, Thousand Oaks (2003)

[14] Croteau, A.M., Bergeron, F.: An Information Technology Trilogy: Business Strategy, Technological Deployment and Organizational Performance. J. Strat. Inf. Syst. 10, 77–99 (2001)

[15] Dagenais, T., Gautschi, D.: Net Markets: Driving Success in the B2B Networked Economy. McGraw-Hill Ryerson Ltd., Toronto (2002)

[16] Gosling, S.D., Vazire, S., Srivastava, S., John, O.P.: Should we Trust Web-Based Studies?: A Comparative Analysis of Six Preconceptions about Internet Questionnaires. American Psychologist 59, 93–104 (2004)

[17] Davila, A., Gupta, M., Palmer, R.: Moving Procurement Systems to the Internet: The Adoption and use of E-Procurement Technology Models. European Management Journal 21, 11–23 (2003)

[18] Huber, B., Sweeney, E., Smyth, A.: Purchasing Consortia and Electronic Markets-A Procurement Direction in Integrated Supply Chain Management. Electronic Markets 14, 284–294 (2004)

[19] Yen, B.P.C., Ng, E.O.S.: Migrating Procurement Onto the Internet. Electronic Commerce Research 2, 113–134 (2002)

[20] Batenburg, R.: E-Procurement Adoption by European Firms: A Quantitative Analysis. Journal of Purchasing and Supply Management 13, 182–192 (2007)

[21] Gunasekaran, A., Ngai, E.W.T.: Adoption of e-Procurement in Hong Kong: An Empirical Research. Int. J. Prod. Econ. 113, 159–175 (2008)

[22] Broadbent, M., Weill, P.: Improving Business and Information Strategy Alignment: Learning from the Banking Industry. IBM Syst. J. 32, 162–179 (1993)

[23] Tanner, C., Wolfle, R., Schubert, P., Quade, M.: Current Trends and Challenges in Electronic Procurement: An Empirical Study. Electronic Markets 18, 6–18 (2008)

[24] Heerwegh, D., Loosveldt, G.: Web Surveys: The Effect of Controlling Survey Access using PIN Numbers. Social Science Computer Review 20, 10–21 (2002)

[25] Conant, J.S., Mokwa, M.P., Varadarajan, P.R.: Strategic Types, Distinctive Marketing Competencies, and Organizational Performance: A Multiple Measures-Based Study. Strategic Manage. J. 11, 365–383 (1990)

[26] Olivia, R.: The Promise of XML. Marketing Management 10, 46–49 (2001)

[27] Ageshin, E.A.: E-Procurement at Work: A Case Study. Production and Inventory Management Journal 42, 48–53 (2001)

[28] Carey, T.T.: A Usability Requirements Model for Procurement Life Cycles. In: Carey, J.M. (ed.) Human Factors in Information Systems: An Organizational Perspective, pp. 89–104. Ablex Publishing Corporation, Norwood (1991)

[29] Kim, J.I., Shunk, D.L.: Matching Indirect Procurement Process with Different B2B e-Procurement Systems. Comput. Ind. 53, 153–164 (2004)

[30] Dai, Q., Kauffman, R.J.: B2B e-Commerce Revisited: Leading Perspectives on the Key Issues and Research Directions. Electronic Markets 12, 67–83 (2002)

Author Index